CULTURAL REMIX
Theories of Politics and the Popular

CULTURAL REMIX
Theories of Politics
and the Popular

EDITED BY
Erica Carter, James Donald
and Judith Squires

LAWRENCE & WISHART
LONDON

Lawrence & Wishart Limited
144a Old South Lambeth Road
London SW8 1XX

First published 1995 by Lawrence & Wishart

Cover design by Jan Brown Designs
Photoset in North Wales by
Derek Doyle & Associates, Mold, Clwyd.
Printed and bound in Great Britain by
Biddles Ltd, Guildford, Surrey.

Contents

CONTENTS

C. DEMOCRACY AND DIFFERENCE

Introduction

In some small corner of publishing history, the early 1990s may in time figure as the moment (not-to-be-missed) of 'the cultural studies reader'. From During and Turner to Grossberg, McGuigan and Gray,[1] editorial energies have been directed towards the delineation both of a tradition and a future trajectory for cultural studies as the Academy's most upwardly mobile discipline.

As the title of this present collection suggests, the articles below – all published in early issues of the journal *New Formations* – circulate around the questions of popular culture, its political possibilities and limitations, that have preoccupied cultural studies since its inception. If, then, *Cultural Remix* is to be read, not as just another cultural studies textbook, but as a text whose reach extends across the critical cultural field, it is worth specifying at this point its relation to cultural studies as the academic market's latest bright young thing – a field characterised, it is sometimes suggested, no longer primarily by cultural-politics, but by the drive for academic hegemony.

NEW FORMULATIONS IN CULTURAL STUDIES

A glance at current higher education curricula reveals cinema courses in departments of history, seminars on comics and women's magazines in contexts stretching from sociology to modern languages and literature. All this signals a new, and surely welcome legitimacy for interdisciplinary and popular cultural studies. Yet there is a troubling political ambiguity in the cultural studies commitment to interdisciplinarity, coupled with its anti-hierarchical reflex – its drive to shift the academic focus from high culture to popular forms. On the one hand, the cultural studies challenge to traditional disciplines has clearly contributed to educational democratisation. Yet simultaneously, the dismantling of established canons which cultural studies demands, meshes all too easily with the new right reshaping of education as consumer marketplace, in which students pick 'n mix their way across

a gift-wrapped curriculum ('get your teen mag module HERE!!...').
The problem with this new educational pluralism is not so much that it has dismantled traditional structures of cultural authority (this must surely be welcomed), but rather that cultural studies has often failed to delineate alternative models of cultural or political value and judgement. Raymond Williams' assertion, 'culture is ordinary', was adopted early on as a motto to underpin cultural studies' sometimes uncritically enthusiastic embrace of 'the popular' in *all* its forms. Critics more recently, however, have begun to question the hedonistic pluralism of a cultural studies that asserts the equal value of all cultural forms. Questioning the canon, it is argued, cannot be synonymous with a wholesale repudiation of authority, value, judgement or differentiation in the aesthetic, ethical or broader cultural domain. There is a point, in other words – as is underlined by Ien Ang, Charlotte Brunsdon and others in this volume – when critical criteria must be formulated, and judgements made.

There are, further, key political difficulties with the cultural studies challenge to the Academy's established markets of certainty. In a 1980 survey of the British cultural studies tradition, Stuart Hall insisted that cultural studies lives or dies by a set of political commitments from which 'fortunately, it has never been, and can never be freed.'[2] The political moment of the articles below (1987-1991) was, however, one of far greater uncertainty about the field's political commitments. Accelerating institutionalisation had posed new questions of the politics of this *arriviste* discipline. What structures of authority and power were established in cultural studies through the discursive procedures of discipline formation: the codification and hierarchisation of objects of study, the formation of a canonical history and tradition? How should teachers negotiate the split logics of cultural studies: the political logic that placed pedagogy in the service of democratic transformation, versus the institutional logic of knowledge acquisition as career ticket?

There were, of course, also wider challenges being posed from the late 1980s to the certainties of cultural studies' political commitments. Following the collapse of marxism-leninism in the East, what (if anything) could now be made of the Gramscian marxism that had formed the bedrock of cultural studies for over a decade? What was the future of cultural and sexual-political radicalism, in the face of their widespread co-option by the new right? What for instance – as Jacqueline Rose asks in her contribution below – were feminists to make of Margaret Thatcher's emergence as brutal emblem of a newly hegemonic authoritarian femininity? What conclusions might be drawn from this and similar cultural developments about the repeated failure of what could no longer confidently be dubbed 'the Left' to elicit popular identification?

It is to these key questions of a popular politics adequate to this *fin-de-siècle* moment that *New Formations* has addressed itself since the late 1980s. *Cultural Remix* takes a cross-section of contributions to that debate: critical readings that rove across the spectrum of contemporary cultural forms. Ranging from toys to television, from automobiles to hairstyles to popular film, the collection might in one sense be read as affirming the cultural studies faith in critical reading and its transformative potential. Against the cultural pessimist equation of commodified popular culture with mass deception, cultural studies has traditionally affirmed the power of social collectivities to transform the meanings and values embedded in existing cultural forms – and thus, potentially at least, to reshape their own conditions of existence. Such utopianism is certainly evident below in Dick Hebdige's account of commodity fetishism as (post)modern echo of the Kantian sublime: or in Kobena Mercer's argument that black hair-styling may be 'politically intelligible as (a) creative response to the experience of oppression and dispossession.' Yet what is most characteristic of the pieces presented here is in the end neither their preoccupation with quotidian cultural forms, nor any advocacy of 'progressive reading' as a strategy for cultural change. As Homi Bhabha observes in his 'Commitment to Theory', critical writings of any kind must be seen as 'forms of discourse, to the extent that they produce rather than reflect their objects of reference.' Most centrally, then, the articles assembled in *Cultural Remix* may be read as the historical traces of critical efforts to produce, out of the political wasteland of the late 1980s, a new field of cultural-political engagement. More specifically, as an early *New Formations* editorial made explicit, the journal was (and continues to be) shaped by the perception 'that new alternatives are produced in the negotiation between theoretical discourses and those of the cultural market-place, the state-funded arts sector, political parties and journalism. It is to this political space that *New Formations* addresses itself, rather than to 'politics' as shibboleth or gesture.'[3]

CULTURE/THEORY/POLITICS

Situating itself thus in a transitional space within contemporary cultural-political debate – in the midst of conflicts, for instance, over often pivotal political terms ('socialism', 'feminism', 'anti-racism', 'democracy', 'the left') – *New Formations* has regularly adopted a politics of address that privileges rupture over closure, dialogue over self-styled 'progressive', yet often entrenched and pre-determined, position-taking. It is characteristic of the journal's perception of the radical contingency of historical truths and political positions that *Cultural Remix* is thus structured, not around a series of illustrative theoretical 'approaches' or conclusive readings. Instead, the three sections below present a set of (still unresolved) *debates* that traversed the journal from the late 1980s. Section A, 'Culture/Theory/Politics', reproduces a tripartite discussion between Homi Bhabha, Jacqueline Rose and Stuart Hall: a discussion initiated in the journal, then continued in a 1989 seminar at the Institute of Contemporary Arts, London (Stuart Hall's contribution is an edited transcript of his response to Bhabha and Rose). Common to all three pieces – despite radical differences in tone, form and theoretical stance – is a perception of the inadequacy of existing critical paradigms to frame the contemporary cultural moment. For Homi Bhabha, it is a matter of especial urgency to rethink the relation between critical writing and aesthetic production (his example is Third Cinema), in a situation where an already established cultural dominance of western 'theory' over Third World 'practice' maps onto and consolidates structures of geopolitical domination. Bhabha draws on poststructuralist understandings of theoretical writing as discursive *event*, to argue for a critical writing that 'opens up a space of "translation": a place of hybridity, figuratively speaking, where the construction of a political object that is new ... properly alienates our political expectations and changes, as it must, the very forms of our recognition of the "moment" of politics.' From the radical poststructuralist perception of the materiality of language – most particularly, of its capacity for the production (as opposed to mimesis) of cultural objects, meanings, collective and individual identities – Bhabha thus concludes that 'theory', though no longer legitimately seen as the bearer of political 'truths', retains its validity as one of a number of contributing forces in the production of new spaces for cultural-political negotiation.

An example here – though not one discussed by Bhabha himself –

might be the moment of 1970s and 80s feminism, when feminist theory was an important catalyst in the transformation of cultures of gender. The example of feminism is perhaps further pertinent here, to the extent that it illustrates the dangers Bhabha and others also highlight of a universalisation of political positions and identities. Over the past twenty-five years, key feminist demands – for labour market equality, for abortion rights, for an end to rape, misogynist violence and discrimination – have without doubt gained greater mainstream legitimacy. At the same time, proto-feminist 'content' of this kind has been dis-articulated from its historical relation to feminism as collective, activist political form. Hence the oft-repeated formula, 'I'm not a feminist, but … I'm appalled by domestic violence, unequal pay' and so on. Through this popular disavowal of the feminist origins of, say, equal opportunities legislation, feminism itself is relegated to the realm of the extra-social and politically deviant. This is not in and of itself a problem: alliances between, say, queer politics and feminism may well bring greater pleasures than the attempted conversion of Tory ladies to feminism. What is required, however (and this not only of feminists) is a greater self-reflexivity about these and similar historical shifts: for if 'there is no given community or body of the people whose inherent radical historicity emits the right signs' (Bhabha), then contemporary politics must involve perpetual, and stringently historicized reflection on the strategic positioning, not only of feminist, but of all radical democratic identities.

To put the case rather crudely, then: radical poststructuralism of the kind espoused by *New Formations* has brought a new awareness of the indeterminacy of individual and collective (political) identities. What this emphatically does not mean, however, is that the task for a reconstructed democratic left is simply to forge alternative role models or figures of positive identification (for example, Bill Clinton as the boy-next-door, jogging-hero democrat for our time). As Jacqueline Rose eloquently argues in her psychoanalytic study of Thatcher's image, what we might usefully take from Freud and Lacan is an awareness of the necessary ambivalence of identifications of this kind: an awareness that might lead in the British context to the unnerving insight, for instance, that 'Thatcher was re-elected [in 1987], not despite the repugnance that many feel for her, but also in some sense because of it.' (In similar vein, Joan Copjec draws on Lacan in her piece later in the collection to argue that Ronald Reagan was loved by US citizens, not in spite of, but precisely because of his demonstrable inadequacy as President.)

This recognition of the perversity of socio-political desires has profound consequences, of course, for any political challenge to right-wing cultural hegemony. As Stuart Hall recognises in the concluding contribution to this section, an acknowledgment of the role of the unconscious in political identification may well undermine the very project of counter-hegemony. That project has traditionally been grounded in efforts to forge an oppositional (rational) collective *will*: a goal that sits uneasily with post-Freudian conceptions of unconscious *desire* as the wellspring of political mobilisation.

In the debate that introduces *Cultural Remix*, then, the question of appropriate political strategies remains (necessarily) open. Bhabha's focus is on the potential of critical writing for rupture, discontinuity, the conceptual break. For Hall, by contrast, the political object must in the end be some form of (temporarily) stabilized meaning and collective identity; for only this – however transitory – allows the construction of political subjects and their collective mobilisation. Where psychoanalysis might thus insist – as does Jacqueline Rose below – on the ambivalence of identifications, their volatile nature, Stuart Hall asks, 'what is it that enables us to identify sufficiently to think what the ground of politics might be? Could there be any kind of collective project which is not constructed around some form of identification?'

The answer to this may well be that an oppositional politics is unthinkable outside the framework of a politics of identification; yet even here, there remain unanswered questions. What cultural strategies are adequate to the radical democratisation of popular desires and identifications? Is there within popular culture the potential for counter-hegemonic transformation? If so, what historical forms might this take, and where are its limitations?

READING THE POPULAR

It is to these issues that *Cultural Remix* turns in the second section, 'Reading the Popular'. In the late 1980s context of Thatcher and Reagan's yuppie boom economies, the question of possible critical responses to New Right popular ascendancy posed itself with particular urgency. In the British case, the 1980s had brought what Stuart Hall for one had insisted were 'revolutionary' rightist cultural transformations.[4] Crippling squeezes on the state-funded cultural sector had been coupled here with the thoroughgoing restructuring of public cultural sites as consumer markets: thus (as we saw above) education-as-shopping-mall came to be conceived as the site *par excellence* of parent/student 'consumer choice'. On the broader cultural front, meanwhile, off-the-peg 'lifestyles' seemed increasingly to displace traditional cultural affiliations and identities. All this had on the one hand apparently (at last?) extinguished romantic leftist fantasies of popular culture as the domain of authentic, and potentially revolutionary working-class (or black, female, lesbian, gay, and so on) identities. But at the same time, these developments seemed equally to undermine even those theorists of the New Left who had long since abandoned authenticity as cultural given; for they still seemed wedded to some notional bond between culture – the domain of the sign – 'the social' (classically in cultural studies, relations of class, 'race' and gender), and 'the political' as extra-textual referent. Earlier Althusserian accounts of, say, working-class youth subcultures as 'imaginary resolutions' to contradictions still rooted in social (class) determinants, for instance, seemed increasingly implausible in the postmodern context of fundamentally dislocated class cultures and identities. Not only had deindustrialisation and post-Fordist restructuring, with their concomitant disorganisation of class and other social identities, radically transformed traditional structures of political allegiance and affiliation (hence, famously, the Thatcherite 'co-option' of the working-class vote). At the same time, the emergence of such apparent political anomalies as Tory anti-racism, or Thatcherite feminists, enforced a postmodern recognition of the necessary disjuncture between social (class, ethnic, gender, sexual) location, and (often mutually contradictory) cultural-political affiliations.

What unites contributions to this section is, then, their common effort to engage the complex cultural shifts conventionally (though often unhelpfully) situated as features of 'postmodernity'. Unlike some earlier cultural studies critics for whom reading a postmodernist article once induced 'an intense physical discomfort – a genuine gut reaction',[5] our contributors conceive the exploration of the postmodern (in its manifestations both as theoretical field, and popular cultural phenomenon) as an opportunity, not to lapse into late twentieth-century nausea or *ennui*, but to reflect constructively on new forms of politicized critique. Though there is certainly no consensus amongst the essayists below on appropriate critical trajectories (Kobena Mercer's and Susan Willis' articles for example occupy opposing positions in a still unresolved debate on black cultures and the commodity form), three key perceptions surface repeatedly across this section. The first involves an emphasis on the specificity of cultural practices and forms: a refusal, then, to harness, say, cultural resistances to larger, eschatalogical projects for political transformation. Thus, for example, Dick Hebdige and Kobena Mercer's focus on commodity consumption as *aesthetic practice* in everyday life allows both authors, first, to bring to bear on a commoditised popular culture contemporary critiques of culture and the aesthetic (Hebdige for instance ranges post-Kantian aesthetic philosophy alongside Bourdieu's sociology of taste, while Mercer situates black hairstyles within postcolonial histories of diasporic identification). What this attention to the particularities of aesthetic forms and cultural identifications allows is, secondly, an escape from facile conflations of consumer pleasure with political resistance; indeed for Hebdige, it is not politics, but the aesthetic that functions as a repository of 'liberatory potentials' – potentials 'residing in that yearning for perfection and the possible which seems to constitute what we might call the aesthetic imperative.' If Kobena Mercer still insists on the 'political intelligibility' of black popular style, then this may be because (as Susan Willis intimates) black people have been traditionally as marginalised within mainstream consumer culture as in what Mercer terms 'official social institutions of representation and legitimation.' Black styles of hair and dress, then, through their re-writing and creolization of mainstream popular cultural forms have 'participated in a popular logic of rupture' (Mercer) that links aesthetic practice to the profoundly *political* disruption of established cultural norms.

This emphasis on specificity in cultural critique produces a second shared perception in the articles below: a stress, that is, on the radical historicity of cultural meanings. From Dick Hebdige's use of autobiography and ethnographic observation, as from Mercer's and Willis' genealogies of black cultural meanings, there emerges an awareness of the local, the particular, the historically specific (not 'grand theory') as points of departure for popular cultural reading. The political urgency of that critical perception is highlighted by Ien Ang in her study of the Dutch TV station VARA as a model of 'progressive television'. Criticising VARA's 'institutional progressivism', Ang argues for a 'progressive television' defined, not by 'content' or origin (the 'right-on' TV station), but by its awareness of the televisual field as a mobile site of cultural contestation. For Ang, what is 'progressive' in culture is situated, not in fixed, formal oppositions to the culturally dominant; instead, it must 'be seen as a temporary and local politico-cultural effect' – one that is, moreover, 'often unpredictable and seemingly accidental.'

Ang's comments bring into focus a third and final critical imperative foregrounded by work in Section C. If there is no pre-existent, 'progressive' identity – no counter-hegemonic bloc as the fixed subject of radical cultural change – then the emphasis of cultural critique shifts to the identification, not of radical content, but of 'spaces' for cultural-political engagement and negotiation. Thus, for instance, Charlotte Brunsdon uses the satellite dish to focus attention on cultural (class) antagonisms in public space: her piece considers the humble dish as a site of public conflict over the hierarchies of taste that consolidate cultural hegemony. The political dimensions of consumer choice in television are highlighted in Brunsdon's identification of the satellite dish as 'a concrete and visible sign of a consumer who has bought into the supranational entertainment space, who will not necessarily be available for the ritual, citizen-making moments of national broadcasting.'

DEMOCRACY AND DIFFERENCE

Charlotte Brunsdon's comments on traditional conceptions of the national citizen reflect a larger preoccupation with questions of democracy and citizenship in *New Formations* since the late 1980s (culminating in a special issue on 'Democracy' in 1991). That turn to political theory was motivated by what might be seen as an epistemological crisis in contemporary cultural critique – or at least, as a fundamental undermining of its key terms and conceptual foundations. The post-marxism that had underpinned cultural studies over two decades was increasingly challenged through the 1980s by (often cataclysmic) transformations in the contemporary political terrain: by socialism's collapse in the East, by a radical redrawing in western politics of traditional boundaries between right and left, by the dissolution of the 'new social movements' that had shaped the Anglo-American New Left, and so on.

In this context, *New Formations* has increasingly addressed itself to a rethinking of the political-theoretical categories that frame cultural analysis. The recasting of a political framework for cultural critique has been facilitated in part by *New Formations*' engagement with theoretical schools and traditions outside the orbit of the Anglo-American New Left (Mladen Dolar's discussion of Foucault and Lacan below – one of many contributions the journal has published over the years from the Slovenian school of Lacanian critique – is one of numerous examples in this collection of that search for new theoretical alliances and configurations).

In *New Formations*' engagement with political theory, two sets of connected questions have surfaced repeatedly. The first relates to conceptualisations of the 'other' and cultural difference: a problematic rooted theoretically in feminist, lesbian, gay and postcolonial theory, and deriving political urgency from contemporary nationalist and radical right persecutions of the alien and different. Hence the inclusion below of Satya P. Mohanty's critique of relativism – his arguments for what might be termed a minimalist universalism as a basis for the political negotiation of antagonism and difference – as well as Anna Marie Smith's exploration of the imaginary logic that situates homosexuality as 'other' to the nation. Chantal Mouffe and Joan Copjec, meanwhile, address a second key question, that of the contemporary viability of the liberal democratic tradition. For Chantal Mouffe, liberal democracy's current triumphalist claims to global hegemony represent a challenge, 'not to provide an apologia for democracy, but to analyse its principles, examine its operation, discover its limitations and bring out its potentialities.' Mouffe herself approaches that goal by reading against the grain one of democracy's most forceful critics, the political philosopher and convert to National Socialism, Carl Schmitt. Joan Copjec's rather different aim, using insights from Lacan, is to account for some at least of the irrationalities surrounding democratic popular opinion (and one can surely only support her view that votes for Reagan had little 'rational' basis ...).

New Formations' preoccupation with political alternatives for the contemporary moment certainly did not cease in 1991, when the most recent of the articles republished in *Cultural Remix* first appeared. This volume takes only a selective look at a journal that has since continued to seek, not some grand project for a brighter political future, but spaces for creative critical engagement.

Eric Carter, James Donald, Judith Squires, Autumn 1994

INTRODUCTION

NOTES

[1] Simon During (ed), *The Cultural Studies Reader*, Routledge 1993: Larry Grossberg, Cary Nelson, Paula Treichler (eds), *Cultural Studies*, Routledge 1992: Jim McGuigan and Ann Gray (eds), *Studying Culture*, Edward Arnold 1993: Graeme Turner, *British Cultural Studies: An Introduction*, Routledge 1990.

[2] Stuart Hall, 'Cultural studies: two paradigms', in Richard Collins *et al.* (eds), *Media, Culture and Society. A Critical Reader*, Sage 1986, pp33-48: p34.

[3] James Donald, 'Introduction: Travelling Theory', *New Formations* 3, Winter 1987, p4.

[4] See for example Stuart Hall's claim that 'this conjuncture (that of 'Thatcherism') has a unique and specific character, and has proved to be *an historic turning point* in postwar British political and cultural life': in his *The Hard Road to Renewal: Thatcherism and the Crisis of the Left*, Verso 1988, p1 (our emphasis).

[5] John Clarke, *New Times and Old Enemies: Essays on Cultural Studies and America*, Harper Collins 1991, p177.

A. Culture/Theory/
Politics

The Commitment to Theory

Homi K. Bhabha

I

In August 1986, the Edinburgh International Film Festival staged a three-day conference on 'Third Cinema' organized by Jim Pines, June Givanni and Paul Willemen. The concerns of the conference were publicized in these terms:

> With the major political and economic changes experienced in both the Euro-American and so-called Third World since the late '70s, the issue of cultural specificity (the need to know which specific social-historical processes are at work in the generation of cultural products) and the question of how precisely social existence overdetermines cultural practices have taken on a new and crucial importance. The complexity of the shifting dynamics between intra- and inter-national differences and power relations has shown simple models of class domination at home and imperialism abroad to be totally inadequate.

Papers by many of the international contributors – both film-makers and theorists – will soon be published in Jim Pines and Paul Willemen (eds), Third Cinema *(London: BFI). This article, based as one of the concluding papers, develops a political response to some of the debates that emerged at Edinburgh.*

There was a damaging and self-defeating assumption circulating at the Edinburgh 'Third Cinema' Conference – and in many influential places beyond it – that theory is necessarily the élite language of the socially and culturally privileged. It is said that the place of the academic critic is inevitably within the Eurocentric archives of an imperialist or neo-colonial West. The Olympian realms of what is mistakenly labelled 'pure theory' are assumed to be eternally insulated from the historical exigencies and tragedies of the wretched of the earth. I believe it ain't necessarily so. Must we always polarize in order to polemicize? Are we trapped in a politics of struggle where the representation of social antagonisms and historical contradictions can take no other form than a binarism of theory vs. politics? Can the aim of freedom or knowledge be the simple inversion of the relation of oppressor and oppressed, margin and periphery, negative image and positive image? Is our only way out of such dualism the espousal of an implacable oppositionality or the invention of an originary counter-myth of radical purity? Must the project of our liberationist aesthetics be for ever part of a totalizing, Utopian vision of Being and History that seeks to transcend the contradictions and ambivalences that constitute the very structure of human subjectivity and its systems of cultural representation?

Deep within the vigorous knock-about that ensued, at times, at Edinburgh, between what was represented as the 'larsony' and distortion of European 'metatheorizing' and the radical, engaged, activist experience of Third World creativity,[1] I could see the mirror image (albeit reversed in content and intention) of that ahistorical nineteenth-century polarity of Orient and Occident which, in the name of progress, unleashed the exclusionary imperialist ideologies of self and other. This time round, the term 'critical theory', often untheorized and unargued, was definitely the Other, an otherness that was insistently identified with the vagaries of the 'depoliticized' Eurocentric critic. Was the cause of radical art or critique best served by the fulminating professor of film who announced, at a flashpoint in the argument, 'We are not artists, we are political activists'? By obscuring the power of his own practice in the rhetoric of militancy, he failed to draw attention to the specific value of a politics of cultural production which, because it makes the surfaces of cinematic signification the grounds of political intervention, gives depth to the language of social criticism and extends the domain of 'politics' in a direction that will not be entirely dominated by the forces of economic or social control. Forms of popular rebellion and mobilization are often most subversive and transgressive when they are created through the identification with oppositional *cultural* practices.

Before I am accused of bourgeois voluntarism, liberal pragmatism, academicist pluralism and all the other -isms that are freely bandied about by those who take the most severe exception to 'Eurocentric' theoretic*ism* (Derrideanism, Lacanianism, post-structuralism ...), I would like to clarify the goals of my opening questions. I am convinced that, in the language of political economy, it is legitimate to represent the relations of exploitation and domination in the discursive division between First and Third Worlds. Despite the claims to a spurious rhetoric of 'internationalism' on the part of the established multinationals and the networks of the new communication technology industries, such circulations of signs and commodities as there are, are caught in the vicious circuits of surplus value that link First World capital to Third World labour markets through the chains of the international division of labour. Spivak is right to conclude that it 'is in the interest of capital to preserve the comprador theatre in a state of relatively primitive labour legislation and environmental regulation':[2] remember Bhopal.

I am equally convinced that in the language of international diplomacy there is a sharp growth in a new Anglo-American nationalism (NATO-nalism?) that increasingly articulates its economic and military power in political acts that express a neo-imperialist disregard for the independence and autonomy of Other peoples and places, largely in the Third World. Think of America's 'backyard' policy towards the Caribbean and Latin America, the patriotic gore and patrician lore of Britain's Falkland Campaign, or the triumphalism of the American and British navies patrolling the Persian Gulf (July 1987). I am further convinced that such economic and political domination has a profound hegemonic influence on the information orders of the Western world, its popular media and its specialized institutions and academies. So much is not in doubt.

What does demand further discrimination is whether the 'new' languages of theoretical critique (semiotic, post-structuralist, deconstructionist etc.) simply reflect those geopolitical divisions and spheres of influence. Are the interests of 'Western' theory necessarily collusive with the hegemonic role of the West as a power bloc? Is the specialized, 'textualized', often academic language of theory merely another power ploy of the culturally privileged Western élite to produce a discourse of the Other that sutures its own power-knowledge equation?

A large film festival in the West – even an alternative or counter-cultural event such as Edinburgh's 'Third Cinema' Conference – never fails to reveal the disproportionate influence of the West as cultural forum, in all three senses of that word: as place of public

5

exhibition and discussion, as place of judgement, and as market-place. An Indian film about the plight of Bombay's pavement-dwellers wins the Newcastle Festival which then opens up distribution facilities in India. The first searing exposé of the Bhopal disaster is made for Channel Four. A major debate on the politics and theory of Third Cinema first appears in *Screen*. An archival article on the important history of neo-traditionalism and the 'popular' in Indian cinema sees the light of day in *Framework*.[3] Among the major contributors to the development of the Third Cinema as precept and practice are a number of Third World film-makers and critics who are exiles or émigrés to the West and live problematically, often dangerously, on the 'left' margins of a Eurocentric, bourgeois, liberal culture. I don't think I need to add individual names or places, or detail the historical reasons why the West carries and exploits what Bourdieu would call its symbolic capital. The condition is all too familiar, and it is not my purpose here to make those important distinctions between different national situations and the disparate political causes and collective histories of cultural exile. I want to take my stand on the shifting margins of cultural displacement – that confounds any profound or 'authentic' sense of a 'national' culture or an 'organic' intellectual – and ask what the function of a committed theoretical perspective might be, once the cultural and historical hybridity of the post-colonial world is taken as the paradigmatic place of departure....

Committed to what? At this stage in the argument, I do not want to identify any specific 'object' of political allegiance – the Third World, the working class, the feminist struggle. Although such an objectification of political activity is crucial and must significantly inform political debate, it is not the only option for those critics or intellectuals who are committed to progressive, political change in the direction of a socialist society. It is a sign of political maturity to accept that there are many forms of political writing whose different effects are obscured when they are divided between the 'theoretical' and the 'activist'. It is not as if the leaflet involved in the organization of a strike is short on theory, while a speculative article on the theory of ideology ought to have more practical examples or applications. They are both forms of discourse and to that extent they produce rather than reflect their objects of reference. The difference between them lies in their operational qualities. The leaflet has a specific expository and organizational purpose, temporally bound to the event; the theory of ideology makes its contribution to those embedded political ideas and principles that inform the right to strike. The latter does not justify the former; nor does it necessarily precede it. It exists side by side with it – the one as an enabling part of the other – like the recto and verso of a sheet of paper, to use a common semiotic analogy in the uncommon context of politics.

My concern here is with the process of 'intervening ideologically', as Stuart Hall describes the role of 'imaging' or representation in the practice of politics in his response to the British election of 1987.[4] For Hall, the notion of hegemony implies a politics of *identification* or the imaginary. This occupies a discursive space which is not exclusively delimited by the history of either the right or the left. It exists somehow in between these political polarities, and also between the familiar divisions of theory and political practice. This approach, as I read it, introduces us to an exciting, neglected moment, or movement, in the 'recognition' of the relation of politics to theory; and confuses the traditional differences between them. Such a movement is initiated if we see that relation as determined by the rule of repeatable materiality, which Foucault describes as the process by which statements from one institution can be transcribed in the discourse of another.[5] Despite the schemata of use and application that constitute a field of stabilization for the statement, any change in the statement's condition of use and reinvestment, any alteration in its field of experience or verification, or, indeed, any difference in the problems to be solved, can lead to the emergence of a new statement: the difference of the same.

In what hybrid forms, then, may a politics of the theoretical statement emerge? What tensions and ambivalences mark this enigmatic place from which theory 'speaks'? Speaking in the name of some counter-authority or horizon of 'the true' (in Foucault's sense of the strategic effects of any apparatus or *dispositif*), the theoretical enterprise has to represent the adversarial authority (of power and/or knowledge) which, in a doubly-inscribed move, it simultaneously seeks to subvert and replace. In this complicated formulation I have tried to indicate something of the complex boundary and location of the event of theoretical critique which does not *contain* the truth (in polar opposition to totalitarianism, 'bourgeois liberalism' or whatever is supposed to repress it). The 'true' is always marked and informed by the ambivalence of the process of emergence itself, the productivity of meanings that construct counter-knowledges *in medias res*, in the very act of agonism, within the terms of a negotiation (rather than a

7

negation) of oppositional and antagonistic elements. Political positions are not simply identifiable as progressive or reactionary, bourgeois or radical, prior to the act of *critique engagée*, or outside the terms and conditions of their discursive and textual address. It is in this sense that the historical moment of political action must necessarily be thought as part of the history of the form of its writing. This is not to state the obvious, that there is no knowledge – political or otherwise – outside representation. It is to suggest that the dynamics of writing – of *écriture* – require us to rethink the logics of causality or determinacy through which we recognize the 'political' as a form of calculation and strategic action dedicated to social transformation.

'What is to be done?' must acknowledge the force of writing, its metaphoricity and its rhetorical discourse, as a productive matrix which defines the 'social' and makes it available as an objective of/for action. Textuality is not simply a second-order ideological expression or a verbal symptom of a pre-given political subject. That the political subject – as indeed the subject of politics – is a discursive event is nowhere more clearly seen than in a text which has been a formative influence on western liberal democratic and socialist discourse – Mill's essay *On Liberty*. His crucial chapter, 'On the liberty of thought and discussion', is almost entirely an attempt to define political judgement as the problem of finding a form of *public rhetoric* able to represent different and opposing political 'contents' or principles as a dialogical exchange in the ongoing present of the enunciation of the political statement. What is unexpected is the suggestion that it is a crisis of identification initiated in the textual performance that displays a certain 'difference' *within* the signification of any single political system, prior to the substantial differences *between* political beliefs. A knowledge can only become political through an agonistic language-game: dissensus, alterity and otherness are the discursive conditions for the circulation and recognition of a politicized subject and a public 'truth':

> [If] opponents of all important truths do not exist, it is indispensable to imagine them– [He] must feel the whole force of the difficulty which the true view of the subject has to encounter and dispose of; *else he will never really possess himself of the portion of truth which meets and removes that difficulty* ... Their conclusion may be true, but it might be false for anything they know: they have never thrown themselves into the *mental position* of those who think differently from them ... and

8

consequently they do not, in any proper sense of the word, *know the doctrine which they themselves profess.* (My emphasis)[6]

It is true that Mill's 'rationality' permits, or requires, such forms of contention and contradiction in order to enhance his vision of the inherently progressive and evolutionary bent of *human* judgement. (This makes it possible for contradictions to be resolved and also generates a sense of the whole truth which reflects the natural, organic bent of the human mind.) It is also true that Mill always reserves, in society as in his argument, the unreal neutral space of the Third Person as the representative of the 'people', who witnesses the debate from an 'epistemological distance' and draws a reasonable conclusion. Even so, in his attempt to describe the political as a form of debate and dialogue – as the process of public rhetoric – that is crucially mediated through this ambivalent and antagonistic faculty of a political 'imagination', Mill exceeds the usual mimetic sense of the battle of ideas. He suggests something much more dialogical: the realization of the political idea at the ambivalent point of textual address, its emergence through a form of political fantasy. Rereading Mill through the strategies of 'writing' that I have suggested above reveals that one cannot passively follow the line of argument running through the logic of the opposing ideology. The textual process of political antagonism initiates a contradictory process of reading 'between the lines'; the agent of the discourse becomes, in the same time of utterance, the inverted, projected, fantasmatic object of the argument, 'turned against itself'. It is, Mill insists, only by effectively assuming the mental position of the antagonist and working through the displacing and decentring force of that discursive difficulty, that the politicized 'portion of truth' is produced. This is a different dynamic from the ethic of 'tolerance' in liberal ideology which has to imagine opposition in order to contain it and demonstrate its enlightened relativism or humanism. Reading Mill against the grain like this suggests that politics can only become 'representative', a truly *public* discourse, through a splitting in the signification of the subject of representation, through an ambivalence at the point of the enunciation of a politics.

I have chosen to demonstrate the importance of the space of writing and the problematic of address at the very heart of the liberal tradition, because it is here that the myth of the 'transparency' of the human agent and the reasonableness of political action is most forcefully asserted. Despite the more radical political alternatives of the right and the left, the popular, common-sense view of the place of the individual in relation to the social is still substantially thought and lived in ethical terms moulded by liberal beliefs. What the question of writing reveals most starkly are the ambivalent and fantasmatic texts that make 'the political' possible. From such a perspective, the problematic of political judgement cannot be represented as an epistemological problem of 'appearance and reality' or 'theory and practice' or 'word and thing'. Not can it be represented as a dialectical problem or a symptomatic contradiction constitutive of the materiality of the 'real' whose difference must be sublated in the progress of history or the political science of Marxism. On the contrary, we are made excruciatingly aware of the ambivalent juxtaposition, the dangerous interstitial, invaginated relation of the 'factual' and the 'fantasmatic', and, beyond that, of the crucial function of the fantasmatic and the rhetorical – those vicissitudes of the movement of the signifier – in the fixing of the 'factual', in the 'closure' of the real, in the efficacy and power of strategic thinking in the discourses of *Realpolitik*. It is this to-and-fro, this *fort/da* of the symbolic process of political negotiation, that we are challenged to think in, and through, what I have called a politics of address. The question of writing and address focuses on the necessity of this ambivalent movement in the construction of political authority, in the fixity and fixation of boundaries of meaning and strategies of action. Its importance goes beyond its unsettling, from the point of view of philosophy, or the essentialism or logocentricism of a received political tradition, in the name of an abstract 'free play of the signifier'.

The first principles of a socialist critique will appear contentious and contradictory to a bourgeois humanist reading, as indeed will be the political intentions of the critic. So much is obvious. In the act of the *écriture* or scription of an oppositional reading, however, we must not expect to recognize the *new* political object, or aim, or knowledge, as simply a mimetic reflection of the *a priori* principle or commitment. Nor should we demand of it a pure teleology of analysis or purport whereby the prior principle is simply augmented, its rationality smoothly developed, its identity as 'socialist' or 'materialist' (as opposed to 'neo-imperialist' or 'humanist') consistently confirmed in each oppositional stage of the argument. Such identikit political idealism may be the symptom of great individual fervour, but it lacks the deeper, if dangerous, sense of what is entailed by the *passage* of history in theoretical discourse. The language of critique is effective not because it keeps for ever separate the terms of the master and the slave, the mercantilist and the Marxist, but to the extent to which it overcomes the given grounds of opposition and opens up a space of 'translation': a place of hybridity, figuratively speaking, where the construction of a political object that is new, *neither the one nor the Other*, properly alienates our political expectations, and changes, as it must, the very forms of our recognition of the 'moment' of politics. The challenge lies in conceiving of the 'time' of political action and understanding as opening up a space that can accept and regulate the differential structure of the moment of intervention without rushing to produce a dialectical unity of the social antagonism or contradiction. This must be a sign that history is *happening* – within the windless pages of theory, within the systems and structures we construct to figure the passage of the historical.

When I talk of *negotiation* rather than *negation*, it is to convey a temporality that makes it possible to conceptualize the articulation of antagonistic or contradictory elements without either the idealism of a dialectic which enables the emergence of a teleological or transcendent History, or the 'scienticism' of symptomatic reading where the nervous tics on the surface of ideology reveal the 'real materialist contradiction' that History embodies. In such a temporality, the act of theory is the process of articulation, and the event of theory becomes the *negotiation* of contradictory and antagonistic instances. These open up hybrid sites and objectives of struggle and destroy those familiar polarities between knowledge and its objects, and between theory and practical-political reason.[7] If I have argued against a primordial and previsionary division of 'right' or 'left', progressive or reactionary, it has been only to stress the fully historical and discursive *differance* between them. I would not like my notion of negotiation to be confused with some syndicalist sense of 'reformism' because that is not the political level that is being explored here. By negotiation I attempt to draw attention to the structure of *interaction* that informs political movements (in both senses of the word), that attempt to articulate antagonistic and oppositional elements without the redemptive rationality of sublation or transcendence.[8]

The temporality of negotiation or translation as I have sketched it has two main advantages. First, it acknowledges the historical connectedness between the subject and object of critique so that there can be no simplistic, essentialist opposition between ideological miscognition and revolutionary truth. The progressive 'reading' is crucially determined by the adversarial or agonistic situation itself; it is effective because it uses the subversive, messy mask of camouflage and does not come like a pure avenging angel speaking the truth of a radical historicity and pure oppositionality. If one is aware of this heterogeneous emergence (not origin) of radical critique, then – and this is my second point, the function of theory within the political referents and priorities – the people, the community, class struggle, anti-racism, gender difference, the assertion of an anti-imperialist, black or third perspective – are not 'there' in some primordial, naturalistic sense. Nor do they reflect a unitary or homogeneous political object. They 'make sense' as they come to be constructed in the discourses of feminism or Marxism or the Third Cinema or whatever, whose objects of priority – class or sexuality or 'the new ethnicity' (Stuart Hall) – are always in historical and philosophical tension, or cross-reference with other objectives.

Indeed, the whole history of socialist thought which seeks to 'make it new and better' seems to be a difficult process of articulating priorities whose political objects can be recalcitrant and contradictory. Within contemporary Marxism, for example, witness the continual tension between the 'English', humanist, labourist faction and the 'theoreticist', structuralist, 'Trotskyist' tendencies. Within feminism, there is again a marked difference of emphasis between the psychoanalytic/semiotic end and those who see the articulation of gender and class as less problematic through a theory of cultural and ideological interpellation. I have presented these differences in broad brush-strokes, often using the language of polemic, to suggest that each 'position' is always a process of translation and transference of meaning. Each objective is constructed on the trace of that perspective that it puts 'under erasure'; each political object is displacing in relation to the other, and displaced in that critical act. Too often these theoretical issues are peremptorily transposed into organizational terms and represented as 'sectarianism'. I am suggesting that such contradictions and conflicts, which often thwart political intentions and make the question of commitment complex and difficult, are rooted in the process of translation and displacement in which the 'object' of politics is inscribed. The effect is not stasis or a sapping of the will. It is, on the contrary, the spur to the 'negotiation' of socialist democratic politics and policies which demand that questions of organization are theorized and socialist theory is 'organized', *because there is no given community or body of the people, whose inherent, radical historicity emits the right signs.*

The emphasis on the representation of the political, on the construction of discourse, is the radical contribution of the 'translation' of theory whose vigilance never allows a simple identity between the political objective (not object) and its means of representation. This emphasis on the necessity of heterogeneity and the double inscription of the political objective is not merely the repetition of a general truth about discourse introduced into the political field. In denying an essentialist logic and a mimetic referent to political representation it is a strong, principled argument against political separatism of any colour, that cuts through the moralism that usually accompanies such claims. There is literally, and figuratively, no space for the 'unitary' or single political objective which offends against the sense of a socialist *community* of interest and articulation.

In Britain, in the 1980s, no political struggle was fought more powerfully and sustained more poignantly on the values and traditions of a socialist community than the miners' strike of 1984-5. The battalions of monetarist figures and forecasts on the 'profitability' of the pits were starkly ranged against the most illustrious standards of the British labour movement, the most cohesive cultural communities of the working class. The choice was clearly between the dawning world of the new 'Thatcherite' city gent and a long history of 'the working man', or so it seemed to the traditional left and the new right. In these class terms the 'mining' women involved in the strike were applauded for the heroic supporting role they played, for their endurance and initiative. But the 'revolutionary' impulse, it seemed, belonged securely to the working-class male. Then, to commemorate the first anniversary of the strike, Beatrix Campbell, in the *Guardian*, interviewed a group of women who had been involved in the strike. It was clear that their experience of the historical struggle, their understanding of the 'historic' choice, was startlingly different and more complex. Their testimonies would not be contained simply or singly within the priorities of the politics of class or the histories of industrial struggle. Many of the women began to question their roles within the family and the community – the two central institutions which articulated the meanings and mores of the *tradition* of the labouring classes around which ideological battle was enjoined. Some challenged the symbols and authorities of the culture they fought to defend. Others disrupted the homes they had struggled to sustain. For most of them there was no return, no going back to the 'good old days'. It would be simplistic to suggest either that this considerable social change was a spin-off from the class struggle or that it was a repudiation of the politics of class from a socialist-feminist perspective. There is no simple political or social 'truth' to be learned, for there is no unitary representation of a political agency, no fixed hierarchy of political values and effects.

My illustration attempts to display the importance of the 'hybrid' moment of political change. Here the transformational value of change lies in the rearticulation, or translation, of elements that are *neither the One* (unitary working class) *nor the Other* (the politics of gender) *but something else besides* which contests the terms and territories of both. This does not necessarily involve the formation of a new synthesis, but a negotiation between them *in medias res*, in the profound experience or knowledge of the displaced, diversionary, differentiated boundaries in which the limits and limitations of social power are encountered in an agonistic relation. When Eric Hobsbawm suggests in *Marxism Today* (October 1987) that the Labour Party should seek to produce a socialist alliance among progressive forces that are widely dispersed and distributed across a range of class, culture, and occupational forces – without a unifying sense of the 'class for itself' – he is acknowledging, as *historical* necessity, the kind of 'hybridity' that I have attempted to identify as a practice in the signification of the political. A little less pietistic articulation of political principle (around class and nation); just a little more of the principle of 'political' articulation....

This seems to be the theoretical issue at the heart of Stuart Hall's arguments for the construction of a counter-hegemonic power bloc through which a socialist party might construct its majority, its constituency; and the Labour Party might (in)conceivably improve its 'image'. The unemployed, semi-skilled and unskilled, part-time workers, male and female, the low-paid, black people, underclasses: these signs of the fragmentation of class and cultural consensus represent, for Hall, both the historical experience of contemporary social divisions, and a structure of heterogeneity upon which to construct his theoretical and political alternative. That is, for Hall, the imperative to construct a new social bloc of different constituencies, through the production of a form of symbolic identification that would result in a collective will. The Labour Party, with its desire to reinstate its traditionalist image – white, male, working-class, trade-union based – is not 'hegemonic enough', Hall writes. He is right; what remains unanswered is whether the rationalism and intentionality that propel the 'collective will' are compatible with the language of 'symbolic image' and fragmentary identification which represent, for Hall and for his 'hegemony'/'counter-hegemony', the fundamental political issues. Can there ever be hegemony 'enough', except in the sense that a two-thirds majority will elect us a socialist government?

It is in intervening in Hall's argument that the necessities of 'negotiation' are revealed, in my attempt to foreground his analytic of fragmentation. The interest and excitement of Hall's position lie in his acknowledgement, remarkable for the British left, that, though influential, 'material interests on their own have no necessary class belongingness'.[9] This has two significant effects. It enables Hall to see the agents of political change as discontinuous, divided subjects caught in conflicting interests and identities. Equally, at the historical level of a Thatcherite 'population', he asserts that divisive rather than solidary forms of identification are the rule resulting in undecidabilities and aporia of political judgement:

> What does a working woman put first? Which of her identities is the one that determines her political choices?

The answer to such a question is defined, according to Hall, in the ideological definition of materialist interests; a process of symbolic identification achieved through a political technology of 'imaging' that hegemonically produces a social bloc of the right or the left. Not only is the social bloc heterogeneous but the work of hegemony – as I see it – is itself the process of iteration and differentiation. It depends on the production of alternative or antagonistic images that are always produced side by side and in competition with each other. It is this side-by-side nature, this partial presence or metonymy of antagonism, and its effective significations, that gives meaning (quite literally) to a politics of struggle *as the struggle of identifications* and the war of positions. It is therefore problematic to think of it as sublated into an image of the collective will.

Hegemony requires iteration and alterity to be effective, to be productive of politicized populations: the (non-homogenous) symbolic-social bloc needs to represent itself in a solidary 'collective' will – a modern image of the future – if those populations are to produce a progressive government. Both may be necessary but they do not easily follow from each other, for in each case the mode of representation and its temporality are different. The contribution of negotiation is to display the 'in-between' of this crucial argument that is *not* self-contradictory, but significantly performs, in the process of its discussion, the problems of judgement and identification that inform the political space of its enunciation. For the moment, the act of negotiation will only be interrogatory. Can such split subjects and differentiated social movements, which display ambivalent and divided forms of identification, be represented in a 'collective will' that distinctively echoes Gramsci's enlightenment inheritance and its rationalism?[10] How does the language of the will accommodate the vicissitudes of its representation, which is its construction through a symbolic majority where the have-nots identify themselves from the position of the haves? How do we construct a politics based on such a displacement of affect or strategic elaboration (Foucault), where political positioning is ambivalently grounded in an acting-out of political fantasies that require repeated passages across the differential boundaries between one symbolic bloc *and an other*, and the positions available to each? If such is the case, then how do we fix the counter-image of socialist hegemony to reflect the divided will, the fragmented population? If the polity of hegemony is, quite literally, *unsignifiable* without the metonymic representation of its agonistic and ambivalent structure of articulation, then how does the collective will stabilize and unify its address as an agency of *representation*, as representative of a 'people'? How do we avoid the mixing or overlap of images, the split screen, the failure to synchronize sound and image? Perhaps we need to change the ocular language of the image in order to talk of the social and political identifications or representations of a 'people' – it is worth noting that Laclau and Mouffe have turned to the language of textuality and discourse, to *différance* and enunciative modalites, in attempting to understand the structure of hegemony.[11] Paul Gilroy also refers to Bakhtin's theory of narrative when he describes the performance of black expressive cultures as an attempt to transform the relationship between performer and crowd 'in *dialogic* rituals so that spectators acquire the active role of participants in collective process which are sometimes cathartic and which may symbolize or even create a community' (my emphasis).[12]

Such negotiations between politics and theory make it impossible to think of the place of the theoretical as a metanarrative claiming a more total form of generality. Nor is it possible to claim a certain, familiar 'epistemological' distance between the *time and place* of the intellectual and the activist, as Fanon suggests when he observes that 'while politicians situate their action in actual present-day events, men of culture take their stand in the field of history'.[13] It is precisely that popular binarism between theory and politics, whose foundational basis is an epistemological view of knowledge as totalizing generality and everyday life as experience, subjectivity, or false consciousness, that I have tried to erase. It is a distinction that even Sartre subscribes to when he describes the committed intellectual as 'the theoretician of practical knowledge' whose defining criterion is rationality and whose first project is to combat the irrationality of ideology.[14] From the perspective of negotiation and translation, *contra* Fanon and Sartre, there can be no final discursive *closure* of theory. It does not foreclose on the political, even though battles for power-knowledge may be won or lost to great effect. The corollary is that there is no first or final act of revolutionary social (or socialist) transformation – just as, in Lacan's account of the process of subjectivity in language, there is no fixed point of identity, for the 'signifier represents a subject for another signifier'.

I hope it is clear that this erasure of the traditional boundary between theory/politics, and my resistance to the en-*closure* of the theoretical whether it is read negatively as élitism or positively as radical supra-rationality, does not turn on the good or bad faith of the activist agent or the intellectual *agent provocateur*. I am primarily concerned with the conceptual structuring of the terms – the 'theoretical' / the 'political' – which inform a range of debates around the place and time of the committed intellectual. I have therefore argued for a certain relation to knowledge which I think is crucial in structuring our sense of what the *object* of theory may be in the act of determining our specific political *objectives*.

II

What is at stake in the naming of critical theory as 'Western'? It is, obviously, a designation of institutional power and ideological Eurocentricity. Critical theory often engages with Third World texts within the familiar traditions and conditions of colonial anthropology either to 'universalize' their meaning within its own cultural and academic discourse, or to sharpen its internal critique of the Western logocentric sign, the idealist 'subject', or indeed the illusions and delusions of civil society. This is a familiar manoeuvre of theoretical knowledge, where, having opened up the chasm of cultural 'difference'

17

– of the indeterminacy of meaning or the slippage of the signifier – a mediator or metaphor of 'otherness' must be found to contain that 'difference'. In order to be institutionally effective as a discipline, the knowledge of cultural difference must be made to 'foreclose' on the Other; the 'Other' thus becomes at once the 'fantasy' of a certain cultural space or, indeed, the certainty of a form of theoretical knowledge that deconstructs the epistemological 'edge' of the West. More significantly, the site of cultural difference becomes the mere phantom of a dire disciplinary struggle in which it has no space or power. Montesquieu's Turkish Despot, Barthes's Japan, Kristeva's China, Derrida's Namibikwara Indians, Lyotard's Cashinahua 'pagans' are part of this strategy of containment where the Other text is forever the exegetical horizon of difference, never the active agent of articulation. The 'Other' is cited, quoted, framed, illuminated, encased in the shot-reverse-shot strategy of a serial enlightenment. Narrative and the *cultural* politics of difference become the closed circle of interpretation. The 'Other' loses its power to signify, to negate, to initiate its 'desire', to split its 'sign' of identity, to establish its own institutional and oppositional discourse. However impeccably the content of an 'other' culture may be known, however anti-ethnocentrically it is represented, it is its *location* as the 'closure' of grand theories, the demand that, in analytical terms, it be always the 'good' object of knowledge, the docile body of difference, that reproduces a relation of domination and is the most serious indictment of the institutional powers of critical theory.

There is, however, a distinction to be made between the institutional history of critical theory and its conceptual potential for change and innovation. Althusser's critique of the temporal structure of the Hegelian-Marxist expressive 'totality', despite its functionalist limitations, opens up the possibilities of thinking the 'relations of production' in time of differential histories. Lacan's location of the signifier of desire, on the cusp of language and the law, allows the elaboration of a form of social representation that is alive to the ambivalent structure of subjectivity and sociality. Foucault's archaeology of the emergence of modern, western 'man' as a problem of finitude, inextricable from its afterbirth, its Other, enables the linear, progressivist claims of the social sciences – the major imperializing discourses – to be confronted by their own historicist limitations. These arguments and modes of analysis can be dismissed as internal squabbles around Hegelian causality, psychic representation,

18

or sociological theory. Alternatively, they can be subjected to a translation, a 'transformation of value' as part of the questioning of the project of modernity in the great, revolutionary tradition of C.L.R. James *contra* Trotsky, or Fanon, *contra* phenomenology and existentialist psychoanalysis. In 1952, it was Fanon who suggested that an oppositional, differential reading of Lacan's Other might be more relevant for the colonial condition than the marxisant reading of the master-slave dialectic.

It may be possible to produce such a translation or transformation if we understand the tension within critical theory between its institutional containment and its revisionary force. The continual reference to the horizon of Other cultures which I have mentioned earlier is ambivalent. It is a site of 'citation', but it is also a sign that such critical theory cannot for ever sustain its position in the western academy as the adversarial cutting edge of western idealism. What is required is to demonstrate another territory of translation, another testimony of analytical argument, a different engagement in the politics of and around cultural domination. What this other site for theory might be will become clearer if we first see that many of these post-structuralist ideas are themselves opposed to western Enlighten-ment humanisn and aesthetics. They constitute no less than a deconstruction of the moment of the modern, its legal values, its literary tastes, its philosophical and political categorical imperatives. Secondly, we must rehistoricize the moment of 'the emergence of the sign', or 'the question of the subject', or the 'discursive construction of social reality', to quote a few popular topics of contemporary theory. And this can only happen if we relocate the referential and institutional demands of such theoretical work in the field of cultural difference – *not cultural diversity*.

Such a reorientation may be found in the historical texts of the colonial moment in the late eighteenth and early nineteenth centuries. For at the same time as the question of cultural difference emerged in the colonial text, discourses of 'civility' were defining the doubling moment of the emergence of western modernity. Thus the political and theoretical genealogy of modernity lies not only in the origins of the *idea* of civility, but in this history of the colonial moment. It is to be found in the resistance of the colonized population to the Word of God and Man – Christianity and the English language. The transmutations and translations of indigenous traditions in their opposition to colonial authority demonstrate how the 'desire of the

19

signifier', the 'indeterminacy' or intertextuality, is deeply engaged in the struggle against dominant relations of power and knowledge. In the following words of the missionary master we hear, quite distinctly, the oppositional voices of a culture of resistance; but we also hear the uncertain and threatening process of cultural transformation. I quote from A. Duff's influential *India Missions* (1839):

> Come to some doctrine which you believe to be peculiar to Revelation; tell the people that they must be regenerated or born again, else they can never 'see God'. Before you are aware, they may go away saying, 'Oh, there is nothing new or strange here; our own Shastras tell us the same thing; we know and believe that we must be born again; it is our fate to be so.' But what do they understand by the expression? It is that they are to be born again and again, in some other form, agreeably to their own system of transmigration or reiterated births. To avoid the appearance of countenancing so absurd and pernicious a doctrine, you vary your language, and tell them that there must be a second birth – that they must be twice-born. Now it so happens that this, and all similar phraseology, is preoccupied. The sons of a Brahman have to undergo various purificatory and initiatory ceremonial rites, before they attain to full Brahmanhood. The last of these is the investite with the sacred thread; which is followed by the communication of the Gayatri, or most sacred verse in the Vedas. This ceremonial constitutes, 'religiously and metaphorically, their second birth'; henceforward their distinctive and peculiar appellation is that of the twice-born, or regenerated men. *Hence it is your improved language might only convey the impression that all must become perfect Brahmans, ere they can 'see God'.* (My emphasis)

The grounds of evangelical certitude are opposed not by the simple assertion of an antagonistic cultural tradition. The process of translation is the opening up of another contentious political and cultural site at the heart of colonial 'representation'. Here the word of divine authority is deeply flawed by the assertion of the indigenous sign and in the very practice of domination the language of the master becomes hybrid – neither the one thing nor the other. The incalculable colonized subject – half acquiescent, half oppositional, always untrustworthy – produces an unresolvable problem of cultural difference for the very address of colonial cultural authority. The 'subtile system of Hinduism', as the missionaries in the early nineteenth century called it, generated tremendous policy implications for the institutions of Christian conversion. The written authority of the Bible was challenged and together with it a post-Enlightenment notion of the evidence of Christianity and its historical priority, which was central to evangelical colonialism. The Word could no longer be trusted to carry the truth when written or spoken in the colonial world by the European missionary. Native catechists therefore had to be found, who brought with them their own cultural and political ambivalences and contradictions, often under great pressure from their families and communities.

This revision of the history of critical theory rests, I have said, on the notion of cultural difference, not cultural diversity. Cultural diversity is an epistemological object – culture as an object of empirical knowledge – whereas cultural difference is the process of the *enunciation* of culture as 'knowledge*able*', authoritative, adequate to the construction of systems of cultural identification. If cultural diversity is a category of comparative ethics, aesthetics, or ethnology, cultural difference is a process of signification through which statements *of* culture or *on* culture differentiate, discriminate, and authorize the production of fields of force, reference, applicability, and capacity. Cultural diversity is the recognition of pre-given cultural 'contents' and customs, held in a time-frame of relativism; it gives rise to anodyne liberal notions of multiculturalism, cultural exchange, or the culture of humanity. Cultural diversity is also the representation of a radical rhetoric of the separation of totalized cultures that live unsullied by the intertextuality of their historical locations, safe in the Utopianism of a mythic memory of a unique collective identity. Cultural diversity may even emerge as a system of the articulation and exchange of cultural signs in certain early structuralist accounts of anthropology.

Through the concept of cultural difference I want to draw attention to the common ground and lost territory of contemporary critical debates. For they all recognize that the problem of the cultural emerges only at the significatory boundaries of cultures, where meanings and values are (mis)read or signs are misappropriated. Yet the reality of the limit or limit-text of culture is rarely theorized outside of well-intentioned moralist polemics against prejudice and stereotype, or the blanket assertion of individual or institutional racism – that describes the effect rather than the structure of the problem. The need to think the limit of culture as a problem of the enunciation of cultural difference is disavowed.

21

The concept of cultural difference focuses on the problem of the ambivalence of cultural authority; the attempt to dominate in the *name* of a cultural supremacy which is itself produced only in the moment of differentiation. And it is the very authority of culture as a knowledge of referential truth which is at issue in the concept and moment of *enunciation*. The enunciative process introduces a split in the performative present, of cultural identification: a split between the traditional culturalist demand for a model, a tradition, a community, a stable system of reference – and the necessary negation of the certitude in the articulation of new cultural demands, meanings, strategies in the political present, as a practice of domination, or resistance. The struggle is often between the teleological or mythical time and narrative of traditionalism – of the right or the left – and the shifting, strategically displaced time of the articulation of a historical politics of negotiation which I suggested above. The time of liberation is, as Fanon powerfully evokes, a time of cultural uncertainty, and, most crucially, of significatory or representational undecidability:

> But [native intellectuals] forget that the forms of thought and what [they] feed ... on, together with modern techniques of information, language and dress have dialectically reorganised the people's intelligences and *the constant principles (of national art)* which acted as safeguards during the colonial period are now undergoing extremely radical changes ... [We] must join the people in that fluctuating movement which they are *just* giving a shape to ... which will be the signal for everything to be called into question ... it is to the zone of *occult instability* where the people dwell that we must come. (My emphasis)[15]

The enunciation of cultural difference problematizes the division of past and present, tradition and modernity, at the level of cultural representation and its authoritative address. It is the problem of how, in signifying the present, something comes to be repeated, relocated, and translated in the name of tradition, in the guise of a pastness that is not necessarily a faithful sign of historical memory but a strategy of representing authority in terms of the artifice of the archaic. That iteration negates our sense of the origins of the struggle. It undermines our sense of the homogenizing effects of cultural symbols and icons, by questioning our sense of the authority of cultural synthesis in general.

22

This demands that we rethink our perspective on the identity of culture. Here Fanon's passage – somewhat reinterpreted – may be helpful. What is implied by his juxtaposition of the constant national principles with his view of culture-as-political-struggle, which he so enigmatically and beautifully describes as 'the zone of occult instability where the people dwell'? These ideas not only help to explain the nature of colonial struggle. They also suggest a possible critique of the positive aesthetic and political values we ascribe to the unity or totality of cultures, especially those that have known long and tyrannical histories of domination and misrecognition. Cultures are never unitary in themselves, nor simply dualistic in relation to Self and Other. This is not because of some humanistic nostrum that beyond individual cultures we all belong to the human culture of mankind; nor is it because of an ethical relativism that suggests that in our cultural capacity to speak of and judge Others we necessarily 'place ourselves in their position', in a kind of relativism of distance of which Bernard Williams has written at length.[16]

The reason a cultural text or system of meaning cannot be sufficient unto itself is that the act of cultural enunciation – the *place of utterance* – is crossed by the *différance* of writing or *écriture*. This has less to do with what anthropologists might describe as varying attitudes to symbolic systems within different cultures than with the structure of symbolic representation – not the content of the symbol or its 'social function', but the structure of symbolization. It is this 'difference' in language that is crucial to the production of meaning and ensures, at the same time, that meaning is never simply mimetic and transparent.

The linguistic difference that informs any cultural performance is dramatized in the common semiotic account of the disjuncture between the subject of a proposition (*énoncé*) and the subject of enunciation, which is not represented in the statement but which is the acknowledgement of its discursive embeddedness and address, its cultural positionality, its reference to a present time and a specific space. The pact of interpretation is never simply an act of communication between the I and the You designated in the statement. The production of meaning requires that these two places be mobilized in the passage through a Third Space, which represents both the general conditions of language and the specific implication of the utterance in a performative and institutional strategy of which it cannot 'in itself' be conscious. What this unconscious relation introduces is an ambivalence in the act of interpretation. The pronominal I of the proposition cannot be made to address – in its own words – the subject of enunciation, for this is not 'personable', but remains a spatial relation within the schemata and strategies of discourse. The meaning of the utterance is quite literally neither the one nor the Other. This ambivalence is emphasized when we realize that there is no way that the content of the proposition will reveal the structure of its positionality; no way that context can be mimetically read off from the content.

The implication of this enunciative split for cultural analysis that I especially want to emphasize is its temporal dimension. The splitting of the subject of enunciation destroys the logics of synchronicity and evolution which traditionally authorize the subject of cultural knowledge. It is taken for granted that the value of culture as an object of study and the value of any analytical activity that is considered cultural lie in a capacity to produce a cross-referential, generalizable unity that signifies a progression or evolution of ideas-in-time, as well as a cultured self-reflection on their premises. It would not be relevant to pursue the detail of this argument here except to demonstrate – via Marshall Sahlins's *Culture and Practical Reason* – the validity of my general characterization of the western expectation of culture as a disciplinary practice of writing. I quote Sahlins at the point at which he attempts to define the difference of Western bourgeois culture:

> We have to do not so much with functional dominance as with structural – with different structures of symbolic *integration*. And to this gross difference in design correspond differences in symbolic performance: between an *open expanding* code, responsive by *continuous* permutation to events it has itself staged, and an apparently *static* one that seems to know not events, but only its own preconceptions. The gross distinction between 'hot' societies and 'cold', development and underdevelopment, societies with and without history – and so between large societies and small, expanding and self-contained, colonizing and colonized.... (My emphasis)[17]

The intervention of the Third Space, which makes the structure of meaning and reference an ambivalent process, destroys this mirror of representation in which cultural knowledge is continuously revealed as an integrated, open, expanding code. Such an intervention quite properly challenges our sense of the historical identity of culture as a homogenizing, unifying force, authenticated by the originary Past, kept alive in the national tradition of the People. In other words, the disruptive temporality of enunciation displaces the narrative of the Western nation which Benedict Anderson so perceptively describes as being written in homogeneous, serial time.[18]

It is only when we understand that all cultural statements and systems are constructed in this contradictory and ambivalent space of enunciation, that we begin to understand why hierarchical claims to the inherent originality or 'purity' of cultures are untenable, even before we resort to empirical historical instances that demonstrate their hybridity. Fanon's vision of revolutionary cultural and political change as a 'fluctuating movement' of occult instability could not be articulated as cultural *practice* without an acknowledgement of this indeterminate space of the subject(s) of enunciation. It is that Third Space, though unrepresentable in itself, which constitutes the discursive conditions of enunciation that ensure that the meaning and symbols of culture have no primordial unity or fixity; that even the same signs can be appropriated, translated, rehistoricized, and read anew.

Fanon's moving metaphor – when reinterpreted for a theory of cultural signification – enables us to see not only the necessity of theory, but also the restrictive notions of cultural identity with which we burden our visions of political change. For Fanon, the liberatory 'people' who initiate the productive instability of revolutionary cultural change are themselves the bearers of a hybrid identity. They are caught in the discontinuous time of translation and negotiation, in the sense in which I have been attempting to recast these words. In the moment of liberatory struggle, the Algerian people destroy the continuities and constancies of the 'nationalist' tradition which provided a safeguard against colonial cultural imposition. They are now free to negotiate and translate their cultural identities in a discontinuous intertextual temporality of cultural difference. The native intellectual who identifies the people with the 'true national culture' will be disappointed. The people are now the very principle of 'dialectical reorganization' and they construct their culture from the national text translated into modern western forms of information technology, language, dress. The changed political and historical site of enunciation transforms the meanings of the colonial inheritance into the liberatory signs of a free people of the future.

I have been stressing a certain void or misgiving attending every

25

assimilation of contraries – I have been stressing this in order to expose what seems to me a fantastic mythological congruence of elements – and if indeed therefore any real sense is to be made of material change it can only occur with an acceptance of a concurrent void and with a willingness to descend into that void wherein, as it were, one may begin to come into confrontation with a spectre of invocation whose freedom to participate in an alien territory and wilderness has become a necessity for one's reason or salvation.[19]

This meditation by the great Guyanan writer Wilson Harris on the void of misgiving in the textuality of colonial history reveals the cultural and historical dimension of that Third Space of enunciation which I have made the precondition for the articulation of cultural difference. He sees it as accompanying the 'assimilation of contraries' and creating that occult instability which presages powerful cultural changes. It is significant that the productive capacity of this Third Space have a colonial or post-colonial provenance. For a willingness to descend into that alien territory – where I have led you – may reveal that the theoretical recognition of the split-space of enunciation may open the way to conceptualizing an *inter*national culture, based not on the exoticism or multi-culturalism of the *diversity* of cultures, but on the inscription and articulation of culture's *hybridity*. To that end we should remember that it is the 'inter' – the cutting edge of translation and negotiation, the *in-between*, the space of the *entre* that Derrida has opened up in writing itself – that carries the burden of the meaning of culture. It makes it possible to begin envisaging national, anti-nationalist, histories of the 'people'. It is in this space that we will find those words with which we can speak of Ourselves and Others. And by exploring this hybridity, this 'Third Space', we may elude the politics of polarity and emerge as the others of our selves.

NOTES

[1] See Clyde Taylor, 'Eurocentrics vs. new thought at Edinburgh', *Framework*, 34 (1987) for an illustration of this style of argument. See particularly footnote 1 (p148) for an exposition of his use of 'larsony' ('the judicious distortion of African truths to fit western prejudices').
[2] Gayatri C. Spivak, *In Other Worlds* (London: Methuen, 1987), 166-7.
[3] See Teshome H. Gabriel, 'Teaching Third World cinema' and Julianne Burton, 'The politics of aesthetic distance – *Sao Bernardo*', both in *Screen*, 24, 2 (March-April 1983), and Ashish Rajadhyaksha, 'Neo-traditionalism: film as popular art in India', *Framework*, 32/33 (1986).

[4] Stuart Hall, 'Blue election, election blues', *Marxism Today* (July 1987), 30-5.

[5] Michel Foucault, *The Archaeology of Knowledge* (London: Tavistock, 1972), 102-5.

[6] J.S. Mill, *On Liberty* (London: Dent & Sons, 1972), 93-4.

[7] For a significant elaboration of a similar argument, see Ernesto Laclau and Chantal Mouffe, *Hegemony and Socialist Strategy* (London: Verso, 1985), ch. 3.

[8] For a philosophical underpinning of some of the concepts I am proposing here, see Rodolphe Gasché, *The Tain of the Mirror* (Cambridge, Mass.: Harvard University Press, 1986), especially ch. 6: 'The Otherness of unconditional heterology does not have the purity of principles. It is concerned with the principles' irreducible impurity, with the difference that divides them in themselves against themselves. For this reason it is an impure heterology. But it is also an impure heterology because the medium of Otherness – more and less than negativity – is also a mixed milieu, precisely because the negative no longer dominates it.'

[9] Hall, *op.cit.*, 33.

[10] I owe this point to Martin Thom.

[11] Laclau and Mouffe, *op.cit.*, ch. 3.

[12] Paul Gilroy, *There Ain't No Black in the Union Jack* (London: Hutchinson, 1987), 214.

[13] Frantz Fanon, *The Wretched of the Earth* (Harmondsworth: Penguin, 1967 [1961]), 168.

[14] Jean-Paul Sartre, *Politics and Literature* (London: Calder/Boyars, 1973), 16-17.

[15] Fanon, *op.cit.*, 182-3.

[16] Bernard Williams, *Ethics and the Limits of Philosophy* (London: Fontana, 1985), ch. 9.

[17] Marshall Sahlins, *Culture and Practical Reason* (Chicago: Chicago University Press, 1976), 211.

[18] Benedict Anderson, *Imagined Communities* (London: Verso, 1983), ch. 2.

[19] Wilson Harris, *Tradition, the Writer, and Society* (New Beacon, 1973), 60-3.

Margaret Thatcher and Ruth Ellis

Jacqueline Rose

An act of barbarism that is deeply *republic* [sic] (correction) *repugnant* to all civilised people.
Margaret Thatcher to the House of Commons after the execution of Farzad Bazoft, journalist, in Iraq, 15 March 1990.

It has been the strength of feminism to produce a recognition of the political importance of sexuality and subjectivity in the face of more traditional political or Marxist analyses which have consistently left them out of account. The dialogue between psychoanalysis and feminism belongs in that political space. But the very success of that intervention may in turn be in danger of producing an unintended consequence: that the domain of what is more easily and conventionally defined as the political can continue to be analysed as if it were free of psychic and sexual processes, as if it operated outside the range of their effects. The re-election of Margaret Thatcher to a third term and the resurgence of right-wing ideologies seemed the appropriate moment to take up this issue – a moment when those very processes revealed themselves more and more to be crucial determinants or at least components of the political scene, a moment when we found ourselves witnessing the pressure of fantasy on our collective political life. If Margaret Thatcher throws up this question, she also does so in a way which is especially difficult for feminism because she is a woman, one furthermore who embodied some of the worst properties of what feminism has identified as a patriarchal society and state. This very difficulty can, however, perhaps serve as a caution to what has become, in many discussions of psychoanalysis and feminism, an idealization of the unconscious, whether as writing or preoedipality, or both. This chapter attempts to situate Thatcher in the domain of what psychoanalysis calls the realm of symbolic possibility; that is, the general forms of psychic cohesion which societies engender and on which they also come to rely. For feminism the symbolic order is always gendered. This chapter is therefore an attempt to run two propositions together: that the symbolic order is gendered, and that right-wing ideologies thrive on and strain against the furthest limits of psychic fantasy. It then adds to these two a further consideration: how to analyse both these factors when it is a woman at the summit of political power who comes to embody them at their most extreme.

> Are women more apt than other social categories, notably the exploited class, to invest in the implacable machinery of terrorism? ...
>
> The habitual and increasingly explicit attempt to fabricate a scapegoat victim as foundress of a society or countersociety may be replaced by the analysis of the potentialities of *victim/executioner* which characterize each identity, each subject, each sex. (Julia Kristeva, 'Women's Time'[1])

These quotations from Julia Kristeva raise the question of women and violence. They are taken from an article 'Women's Time' which has often been quoted as heralding a third stage of feminism which will follow feminism's demand for equality and then for separation and difference. In this third stage, sexual difference itself will be exposed as a metaphysical category. If this is not the Derridean position to which it bears a striking resemblance, it is because of the concepts of subjectivity and psychic reality to which Kristeva holds and which here, as elsewhere in her writing, she pushes to a type of extreme. In this article, Kristeva's most explicit discussion of the history of feminism is conducted for a large part through an examination of the question of violence for women; that is, the way that women situate themselves in response to a crisis in what she calls the socio-symbolic contract, a contract to which they are subjected, from which they are also excluded, and which they can also embody in the words of its effects. For Kristeva, that contract is founded on a moment of violence, the violence of primitive psychic separation which precipitates subjects into language and the violence of a social order which has sacrifice as its symbolic base. We can add to that the violence of sexual difference itself, meaning both the trauma of its recognition and the worst forms of its social enactment in the real. For Kristeva, it is feminism's importance that it confronts the furthest extremities, or perversion, of what it is that constitutes the social bond. Women can refuse that social bond (the feminism of difference) or they can take it on, in the two meanings of identification (the feminism of equality) and assault (terrorism). A third stage would idealize neither the social nor the concept of its antithesis, but would instead turn its attention to the violence of the subjectivity which upholds it. Far from heralding a new dawn, therefore, the deconstruction of sexual difference leads us straight back to the heart of violence itself, to 'the victim/executioner' in us all.

Why does Kristeva conduct her discussion of feminism in terms of this question of violence – a connection in her argument which, for the most part, has been ignored or overlooked? What leads her to produce such a dangerous proximity between women and terrorism and death? We can perhaps try to answer these questions not directly with reference to Kristeva, but by looking at that place within English culture where the issue of women, power, and violence presents itself with particular force. I am referring to Margaret Thatcher, whose re-election to a third term brought into special focus the question of what happens when it is a woman who comes to embody the social at its most perverse. The difficulty is that any discussion of Thatcher which relates specifically to her as a woman constantly risks a slide into misogyny (of which, it should be said, Kristeva has been accused). But something about Thatcher's place in the collective imaginary of British culture calls out for an understanding of what it is she releases by dint of being a woman and of the forms of fantasmatic scenario which she brings into play. Is there something in that scenario which touches on the most extreme edge of the social, of what it is that has to be secured and regulated to ensure the very possibility of our collective social life? And did Margaret Thatcher draw part of her imaginary power from the way that she operated, or appeared to operate, in that space? More fundamentally, can her re-election be used to understand something about the place of fantasy in our collective political life?

Discussion of the election result on the left came very close to acknowledging this as an issue of importance. In the first of what has become a set of key articles on Thatcher's third term, Stuart Hall argued in the July 1987 issue of *Marxism Today* that the Conservative victory needed to be understood not just in terms of material interest, but in terms of images and identifications. The Conservatives were unpopular in terms of policies, but had managed to mobilize a new ideological constituency. Political identities, he argued, are formed not just on the basis of 'so-called "real" majorities but on (equally real) "symbolic" majorities'.[2] The left weakens itself politically by failing to take images seriously, leaving the important field of these symbolic identifications to the right. Politics, Hall was effectively arguing, is not only, but also, a matter of fantasies, in which the way that people 'imagine' themselves occupies a crucial place. His analysis therefore picked up on a problem which has a history going back at least to the 1930s, when the left had to ask itself why, in the face of increasing political oppression, large sectors of people, including those who are most exploited, move not to the left but to the right. Thatcherism – and the analogy is more than gratuitous – forces us up against something Wilhelm Reich was the first to call the mass psychology of fascism.

Hall's analysis was crucial for addressing the issue of fantasy and political identities. But it raises a problem for me – one that suggested the need to extend that basic insight – in so far as the argument about identification remained within the framework of rational calculation: 'far from this being a sign of voter irrationality, there are a number of quite "rational" reasons why there should be a trend in this direction.'[3] Avoiding the image of the irrational or, as Hall puts it elsewhere, the 'endlessly deceived, or endlessly authoritarian masses',[4] the article could be read as producing the counter-image of another: the always reasoned political subject. Subjects identify not with their immediate material interest, but with the place from which they can see themselves as potentially making good. The article was then criticized on the grounds that many voters hated the image of Thatcherism but voted for her policies as most likely to secure that good, as well as for a potential pessimism (if politics are determined by a kind of long-term fantasmatic version of individual self-interst, what is to prevent an eternity of Toryism?). It is crucial, however, that these criticisms not allow the political issue of identification and the image raised by Hall to be lost. For only if you are operating with a rationalist concept of fantasy will the dislike of Thatcher automatically dispense with the idea that something about her image is at work in the political processes that returned her to power. What if Thatcher was re-elected not despite the repugnance that many feel for her image, but also in some sense because of it? What if that force of identity for which she is so severely castigated somewhere also operates as a type of pull?[5]

That is not to argue that this is necessarily the case, but simply to point to the fact that the area of symbolic identifications, once it has been broached, cannot be halted at the level of the rational. One of the key characteristics of both identification and the image is their tendency to operate in a contradictory fashion, which means psychoanalytically that there is no stopping the potential range of their aberrant causes or effects. The attempt of the social order to secure its own rationality and its constant failure to do so may be one of the things that Thatcher brings most graphically into focus. If this is the case, any discussion of collective identifications which remains within the terms of the rational may find itself inadvertently reinforcing one of the most powerful myths carried by the image of Margaret Thatcher herself.

The centrality of Thatcher to the problem of this political moment therefore obliges us to take up the legacy of the debate about fantasy and the right. But it throws in a new factor for consideration: what might it be about a woman in power that brings us up against the furthest and most perverse – Kristeva's terms are 'irreducible and deadly' – extremities of the social bond?

Ruth Ellis was the last woman to be hanged in England. She died in 1955. She was brought back to public attention in 1983, at the time of the vote on capital punishment which Thatcher allowed in Parliament almost immediately after the election victory which secured her second term. Ruth Ellis was not the last person to be executed in England, but in the publicity over the vote and the accompanying debate her image was central. Film and photographs of protests at her hanging appeared on television and in the Press; Renée Short referred in the House to the 'judicial murder' of Ruth Ellis as the event which had brought home to the country as a whole the enormity of capital punishment.[6] It was of course because Ellis was a woman that she aroused this interest, which appeared more and more as curiosity, both about the spectacle of hanging and also about the sexual nature of her crime (she shot her lover). The object of a voyeuristic attention (a film, *Dance with a Stranger*, was made about her life in 1984), Ruth Ellis, or rather the focus on her, seemed to be demonstrating the power of spectacle, femininity, and violence and their mutual association in public fantasy life. The protest at the hanging – the mobilization of Ellis for the case against state violence – found itself repeating the drama of the original event. Death by hanging became a symbol of contention centring on two women: Thatcher, who supported the restoration of capital punishment, and Ellis, who was called up to demonstrate its inhumanity, but who seemed equally to release something of that peculiar pleasure which the idea of execution always seems to provoke.[7]

In one sense there is no common point or even dialogue between these two women: from different historical moments and opposite ends of the social spectrum, they stand respectively for criminality and the law. (Thatcher was a barrister before, and during the early stages of, her political career.) To this extent they could be said to illustrate the emptiness of the category 'woman' as a totality which denies the crucial differences of identity and class between women. To link them is therefore to constitute a fantasy in itself.[8] Yet Margaret Thatcher and Ruth Ellis were brought together at this historical moment in a scenario whose imaginary basis may well be what constitutes its importance and force. 'Victim' and 'executioner', they meet at that point of violence where the ordering of the social reveals something of the paradox on which it is based: the fact that civilization, as Freud puts it, 'hopes to prevent the crudest excesses of violence by itself assuming the right to use violence against criminals'.[9] René Girard makes this point the basis of his discussion of violence and the sacred: 'All the procedures that allow men to moderate their violence are analogous in that none of them are strangers to violence.'[10] That 'men' is of course eloquent, apparently expressive of the desire to 'protect' women from violence in both senses of the term. In that moment of symbolic encounter between Margaret Thatcher and Ruth Ellis, however, it was not men, but two women who stood for the violence which both Freud and Girard situate structurally on either side of the law. Drawing attention to themselves precisely *as* women, they could serve to gloss over that double and paradoxical location of violence; the perversion of the State in relation to violence could be transposed on to the perversity of the woman, its more troubling implications then siphoned off and ignored.

The 'perversity of the woman' refers here as much to Thatcher as to Ellis, for the woman supporter of capital punishment is as grotesque for the dominant stereotypes of femininity as for a feminist critique of the State as the embodiment of phallic power. We should not forget, however, that Thatcher initiated the debate on capital punishment after an election result secured by the Falklands victory. Her resoluteness over the machinery of war seemed to turn her from the most unpopular prime minister since the last World War to one guaranteed a return to power. In that second election, at least, there can be no doubt that one of the things which Thatcher stood for was the desirability of war. We may therefore be able to turn this episode to account by asking what may the bizarre nature of the woman's position within it reveal about the paradox in the definition and regulation of the limits of the social itself?

The trial of Ruth Ellis was described at the time as 'one of the most one-sided legal battles ever to be fought in the number one court'.[11] She was convicted, by all accounts, at the moment when she stated in court that she had 'a peculiar feeling I wanted to kill him', repeating on being questioned, 'I had an idea I wanted to kill him.'[12] This supreme clarity on the part of Ruth Ellis ('she felt completely justified') destroyed any possibility of reducing the charge from murder to manslaughter.[13] Only if she had been out of control, 'the subject of such emotional disturbance operating upon her mind so as for the time being to unseat her judgment, to inhibit and cut off those censors which normally control our conduct,' might she have been found not guilty of the charge.[14] Premeditation therefore signifies here the rationality of a subject who knows her own mind, meaning that she knows – rather than simply experiencing as something beyond her – that part of the mind controlled by the censors which is normally cut off. In relation to desires effectively acknowledged here as universal, Ruth Ellis is a woman who knows too much.

At the time of Ruth Ellis's trial, the defence of insanity could be mounted only under the McNaghten Rules of 1843. These were applicable if 'the accused was labouring under such a defect of reason, from disease of the mind, as not to know the nature and quality of the act, or, if he did know it, that he did not know that he was doing wrong'.[15] The legal definition of insanity therefore rests on something we could describe as a knowledge relation. Those who are insane act not without reason, but without that reason which should provide them with correct knowledge of what they are doing. This is, as has often been pointed out, a legal rather than a medical account of insanity. The law adjudges the nature of the act, excuses those who are deficient in that knowledge, and condemns those who share that knowledge and act on it. The law therefore condemns the murderer to the extent that she or he can identify with its own adjudication. Thus Ellis's supreme rationality mimics the reason of the law.[16]

This rationality of Ruth Ellis clearly threatened a crisis of sexual difference. 'You will hear – and I am going to call a very eminent psychiatrist to tell you', the defence announces, 'that the effect of jealousy upon a female mind can so work as to unseat the reason and can operate to a degree in which a male mind is quite incapable of operating.'[17] Women, according to the psychiatrist's testimony, are 'inclined to lose some of their inhibitory capacity and solve their problems on a more primitive level. This is not applying to women in general, but if they do have hysterical reactions, they are more prone to hysterical reactions than men.'[18] When a man is hysterical, on the other hand, he is so in the service of self-interest, like the men in the firing line in the war whose hysterical paralyses ensured their removal from the front (the discussion of male hysteria was stopped by the judge). The problem with Ruth Ellis was that she was not 'hysterical *enough*' – lacking a 'sufficiently hysterical personality to solve her problems by a complete loss of memory'.[19] Showing no emotion, Ellis was described later by her counsel as having got herself into a 'stratosphere of emotion', as if some notion of her total strangeness had to be produced to cover the lack of hysteria, of the appropriate feminine affect.[20] It is a case in which a woman fails to mobilize a stereotype in her defence. She is outside the bounds of the law and of conventional expectation only by being not quite far outside enough.

What we see here is the way femininity is being used to draw a line around the limits of what a society will recognize of itself. Femininity, like insanity, is a type of mitigating circumstance. Subjects who commit murder must be feminine and/or out of control. The murderer who acts wilfully and in full knowledge of her or his emotions is rather like the psychoanalyst who, in defiance of the censors and in the name of forbidden knowledge, brings our guilty secrets to light.

Ruth Ellis was a problem for the court because her femininity did not come into play at the right point. Femininity failed to secure a limit-definition of violence: murder as the limit of what a society can recognize of itself, murder beyond the limit as the only form of murder it can accept. Because it did not guarantee this definition of violence, because it would not respect the existing conceptual boundaries, Ellis's femininity could appear only as an outrage, as something inappropriate and out of place – the peroxide she insisted on for her hair for her appearance in court, for example. If not essence, femininity can only be trapping or mere show.[21]

The trial of Ruth Ellis presents us with a unique combination of the terms of femininity, rationality, and violence in both their symbolic and concrete weight (the second as an effect of the first). It also forced their realignment in ways that I shall go on to describe. The woman who murders with reason (ambiguity intended) produces a particular form of crisis, doubling over with the fact of her sexuality that disturbing conflation of rationality with the most violent of crimes. In doing so, she provokes a sexualized version of the question produced by the category of 'reasoning madness' in nineteenth-century France: 'In what way rationality could be criminal, and how it all, crime and knowledge, could be "borne" by what was called the "social order".'[22] If rationality can be criminal, not, note, if crime can be rational: if murder can be reasoned – the question is almost asked – then what price the insight that reason might be murderous in itself?

What then happened in response to the case of Ruth Ellis is a realignment of the terms of criminality, reason, and madness on which the judgment had turned, terms organized so as to secure an image of the social but which the spectacle of the trial and execution had instead seemed to question or even undermine. Thus the year after her trial, the Conservative government was defeated on an opposition motion to abolish capital punishment (it had defeated such a motion just months before the trial, although the later vote was overturned in the Lords and capital punishment was not finally abolished until 1969). But the McNaghten Rules were altered by a new Homicide Act which introduced the category of 'diminished responsibility' – a borderline category in the legal definition of reason, since it is the only instance in law which recognizes a middle position between full responsibility for a criminal act and a total absence of responsibility. It was as if the trial and execution of Ruth Ellis had tested the limits of a set of key concepts through which we secure the 'sanity' of our collective social life. In doing so, the case led to a redefinition of violence: the violence not only of the criminal, but also of the due processes of the law.[23] The irony was that Margaret Thatcher would return to the issue of capital punishment, calling up the collective memory of Ruth Ellis, as part of an attempt to put back in place the very terms which that earlier moment had put so definitively under threat.

The NcNaghten Rules of 1843 had required that the defence establish the insanity of the act. The concept of diminished responsibility applied more to the insanity of the person: 'such abnormality of mind (whether arising from a condition of arrested or retarded development of mind or any inherent causes or induced by disease or injury) as substantially impaired his mental responsibility for his acts or omissions'.[24] The Rules complete the pathologization and infantilization (feminization?) of the murderer, which locates

37

criminality in the very nature of the criminal and her or his history. In Foucault's terms, this would bring the wheel full circle, from the idea dominant in the eighteenth century that the more aberrant the act, the more guilty the criminal, to the idea which emerged with the increasing psychiatrization of justice in the nineteenth century that only aberration is an excuse for violent crime.[25]

Unlike Foucault, however, I see this not just as the pathologization of criminality, but also as the criminalizing of pathology. By that I do not mean a simple reconstitution of the earlier institutional link between delinquents and the mentally ill, but rather a move by the legal system of recognition and denial: both murder and pathology are outlawed; but the effect is to bring murder into the realm of the psychic, thereby releasing the potential recognition that the psyche might be murderous in itself. Foucault himself acknowledges that – beyond the specific histories produced by these definitions, which they also reflect – we seem to be dealing with something universal, collective, a property of the social as such: 'the collective fear of crime, the obsession with this danger which seems to be an inseparable part of society itself'.[26] Psychoanalysis would recognize in such a collective obsession a way of disposing of a collective guilt. The guilt of the criminal establishes the innocence of the society; but, like all oppositions, it risks a potential identification between its basic terms.

The trial of Ruth Ellis, the changing legal account of responsibility which followed, and the debate about capital punishment which she helped to provoke all make it clear that the question of social regulation threw up a problem of delimitation in the fullest psychic sense of the term. This involved delimitation not only of the social, but also of the psychic, as well as of the boundaries and links between the two. It was a problem that had already been graphically underlined by the testimony of the Institute of Psycho-Analysis to the Royal Commission on Capital Punishment which had met from 1949 to 1952. Their question was what murder might mean to, or more exactly, in what sense we – that is, technically the non-murderers – might recognize ourselves in this most violent of crimes, not just at the level of spectacle, but in terms of the identification which it might uncover and provoke. Here 'identification' implies that crucial sense of an active self-recognition where what is at stake is a conflation of identities not just played out by the discourse, but positively sought after or desired.

In their strange encounter with the Commission, the analysts argued that most people react to murder as an unconscious threat to the security of their repressions. The murderer cannot be called 'abnormal' in so far as murder is potentially present in the very regulation of drives. For psychoanalysis, the subject's own aggression is an object of fear, and the child has two ways of preserving his fantasied world from its attacks. Either the aggression can be transformed into conscience, or it can be neutralized by the erotic drives. But both these solutions contain their own dangers. The first can lead to suicidal impulses if the aggression is turned against the self, and the second can lead to sexual murder if the sexual impulses find themselves eroticizing the very violence they were meant to control ('the presence of the erotic component shows clearly in the sexual nature of the crime'[27]).

Nor can the analysts predict with any certainty which of these outcomes is more likely to occur. What emerges from their testimony is a failure of discrimination between normal and abnormal at a psychic level as far as murder is concerned. The force of the psychoanalytic argument, its power of explanation, produces as its effect that, in relation to the most dangerous of crimes, the category of what is normal starts to fade and even disappear. It was a particular scandal of their testimony that one analyst found himself talking quite happily of the 'normal murderer' as the most important in psychoanalytic terms. This analyst was then hastily corrected by a colleague who insisted that between those who murder and those who don't there must finally be a difference in the impulses involved. The evidence of the analysts seemed, therefore, to repeat that mechanism of partial recognition and denial that they themselves had identified in the public response to the crime.[28]

The problem is of course the category of normality itself. What we can see here is a paradox inherent in psychoanalysis operating in the region of the law – that the concept of the unconscious at once dispenses with, yet still relies on, the concept of the normal mind. For Ernest Jones, writing in 1942 in an article entitled 'The Concept of the Normal Mind', it remains an ideal concept, and can be stated categorically not to exist, even if psychoanalysis can describe the conditions for its production.[29] Nor does he claim to know whether it might exist in the limited and clinical sense that he describes. In this context, the murderer merely highlights the problem, which has been accentuated with the understanding of infantile psychotic states developed after Freud, that the more you identify the aberrational and extravagant in the most fundamental workings of the mind, the harder

39

it becomes to use those categories to secure a social classification – to secure the social itself. The trial and execution of Ruth Ellis, however, brought all this too close: 'The breakfast table is no place for a refresher course on the abnormal' – a beautiful parody of the link that psychoanalysis establishes between the crazy and the domestic, between psycho-pathology and everyday life.[30]

What then of capital punishment itself? What confusions does it in turn engender in relation to the public, the criminal, and the State? For that account of the vicissitudes of the drives offered by psychoanalysis started with the observation that capital punishment is the clearest embodiment of the primitive mechanism whereby the subject expels aggressivity only to experience it as returning from the outside. That is to say, if the murderer threatens a lifting of repression, undoing the relative comfort of a neurotic mechanism on which subjects and statehood survive, then capital punishment acts out a psychotic drama in which the libidinal impulses one thought to be rid of return in the shape of God. This may give its full meaning to the idea of capital punishment as the supreme embodiment of a penalty whose enormity *matches* the hideousness of the crime. For the *Lancet*, writing in 1955 after the execution of Ruth Ellis, an execution whether actually seen or only imagined was bound to be contagious in its effects: 'Small wonder if the youngsters swallowing the poison find the idea of violence dangerously attractive.'[31] It is an act of communal violence which already operates by mimesis (from the criminal to the punishment) and which then passes to the public at large. The argument anticipates the debates about violence which followed the Hungerford massacre in 1987, except that in this instance the contagion was presumed to stem from the violence of the State.

Clearly the issue of capital punishment poses one of the greatest threats to the most basic of social differentiations, because of this relation of mimesis between punishment and crime. Each time the Conservative Party returns to this issue in what became under Thatcher the obligatory annual vote, it therefore places under considerable strain the symbolic limits which a 'civilized' society draws around itself. The motion on the first free vote on hanging after the execution of Ruth Ellis read: 'This House believes that the death penalty no longer accords with the needs or true interests of a civilized society.'[32] If capital punishment is 'barbaric', however, we should note that the desire for its restoration tends in the West to be a characteristic of extreme right-wing governments standing for the fullest authority of the State. It is a paradox expressive of the most fundamental regulation of the social that the government which most fully embodies that authority is closest to its symbolic limits, and therefore most likely to push it over the edge. As one Tory MP put it: 'It's a good red meat issue; it gives us something to chew on, but we won't swallow it.'[33] In the strictest sense, the issue of capital punishment under Thatcher set the limits to the anti-State rhetoric which she so consistently deployed. Specifically, in the 1950s, that free vote had found itself wedged between two imperatives: the distinction between the 'civilization' of England and the 'backwardness' of the colonies and the urgent necessity after Nazism to save the concept of a beneficient State.[34]

It none the less seems that, in strictly legal terms, capital punishment can be seen to represent the limits of judicial authority itself, challenging or exposing as a masquerade the very reason of the law. This is how David Pannick opens his *Judicial Review of the Death Penalty*:

> It was the optimistic belief of the eighteenth-century philosophers of the Enlightenment that all problems could be resolved, and all questions correctly answered, if only we could discover and apply the relevant formula. Leibniz dreamt of a 'logic machine' that would, without debate or delay, supply the right answer to any moral or political controversy. The Encylopaedists worked at producing eighty-four octavo volumes that would provide information to settle any dispute. There remains only one forum where the Enlightenment philosopher would today feel at home: our courts of law.[35]

For Pannick, capital punishment best challenges this logic machine of the courtroom by demonstrating the essentially *hermeneutic* nature of the law, the difficulty it has in defining its own limits, and even the possibility that it might act contrary to its own form. The object of interminable dispute, capital punishment, repeatedly shows the law passing beyond itself.[36] More crucially, according to the very constitution (written or unwritten) which appears to legitimate it, capital punishment may be contrary to the 'due process of the law'. Most of the criteria which could, technically, establish its constitutionality or not (that it is imposed in a 'cruel and painful manner', 'wantonly or freakishly', or by 'caprice or procedural irregularity') are not susceptible to absolute definition.[37] (Note how instability figures as the very content of the key terms.) Capital punishment brings the law up against the *arbitrary* – the arbitrary of its own practice, but through that, and in defiance of the enlightened rationality to which it still holds, the arbitrary as such. In strictly judicial terms, therefore, capital punishment represents that point where the law has the greatest difficulty in securing its own rationality. It provides a strange imitation or acting-out of the problem the law has in establishing the absence or presence of reason in the criminal it is required to judge.

In the case of Ruth Ellis, horror at the execution of a woman also played a crucial part in the reintroduction of the motion against capital punishment and in the subsequent passing of the Homicide Act. It is as if the thinness of the boundary between criminal and legal murder, the uncomfortable proximity between them, presents itself too starkly when it is a woman who is executed. It seems also that the spectacle of execution – 'seen or imagined' (*Lancet*) – is too powerful when it is a woman, because her status as spectacle in the more general culture threatens to turn this moment of a society's most precarious self-regulation into nothing but show (the classical and repeated ambiguity of the woman as spectacle, focus of a displaced anxiety which she always threatens to provoke).[38]

Returning to Margaret Thatcher, we can perhaps see now something of the extraordinary nature of having a woman in power who unequivocally supported the return of capital punishment, a woman who chooses to embody the State at that very point where it rests its authority on the right to kill, but does so by means of a language which is one of consistency, rationality, and control. One of the things that Thatcher presented us with is an inflated version of the rationality which can be the only basis for distinguishing between legal and illegal violence. For if the law partly allows for the murderer who is deemed to be out of her or his mind, punishing above all a violence which stems from a self-knowing calculation, it is also because violence as rational is the form of violence which it reserves to itself. It is her utter certainty of judgement which allowed Thatcher to release into our public fantasy life, with no risk of confusion, the violence which underpins the authority of the State. If femininity is opposed to violence according to one stereotype – women are not violent – Thatcher presented a femininity which does not serve to neutralize violence but allows for its legimitation.[39]

It is a grotesque scenario – one which mimics that of Ruth Ellis in reverse – where a woman who stands for a super-rationality writes violence into the law (or would do so), instead of being executed by it:

> Allowing the repressed – the drive if you like, or the death drive to get to the point – to be spoken through language is perhaps one way of stopping it from erupting inside the code: for it is that codified, legitimated, eruption which precisely constitutes fascism.[40]

One of the key aspects of Thatcher's image, I would argue, is this symbolic legitimation and rationalization of violence. That this could be the case at the same time as the Conservatives mounted their official onslaught against media violence and crime – 'no procedure against violence that is a stranger to it' (Girard) – merely demonstrates that structure of necessary antagonism which inheres in rationality itself. Writing on American politics, Richard Hofstadter described this mechanism as the 'paranoid style' which produces out of its own system an enemy of super-competence whose 'plots long hatched and deeply premeditated' mirror its own supreme and deadly rationality in reverse.[41] Murderers who premeditate are therefore the most dangerous because they too closely resemble the symbolic and psychic structure written into the legal apparatus that comes to meet them.

A brief look at Thatcher's rhetoric will confirm its investment in its own supreme logic and consistency, the way that she elevated these concepts to the status of general policy and object of desire. (The last chapter of Bruce Arnold's *Margaret Thatcher: a study in power* is called 'The Consistency of Rhetoric'.[42]) To take just one speech, the New Year's message of 1984, and deliberately and wildly extract from it the key images on which it turns:

> Our commitment remains as strong as ever ... the defence of the realm and the rule of law ... We have already made considerable progress ... We have shown what can be done ... this is only the beginning of the revival of Britain ... We have embarked on our second term with the same enthusiasm ... The British people now know that we are as good as our word and the rest of the world is beginning to know it too ... They know that this government will never hesitate to stand up for Britain's interests. We shall persist ... We want people in all walks of life to set their hopes high and to carry them through into reality ... We shall not

> be afraid … people need a government which follows a consistent and coherent policy and sticks to it … we shall continue to protect the value of your money. We shall continue to control public spending … This government already has a reputation for consistency … No one can accuse this government of complacency. Far from losing our way, we are just getting into our stride. We have stayed right on course. We believe what we say. We say what we believe.[43]

I am not sure that it is necessary to pick out the repeated and central terms of consistency, persistence, and sameness, the refusal of any possible gap between reality and intent (which passes to her subjects 'who set their hopes high and carry them through into reality'), and then, as the inevitable corollary for those who see in this form of rhetoric a denial of the precariousness of language itself, the insistence on the utter coherence of the word ('We are as good as our word … We believe what we say. We say what we believe'). We can call it an inflation and parody of government as reason, an appropriation into the pure *form* of reason of an earlier idealist and more radical tradition which rested its hopes on the idea of a rational State.[44]

It is this quality of consistency and logic that was picked up by commentators on Thatcher's style, whether 'for' ('We will have one of the most logical governments this country has ever had'[45]), or 'against':

> The picture of consistent certainty is a complete one. The fact that it is so free of doubt is unnerving. The fact that it is so well remembered is puzzling. The fact that it is so freely given, and yet in so limited and circumscribed a form, is faintly frightening … The self-assurance, the assured recollection and presentation of self, in one who keeps no diary, retains no personal papers, deals always and emphatically in the present, is itself a kind of consistency.[46]

Compare Hofstadter: 'It is nothing, if not coherent, far more coherent than the real world, no room for mistakes, failures, ambiguities, if not rational intensely rationalistic.'[47] The conviction politician by her own definition, Thatcher made of her own logic, and of logic itself, a type of personality and political cult. The image is uncannily close to that of Ruth Ellis ('She felt completely justified') standing in the dock 'firm, erect and unafraid' (for one correspondent, this in itself was enough to condemn her[48]). The two women, therefore, present the image alternatively of an acceptable and a threatening form of reason in excess – unless it is the case that, according to a logic which is proper to reason, the acceptable form of reason is not opposed to the threatening, but depends on it.

For Hofstadter, it is precisely that super-rationality which takes precedence over, and then releases, the paranoid mode. This is Thatcher:

> We must become aware of the way in which our daily lives, our own thinking, may have become affected, become tainted without our ever realising it, by the ceaseless flood of Socialist and pseudo-Socialist propaganda to which we have been exposed for so long ... The decline of contemporary thought has been hastened by the misty phantom of Socialism ... Socialism has lured [people's] conscience into thinking that the steamroller which is about to flatten them is a blessing in disguise.[49]

> The British character has done so much for democracy, for law, and done so much throughout the world that if there is any fear that it might be swamped people are going to react ... the moment the minority threatens to become a big one, people get frightened.[50]

Power in the adversarial mode: Thatcher seems to be repeating here one of the fundamental psychic tropes of Fascism, which acts out this structure of aggressivity, giving name and place to the invisible adversary which is an inherent part of it, and making fear a central component of strategy. 'People get frightened ... we are not here to ignore people's wishes.' It does not take much to reorganize the semantics of that sentence and to read it as stating that fear in itself is an object of desire. The Falklands War, therefore, simply brought to its logical conclusion a rhetoric whose basic terms were already firmly in place. The film of the Black Audio Film Collective *Handsworth Songs*, made in 1986, makes the link explicit: 'Between Thatcher's "swamping" speech and the Falklands expedition, lies another melodrama of consent: *the war of naming the problem*, the rush to discover the unclubbables, the drug barons, the new black, the black of disorders and mayhem' (my emphasis). The message seems to be, as is the case with paranoia: we have every reason to be frightened, we have everything firmly under control. It is on the back of this that Thatcher reopened the question of capital punishment, which repeats this message with explicit reference to the violence on which its structure depends ('a vehicle for political capital, a scapegoat to illogically appease our society's sense of guilt, fear, passion and vengeance'[51]). In 1986, the first report of the new Conservative Research Department, taking over from the Centre of Policy Studies, argued that retribution is the very meaning of the law. (Compare this, however, with Willie Hamilton in the House of Commons: 'Retribution did not solve the problem ... in desperation the party of law and order put forward these debates to prove its virility.'[52])

Commenting on the sacrificial nature of the social order as described by anthropologists, Kristeva writes: 'But sacrifice orders violence, binds it, tames it.'[53] It also, however, *repeats* it, or binds it in the form of what Girard calls a 'violent unanimity', scapegoating its victim in order to expel violence out into the real and so end it. If this mechanism is the basis of social cohesion, it is the characteristic of a right-wing ideology such as this one not to threaten the social, but to act out its most fundamental symbolic economy. Or, rather, it threatens the social by making that economy too blatant – the object of a renewed investment by the very drives it was intended to regulate or keep underground.[54]

In this context, it seems to me that it is limiting to talk of images and identifications in relation to politics as if what we are dealing with belonged to a straightforward economy of desire. Desire may well be the necessary term, but only if we define it as something which includes not irrationality – what is at stake here is not some rational-irrational dualism – but a logic of fantasy in which violence can operate as a pole of attraction at the same time as (to the extent that) it is being denied. If this logic is 'deadly and irreducible', it is so only in so far as it repeats a paradox inherent to the organization of the social itself. One of the things that Margaret Thatcher was doing, or that was being done through her, was to make this paradox the basis of a political identity so that subjects could take pleasure in violence as force and legitimacy while always locating 'real' violence somewhere else – illegitimate violence and illicitness increasingly made subject to the law. There is, however, always the risk for any right-wing ideology which plays on this scenario that, in the very place where violence and the illicit seem most effectively to have been abolished, they will return: witness the call for the legalization of incest and the songs in praise of the Yorkshire ripper at the conference of the Federation of Conservative Students in 1986.

To return to the question of the woman. In 'Women's Time', Kristeva describes the woman terrorist as the woman who, too brutally excluded from the socio-symbolic, counter-invests the violence she has experienced and takes arms against the State. She also describes the woman who identifies with and consolidates power because she brings to it the weight of the investment consequent on her struggle to achieve it. Without accepting Kristeva's terms as an explanation for women's political activity (it is never clear whether this is a causal analysis or one which crucially describes the affective and unconscious repercussions for women of their participation in political life), we can none the less recognize in Thatcher a hybrid of both these positions: a consolidation of power which is also a violence not of counter-investment, but the violence which underpins power as such. Blatantly drawing on this violence, Thatcher legitimated and encoded it (the real risk of Fascism), but she also laid bare the presence of violence at the heart of the socio-symbolic order. Certainly because she is a woman, she appeared to do both these things – which merely articulate a paradox at the heart of right-wing ideology – separately and together, in the form of an extreme. We can call her an object of fantasy – castrating mother, punitive superego, would be the psychoanalytic terms – only if we stress that the scenario she embodies goes way beyond her to take on the furthest parameters of our psychic and social life.

And Thatcher's own femininity, the way she presents herself as a woman (or not)? We can only note the contradictions: from denial ('People are more conscious of me being a woman than *I* am of being a woman'[55]), through an embracing of the most phallic of self-images (the iron lady), to the insistence on her femininity as utterly banal (the housewife managing the purse-strings of the nation). Predictably these images are mirrored and exceeded by the more or less misogynistic images which she provoked: 'doubtful whether any male PM would have actually seen that Falklands thing through to the end', 'in practice as sentimental as a Black Widow'.[56] It is none the less the case that Margaret Thatcher does deliberately choose to situate herself in the place of such an ambiguus sexual self-fashioning. The paranoid structure which I am describing here no doubt thrives on this ambiguity of a femininity appealed to and denied, a masculinity parodied and inflated. It is the worst of a phallic economy countered, and thereby rendered permissible, by being presented as masquerade.[57]

When Reich wrote *The Mass Psychology of Fascism* in 1933, he described Fascist ideology as mystical and irrational, opposing it to the rationality of a revolutionary ethic which would be based on a shared, democratic organization of sexuality and work. Fascism was repressive and distortive of body and mind, engendering a pathological sexuality and form of thought. Underneath that distortion, Reich saw an ideally untrammelled genitality and mental clarity. It has frequently been pointed out that both of these conceptions effectively dismantled the two poles of Freudian psychoanalysis on which Reich claimed his work was based: an infantile sexuality characterized above all by its perversion and an unconscious which stood for an irreducible splitting of the mind. More important, perhaps, Reich's idea of pure rationality – of rationality *as* purity – rejoined at crucial moments the Fascist ideology to which he opposed it.[58]

Although Thatcherism cannot be equated with Fascism (given the preservation of democratic government, the support of the free market, the rhetoric – at least – of the rolling back of the State), there are of course points of connection that can be made (the glorification of nationhood, the assault on homosexuals, the destruction of local government, and the increasing centralization – despite the rhetoric – of State power). More important, the retributive violence of her ethical absolutism, as I have described it here, echoes a central component of what Reich and others have described. What Thatcher seems to have demonstrated is a taking off, a relative autonomy, of certain psychic tropes beyond their historically attested political and economic base. Crucially, the phenomenon of Thatcher suggests that our understanding of the libidinal undercurrents of political processes can no longer be restricted to the historically recognized moment of Fascism alone – the place to which the possibility of a dialogue between psychoanalysis and politics has traditionally been consigned.

In this context, Reich's analysis, his stress on the irrationalism of Fascist discourse, has left us with a difficulty to which everything I have been describing in this chapter seems to return. It is not the irrationality of Thatcher's rhetoric that strikes me as the problem, but its supreme rationalism, the way that it operates according to a protocol of reason elevated to the status of a law. In this case, we cannot counter that ideology with a greater rationality without entering into one of the predominant fantasies of the ideology itself. This is not of course to argue that the idea of rationality has not been historically mobilized by the left, and to positive effect; but rather that, as a concept, it is inadequate for dealing with the specific force of

48

right-wing ideologies at that point where they harness fantasy to reason, giving reason to what I want to call the flashpoints of the social, the very point where reason itself is at its least secure. If we want to think about the place of fantasy in public life today, we need therefore to avoid or qualify two conceptions: the one that describes fantasy as a projection of individual self-interest (the 'rational' reasons identified by Stuart Hall), but equally the one that sees fantasy as an unbridled irrationalism without any logic, a conception which turns fantasy into a simple counter-image of the law.

For Reich irrationalism meant sexual pathology and perversion, but that was because of the normative, if liberationist, concept of genital sexuality to which he held – normative *because* liberationist, we might argue today. He could therefore argue that the aggressivity mobilized by Fascism stemmed from drives which in an ideal world would move effortlessly into love, work, and health. Gradually the concept of infantile sexuality was replaced by that of adolescent desire, which Fascism rendered pathological because its repressive dictates stopped this desire from fulfilling itself. For Reich, Fascism mobilized above all pre-genital forms of sexuality, but he considered that in a socialist society they would naturally dissipate themselves. But if one no longer believes in this normative account of sexuality, then what form of sexuality can one oppose to that which is mobilized by the right? Even if today we would stress more than Reich did the phallocentric organization of these fantasies, we would still surely recognize that right-wing fantasy also draws on some of the earliest formations of the drives. That seems to place under considerable strain two recent ways of attempting to politicize psychoanalysis: the appeal, especially by a feminist and gay politics, to early sexuality for the pre-oedipal and non-normative possibilities which it appears to permit, which means ignoring the aggressive components of the early drives; or an appeal to a developmental model which recognizes early aggressivity and then seeks reparation from an ego which will gradually organize the drives which support it into sexual and psychic health.

The problem with the first position is its idealization of early psychic life. The problem with the second is not just that it entails a normative concept of sexual development, but also that the category of the ego, far from being independent of the political fantasies which it is being called on to avoid, is deeply implicated in them. Thus the authors of *The Authoritarian Personality*, written after the war as part of an attempt to predict the psychic possibility of Fascism in American, called on the ego as both solution to, and cause of, authoritarianism:

> It is the ego that becomes aware of and takes responsibility for nonrational forces operating within the personality. This is the basis for our belief that the object of knowing what are the psychological determinants of ideology is that men can become more reasonable.
> *Measurement of antidemocratic trends*: ... overemphasis on the conventional attributes of the ego.[59]

This simply means that is not possible to fix the ego unequivocally on either side of the political divide – any more, indeed, than American democracy: 'It has frequently been remarked that should fascism become a powerful force in this country, it would parade under the banners of traditional democracy.'[60] The problem reproduces itself almost exactly in Klaus Theweleit's *Male Fantasies*, which attributes the fantasies of the German Freikorps to the fragmentary nature of the ego which these soldiers seem to display, and then almost immediately locates some of the most pernicious forms of Western logic in the defenders of the 'bourgeois ego struggling to stave off their own demise'.[61]

If, therefore, we recognize in right-wing fantasy a mobilization, and specific economy of aggressivity and its defence; if we allow that it is through the category of rational identity that this economy authorizes (codifies, legitimates) itself, then the political case for a non-normative, pre-oedipal sexuality, as much as for an ego which guarantees normality and reparation, seems to collapse. A key component of the sexuality some of us thought to oppose to the law suddenly appears – and in the worst forms of the social imaginary – enshrined within it. And the ego, which others have invested as the site of our psychic and social health, confronts us in the shape of the worst form of social authority that knows only its own reason and truth. If, as Kristeva suggests, one solution is to let these fantasies be spoken so as to prevent their social legitimation, their acting out in the very framework of the law (the case for psychoanalytic practice), then this can only be on condition that it does not lead into the no less troubling fantasy of a total knowledge and control of the mind. The alternative presents itself with startling clarity at the end of Deborah Cameron and Elizabeth Frazer's 1987 study of the male serial killer, *The Lust to Kill*, when, recognizing the problem of female violence, they argue for nothing less than a total reconstitution of desire.[62]

I should perhaps stress here that psychoanalysis gives us no absolute or consistent theory of violence which could adequately describe it as much in its genesis as in its effects. It is described by Klein as an instinct, by Lacan as a structure inherent in intersubjectivity, by Kristeva as both cause and result of the precipitation of subjects into linguistic form. Nor should we forget Freud's insistence that it is always already attached to the fantasies which it appears to provoke. Rather, the point is to notice that if psychoanalysis is the intellectual tabloid of our culture ('sex and violence' being its chief objects of concern), we have recently privileged – sought, indeed, to base the politicization of psychoanalysis on that privilege – the sex over the violence. (Barbara Ehrenreich makes a related point in the Foreword to *Male Fantasies*.[63])

A question remains about the status of the woman – about that difficult position which Thatcher occupies and, I must acknowledge, in which I have positioned her, thereby repeating what I see as the problem of the way she functions as both authority and fantasy. For anything that might be said about the power which she concretely exerted, with effects that I think most of us would recognize as devastating, starts to join in and be complicit with the forms of projection which, precisely because of that strange and unique position she occupies as a woman, she provokes. Writing on the link which Freud thought he had established between femininity and death, Kristeva comments in *Histoires d'amour*, published four years after 'Women's Time':

> In Freud's later writing, [a paternal] position emerges which resolves the feminine share of subjectivity, by leaving to it the operative place of hatred and death promoted to the status of driving forces of the law. A scandal? Misogyny? Women analysts, starting with Melanie Klein, will recognize here an unconscious truth: their own?[64]

We can reformulate this question in the terms of her own earlier article, and insist on its social implications and determinants – that this association of women with hatred and death is expressive of their peculiar relation to the social in so far as it is grounded symbolically on both. But even if we do so, the question still remains as to whether this is something projected on to the woman or something which corresponds to women's psychic experience as such. Because of the power which she concretely had in reality, Thatcher forces us up against the limits of this problem. Another way of putting this would be to say that Thatcher is both a fantasy and a real event.

For a feminism which has argued for the perversity and even deadliness of the social, and then called it male, Thatcher presents a particular difficulty and anxiety which has perhaps been operating in the form of a taboo. In the scenario I have tried to outline here, the fact that Thatcher is a woman allowed her to get away with murder.

To return finally to the beginning of this chapter, I should stress that none of this is to deny the 'rational' reasons why people may have voted for Thatcher, nor indeed to give to anything I have described here the status of single political determinant or cause. It is, however, to point to a realm no less politically important (perhaps even more important) for not being containable in these terms.

POSTSCRIPT (AUGUST 1992)

It was perhaps inevitable that when Margaret Thatcher resigned as the leader of the Conservative Party in November 1990, it would be represented – and apparently experienced by her and her followers – as something between a political assassination and a palace *coup*, as if she were being confronted, and framed in effigy, by one version of the language of violence, not to say execution, on which she herself had often seemed to thrive: 'a political assassination which it will be hard to forgive'; 'She picked up the pistol after all'; 'The great oak has been brought down'; 'Those who live by the sword shall perish by the sword'; 'It was like when Kennedy was shot. I suppose we'll all remember this.'[65]

Margaret Thatcher was of course neither murdered nor assassinated, but it seemed as if no other language could quite capture or do justice to whatever it was that her own dramas of self-imagining had released. The sexual sub-text of this was explicit: Thatcher as a woman who, *as* woman, had managed to elevate phallic power to new heights: 'Boudicca [Boadicea] riding a Challenger tank'; 'The heroine expired in the night ... many hands have an interest in keeping [the stage] erect' – a basically violent and paranoid structure, as feminism has long argued, which relies on an antagonist to keep itself up: 'Her thrust fizzled because it lacked a black-and-white enemy.'[66] Ironically, but confirming the basic point, the man who has replaced her – his benign greyness is famous – offers self-effacement as the model of masculinity in power. Perhaps it is only a woman leader today who can claim so

52

literally to embody the phallus.

The question then arises of what is left of Thatcher and/or Thatcherism. When, the following year, Thatcher announced her decision to stand down from parliament, the *New Statesman* was quick to insist that Thatcherism was a chimera and largely a creation of one part of the intellectual left.[67] Certainly the fact that the fourth Conservative election victory took place under John Major's leadership suggests that whatever it is that guarantees the triumph of Conservatism cannot be located in Thatcher's psycho-political agenda, her triumphalism, alone. But while it may be true to say that Thatcher was 'as much a creature of Thatcherism as its creator' (on the day after her resignation, the *Independent* listed all the men who had 'made' her), yet it still seems to be the case that Thatcher effected a decisive shift in the British collective imagination, that she managed at some level to fulfil her best (worst) ambition: to 'change, not only the priorities of politicians, but the national soul'.[68] As Eric Hobsbawm argues:

> What difference did Thatcher make? Negatively, probably quite a lot, even if some of the more dangerous and irresponsible changes of the Eighties can be reversed – notably the excessive centralisation of state power and state direction, and the downgrading and destruction of lesser collective autonomies ... The atmosphere of Thatcherism, that conglomerate of egoism, political servility and moral blindness will not be so easy to eliminate.[69]

When the *New Statesman*, for example, argues that social attitude surveys show that there is no evidence of a public opinion shift in favour of State intervention and tax cuts[70] (there were a plethora of such polls during the election all suggesting support for increased public spending and hence a Labour victory), it is ignoring what the concept of 'attitude' is precisely unable to grasp. And that is the set of convictions which hover somewhere between an articulable belief and a fantasy in which collective self-imaginings take shape. That fourth election victory has if anything confirmed, rather than contradicted, the argument that it is in the crucible of subjective identities that political histories are forged – the issue not one of immediate or the most obvious forms of self-interest, but of how subjects 'envision' themselves. As if the fantasy component and legacy of Thatcherism could ride over all the material evidence (the worst recession, the decline if not collapse of health and educational provision, since the war). The difference today seems to me to reside in the fact that it has become harder to separate out what Hobsbawm calls the egoism and moral blindness from valid social and material aspirations; just as in Eastern Europe we are being presented with the split and coalescence of legitimate claims to national self-determination and autonomy with the absolutes of ethnic purification and hatred. How to distinguish them may be one of the most important political questions of today.

It seems to me far too easy, then, to say that what Thatcher carried psychically has now gone away; too easy to load on to her something which, in the course of her administrations, seemed at moments out of control if not mad. If Thatcher thrived on the ideology and mechanism of the scapegoat (the victim to be expelled), it would be a strange irony now to see ourselves as innocent of that process because we have so entirely lodged it in her: 'Is she going off her rocker? The inhabitants of the bar divide evenly between the "I've always said she was barking mad anyway" school and those who drool at the prospect of Maggie going publicly berserk and being escorted away in kindly fashion by men in white coats ... We are simply waiting for Krakatoa to erupt.'[71] Which is not to say that Thatcher did not operate in that space of fantasy where terrors are evoked, paradoxically but effectively, as part of a message and strategy of reassurance and control. Nor to suggest that what she enacted could not be described as politics in the paranoid mode. But what matters in all this is the structure or underside of *legitimate* power which Thatcher laid bare at its most extreme.

In a small news item tucked away at the bottom of the front page on the day of Thatcher's resignation, the *Independent* reported that one of the last things she had done before resigning was to double the British presence in the Gulf. It is notorious that the Gulf War – or at least the buildup to it – was partly a result of her egging Bush on ('Don't be a wimp, George'). In the last few weeks, Thatcher has been the first and the loudest to call for military intervention in Bosnia, echoing without qualification the strongest anti-Serbian rhetoric, in the face of the mounting evidence that this is not in any simple sense a one-sided situation, that the Serbs are becoming racial parodies and psychological scapegoats for a crisis in which they are not the sole agents of violence and in which Western Europe (past and present) has, at the very least, played its part. It does not seem to me to be a time when dismissal of Thatcher and her psychic agendas is appropriate. The risk is that, like any good – or rather bad – act of repression, the extent to which we require her to bear the burden will be in exact proportion to the grotesqueness with which those agendas return.

NOTES

[1] Julia Kristeva, 'Women's Time', trans. Alice Jardine and Harry Blake, in *Feminist Theory, A Critique of Ideology*, ed. Nannerl O. Keohane, Michelle Z. Rosaldo, and Barbara C. Gelpi (Chicago: University of Chicago Press, 1981; Brighton: Harvester, 1982), pp47, 52.
[2] Stuart Hall, 'Blue Election, Election Blues', *Marxism Today* (July 1987), p33. An edited version was published as 'When It's the Only Game in Town, People Play It', *Guardian*, 6 July 1987; see also correspondence, 8 July.
[3] *Ibid.*, p31.
[4] Hall, 'The Toad in the Garden: Thatcherism among the theorists', in *Marxism and the Interpretation of Culture*, ed. Cary Nelson and Lawrence Grossberg (Urbana, Ill. and Chicago: University of Illinois Press, 1988), pp35-73; the phrase was used by Hall specifically in response to a question about Wilhelm Reich (p72). These articles are just two from a series by Stuart Hall which, together with those by Sarah Benton (see n. 5 below), represent for me the most sustained and valuable critique of Thatcherism overall. See also 'The Great Moving Right show', in *The Politics of Thatcherism*, ed. Stuart Hall and Martin Jacques (London: Lawrence and Wishart, 1983), pp19-39.
[5] Sarah Benton makes this point in her analysis of Thatcher, 'The Triumph of the Spirit of War', when she talks of Thatcher as 'loathed with a rare passion', while also commenting on the way that Thatcher has been able to feed on the (feminist) insight that 'hitherto private feelings and fantasies can, once uttered, strike an unexpected public response' (*New Statesman*, 29 May 1987, p14).
[6] *The Times*, 14 July 1983.
[7] The strange relation between women and hanging in classical Greece is examined by Eva Cantarella, 'Dangling Virgins: myth, ritual, and the place of women in ancient Greece', in *The Female Body in Western Culture*, ed. Susan Suleiman (Cambridge, Mass., and London: Harvard University Press, 1986), pp57-67.
[8] In fact it is the points of connection and difference that are so striking. The two women were born within a year of each other (Ellis in 1924, Thatcher in 1926). Ellis's father came from a successful and respected middle-class family which had made its money out of weaving. His own father was a musician (a cathedral organ player), and he himself was a cellist and cinema musician until the advent of speaking pictures drove him down the social scale into unemployment, and then work as a porter, caretaker and chauffeur. Her mother was a Belgian-French refugee. Ellis could be said to have tried to make her way as a woman back up that scale by working as a model and then a club hostess. In that post-war period which was so decisive for the two women, therefore, Ellis had strong aspirations to social mobility not dissimilar in kind, although unlike in trajectory, Thatcher's own. As James Donald put it, they can be seen to represent the 'seedy' and 'golf club' sides of the petty

bourgeoisie, and have in common the same iconography of meticulous artificiality and precision (on Ellis's hair in court, see p51).

[9] Sigmund Freud, *Civilisation and its Discontents*, 1930 (1929), in *Standard Edition*, vol. 21, p112. Cf. also: 'Thus we see that right is the might of a community. It is still violence, ready to be directed against any individual who resists it; it works by the same methods and follows the same purposes. The only real difference lies in the fact that what prevails is no longer the violence of an individual but that of a community' ('Why war?', in *Standard Edition*, vol. 22), p205.

[10] René Girard, *La Violence et le sacré* (Paris: Grasset, 1972), p41.

[11] Laurence Marks and Tony van den Bergh, *Ruth Ellis: a case of diminished responsibility?* (London: Macdonald and Jane's, 1977), p105; for a full account of the trial, see Jonathan Goodman and Patrick Pringle, *The Trial of Ruth Ellis* (Newton Abbot: David and Charles, 1974).

[12] Marks and van den Bergh, *Ruth Ellis*, p87.

[13] Dr Duncan Whittaker, psychiatrist, quoted in *ibid.*, p104. Cf. also Ellis's defence counsel's later remarks: 'She had got into a very calm state of mind ... in which she thought everything she did was right and justified ... that there was no other course open to her' (p127).

[14] Opening statement by the judge, cited in *ibid.*, p117.

[15] Quoted in *Royal Commission on Capital Punishment*, 1949-52 (London: HMSO), p3.

[16] The French newspaper *Le Monde* commented at the time of the trial: 'English law does not at the moment recognize any intermediate stage between the rational and balanced being who kills in perfect awareness of what he is doing and the total lunatic who is not conscious of his own acts. As everyone knows, the Englishman is – or believes himself to be – a creature of sang-froid, and the legal system in force supports this fiction' (cited in Marks and van den Bergh, *Ruth Ellis*, p134).

[17] *Ibid.*, p118.

[18] *Ibid.*, p125.

[19] Cited in Goodman and Pringle, *Trial of Ruth Ellis*, p119.

[20] Cited in Marks and van den Bergh, *Ruth Ellis*, p127.

[21] In a review of *Myra Hindley: inside the mind of a murderess* (London: Angus and Robertson, 1988), Helen Birch points to the analogies that can be drawn between Hindley and Ellis, on the question of both their 'sanity' and their 'femininity', when commenting on the public obsession with Hindley, compared with other women this century who have murdered children: 'Hindley, on the other hand, is viewed as sane – "a calculated pretty cool operator" in the words of the prosecution ... the story goes that she sat impassive throughout the trial, in smart clothes, full make-up, with newly dyed hair. There are echoes here of the case of Ruth Ellis ... Feminists have since argued that one of the reasons Ellis was sent to the gallows was because, in the eyes of the all-male jury, her appearance did not match the line of her defence' (*New Statesman*, 18 March 1988), p25.

[22] Alexandre Fontana, 'The Intermittences of Rationality', in *Pierre Rivière*, ed. Michael Foucault (Harmondsworth: Peregrine, 1978), p273: 'Is it possible for a criminal to keep his reason entire or lose it for an instant and then recover

it? Was he aware of what he was doing? Did he harbour delusions about a single subject only, keeping the remainder of his faculties intact? Was only one of his faculties affected to the exclusion of all the others? ... Reasoning madness and monomania were the flaw, the twilight zone, the point of opacity in the system'; first published in French in *Moi, Pierre Rivière, ayant égorgé ma mère, ma soeur, et mon frère ... un cas de parricide au XIXe siècle* (Paris: Gallimard, 1973).

[23] The defence counsel later said that he was convinced that the trial had led to the new law of diminished responsibility (cited in Marks and van den Bergh, *Ruth Ellis*, p127). The authors open their book with this statement by Muriel Jakubait, sister of Ruth Ellis, to whom the book is dedicated: 'When any child is murdered in England today, I am the subject of attack. They say that if it weren't for my sister, we would still have the death penalty ... and then that child would have lived.' Cf. also Goodman and Pringle: 'There is little doubt that the execution of Ruth Ellis played a major part in bringing about the abolition of capital punishment' (*Trial of Ruth Ellis*, p77).

[24] Cited on the opening page of Marks and van den Bergh, *Ruth Ellis*.

[25] Michel Foucault, 'About the Concept of the "Dangerous Individual" in Nineteenth-Century Legal Psychiatry', trans. Alain Baudot and Jane Couchman, *International Journal of Law and Psychiatry*, 1 (1978), pp1-18.

[26] *Ibid.*, p12.

[27] 'Memorandum submitted by the Institute of Psycho-Analysis', 23rd day, Thursday, 1 June 1950, in *Royal Commission on Capital Punishment*, p546.

[28] Dr Carroll ('We would stress the need to cover the normal murderer') was interrupted on this point by Dr Gillespie ('It depends on what you mean by "normal", because if one assumes most people have murderous impulses but very few people give way to them and so become murderers, then statistically speaking the murderer cannot be called normal'). Roger Money-Kyrle then added: 'In a precise way [normal] would mean a very high degree of integration of personality. I think we at the Institute would all agree that a normal person in that sense would very rarely commit a murder' (*ibid.*, p548). The memorandum also states that this outcome will depend on 'the relative strengths of the aggressive and loving impulses ... determined by both inborn factors and environmental experience, especially during the first months and years of life' (p546). See also n. 29 below.

[29] Ernest Jones, 'The concept of the Normal Mind', *International Journal of Psycho-Analysis*, 23, pt 1 (1942), pp1-8. See also Ernest Jones, *Hamlet and Oedipus* (New York: Norton, 1949; Anchor edition, 1954), where he states that psychoanalysis confuses the division 'which until our generation (and even now in the juristic sphere) separated the sane and responsible from the irresponsible insane' (p76). Arthur Koestler and C.H. Rolph quote this passage from the Commission in their campaigning book *Hanged by the Neck: an exposure of capital punishment in England* (Harmondsworth: Penguin Special, 1961): 'There is no sharp dividing line between sanity and insanity ... the two extremes shade into one another by imperceptible gradations. The degree of individual responsibility varies equally widely; no clear boundary can be drawn between responsibility and irresponsibility. Likewise crimes of passion shade without a sharp division into crimes due to mental disease'

(p136). Roger Money-Kyrle, who spoke at the Commission in defence of the category of 'normality', quotes Jones's article on 'The Concept of the Normal Mind' in his book *Psychoanalysis and Politics, A Contribution to the Psychology of Politics and Morals* (London: Duckworth, 1951), where he makes much more explicit the relation of the concept of the 'normal' to 'rationality': 'For if the "normal" is equivalent to the "rational", and if there is a type of conscience common to normal people which differs from the consciences of abnormal people, then this type is an attribute of rationality' (p19).

[30] Letter from R.C. Webster, Todmorden, Lancashire, cited in Marks and van den Bergh, *Ruth Ellis*, appendix 3, p143.

[31] 'The Death Penalty', *Lancet* (23 July 1955), reprinted in Marks and van den Bergh, *Ruth Ellis*, appendix 3, 138-40.

[32] Cf. also the correspondence on the execution of Ruth Ellis: '[Capital punishment] is *not* rational: it is barbaric'; 'the barbaric penalties of execution'; 'the medieval savagery of the law'; all in Marks and van den Bergh, *Ruth Ellis*, appendix 3, pp147, 128, 129.

[33] Cited in 'Another Defeat Expected for Pro-Hanging Lobby', *Independent*, (27 May 1988). For an 'aesthetic' defence of capital punishment, or rather a defence of capital punishment *as* aesthetic, however, see Walter Berns, *For Capital Punishment, Crime and the Morality of the Death Penalty* (New York: Basic Books, 1979): 'Can we imagine a world that does not take its revenge on the man who kills Macduff's wife and children? ... Can we imagine a world that does not hate murderers? To ask these questions is to ask whether we can imagine a world without Shakespeare's poetry ... punishment may be likened to dramatic poetry or the purpose of punishment to one of the intentions of the great dramatic poet' (p168).

[34] The distinction is not as straightforward as it seems however; see Hannah Arendt's discussion of the concept of *raison d'état* in Postscript to *Eichmann in Jerusalem* (Harmondsworth: Penguin, 1977 (1963; 1965)), pp290-1.

[35] David Pannick, *Judicial Review of the Death Penalty* (London: Duckworth, 1982), p1.

[36] See also Mark Cousins, '*Mens rea:* a note on sexual difference, criminology and law', in *Radical Issues in Criminology*, ed. Pat Carlen and Mike Collinson (Oxford: Martin Robertson, 1980): 'Certain forms of traditional jurisprudence can unify [the law] as the expression of an unfolding rationality. Legal positivism could represent it through the unity of a command of a sovereign. Pashukanis will reply to this by making it the space of rights of the subject of possession. But each of these positions requires to be supported theoretically, and each of them will face analytic problems of where the boundaries of the unity lie, where law suddenly passes beyond itself' (p115). Cousins is reviewing Carol Smart, *Women, Crime and Criminology* (London: Routledge and Kegan Paul, 1976), a feminist critique of the category of the woman criminal. The point about the limits of the law was made quite explicitly with reference to Ruth Ellis: 'Judges have often pointed out that the courts are courts of law, *not* courts of morals. The McNaghten rules are really based on moral theology, which assesses human acts on the basis of gravity of the act, knowledge of the agent, and volition of the agent' (R.C. Webster, cited in Marks and van den Bergh, *Ruth Ellis*, appendix 3, p143).

[37] Pannick, *Judicial Review*, p65; he is describing specifically the American and Indian judiciary. The other two criteria are 'That it is mandatory for a defined offence' (this would rule out the attempt in England to make the death sentence mandatory for terrorism), and 'That it is grossly disproportionate to the offence' (this immediately comes up against the problem of proportionality: 'One must be careful not to assume "the role of finely tuned calibrator of depravity, demarcating for a watching world the various gradations of dementia"' (p145), quoting *Godfrey* vs *Georgia* [1980]). All these difficulties have not prevented courts from claiming that they have provided the means to 'promote the evenhanded, rational and consistent imposition of death sentences under law': *Jurek* vs *Texas*, cited on p179.

[38] 'Not since the condemnation of Mrs Edith Thomson in 1923 had such a storm of public protest been aroused against the hanging of a woman' (Duncan Webb, *Line up for Crime* (London: Frederick Muller, 1956), p203). The horror, however, was clearly ambivalent: 'Children in a school near the prison are described by one of their teachers as being in a ferment: "Some claim to have seen the execution from a window, others spoke with fascinated horror of the technique of hanging a female"' ('The Death Penalty', p140).

[39] It is a stereotype which, specifically in relation to capital punishment, is written into the history of the law; see William Blackstone, *Commentaries on the Laws of England*, facsimile of the first edition of 1765-9, vol. 4 (Chicago and London: University of Chicago Press, 1979): 'Was the vast territory of all the Russias worse regulated under the late Empress Elizabeth, than under her more sanguinary predecessors? Is it now, under Catherine II, less civilised, less social, less secure? And yet we are assured, that neither of these illustrious princesses have, throughout their whole administration, inflicted the penalty of death' (p10).

[40] Julia Kristeva, in discussion at the colloquium 'Psychanalyse et politique', Milan, 1973, published as *Psychanalyse et politique* (Paris: Seuil, 1974), p40.

[41] Richard Hofstadter, *The Paranoid Style in American Politics and Other Essays* (London: Cape, 1966), quoting Barnuel (p12). In a series of articles starting in 1984, Sarah Benton has commented on the 'cultivated paranoia' on which the Conservative Party relies: 'Press a placid Tory, who wants nothing more than a world in which there is no argument, no interference with the natural way of doing things, no disturbing questions on war, economics or sex, and out comes a flow of nightmare fears and anecdotes ... [they feel part of] a mystical national good. Such a belief can only derive coherence from the conjuring up of the Alien, a force whose shape you never quite see but which lurks in every unlit space ready to destroy you; and is incubated, unnoticed, in the healthy body politic' ('Monsters from the Deep', *New Statesman*, 19 October 1984, pp10-12). Benton was arguing here that the Brighton bomb fulfilled these persecution fantasies; compare Tebbit, quoted in *The Times*, (19 December 1984), as saying that the bomb was not an 'isolated incident' but 'part of an irrationality that had crept into politics and society'. See also Benton, 'The Triumph of the Spirit of War', and 'What are They Afraid of?', (*New Statesman*, 11 March 1988), pp14-15.

[42] Bruce Arnold, *Margaret Thatcher: a study in power* (London: Hamish Hamilton, 1984), pp269-74.

[43] Printed in full in *The Times*, 31 December 1983; compare also this comment from the *Observer*'s leading article, (29 May 1988): 'She is a woman who not only says what she means but, to a degree unusual in politicians, actually means what she says.'

[44] The most important examination of this concept of rationality is Herbert Marcuse's *Reason and Revolution: Hegel and the rise of social theory* (London: Routledge and Kegan Paul, 1969 (1941)).

[45] Ernle Money, *Margaret Thatcher, First Lady of the House* (London: Leslie Frewin, 1975), *Margaret Thatcher*, p134.

[46] Arnold, *Margaret Thatcher*, p271.

[47] Hofstadter, *Paranoid Style*, pp36-7; see also N. McConaghy, 'Modes of Abstract Thinking and Psychosis', *American Journal of Psychiatry*, 117 (August 1960), pp106-10 (this article is cited by Hofstadter), and also Robert Waelder, 'The Structure of Paranoid Ideas', *International Journal of Psycho-Analysis*, 32 (1951), pp167-77, especially on why the paranoiac correctly fears, and must therefore fight off, the defeat of his or her own system: 'It is a fight in which all the initial advantages are with the paranoiacs, but which they are bound to lose, because of their lack of elasticity, unless they can turn initial advantages into complete victory' (p167n). This description by Hofstadter sounds uncannily like Thatcher: 'The passion for factual evidence does not, as in most intellectual exchanges, have the effect of putting the paranoid spokesman into effective two-way communication with the world outside his group – least of all with those who doubt his views. He has little real hope that his views will convince a hostile world. His effort to amass it has rather the quality of a defensive act which shuts off his receptive apparatus and protects him from having to attend to disturbing considerations that do not fortify his ideas. He has all the evidence he needs; he is not a receiver, he is a transmitter' (p38).

[48] Letter from L. Webb, cited in Marks and van den Bergh, *Ruth Ellis*, appendix 3, p132.

[49] Speech to the Junior Carlton Club, 4 May 1976, quoted in Patrick Cosgrave, *Margaret Thatcher: a Tory and her party* (London: Hutchinson, 1978), p215.

[50] Remarks made during an interview on *World in Action* (Granada TV, January 1978), quoted in Penny Junor, *Margaret Thatcher: wife, mother, politician* (London: Sidgwick and Jackson, 1983), pp116-17; when challenged on this speech by Kenneth Harris in an interview in the *Observer*, Thatcher replied, 'I *never* modified it! I stood by it one hundred per cent. Some people have felt swamped by immigrants. They've seen the whole character of their neighbourhood change. I stood by that statement one hundred per cent' (*Margaret Thatcher Talks to the* Observer, published as a separate booklet, January 1979).

[51] From *State* vs *Dixon*, 1973, cited in Pannick, *Judicial Review*, p71n.

[52] *Confidence in the Law*, Conservative Study Group on Crime, Conservative Research Department, vol. 1 (January 1986). William Hamilton, speaking in the debate on capital punishment in the House of Commons, reported in *The Times*, 14 July 1983.

[53] Kristeva, 'Women's Time', p47.

54 See Georges Bataille, 'The Psychological Structure of Fascism', in *Visions of Excess: selected writings 1927-1939*, ed. Allan Stoekl, trans. Allan Stoekl with Carl R. Lovitt and Donald M. Leslie Jr (Minneapolis: University of Minnesota Press, 1985), pp137-60. In a very different, recent article specifically on the Conservative Party and violence, Frank Burton argues, within a Foucauldian framework, that the Conservative rhetoric of coercion is deceptive, and merely expressed a 'rationalization of the administration of justice'; but he does acknowledge that the free vote on capital punishment does not quite fit into this frame. ('Questions of Violence in Party Political Criminology', in *Radical Issues in Criminology*, ed. Carlen and Collinson, pp123-51).

55 Harris, *Margaret Thatcher Talks to the* Observer.

56 John Nott, interviewed on the BBC *Panorama* programme *300 Days*, which marked Thatcher's becoming the longest-serving prime minister this century (4 January 1988); Robert Harris, '*Prima donna inter pares*', *Observer*, 3 January 1988.

57 On the question of Thatcher as a woman, see Beatrix Campbell, 'To Be or Not To Be a Woman', in *The Iron Ladies: why do women vote Tory?* (London: Virago, 1987), ch. 9, pp233-47, and Benton, 'Triumph of the Spirit of War'.

58 Wilhelm Reich, *The Mass Psychology of Fascism*, trans. Theodore P. Wolfe, 3rd edn (New York: Orgone Institute Press, 1946); retrans. Vincent R. Carfagno (New York: Farrar, Straus and Giroux, 1970; Harmondsworth: Penguin, 1975).

59 T.W. Adorno, Else Frenkel-Brunswick, David J. Levinson, and R. Nevitt Sandford, in collaboration with Betty Araon, Maria Hertz Levinson, and William Morrow, *The Authoritarian Personality*, Studies in Prejudice series, ed. Max Horkheimer and Samuel H. Flowerman (New York: Harper and Row, 1960; Science Editions, 1964), vol. 2, p228.

60 *Ibid.*, p50; compare, however, the last lines of the book: 'If fear and destructiveness are the major emotional sources of fascism, eros belongs mainly to democracy' (p976).

61 Klaus Theweleit, *Male Fantasies*, vol. 1, trans. Stephen Conway in collaboration with Chris Turner and Erica Carter (Minneapolis: University of Minnesota Press; Cambridge: Polity Press, 1987), pp208, 219.

62 Deborah Cameron and Elizabeth Frazer, *The Lust to Kill* (Cambridge: Polity Press, 1987): 'We insist that there can be a vision of the future in which desire will be reconstructed totality' (p176).

63 Barbara Ehrenreich, Foreword to Theweleit, *Male Fantasies*, pxii.

64 Julia Kristeva, *Histoires d'amour* (Paris: Denoël, 1983), p121n; trans. Leon S. Roudiez, *Tales of Love* (New York: Columbia University Press, 1987).

65 *Daily Telegraph, The Times, Daily Mail, Independent*, 23 November 1990.

66 Colin Hughes, 'The Woman who Transformed Britain', *Independent*, 23 November 1990; Ross McKibbin, 'Diary', *London Review of Books*, 6 December 1990, p25.

67 'The End of an Error', Editorial, *New Statesman*, 5 July 1991, pp4-5.

68 Hughes, 'Woman who Transformed Britain'.

69 Eric Hobsbawm, 'What Difference Did She Make?', *London Review of Books*, 23 May 1991, pp3-6.

[70] 'End of an Error'.
[71] R.W. Johnson, 'The Human Time Bomb – Is the Former Prime Minister Going off her Rocker?', *New Statesman*, 22 March 1991, p10.

Fantasy, Identity, Politics

Stuart Hall

This is based on a transcript of a talk given by Stuart Hall in response to Homi Bhabha and Jacqueline Rose. The discussion took place at the ICA, London, 25 January 1989.

Rather than go over the ground that I share with both Jacqueline and Homi, I prefer to consider the implications of what they have said for my own positions. The central question they raise, I think, concerns the nature of the subjectivity that underpins identification and politics. I agree with them about the need to move away from conceptions of the political subject and political action based on an unified identity and the rationalist calculation of interests. But I have reservations about *how far* we can or should move. I shall try to say what my areas of reservation are, even if I cannot give a very theorised account of them.

In her essay on Thatcherism, Jacqueline analyses the appeal of a form of political paranoia which yokes together apparently deeply contradictory elements. In a different way, that is a question I have continually come back to over the past five years. Working on Thatcherism has made it patently clear that a rationalist conception of ideology simply has no purchase on what is going on politically. You can't make sense of Thatcherism as an ideology that interpellates subjects through a rational calculus of interests. Equally, against explanations of Thatcherism as irrational false consciousness, I have often argued that political identification and subjectivity are inherently fragmented. Far from being false consciousness, there are perfectly *rational* reasons why people respond to aspects of Thatcherism, and identify with them as they do. Even though I always put that 'rational' in quotation marks, the question Jacqueline raises for me is, what is that rationality? If it is not the rationality of calculable material interests from which one can read off people's political positions and around which one can build a contractual political programme, what is rational about it? Why not just drop the notion of rationality?

This may seem a quibble, but it does not help our understanding to think of people's political identifications as *irrational* in the dismissive sense – in short, that ideology is something that comes from outer space, that it has no logic to it, that there is nothing that can be done about it. These things do have a logic. Again, I save myself by putting 'logic' in quotation marks: I don't mean a series of logically entailed propositions, but rather a *discursive* logic, a way of connecting one statement to another. Although people's political identifications may well contain contradictory strands, they nonetheless have a form, a structure, a shape and are always 'motivated' by powerful, unconscious investments. They have some sequential element built into them. If you want to understand the 'logic' of Thatcherism, for example, you will get closer to it by thinking in terms of the logic of a dream rather than the logic of philosophical investigation. It is absurd to say that Thatcherism cannot work because it is internally contradictory. The beauty or the symmetry of the operation lies in its capacity to condense and display contradictory symbolisations in the same space.

Now, where does this logic of identification operate? Is it simply another level of (secondary) political rationalisation produced on top of unconscious processes which cannot be named within any form of symbolic representation or language? I wouldn't go that far. I would say that there is a domain of discursive operations in which extremely important forms of social and political action take place, that these of course are connected to what Jacqueline calls psycho-sexual processes, and that they cannot therefore be understood without reference to the imaginary or to the unconscious. But they are not simply repetitions or reiterations of psychic processes. They also have a reality and acquire a social logic in the world. They have some purchase in terms of social action and social behaviour.

The reason I want to save that residue is that without it I don't understand where politics is located. That is my hesitation. What I have learned from psychoanalytic perspectives, from feminism particularly (and especially from Jacqueline's work), is the importance of thinking the articulation between the unconscious and political processes without hoping, as it were, ever to square up those two

64

continents as equivalents. The unconscious itself acts as a bar or a cut between those two continents: it becomes the site of a perpetual postponement or deferral of equivalence. It is therefore impossible to understand politics without taking account of both the unconscious and the social, but it is equally impossible simply to translate either set of processes into the other.

But, although I see all the theoretical problems involved in saying this, I do still want to understand how the relations between the two continents have real consequences in the space we refer to as 'the political'. This is the point at which I use the term identity – perhaps in a different way from Homi. By *identity*, or *identities*, I mean the processes that constitute and continuously re-form the subject who has to act and speak in the social and cultural world. Identity is the meeting point, or the point of future, between, on the one hand, the ideological discourses which attempt to interpellate or speak us as social subjects, and, on the other, the psychological or psychical processes which produce us as subjects which can be spoken. So I certainly don't want to restore the notion of identity as unified essence, something continuous with the self, an inner truth that can be discovered. On the contrary, I understand identies as points of suture, points of *temporary* attachment, as a way of understanding the constant transformations of who one is or as Foucault put it, 'who one is to become'. You only discover who you are because of the identities you are required to take on, into which you are interpellated: but you must take up those positionalities, however temporarily, in order to act at all. Identities are, as it were, the forms in which we are obliged to act, while always knowing that they are representations which can never be adequate to the subject processes that are temporarily invested in them. Identities also have histories, within the discourses which construct or narrate them, and they are going to be transformed. The next time I act politically it will not be within the form of identification which on the previous occasion seemed – how can I put it? – to represent enough of me at that moment to get to the next place.

In that sense, identity is like a bus! Not because it takes you to a fixed destination, but because you can only get somewhere – anywhere – by climbing aboard. The whole of you can never be represented by the ticket you carry, but you still have to buy a ticket to get from here to there. In the same way, you have to take a position in order to say anything, even though meaning refuses to be finally fixed and that position is an often contradictory holding operation rather than a position of truth. And I recognise that such positional identities are narratives, that they are stories we tell ourselves about ourselves. They are necessarily fictional. They are the necessary fiction of action, the necessary fictions of politics. They are also a kind of recognition after the event. All the identities I can think of in my life have been after the event. Long after you have acted in their name, someone says, 'That's what you are.' And you say, 'My God! That's what I am!' At that moment, you can be pretty certain you are in the transition to becoming something else.

So identities are sliding, but they are not infinitely sliding. It is their fictional and retrospective nature that allows us to see them as over-invested, as an arbitrary in the linguistic sense. You have to stop, because if you don't you cannot construct meaning. You have to come to a full stop, not because you have uttered your last word, but because you need to start a new sentence which may take back everything you have just said.

What conception of politics emerges from this line of thinking? It undermines any notion of a politics constructed around fixed identities or 'real' interests. Political collectivities are always partly the result of imaginary identifications. They are imagined communities; and none the less important or effective for that. It is *because* they are imagined – because they constructed between the real and desire – that such communities can act as a mobilising political force.

This does not imply that political identifications are free-floating. I can illustrate by an analogy with ideology and language. These two are not synonymous, because ideology is the thing that *cuts* language. By that I mean that, although language contains an infinite semiosis or plenitude of meaning, to become meaningful it has to be fixed in the form of a statement or utterance. It has to take up a position in meaning if it is to get something said/done in the world, and that is when its plenitude is cut by ideology. In a similar way, I cannot conceptualise a politics has no 'frontier effects', which doesn't involve symbolically staging the line between 'us' and 'them'. That is quite different from assuming that 'us' and 'them' are eternal essences, but it does recognise the necessity of saying that just now, conjunctionally, this line matters. The drawing of the line is never final, never absolute. Part of us is already on the other side of the barricades, and part of the Other, even of the Enemy, is already inside us. Nevertheless, in the positional play of politics, the line sometimes has to be drawn. What I am trying to imagine is a politics which can recognise the arbitrariness of that cut. What would be the nature of a politics in which people know every commitment to be partly a fiction, but are still able to act?

You may think this is me wanting to have my cake and eat it too. Maybe it is, but I want to defend the position, while responding to Homi's arguments, by talking about some disturbing recent events. One, obviously, is what is happening around *The Satanic Verses*. The *fatwah* is horrendous, an obscenity. But I'll tell you another, more hilarious version of the same thing, which I suspect Salman Rushdie would enjoy.

I know nobody here is a regular reader of the *Daily Mail*. But last week it ran a series of features under the title, 'Who are the British?' Who keeps up British standards today? they asked. Who believes in the nuclear family? Who maintains moral values? Who is opposed to extra-marital sex? Who is disgusted by the practices of gay and lesbian people? If you want to know who now stands for the values the English are losing, said the *Daily Mail*, the answer is – Muslims.

I present this as a joke, but at another level it is not at all funny. The reason it has troubled me profoundly is that, at the same time as I have been trying to rethink *identity*, I have also been trying to rescue some notion of *ethnicity* as a necessary but not sufficient way of thinking about cultural identities. I have been arguing for new conceptions of ethnici*ties* which recognise that people are placed in a history, in a culture, in a space, that they come from somewhere, that enunciation is always located. I have been asking whether ethnicity could be a term which would enable us to recognise that placing of enunciation in a very different way from the embattled, aggressive ethnicities that have rampaged through our world.

This week, after the reversals around questions of ethnic identification, especially in connection with *The Satanic Verses*, my commitment to the notion of rethinking ethnicity is somewhat weaker. But, although what has happened has shaken me politically, I have to say that it has not shaken me theoretically. If you reject any notion of essential ethnicity or fixed identity, and if you accept the contradictoriness of cultural, political and representational practices, then even a transformation as bizarre as the *Mail* being able to recognise itself in the Muslim identity has always been on the cards.

Sometimes the cycle of articulation, disarticulation and rearticulation seems to offer a comforting new political logic. But rearticulation is attractive only so long as we think *we* are going to do the rearticulating. When it is we who are rearticulated, we don't like it so much. That has happened not only in these two horrendous examples, it has been happening to us perpetually over the past ten years. That is how, in my view, Thatcherism has understood hegemony much better than anybody on the Left. Its effectiveness shows that disarticulation and rearticulation need not necessarily be directed towards any progressive, humane or socially just end. It has no necessary political belongingness. But that should not disturb us *theoretically*.

In that spirit, I agree with almost everything that Homi has said, so eloquently, about the ambivalence of identification and the moments of splitting and doubling that it always entails. I do not need to go through that argument, because I am at one with him on that. What I want to know is how one can think politics in the teeth of those insights. Given the ambivalence and splitting involved in the process and structure of identification, what is it that enables us to identify sufficiently to think what the ground of politics might be? Could there be any collective project which is not constructed around *some* form of identification?

I don't know the answer to that. But I am convinced that we won't know a new form of politics until we can think those questions. It is really the same question I raised in relation to Jacqueline's arguments: how can you think identity *through* difference? Difference means that identification must always be a matter of sliding. There will always be things which are excessive; you will always try to polarise the world. And that draws you into the logic of *différance* rather than the logic of difference.

But I am not sure that we should try to transcend difference. I think it is still possible to imagine forms of political action that take account of the always provisional, necessarily contingent, and never sufficient nature of those identifications which are *in* difference. I think that is possible, although I cannot find the language to express the argument adequately and I don't know what policies and practices flow from it. But if what we have been saying is right, that must be the next step. Either we give up on the question of politics, or we have to rethink politics in these ways.

A question raised by Homi's article is how one might rethink the notion of hegemony in the light of all this. If political identification is contingent and contradictory, how can one talk about hegemony? What collective will could be constructed out of these endlessly fragmented subjectivities? That partly depends on how you interpret hegemony. I have always understood hegemony as *operating through* difference, rather than *overcoming* difference, but I have never really been able to get that notion across. People imagine that the subordinate groups in a hegemonic formation must be reconstituted in the image of the dominant formation. On the contrary, hegemony is an authority which can be constructed *only* by continuing to recognise difference. Patriarchal hegemony does not remake women in the image of men, for example: it provides the secondary or subaltern place for that which it recognises as different. So hegemony need not imply a collective will that is uniform, that is imposed, that obliterates difference. Hegemony is the process, never complete, of trying to create some formation out of persistent, contradictory differences which continue therefore to need the work of 'unifying' – again in quotation marks, since no self-sufficient unity or totality can ever be produced.

But I do recognise that the versions of 'identities' and 'subjectivities' I am now using take me two or three steps even beyond that provisional notion of hegemony. Am I giving it up? Well, not yet ...

B Reading the Popular

The Impossible Object: Towards a Sociology of the Sublime

Dick Hebdige

A Klee painting named *Angelus Novus* shows an angel looking as though he is about to move away from something he is fixedly contemplating. His eyes are staring, his mouth is open, his wings are spread. This is how one pictures the angel of history. His face is turned towards the past. Where we perceive a chain of events, he sees one single catastrophe which keeps piling wreckage upon wreckage and hurls it in front of his feet. The angel would like to stay, awaken the dead, and make whole what has been smashed. But a storm is blowing from Paradise; it has got caught in his wings with such violence that the angel can no longer close them. This storm irresistibly propels him into the future to which his back is turned while the pile of debris before him grows skyward. This storm is what we call progress.

(Walter Benjamin, 'The 9th thesis on the philosophy of history')

Cosmogony Legends. Like almost all Indians, the Algonquin tribes believe in the Thunder Bird, a powerful spirit whose eyes flash lightning, while the beating of his wings is the rolling of thunder. He it is who prevents the earth from drying up and vegetation from dying.

(Robert Graves (ed.), *New Larousse Encyclopaedia of Mythology*)

I

In recent years, the reappraisal of political and intellectual priorities which has been forced upon us by a whole series of cultural, political and epistemological crises has led to a renewal of interest in the genealogy and origins of contemporary modes of thought, ways of seeing and saying. As part of this process of critical, reflexive practice – a movement back which can involve either a painful but necessary return to primary questions or a wilful retreat from the challenge of the present – there has been a renewal of interest in the origin and meaning of the aesthetic experience. Attention has been concentrated on two founding moments: the origin of western philosophy in ancient Greece and the birth of formal aesthetics in the Enlightenment when the categories of the Sublime and the Beautiful were first used to differentiate the varieties of aesthetic experience.

At the same time, the rhetoric of postmodernism has helped to induce and articulate a generalized 'sense of an ending' which is focused around a refusal of totalities, explanatory systems, older certainties of all kinds. Often, and paradoxically, the genealogical impulse has here been combined with a tendency to engage in what Jean Baudrillard calls 'science fiction': a sense of play and prophecy, along with forms of parable and allegory, has entered 'serious' critical discourse, sometimes in the shape of highly schematic diagnoses of our present 'condition'. In this spirit, some commentators have deconstructed the 'aesthetic', and in a Derridean flourish turned it inside out, presenting in its place a critical postmodern 'anti-aesthetic'.[1]

Taking advantage in what follows of the critical licence opened up within the Post I shall move back and forth across this landscape mobilizing different kinds of knowledge, different voices, different kinds of writing, to reflect upon the provenance in the modern period of the idea of aesthetics and aesthetic judgement and to summarize two different but related critiques of the 'aesthetic': on the one hand, Pierre Bourdieu's work on the social origin and functions of aesthetic taste and, on the other, the postmodernist promotion, following Nietzsche, of an 'anti-aesthetic' based on a rejection of the Enlightenment idea of beauty. At the same time, by cutting back at regular intervals to more grounded 'ecological' descriptions of the street in London where I live, by concentrating in particular on the heterogeneous (sub)cultural-ethnic mix that constitutes the local demography, I hope to 'bring home' – in both the literal and figurative senses of the phrase – the implications of issues raised in these larger debates on taste, aesthetics, postmodernism. This weaving together of incommensurable levels, tones, objects, represents an attempt to engage *suggestively* in those debates, to alternate between on the one hand the personal, the confessional, the particular, the concrete, and the other the public, the expository, the general, the abstract: to walk the flickering line between vertigo and ground.

The ghost of a totality hangs in the air like the shadow of Klee's Angel over the discourse(s) of the Post but the Angel also has another side and a different name. (In other places it answers to the name of Thunder Bird.) This article, centred as it is on the reverie of the impossible object (a sociology of the Sublime is, after all, impossible) is also intended as an invocation of the Thunder Bird: as a tracking of the Angel's brighter aspect. The invocation ends with a question: if sociology is concerned with the discovery and examination of invisible, impalpable structures which cannot be directly apprehended in experience but which none the less condition everything that passes as *social* experience, then what can sociology do with the unconscious, what can it do with those invisible, impossible, imaginary structures we inhabit every night as we sleep? What kind of sociology would take dreams as 'data'?

2

There is a paradox in the historical development of the word 'taste'. Originally denoting physiological sensations, the word was generalized from meaning essentially passive physiological responses (primarily palatal) to given stimuli, to a sense either of the active attribution of value to aesthetic objects or of the more or less codified rules of polite society – so-called 'good taste'. By the eighteenth century, according to Raymond Williams,[2] the word had been, as it were, etherialized so that it no longer referred to the physical senses but rather to the underlying principles which are taken to govern the laws of conduct and aesthetics alike. From that time onwards, taste can be taken to refer to the judgement of either social or formal values, while the 'laws' or 'rules' which are invoked to legitimate and authorize those judgements are in both cases typically seen as God-given, universal, timeless.

It is that confusion surrounding the term – a term which can designate at once physical sensations of attraction and repulsion and the elaboration of both social and formal codes – which provides the starting-point from which subsequent debates on taste proceed. The entire fragile edifice of modern aesthetics could be said to rest upon the founding set of contradictions and oppositions traced out during the eighteenth century around the word 'taste'. A struggle over the meaning of the term begins in earnest in the latter part of the century. The romantic poets, for example, as part of their resistance to the commercialization and commodification of literature – itself linked to the decline of aristocratic patronage and the rise of the literate mercantile and industrial middle classes – begin to articulate a mythology of artistic production around the solitary figure of the alienated and marginalized poet-prophet. This romantic archetype of the isolated creative genius, estranged from urban 'polite society', temperamentally aligned with Nature and the Folk (as opposed to the Public), develops in explicit opposition to the cultural aspirations of those sections of the emergent bourgeoisie which are seeking to emulate aristocratic models, to gatecrash 'high society', to codify and generalize the rules of taste and manners so that they can consolidate their economic ascendancy in the cultural field. The conflict arises, then, between those who resist any attempt to submit or reduce literature and the arts to the laws of the market, and those fractions of the emergent élites who seek to conceal and euphemize the 'vulgar' sources of their wealth in industry and commerce and to raise themselves and their offspring to a 'higher', more spiritual level. For Wordsworth, who in the preface to the *Lyrical Ballads* had referred contemptuously to those 'who will converse with us as gravely about a *taste* for Poetry, as they express it, as if it were a thing as indifferent as a taste for rope-dancing, or Frontiniac or Sherry',[3] only the poets, men (*sic*) of principle and insight, in tune with Nature and the eternal verities, pledged to defend and renew the living language through their poetry, should be entrusted with the sacerdotal role of distinguishing the good from the bad, the beautiful from the ugly, the enduring from the transitory. And these oppositions develop, in the succeeding decades, alongside other ideologically weighted distinctions between, for instance, 'art' and 'industry', 'individual' and 'mass', 'organic' and 'mechanical', 'high' and 'low' culture. In other words, they develop alongside and in parallel with all those structured oppositions which form around the superordinate polarity between culture and society which Raymond Williams shows to have dominated literary-critical and aesthetic discourse in England from the latter part of the eighteenth century until the middle of the twentieth.[4]

But the question of taste, of discrimination, of the generalizability or otherwise of aesthetic judgements, is posed much further back, at the root of the western philosophical tradition, in the Platonic concept of ideal forms, where the objects which we encounter in sensory experience are held to be mere tokens: imperfect, mortal echoes of the absolute forms of the Good, the True and the Beautiful which are said to exist beyond the reach of our senses, 'on the other side' of sensory experience, beyond time and change. In a famous series of metaphors, of which the fable of the cave is the most developed and concise, Plato argued that the phenomenal forms of perception were mere shadows of the Real, of the absolute and timeless Forms which lay beyond sensory perception. Implicit in this distinction between the ideal and the actual, reality and appearance, soul and body – the distinctions upon which western conceptual dualism, monotheism and metaphysics are generally assumed to have been founded – is the assumption that there can be an ideal knowledge of what is and is not beautiful, that the Beautiful, the Good and the Just can be ascertained through the dialectics of rational argument and enquiry.

In Plato's ideal Republic, it is the philosophers who sit at the top of the societal pyramid. Only they can be entrusted with the exalted role of discriminating between the good and the bad, the beautiful and the ugly. The prominent social role proposed by Wordsworth for the poet is a variation on this Platonic theme of the philosopher-as-arbiter-of-value. It is this figure which is reinvoked by literary intellectuals throughout the modern period in the form of Coleridge's clerisy, Matthew Arnold's priesthood, Leavis's enlightened army of critics capable of 'unprompted first-hand judgement', who are presented as the redeemers of a fallen industrialized world – as the defenders of properly authentic values.

3

European aesthetics proper – as the systematic elaboration of a rational approach to the questions posed around the term 'taste' – is a product of the Enlightenment. It is generally held to have its origins in the eighteenth century, in a text called *Aesthetica Acromantica* (1750) by Alexander Baumgarten. Immanuel Kant's *Critique of the Judgement of Taste* was in part a response and a riposte to this book and to Edmund Burke's *Philosophical Enquiry into the Origin of Our Ideas of the Sublime and the Beautiful*.[5] Kant argues against Burke's empiricism and his physiologism – his insistence on referring aesthetic experience back to bodily sensations – because such an orientation effectively invalidates the possibility of any higher ordering principle or Reason. Kant argues against both Burke's physiologism and Baumgarten's notion that aesthetic pleasure is based in a conceptually determined relationship to the work of art. If Burke is too coarse, too physical for Kant, then Baumgarten is too pedantic and mentalist.

Kant rejects Baumgarten's theory as mechanical and narrow because it proposes that the exercise of taste involves categorical judgements rather than reflective ones. Reflective judgements, Kant argues, move from the particular to the universal, from the work of art to the judgement of it, whereas categorical judgements proceed in the opposite direction, from the universal, the rule, to the particular case. Reflective judgements are to do with the contemplation of an indeterminate, relatively open and free relationship among the internal properties and overall order of a work of art or of a pleasing natural phenomenon; but that pleasure is not a 'mere' corporeal, bodily or carnal pleasure such as we derive, for instance, from eating or sex. It is of a more refined order, kindled by a free harmony or interplay between the function of images and the function of concepts; and beauty itself is a symbol of the morally good in so far as it consists in the transposition of aesthetic and moral terms which is reckoned to be immediately and intrinsically pleasing.

Kant introduced a number of influential distinctions and axioms:

1) that aesthetic judgement is predicated upon the detachment of form from any purposes. The proper object and goal of all authentic high art is 'purposiveness without purposes' – the work of art has that effect of intentionality, that compelling sense of destination, of going somewhere but it doesn't actually *do* anything; it serves no external or ulterior purpose or interest. The sense of beauty is 'without any interest whatsoever'.

2) that a work of art is like an organism – a unity surrounding a manifold of perception: a totality which is more than the sum of its parts.

3) that, following Burke, a distinction can be made between the sublime and the beautiful. Whereas the form of the beautiful is said to consist in limitation (contemplation of a framed picture, a bounded narrative, etc.), the sublime challenges the act of judgement itself by suggesting the possibility of limitlessness. The sublime mixes pleasure and pain, joy and terror, and confronts us

with the threat of the absolute Other – the limitations of our language and our capacity to think and judge, the fact of our mortality. In Burke's and Kant's category of the sublime, reason is forced to confront its incapacity to deal rationally with the infinite.

More crucial still for the present argument, Kant claimed that a judgement of aesthetic taste may either express a mere liking (or aversion) which remains an individual preference, or may in addition claim universal validity. Whereas to say a picture seems beautiful to me does not imply a general assertion of its aesthetic value, to say a picture *is* beautiful is to claim that those who disagree are wrong.

These categories and distinctions have recently received a great deal of critical attention. For example, Peter Fuller has attempted to retrieve the idea of the universal validity of 'legitimate' aesthetic judgements.[6] Confronted by what is for him the disastrous collapse of a common visual aesthetic beneath a welter of competing styles – a collapse which has been facilitated by the profane intrusion of advertising motifs and values into fine art and the manic neophilia of the art market – Fuller combines anthropological and psychoanalytic approaches to argue the aesthetic sense back to its 'natural' source and point of origin in the perception of the human body. In his fundamentalist quest for universal aesthetic values, Fuller goes even further than his Enlightenment forebears, claiming that Kant was wrong to discount the possibility that even preferences for particular foods or for 'good' wine over 'plonk' are rationally verifiable and generalizable.

Fuller claims, further, that the hegemony of a modernist design aesthetic like Bauhaus functionalism – what he calls the inhuman 'taste of the machine' – has been superseded by an even more debilitating and wrongheaded dogma, an untenable and anti-human ideology of arbitrariness and 'anything goes' (what, I think, other people call postmodernism). Fuller has also called for the restoration of reason and order through the establishment of independent institutional bodies (commissions) staffed by accredited experts equipped with the necessary refinement, taste and knowledge to legislate on what is and is not good art and design, to decide what should and should not be manufactured, exhibited, worn. In other words, Fuller proposes a return to the *Republic* with the art critic replacing the philosopher at the apex of the social hierarchy. Although Fuller's utopianism – his prophetic and denunciatory tone – has drawn fire from both left and right, the patent absurdity of some of his arguments should not be allowed to obscure the force, consistency and strategic value of his overall position at a time when the New Right is intent on giving such ideas an explicitly authoritarian inflection; at a time, too, when attacks on the arts in general and on art education in particular are being justified in terms of the narrowest and crudest kinds of market-oriented logic.

The influence of Kant's critique of aesthetic judgement, however, stretches far beyond such local controversies and debates. Kant's distinctions and axioms were fundamental in the formation both of European aesthetics as an academic discipline and of *aestheticism* – that structure of feeling that might be more accurately termed a 'feeling for structure': a sensibility which systematically privileges form over content or function, style over substance, abstraction over representation, and means of representation over thing represented. It is this sensibility, this set of preferences for form, style, abstraction, means over content, function, substance, matter, which recurs again and again from the 1840s onwards, to animate a long line of metropolitan European literary and aesthetic avant-gardes from Baudelaire and the cubists to the abstract expressionists and Jean-Luc Godard. Such a sensibility, such a set of preferences, might be said to inform much of what gets defined as today's 'post avant-garde': the collage writing of Kathy Acker, for instance; the flat post-Pop representational style and knowing parody of Biff cartoons; the found sounds and quotation aesthetics of Talking Heads, Brian Eno, Malcolm McLaren. It might also be said to animate the academic and critical equivalents of those avant-gardes – those intellectual tendencies from Russian formalism to Swiss and French structuralism, Barthesian and Kristevan poststructuralism, Derridean deconstructionism. All these tendencies focus attention on form, pattern, style, structure or on the other side of what is, after all, the same coin: polysemy and *significance* – the escape from structure, the unrestricted play of signifiers unconstrained by external referents.

While many of these terms and the tendencies they designate would seem to cut right against the grain of Kant's project (explicitly so, in the case of Derrida and the post-structuralists), they none the less share many of the features of what Althusser might have called the Kantian 'problematic'. They are all based on the assumption that aesthetic pleasure should be dispassionate, disinterested, detached ('critical') and rooted in a relationship defined by distance, by the refusal of identification or merger with the object. The favoured aesthetic response is a 'pure gaze' cleansed of any involvement with or immersion in the subject-matter, in the fictional or imaginary worlds that art makes possible. The only surrender which is permissible is the surrender to the 'text', to the radical 'undoing' of the subject in a 'pure' play of language. Such facile pleasures as identification should be blocked, refused, deconstructed. The properly aesthetic experience has to be bracketed off from those forms and practices which are merely decorative, distracting, recreational or straightforwardly enjoyable and therefore 'vulgar', in the original sense of the word: i.e. 'in common use, ordinary, popular'. This aversion to a relation of ease between the spectator and the art work may itself be rooted in a more general mistrust of the visible and of visual representations which in turn has been traced back to the Talmudic prohibition on graven images.

There is a further connection with Kant, in so far as all these critical and terroristic avant-gardes concur in the assumption that art should be addressed to the 'higher faculties', to the spirit, or its modern equivalent, the intellect. Even when the body figures prominently, as in Barthes, it is in a highly abstracted, intellectualized though eroticized (eroticized *because* intellectualized) form. Art should be serious. Art should be improving – even if the improvement now has no moral pretensions beyond the destruction of the notion of morality as such; even where the intention is to dismantle or destroy the *doxa* (Barthes) or to deconstruct the metaphysics of Presence (Derrida).

Most importantly, all these avant-gardes share with Kant a refusal of the popular, the vulgar. They share, too, his repugnance for the body and the body politic, the common herd – even when this repugnance presents itself in critical, Marxist or anarchistic guise as a critique of the 'culture industry'; a repudiation of 'mass society', a hostility towards the ideological or metaphysical residues lurking at the heart of *common* sense. In other words, all these avant-gardes could be said to share with Kant a literal *élitism*. This élitism, furthermore, is not incidental. On the contrary, it is essential.

4

In his essay of 1954, 'Building, dwelling, thinking', Martin Heidegger provides us with a critical vantage point from which to behold this (modern) phenomenon of universal placelessness. Against the Latin or, rather, the antique *abstract* concept of space as a more or less endless continuum of evenly subdivided spatial components or integers – what he terms the *spatium* and *extensio* – Heidegger opposes the German word for space (or rather, place), which is the term *Raum*. Heidegger argues that the phenomenological essence of such a space/place depends upon the *concrete*, clearly defined nature of its boundary, for as he puts it, '*A boundary is not that at which something stops, but, as the Greeks recognised, the boundary is that from which something begins its presencing*' [my emphasis]. Apart from confirming that western abstract reason has its origins in the Mediterranean, Heidegger shows that etymologically the German gerund *building* is closely linked with the archaic forms of *being, cultivating*, and hence *dwelling*, and goes on to state that the condition of dwelling and hence ultimately of being can only take place in a domain that is clearly bounded.

(Kenneth Frampton, 'Towards a critical regionalism', in Hal Foster (ed), *Postmodern Culture*)

When I moved two years ago into the house where I now live, I had to go through the usual process of acclimatization, of boundary-marking and boundary-acknowledgement. Moving house involves far more than the mere transplantation of oneself and one's possessions from one blank site to another. The move requires quite specific social and cognitive skills if it is to be accomplished successfully. In order to find out where you really *are – as opposed to where you are geographically (to use Heidegger's terms, to 'find yourself' in relation to* Raum *rather than* spatium*) – you have to develop the kind of fortitude, resourcefulness and map-reading skills needed in orienteering – that sport in which one gets dropped in an unfamiliar location with a fragment of a map and has to match the symbolic to the real in order to 'get home' to the prescribed destination. When it comes to socio-cultural orienteering, to borrow a phrase from London cab drivers' slang, you have to 'do the knowledge': learning how the place fits together as a social space through experience on the ground. You have to actively interpret and internalize significant features of the local environment through a process of osmosis, to learn how to gauge and judge the terrain, to develop a working topography, before you can act effectively within that environment and upon it. You have to become sensitive to the finely drawn boundaries and distinctions in social and physical space (and to the relations between them) before you can even attempt to establish your own boundaries: to impose your own presence, to be properly 'at home' in the neighbourhood.*

I had to compare and contrast the suitability of particular places – e.g.

shops, pubs – for my needs. The alternatives had to be weighed in the balance: this shop is cheaper than that shop, this pub is nearer than that one. As I acquired more information, it became possible to qualify these purely quantitative assessments: the cheap shop sells old vegetables; this pub is nearer but the clientele is disproportionately white given the ethnic composition of the locale (a rumour circulates that it's used as a meeting place for the racist National Front party). To 'fit in' I had to be able, in other words, to decipher the signs and memorize the relations between them, to marry forms to contents. To borrow Clifford Geertz's term, I had to internalize increasingly 'thick descriptions'[7] of the local cultural scene. Crucially, I had to try to surmise with a fair degree of accuracy the intentions – conscious or otherwise – behind the communications of my neighbours.

In some cases, form, content and intention seemed to fit together neatly: there was a perceptible 'homology' between these different communicative levels or 'moments'. I soon learned there was a homology between the form of the house two doors down – rubbish in the front garden, unwashed windows, peeling paint, an absence of (the statutory respectable working-class) net curtains, and a gaunt, forbidding stencilled face on the front door – and the occupants of the house – the group of anarcho post-punk musicians who lived there and who were given to playing loud discordant 'Dark Wave' music every night (except Fridays and Saturdays) between three and seven o'clock in the morning. In this case, there seemed to be a direct or transparent connection between the form, content and manifest intention, i.e. to destroy the 'straight world' by demoralizing what remains of the local workforce (1 in 5 local people are currently (early 1986) out of work) by keeping it awake every night of the working week. Put less facetiously, the probable intention behind this particular organization of visual and audible signals – the dishevelled façade, the deafening anti-music – is to mark out territory. The absence of curtains and the presence of noise are the recto and verso of the same sheet of paper upon which is scrawled the message: WE ARE NOT YOU. (It is an ambiguous message, i.e. 'We are not (the same) as you', or in a more aggressive inflection, one which is foregrounded whenever I've been round to complain, 'We are. (But) you aren't.') The decayed frontage of the house and the 'decadent' noise produced by its occupants function to signal the difference the post-punks perceive between their bohemian freedom and our bourgeois confinement within the norm; to signal the distance between the wilderness, the nature, the libertarian chaos of a short-life squatted tenancy and our culture, the constriction and order of the straight world of the owner-occupiers and permanent council tenants who make up the rest of the street's population. Their visual and aural 'noise' serves to mark off this household – symbolically and actually – from all the other households in the street – the more or less respectable, more or less working-class families of Asians, West Indians, Africans and Irish who dominate the street numerically. (There is a slight majority of Sikh households in our section of the street at the moment; slightly fewer households of people of West Indian descent, together with a scattering of London Irish, African and white working-class families and single people.) It is also used to mark the difference between themselves and people like myself – the upwardly mobile gentrifiers who represent one potential future for the locality in general – a future they intend to resist with all the wattage they can muster.

The public space of the street itself is perhaps the single most important focus of attention for the newcomer anxious to fit in and feel at home on the local 'manor'. I soon noticed that access to the public space of the street where I live is unevenly divided btween the Asian boys and girls. Whereas during the day the air is filled with the boys' cries and their footballs, the pavements blocked by their BMX bikes, the Asian girls are only visible to me as faces glimpsed between the curtains and the window panes staring down – one hand underneath the chin – watching their brothers staking out the domain from which they themselves have already been excluded.

But to 'thicken' the description a little: a number of factors intervene to complicate or obscure my 'readings' of the street. Whereas I felt I could assume the legibility and transparency of my interactions with my (white) post-punk neighbours and their 'obvious', 'anti-social' 'refusals' of order, the interactions which took place between the various ethnic social and familial groups on the street itself proved relatively impenetrable. The street is the stage on which regular dramas of cross-cultural contact and subcultural conflict are enacted. Within the patriarchally ordered territory of the street, cars function as the major currency and medium of these exchanges. The maintenance of cars, their finish, their make and their performance are relentlessly monitored by the males and made to signify within a more or less common but none the less unstable system of codes, values and strictly ranked preferences. There is, as is to be expected, a pecking order and a status game. Number plates are highly 'expressive' counters in this game indicating as they do the age of the vehicle and hence the likely

84

resale value. There is nothing unique in this either. Cars function universally in this way in the industrial, semi-industrial and post-industrial worlds as loaded signifiers of masculinity representing – at least in relatively 'unsophisticated' communities – a crude phallic mastery of space and time. (Amongst 'sophisticated', design- or ecology-conscious middle-class communities and those aristocratic groupings which define their superior taste against 'vulgar ostentation', it is possible for this to be inverted with the maxim 'Less is more'.) As Barthes,[8] Wolfe,[9] Packard,[10] and others have indicated, highly structured sets of rules govern the uses and meanings of cars and they function as much as means of communication as modes of transport, conveying 'messages' as well as passengers.

On the street in which I live, the rules of the car game have mutated in a particular way in response to local circumstances. The amount of time and energy expended on competitive display (car cleaning, customizing, repairing and respraying bodywork, fine-tuning, general maintenance) increases in line with the rising unemployment rate. The high proportion of unemployed or casually employed young car owners who live in the vicinity have relatively more time to spend working on the stationary object than they have money to spend on petrol to make it move.

Another factor complicating the car game in my street is the heterogeneous cultural-ethnic mix (the clash of different cultural-ethnic codes contributes to the relative instability of the system). Amongst the more affluent and street-wise West Indian and black British youths, the car tends to function as an extension of the body: as a kind of phallic carapace. Highly polished and often with the protective plastic covers still adhering to the seats, the car can be a mobile alternative to the parental home: a complete living space equipped with a hi-fi tape deck or a radio tuned to one of the local pirate radio stations and often a rack of drycleaned clothes in plastic bags on hangers in the back. The formerly popular Ford Cortina which for the last ten years or so has been associated with working-class youth culture particularly in North London,[11] is losing favour as the prime symbol of a solvent and cool bachelorhood. There are fewer signs of Cortina culture nowadays (e.g. furry lucky dice hanging over a windscreen on which the owner's nickname – MIKEY, EXTRA CLASSIC, LEE VAN CLEEF, etc. – has been stencilled in white letters). Now the more self-consciously stylish West Indian and black British young men (who tend to be the style leaders throughout North London) seem to prefer Triumphs, old

Rovers, foreign cars and Japanese 'Range Rover' replicants. (The replicants form part of an 'English County look' ensemble, other elements of which include deerstalker hats, Burberry raincoats, 'classic' tweed and expensive umbrellas. The entire ensemble has been ironically appropriated by some black British youths as a signifier of 'class' (i.e. quality) and 'traditional Englishness'.) With the windows wound down and the bodywork gleaming, the street filled with the pulsing rhythms of reggae or (more commonly these days) the stuttering beat of rap, electro funk and jazz, the car serves as an assertion of the owner's physical presence, of corporeal pleasure against the work ethic and as a provocation to the police who in my neighbourhood still insist on regarding cars driven by young black men as stolen property.[12] Here – amongst the young single men, both black and white – the car can be used to perpetuate the fantasy of the male as a self-sufficient, possibly dangerous predator, the 'Wanderer' (Dion) out to get what's his.

On the other hand, among the adult population – particularly among Muslims (Pakistanis and Turkish Cypriots, for instance) – the car tends to be seen first and foremost as a reflection of the status of the family headed by its owner. In this context, the car may signify within the Islamic code of Izzat – a term which corresponds in some ways to the Chinese concept of 'face' and which combines the ideas of masculine pride, family honour, dignity and proper bearing in public. As for myself, as a non-driver I fail to figure in either system. Instead I am perhaps consigned to a no man's land beyond or beneath gender and the order of things. As a lecturer-writer-researcher, I occupy, to use Pierre Bourdieu's terminology, a different class habitus – a different constellation of moral and aesthetic dispositions, of institutionalized pressures and 'background expectancies' which, according to Bourdieu, can determine everything from my physical posture and 'body hexis' to the way I classify the social world and am in turn classified within it.

5

Bourdieu has argued that it is only by understanding the social function of bourgeois *and* ostensibly anti-bourgeois, 'radical', avant-garde tastes what we can properly grasp the significance and the long-term effects of Kant's work on aesthetics.[13] For according to Bourdieu, the pure aesthetic taste constitutes itself precisely in the refusal of impure taste and sensation, in the refusal of the 'vulgar' 'taste of the tongue, the palate and the throat'. Bourdieu traces the origin of the pure, detached aesthetic gaze historically to the emergence of an autonomous field of artistic production in the late nineteenth century – a development which reaches its apogee in the production first by poets, then by painters, of 'open works' which are intrinsically and deliberately polysemic.

The implication of Bourdieu's argument is that there is nothing particularly novel, still less 'revolutionary', in the post-structuralist privileging of the signifier over the signified. Post-structuralism is seen merely as an especially explicit and elaborated moment in a long-term tendency to formalism which by definition characterizes all aesthetic discourse. Bourdieu suggests, then, that the trajectory from the neo-Kantian fascination with form which typifies the 'classic' Lévi-Straussian phase of structuralism to the demolition of the signified undertaken in different ways at a later moment by Derrida, Barthes and the *Tel Quel* group is not a movement 'beyond' Kant at all but rather a natural or logical progression from Kant's initial propositions and premisses.

From the point when artists in Europe deliberately set out to explore polysemy, Bourdieu argues, art no longer requires an outside (a referent or a public). It revolves increasingly around a concern with its own histories, codes and materials and it addresses an audience equipped with the philosophical, art historical, critical and/or literary competences which the viewer or reader needs to get something out of such an art work. Bourdieu suggests that this audience is as concerned in the final analysis as the artists themselves are to distance itself both from the 'vulgar' mob or mass and the 'commercial' bourgeoisie. The avant-garde and the marginals, intellectuals and dilettantes which it services are defined by Bourdieu as the 'dominated fractions of the dominant class' (i.e. the petit bourgeoisie, the déclassés, the shabby gentry, etc.) who are high on cultural capital (education, qualifications, [high] cultural expertise, 'sensibility', etc.) but low on economic capital and political power.

Through a massive empirical survey in which Parisians of all classes, occupations and ages were interviewed and tested on their cultural knowledge and taste preferences, Bourdieu sets out to provide a quasi-positivist sociological answer to and refutation of Kant's critique of the judgement of taste. He demonstrates that all cultural pursuits are conditioned by, first, the level, duration and quality of the education of those engaging in such pursuits and second, by their social origin and class *habitus*. Bourdieu distinguishes four basic taste formations:

legitimate, middlebrow, popular, pure. Legitimate taste – the preference for and knowledge of the accredited 'classics' and the 'most legitimate of those arts that are still in the process of legitimation (e.g. cinema, jazz)' increases 'with educational level and is highest in those fractions of the dominant class that are richest in educational capital'. Middlebrow taste which brings together 'the minor works of the major arts' and the 'major works of the minor arts ... is more common in the middle classes than in the working classes or in the "intellectual" fractions of the dominant class'. Popular taste, signalled by the choice, for instance, 'of so-called "light" music or classical music devalued by popularization ... and especially songs totally devoid of artistic ambition or pretension ... is most frequent among the working classes and varies in inverse ratio to educational capital (which explains why it is slightly more common among industrial and commercial employers or even senior executives than among primary school teachers and cultural intermediaries)'. Finally the 'pure' aesthetic disposition which is most clearly dependent on the acquisition of a specific 'aesthetic' competence is capable 'of applying to *any* object the pure intention of an artistic effort which is an end in itself'. The pure gaze perceives as art that which it nominates as art and involves the categorical assertion of the primacy of form over function.

Using these categories as broad guidelines in his interpretation of the empirical data, Bourdieu sets out to demonstrate how taste 'classifies the classifier' and he finds systematic correlations between social class, occupation, education and cultural and aesthetic preferences in food, music, photography, fiction, etc. When confronted with an unidentified photograph of the Lacq gas refinery taken at night, manual workers indicated bewilderment ('I can't make head or tail of it'); small employers were hostile because they saw it as 'experimental' ('That stuff leaves me cold'); junior executives were disconcerted but sought to disguise their discomfort by being non-committal and confined their remarks to technical rather than aesthetic matters ('It's just light captured by the camera'). Only members of the highly educated dominant class (professors, senior civil servants, etc.), often recognizing the object represented, accepted such photographs as 'art' ('It's aesthetically pleasing'). In the same way, a photograph of an old peasant woman's hands elicited an empathetic and/or ethical response from manual workers ('The poor old girl') but never an aesthetic judgement. Lower middle-class clerical and technical workers oscillated between sympathy, populist sentimentality and a concern for aesthetic properties ('The sort of hands you see in early Van Goghs'). At higher levels in the social hierarchy the remarks became more abstract 'with [other people's] hands, labour and old age functioning as allegories or symbols which serve as pretexts for general reflections on general problems ("It's the very symbol of toil")'. Thus Bourdieu claims that taste, far from being purely personal – a mysterious unclassifiable faculty exercised by freely choosing sovereign subjects – is a quintessentially social phenomenon, that social differences are reinforced, perpetuated, reproduced by antagonistic judgements of taste – that taste always operates as a differentiating agent in the social field.

While the contents of the categories – legitimate, middlebrow, popular, pure – may change over time (Bourdieu cites jazz, 1940s' *film noir*, American pop kitsch and science fiction passing up from the popular via the pure to the legitimate, while certain styles of painting, etc., drop down in the same period from the legitimate via the middlebrow to the popular), none the less the relations between these taste formations remain constant. Invariably those relations are antagonistic and antithetical. Taste is a purely negative category in Bourdieu. Each taste formation is constituted in the refusal of other tastes, particularly in the refusal of adjacent formations. Popular taste, for instance, is defined as 'the refusal of the refusal of pure taste'.

Against the rigours and austerity of the avant-garde, popular taste is marked by a Rabelaisian mood of insolence, carnival and category inversion. It celebrates the body, the emotional and sentimental properties of life and art, seeking out the moment not of distanced contemplation but of the loss of individuality in the collective, the suspension of disbelief as the self is dissolved not in the 'play of signifiers' – far from it – but rather in the remorseless narrativity that characterizes much popular art. Furthermore, Bourdieu suggests that these differences and antagonisms are far from innocent. Popular taste is predicated on a knowledge that it is both plundered and despised by its 'betters' and that the difficulty of avant-garde art and legitimate taste (despite the protestations of their adherents that they long to 'educate' and 'elevate' the public and to 'popularize' the classics) derives, on the contrary, *precisely from the will to keep the masses out*.

The distinctions and antagonisms penetrate as far as the dining table and the kitchen. The working-class man as represented in Bourdieu's survey favours substance over style of presentation, is encouraged by the female (mother/wife), who prepares his food, to eat with gusto, to get silently lost in his plate, is often licensed to make appreciative smacking sounds with his lips, is inclined to relish good, simple French food taken in the prescribed Gallic sequence – hors-d'oeuvre (charcuterie for the men, crudités for the women and children!), main dish and dessert – and rejects fish as too delicate and insubstantial. (One is reminded of Richard Hoggart's description of the 'traditional' working-class dietary emphasis on strong tastes, bulk and meat whenever possible.[14]) The bourgeois French person, on the other hand, focuses attention on the style of presentation, on the cutlery, the table-cloth, the glasses, flowers, etc., on the look of the food not its quantity (think of *nouvelle cuisine*), will often skip a course electing to 'taste' (but not consume) one or two 'specialities' – refined, rare or exotic (even foreign!) dishes – and claims to relish the conversation as much as if not more than the food. The differences – presented in this way – are virtually symmetrical: they are 'structured in dominance' around those social class distinctions which they serve to duplicate and dramatize. The oppositions are right underneath our noses. In fact they even extend to the way in which we clear that organ:

> It would be easy to show ... that Kleenex tissues, which have to be used delicately, with a little sniff from the tip of the nose, are to the big cotton handkerchief, which is blown into sharply and loudly, with the eyes closed and the nose held tightly, as repressed laughter is to a belly laugh, with wrinkled nose, wide-open mouth and deep breathing ('doubled up with laughter') as if to amplify to the utmost an experience which will not suffer containment, not least because it has to be shared, and therefore clearly manifested for the benefit of others.[15]

Bourdieu sums up the system of distinctions by resorting to a paradox – suggesting that those at the lower end of the social ladder are compelled to 'choose the necessary' in the form of 'simple pleasures' – the straightforward satisfaction of primary needs – whereas those who lay claim to the 'aesthetic disposition' can literally *afford* to sublimate primary needs in such a way that the detachment of the pure gaze could be said to be conditioned by negative economic necessities – a life of ease – that tends to induce an active distance from the principle of necessity itself. He concludes that the classificatory boundaries between culture and nature, higher and lower, body and soul serve to reproduce and legitimate social inequalities, to naturalize the idea that hierarchically ranked social distinctions are simply *there* – are not subject to modification – and that systems of social stratification are in themselves nothing more than the natural order of things transposed to the social domain. He concludes:

> The opposition between the tastes of nature and the tastes of freedom introduces a relationship which is that of the body and the soul, between those who are 'only natural' and those whose capacity to dominate their own biological nature (through sublimation, the search for 'higher truths') affirms their legitimate claim to dominate social nature ... the theory of pure taste (then) has its basis in a social relation: the antithesis between culture and corporeal pleasure (or nature if you will) and is rooted in the opposition between a cultivated bourgeoisie and the people.[16]

Or put another way, the 'pure aesthetic' – the apparently disinterested contemplation and appreciation of 'purposiveness without purposes' – itself serves a 'higher' (baser) purpose: the perpetuation of social distinctions, the justification of the very principle of inequality.

Although his work on taste has had a very uneven impact in Britain and has generally, perhaps predictably, been less enthusiastically received by those professionally engaged in textual criticism (literature, art, film studies) than the work produced by other more Kantian and text-fixated French intellectuals, none the less Bourdieu's scepticism concerning the adequacy of non-reflexive, non-sociological accounts and critiques of the aesethetic field has been welcomed by those working within cultural studies who seek to move beyond the formal and philosophical preoccupations of post-structuralism and deconstructionism and to rethink popular culture in more positive, less proscriptive ways. Like Bakhtin,[17] Bourdieu is often invoked to puncture the pretensions of more ascetic or solipsistic Parisian *philosophes*, and both writers have often been recruited by those (myself included) who have set out to question the dominant paradigms of what taste is and how it functions, and to describe instead a more dynamic, heterogeneous and socially variegated cultural field – one in which, for instance, social groups are seen to establish public identities through shared commodity and 'lifestyle' preferences.[18]

Perhaps the myth of the inert masses is in danger of being replaced by a counter-myth of the robustly iconoclastic, healthily corporeal and debunking culture of the popular classes. A kind of inverted snobbery is sometimes operative here. Just how applicable Bourdieu's analysis is to the very different field of British culture is in any case hard to establish in the absence of an equivalent empirical survey of indigenous tastes. The generalizability of his thesis is further thrown into question by the time-lag. Although appearing in translation for the first time in 1984, Bourdieu's *Distinction* is based on research conducted in Paris in the early 1970s. The confidence with which he links class, culture and occupation would perhaps be misplaced in the 1980s with the recomposition of social classes, the restructuring of work, the decline of the manual sector and the growth of the service industries. It would be less easy now than it was even ten years ago to give centre stage to the manual worker in any definition of either popular culture or the popular classes. Still less would it seem appropriate to present the working class as essentially male, as Bourdieu tends to do, or to proffer the working-class male as the wholesome touchstone of immutable good sense, as a kind of bucolic embodiment of tough unsentimental folk wisdom.

None the less, Bourdieu's project provides a healthy counter to the more formalist and text-centred approaches which till now have tended to dominate discussions of the aesthetic response. However, if Bourdieu's work is easily distinguishable in its tone, intentions and objectives from the positions of other prominent French intellectuals, it inevitably shares a certain amount of common ground with them. Despite the hostility to structuralism which, here as elsewhere,[19] forms one persistent strand of Bourdieu's polemic, the stress in *Distinction* on system, pattern, symmetry and difference is likely to strike the English reader as being pre-eminently structuralist. In the same way, while the concept of class *habitus* opens up a limited space for social subjects as reflexive agents capable of formulating strategies of self-enhancement, calculating the probable outcomes of specific lines of action and shaping their own lives accordingly, it still places a great deal of emphasis – for those trained in more strictly Anglo-American traditions of enquiry, perhaps an inordinate degree of emphasis – on the *systematic* overdetermination of people's life options by institutional factors.

However, it is the way in which Bourdieu places himself in relation to the great continental traditions of social theory and philosophy which distinguishes him most clearly from British sociologists with more positivist, straightforwardly empiricist or culturalist leanings and which draws him closer to those intellectual figures whose positions his book sets out expressly to critique.

6

When I first moved into my present home, I was intrigued by one car in the street – a great spotless Thunderbird, its maroon bodywork and sculptured chromium accessories glistening all the year round, irrespective of the weather. This Thunderbird is the single most conspicuous anomaly in the Victorian terraced street in which I live. It is a cathedral among hovels. It is out of scale, out of place (its real home is Detroit or Dallas), out of time (its real time is pre-1974, pre the Oil Crisis). I immediately assumed – drawing on my stock of Hollywood-derived cultural stereotypes – that the car belonged to a pimp, a gangster or a 'big shot' of some kind, that it should be referred to the young man's code of phallic braggadocio, *that it was a boast in three dimensions. These assumptions turned out to be unfounded. The car is owned by one of the gentlest, most gracious and modest men I know. Mr H. is a slight, mild-mannered Turkish Cypriot who lives with his wife in a run-down, sparsely furnished ground-floor flat in the house opposite. He rents the apartment from the Hindu family who own it and who occupy the rest of the house. Mr H. is in his 50s, short and thin, speaks broken English very softly and is usually dressed in (unfashionable) flares and a pullover. There is nothing remotely 'flash' or ostentatious about his appearance and demeanour. His car is his only conspicuous luxury. He is a believer in Allah but is not dogmatic and smoked Bensons all the way through Ramadan explaining: 'Some pretend not eat, not smoke, not drink – just for show. It's what is in the heart that matters.' He has given us a vine and a jasmine plant as a gift from his garden to ours, has sent us a card and a plateful of honey-drenched, almond-speckled cakes baked by his wife at Christmas.*

Mr H. is the local car doctor. A semi-pro mechanic, he sits by the window behind the net curtains in his front room and in his own words he 'listens to the street' – to the rush and whirr of cars as they sweep past, to the cough of ignition keys being turned and engines being revved. He can diagnose a sick motor just by the sound. In reasonable weather he spends as much time on his car (though not in it) as he does inside his flat. At least three times a day – more if there are showers – he washes and polishes his beloved Thunderbird, tunes and tunes and retunes the engine.

From his vantage point beside or underneath the car, Mr H. can socialize with neighbours as they pass by on their way to the shops or to work and he can keep an eye on neighbours' houses to make sure that there are no break-ins. Once a week or so – usually on a Sunday – he emerges from the house followed by his wife who as a conventional Muslim keeps a few paces behind him. They get into his car and Mr H. sinks into the white leather upholstery of the driver's seat, grasps the enormous wheel and takes her (the car/his wife) for a short and what I suspect is a quite nerve-wracking drive – nerve-wracking because of the Thunderbird's loose, wide-open steering and its size in relation to the narrow London streets.

7

There is something curiously Derridean in Bourdieu's 'sociological' deconstruction of Kant. Bourdieu's work is clearly linked to the projects of Marx, Durkheim and Weber; but it can also be seen – though this is not explicitly acknowledged by Bourdieu himself – as an extension of Nietzsche's corrosive anti-metaphysical attack on the fundamental premisses of post-Socratic philosophy. His insistence on the health and vitality of popular culture may not be very Nietzschian, but his physiologism certainly is. For Nietzsche, the difference between the beautiful and the ugly is entirely dependent on and derivative from primary phylogenetic drives. It is determined by the imperative of species preservation. The sense of the beautiful, the intuition of the good in Nietzsche's account have nothing whatsoever to do with other-worldly forces or values, with a transcendental 'above' or 'beyond', with imperfect, ghostly memories of the Ideal or the Divine. They simply serve to valorize all that is life-enhancing, beneficial, species-preserving. Ugliness for Nietzsche is merely all that which is harmful, dangerous, worthy of suspicion: the decadent, the demeaning, the rotten. Aesthetics is, to use his own words, 'nothing but applied physiology' and his objections to Wagner after he turned against his former friend and mentor in 1876 were, he claimed, not ideological or aesthetic, political or ethical, but simply physiological:

> My objections to Wagner's music are physiological objections: why conceal them under aesthetic formulas? My 'fact' is that I no longer breathe easily as soon as this music begins to affect me.[20]

Nietzsche's physiologism, his contempt for euphemism, pretension and cant, his refusal of the transcendental and utopian claims of art, his insistence on the ineluctable pressures of necessity and the power of sublimation – all these are strongly recalled in Bourdieu's tone and thesis (though Bourdieu declines, unlike many French literary intellectuals, to adopt Nietzsche's enigmatic, aphoristic style, arguing instead that glib 'smart' literary effects would actively subvert the scientific, anti-aesthetic ambition which motivates his project).[21]

The Nietzschian legacy is felt not only here. The debt to Nietzsche has been acknowledged by those writers from Foucault to Derrida, from Deleuze to Baudrillard, who together – thought not in unison and from quite different directions – have opened up and occupied the discursive spaces of the Post (post-structuralism, postmodernism). To take just one example – an untypically demonstrative moment in that trajectory from Marx to Nietzsche – Barthes writing in 1969 recommended a move from 'mythoclasm' (ideology of revelation) to 'semioclasm' (destruction of the sign, the symbolic order and the subjectivities it allegedly supports and 'positions'), thereby sketching out a kind of abbreviated manifesto for the Post (at least for its reformed (i.e. 'post-Marxist') libertarian wing):

> In an initial moment, the aim was the destruction of the (ideological) signified; in a second, it is that of the destruction of the sign: 'mythoclasm' is succeeded by 'semioclasm' which is much more far-reaching and pitched at a different level. The historical field of action is thus widened: no longer the (narrow) sphere of French society but far beyond that, historically and geographically, the whole of Western civilisation (Graeco-Judaeo-Islamic-Christian), unified under the one theology (Essence, monotheism) and identified by the regime of meaning it practises – from Plato to *France-Dimanche*.[22]

Widened indeed ... The Nietzschian disposition, so clearly in evidence here, is central to the cultural, political and existential 'decentring' which constitutes – as ideal goal – the project of the Post and which in the years after 1968 forms – as socio-political 'fact' – the object of its multiple enquiries and de-scriptions. The Nietzschian problematic is inscribed in the very prefix 'post' and the elements of that problematic shape the characteristic concerns of Post discourse: the preference for questions of genealogy and origin over those of prediction and agency; the emphasis on *agon* and process; the suspicion of all models of historical causality and progress. Some have argued that the distinction between post-structuralism and postmodernism is crucial[23] and definitive, and it is clear that not all the strands that are woven round the Post are made of the same thread. Similarly, the moment of supersession (of structuralism, of modernism) can be differently periodized depending on which particular history, movement or historic aspiration is being defined as finished or on the point of exhaustion. However, the apocalyptic tone is unmistakable throughout the literature. The founding proposition of the Post – shouted Zarathustra-style from the various disciplinary peaks from which Post intellectuals gain access to their exalted 'overviews' – is that God is dead, though different gods are decreed dead from different mountain-tops. God can be (i.e. 'has been') Marx, the Logos, Hegel's World spirit, Brecht, Breton, Freud, the Enlightenment project, European rationalism, the Party, the Law of the Father, the Transcendental Signified. But whoever or whatever He or It was, the fact of His/Its passing – the proclaimed sense of an ending – and the programmatic tone in which the announcement is made tend to be quite similar.

It is around the term 'postmodernism' that debates about the visual arts, about the general theory of aesthetics and the broader issues raised in the deployment and critique of culture as an anthropological and analytic category, have most clearly and consistently revolved. Most notably Jean-François Lyotard has been engaged in a lengthy meditation on these issues within the domain of art theory and philosophy, and it is he who has been most influential in focusing critical attention in recent years on the question of the sublime. As part of his critique of the utopian impetus within the Enlightenment project – a project defined here as a twofold aspiration towards universalization (Reason) and social engineering (Revolution) – Lyotard defines the European modernist achievement as a series of gestures motivated by the intention to 'present the unpresentable'.[24] This elevation of the sublime as the originary impulse within modernism involves an explicit rejection of the relatively facile pleasures of the beautiful – that which can be represented, framed, assimilated. More importantly, Lyotard also uses it to question the viability of the project of modernity and the accompanying ideologies of 'historical necessity' and 'guaranteed progress'. For Lyotard uses the notion of the sublime as a kind of metaphor for the *absolute* nature of those limitations placed on what can be said, seen, shown, presented, demonstrated, put into play, put into practice and he implies that each encounter with the sublime in art provides us with the single salutary lesson that complexity, difficulty, opacity are always there in the same place: *beyond our grasp*. The inference here in the insistence on the palpability of human limitation is politically nuanced at those points when Lyotard talks about the disastrous consequences which have flowed from all attempts to implement the 'perfect (rational) system' or to create the 'perfect society' during what he calls the 'last two sanguinary centuries'.[25]

These arguments have been developed in the context of the French philosopher's protracted debate with Jürgen Habermas who whilst distinguishing his own position from Marcuse's has none the less stressed the emancipatory dimensions of art favouring an aesthetics of the beautiful. From this latter position, the fact that the harmonious integration of formal elements in an art work gives us pleasure indicates that we are all drawn ineluctably by some internal *logos* (reason reflexively unfolding/folding back upon itself through the dispassionate contemplation of form), that we are, in other words, drawn towards the ideal resolution of conflict in the perfection of good form. Here our capacity both to produce and to appreciate the beautiful stands as a kind of 'promissory note' for the eventual emancipation of humanity. Lyotard, on the other hand, in a move which is reminiscent of the deconstructive strategies exemplified by Derrida, takes the relatively subordinate, residual term, the 'sublime' in the binary coupling upon which Enlightenment aesthetics is based – the beautiful: the sublime, where the sublime functions as that-which-is-aesthetic-but-not-beautiful – and privileges it to such an extent that the whole edifice of Enlightenment thought and achievement is (supposedly) threatened. For whereas the idea of the beautiful contains within it the promise of an ideal, as yet unrealized, community (to say 'This is beautiful' is to assert the generalizability of aesthetic judgements and hence the possibility/ideal of consensus), the sublime in contrast atomizes the community by confronting each individual with the prospect of his or her imminent and solitary demise. In Lyotard's words, with the sublime 'everyone is alone when it comes to judging'.[26]

The sublime functions in Lyotard's work as a means of corroding the two 'materialist' faiths (positivism and Marxism) which characterize the superseded modern epoch.[27] Embracing paradox, computational logics and simulations, he identifies himself (and the 'postmodern condition') with the production of *les immatériaux*,[28] and speculates upon those abstract structures and invisible forces which shape and constitute human experience whilst remaining inaccessible to that experience. Lyotard associates the revolutionary animus of the modern period with that litany of abominations which Adorno called simply 'Auschwitz' and argues that, from the time of Robespierre on, disaster has followed in the wake of the succession of revolutionary vanguards and tribunals which have set themselves up as the subjects and agents of historical destiny. In that sublime presumption to 'speak for' (i.e. 'make') history, these vanguards and 'people's courts' have sought to place themselves outside the normative framework provided by the web of 'first order narratives' in which popular thought, morality and social life are properly grounded.[29] Those moments when men and women believed themselves to *be* Benjamin's Angel of History who 'would like to stay, awaken the dead, and make whole what has been smashed',[30] moments of illusory omnipotence and certainty, are, for Lyotard, the dangerous moments of supposedly full knowledge, when people feel fully present to themselves and to their 'destiny' (the moment, say, when the class in itself becomes a class for itself). The sublime remains the prerogative of art alone: the *socio-political aspiration* to 'present the unpresentable', to embody in the here and now the that-which-is-to-be, is deemed untenable: 'paranoid'.[31] The sublime by definition is *das Unform*[32] – that which is without form, hence that which is monstrous and unthinkable – and rather than seeking to embody universal values of truth, justice and right, finding the licence for such pretensions in the great metanarratives ('the pursuit of freedom or happiness'[33]), Lyotard recommends that we should instead think of the human project in terms of the 'infinite task of complexification ... complexifying the complexity we are in charge of'.[34]

8

Lying in bed at 4 a.m. on one occasion unable to sleep because of the racket emanating from the squatters' house I decided to 'have it out' with them 'once and for all'. I got dressed and walked into the night air which was filled with the whine and screech of feedback and guitar. Having failed to rouse them by knocking on the door and shouting through the letter-box, I picked up an empty beer can and threw it at the first-floor window. The noise died off suddenly as the window was thrown open and a line of faces appeared. In the course of the ensuing argument I yelled (and I could hear the old man in my voice): 'Can't you turn the amplifiers down?' This seemed to strike a note of discord. There was a brief hiatus (was 'amplifier' an obsolete term? didn't musicians use amplifiers any more?) and then the response came loud and clear: 'You don't understand.' Opting like an irate father for a well-worn strategy – one that had been used on myself by older 'authority figures' many times in the past – I shouted back: 'I don't care whether I understand or not! Just keep the —— noise down! There are families with young babies in this street.' The absurdity (and the irony) of this exchange between the members of 'an anarchic youth subculture' and a 'former expert on subcultural resistance' was lost on me at the time but walking back towards my house five minutes later, I felt strangely elated, lighter on my feet: I was turning my back not only on a quieter scene, but also on an earlier incarnation. Released from the obligation to 'understand', I was free to sleep – at last! – the dreamless sleep of the senex or the fool.

9

Lyotard ends by dissolving dialectics into paralogy and language games but there are within the debates in France on post-structuralism, postmodernism and postmodernity other variations on the Nietzschian theme of the end of the western philosophical tradition. In some ways, those discourses from Foucault to Derrida, from the Barthes of the *Tel Quel* phase to the Jacques Lacan of *Ecrits* might be said to be posited following Nietzsche on the no man's land (the gender here *is* marked!) staked out between the two meanings of the word 'subject': first, 'I' the self-present subject of the sentence; secondly, the subjected subject of the symbolic order: the subject of ideology. This no man's land is just that – a land owned by nobody in the space between the *énoncé* and the *énonciation* where questions of agency, cause, intention, authorship, history become irrelevant. All those questions dissolve into a sublime, asocial Now which is differently dimensionalized in different accounts. For Derrida in grammatology, that space is called *aporia* – the unpassable path – the moment when the self-contradictory nature of human discourse stands exposed. For Foucault, it is the endless recursive spirals of power and knowledge: the total, timeless space he creates around the hellish figure of the Panopticon: the viewing tower at the centre of the prison yard –

the *voir* in *savoir/pouvoir*, the looking in knowing. For *Tel Quel* it is the moment of what Julia Kristeva calls *significance*: the unravelling of the subject in the pleasure of the text, the point where the subject disintegrates, moved beyond words by the materiality, productivity and slippage of the signifier over the signified. And for Lacan, it is the Real – that which remains unsayable and hence unbearable – the boundless, inconceivable space outside language and the Law beyond the binaries of the Imaginary register: the Real being the promise/threat of our eventual (unthinkable) disintegration, our absorption into flux. The sublime is here installed in each case as the place of epiphany and terror, the place of the ineffable which stands over and against all human endeavour, including the project of intellectual totalization itself. Lacan's Real, Foucault's power-knowledge spirals, Kristeva's *significance*, Derrida's *aporia*, Barthes's text of bliss: all are equivalent, in some senses reducible to Lyotard's category of the sublime.

The elevation of the sublime (which has its more literal, or crass, quasi-empirical corollary in the cult of schizophrenia – the cult, that is, of dread, of the sublime mode of being in the world) could be interpreted as an extension of the aspiration towards the ineffable which has impelled the European avant-gardes at least since the symbolists and the decadents and probably since the inception in the 1840s of metropolitan literary and artistic modernism with the 'anti-bourgeois' refusals of Baudelaire. It implies a withdrawal from the immediately given ground of sociality by problematizing language as tool and language as communicative medium, by substituting models of signification, discourse and decentred subjectivity for these older humanist paradigms and by emphasizing the *im*possibility of 'communication', transcendence, dialectic, the final determination of origins and outcomes, the fixing or stabilization of values and meanings. The moment which is privileged is the solitary confrontation with the irreducible fact of limitation, Otherness, 'differance' (Derrida), with the question variously of the loss of mastery, 'death in life' (Lyotard), of the 'frequent little deaths' or 'picknoleptic interruptions' of consciousness by the unconscious (Virilio).

The conversion of asociality into an absolute value can accommodate a variety of more or less resigned postures: scepticism (Derrida), stoicism (Lyotard, Lacan, Foucault), libertarian anarchism/mysticism (Kristeva), hedonism (Barthes), cynicism/nihilism (Baudrillard). However, such a privileging of the sublime tends to militate against the identification of larger (collective) interests (the isms of the modern epoch e.g. Marxism, liberalism, etc.). It does this by undermining or dismissing as simplistic or 'barbaric'[35] what Richard Rorty has recently called 'our untheoretical sense of social solidarity[36] and by bankrupting the liberal investment in the belief in the capacity of human beings to emphathize with each other, to reconcile opposing 'viewpoints', to seek the fight-free integration of conflicting interests. There is no room in the split opened up in the subject by the Post for the cultivating of 'consensus' or for the development of a 'communicative community', no feasible invocation of a possible progress towards an 'ideal speech situation' (Habermas). The stress on the asocial sublime further erodes the sense of destination and purposive struggle supplied by the 'optimistic will' (Gramsci) and the theoretical means to recover (that is, to emancipate) a 'reality' outside discourse obscured by 'something called "ideology" (created by power) in the name of something called "validity" (not created by power)'[37] (Habermas again). The stress on the impossible tends, in other words, to seriously limit the scope and definition of the political (where politics is defined as the 'art of the possible'). A series of elisions tends to prescribe a definite route here (though it is a route taken by more disciples than master-mistresses). First there is the absolute conflation of a number of relatively distinct structures, paradigms, tendencies: the emergence of industrial-military complexes, the Enlightenment aspiration to liberate humanity, the rise of the bourgeoisie and the modern 'scientific' episteme, the bureaucratic nation-state, and 'Auschwitz'. Next these discrete and non-synchronous historical developments are traced back to the model of the subject secreted at the origin of western thought and culture in transcendental philosophy. Finally an ending is declared to the 'tradition' thus established and the equation is made between this ending (the end of philosophy) and the ending of history itself.

10

One day someone ran a key along one side of the Thunderbird, scratching a line across the paintwork of one of the panels. Mr H. sent off to Detroit and had a replacement for the damaged section crated up and sent over at a cost somewhere in excess of £600. Another time the mentally retarded son of Mr H.'s landlord accidentally threw a stone which made a minute hole in the centre of the windscreen. Mr H. sent off to the States for another replacement, though he claimed the next day that the windscreen had miraculously healed itself – he surmised that it contained a special fluid which had set overnight across the tiny aperture.

Mr H. demanded satisfaction: a confession from the boy, an apology from the father. There were threats of court action. (Honour was at stake here, Mr H. explained, not just property. He didn't want the boy to be punished. He knew he wasn't really responsible for what he'd done. But he couldn't bear to hear the father denying what had really happened). One day the boy appeared at our door. He seemed distraught. He looked across the street towards his father's house. (Was someone watching from the window? Had he been sent by his family to enlist our support in the battle with Mr H.?) The boy seemed confused, close to tears (under normal circumstances he's more prone to song and to sudden gusts of laughter). Now his shoulders were stooped. His long thin arms hung listlessly at his sides. He stood on the doorstep glancing back from time to time towards the net curtains in the windows of the house opposite. Could he come here? he asked. Could he go up there? He pointed up the stairs behind me. He said he wanted to go home. 'You know where you live, J.,' I said, pointing to his house. 'You live over there.' The boy refused to turn around. He said he could get home by going through our house and climbing over the garden wall at the back. The garden wall borders a railway line (did he know this?). It faces in a direction which is diametrically opposed to his parents' house.

11

Schizophrenia is often identified as the psychic state which most clearly embodies the subjective response to the 'postmodern condition'. The word 'subjective' is problematic in this context: schizophrenia is the ghost that rises from the corpse of 'authentic' subjectivity. It is the only (valid?) 'life' that's left after the 'death of the subject' (see Deleuze and Guattari, Baudrillard, Jameson). The binary structures on which post-Socratic thought, and hence western civilization and culture, are reckoned to be based – reality v. appearance, real relations v. phenomenal forms, science v. object, etc. – are systematically dismantled as the 'depth model' disappears along with the exalted vantage point and the 'penetrating insights' of the totalizing intellectual-as-seer. The implication is that we are left stranded in a world of meaningless surfaces: 'lured' this way and that by the 'fatal' fascination exercised upon us by mirrors, icons, images.

As the production economy of an earlier epoch with its 'technocratic' or 'instrumental' rationality, its purposive strategies, its regulated sexuality folds into the consumption economy of the Post, we move into an unbounded space of unconstrained imaginaries, licensed promiscuity, drift and dreamwork where subjects and objects, mainstreams and margins are inextricably merged. In an economy geared towards the spinning of endlessly accelerating spirals of desire, consumption allegedly imposes its own 'ecstatic' or pluralist (dis)order (Jameson's 'heterogeneity without norms'[38]). Baudrillard's 'obscene' 'ecstasy of communication' involves an 'implosion of meaning' such that all distinctions are flattened out in the 'hyperreal' where the precession of image-bloated simulacra work to substitute the model for the real.[39] For Jameson, there is the schizophrenic consumer disintegrating into a succession of unassimilable instants, condemned through the ubiquity and instantaneousness of commodified images and instants to live forever in *chronos* (this then this then this) without having access to the (centring) sanctuary of *kairos* (cyclical, mythical, meaningful time). And for Deleuze and Guattari there is the homeless wandering 'nomad' drawn 'like a schizophrenic taking a walk' across *milles plateaux* from one arbitrary point of intensity to the next.[40]

Postmodernity is presented in each case as positively schizogenic: a grotesque attenuation – possibly monstrous, occasionally joyous – of our capacity to feel and to respond. Within this grim scenario, as psychosis replaces neurosis as the emergent psychic norm, the dominant subjective modality of our current 'condition', postmodernity becomes nothing more than modernity without the hopes and dreams which made modernity bearable.

The tendency within such accounts to flatten the temporal-sequential dimension beneath spatial metaphors, to outlaw progressive models of history, to engage in general arguments, to adopt postures of cultural and political pessimism can all be read back to the Nietzschian problematic in which the discourse(s) of the Post remain embedded. From such a perspective it is impossible to countenance the prospect of any historically constituted collective (any putative 'We') changing anything for the better. A 'constant (postmodern) condition'[41] has to be confronted, negotiated, come to terms with. By definition, it will not be modified, changed, still less 'transcended' or 'resolved'. Alternatively, within the diagnosis of postmodernism as a condition peculiar to 'late capitalism', in the absence of any identifiable sources of renewal or resistance there can be no 'elsewhere' – no 'better place' –

to move towards. The word 'post' suggests that the clock has stopped and without a clock it is difficult to estimate just how 'late' it is in 'late capitalism'.

And yet, however dramatic the changes in the deployment and accumulation of capital in the post-war period; however dramatic the changes in the production and the uses of new technologies, in the organization of the work process or in the level of investment in communications, data banks, information, image; however prevalent pastiche and parody in the arts, in critique, in film, TV and advertising it is surely palpably misguided to expect to find these shifts automatically re-enacted in (the dissolution of) the individual human psyche, or in the total transformation of the cultural sphere. We might look to a less general crisis afflicting particular academic institutions to understand the broader historical significance of such a 'sense of an ending'. For the varieties of postmodernist critique which abjure all hope might be said to presage the historic decline not of politics, or meaning in general, but rather of a specific professional intellectual formation. What is perhaps most clearly intimated in such accounts is the impotence of negative critique. Rather than surrender mastery of the field, the critics who promulgate the line that we are living at the end of everything (and are *all* these critics men?) make one last leap and resolve to take it all – judgement, history, politics, aesthetics, value – out of the window with them. In a gesture redolent of Nietzsche's own decline into insanity and silence, they propose that we live the penultimate negation.[42] The implication seems to be that if they cannot sit at the top of Plato's pyramid, then there shall be no pyramid at all. And in the final analysis, in our appraisal of the claims made on behalf of the 'anti-aesthetic', do we honestly believe in the schizophrenic as the contemporary answer to the Cartesian monad? Is the widespread 'waning of affect'[43] an historical reality?

None of this is to deny the pertinence of postmodernism *per se*. These post-modernist accounts offer in an extraordinarily compact and vivid way a description of what it *feels* like to be alive in western Europe in the late 1980s. The issues raised within the discourse(s) of the Post – about the collapse of Marxism as a total explanatory system, about representation and sexual identity, about who has the right to speak for whom – are crucial ones. They have to be addressed, confronted, lived through. It is vital, for instance, that we – all of us, but most especially us men – strive to open ourselves up to that which is just beginning, that we become more flexible, more sensitive to difference, that we become alert to the dangers of speaking from a position of unacknowledged mastery, or 'speaking for' a universal subject, for history and unchallengeable truth, that we become in other words, and most especially, alert to the possibilities inscribed on the other, hidden side of crisis and decay.

12

Mr H. is not a rich man, he owns very little. His one indulgence is the Thunderbird. It is an indulgence he can ill afford in material terms. The car is the object of a devotion which whilst not being in the least idolatrous (Mr H. is no worshipper of Baal) none the less does have a religious, transcendental component. The car is a love object: the literal embodiment of an ideal. The attention he lavishes upon it is a public declaration of his commitment to the quality of life and to the ideal of quality as something that is not given, that cannot just be bought with money but that has to be striven for, worked for, achieved through dint of effort, saving, self-denial.

How would Baudrillard or Bourdieu deal with such an excessive relation to such an ostentatious object? In an essay which predates his immersion in the Post, Baudrillard set out to investigate how objects function to externalize social values, to objectify social distinctions and to embody aspirations and fantasies, how they act, to use his own words, as 'carriers of indexed social significations of a social and cultural hierarchy'.⁴⁴ He looks at the contents of a room or a house and notes that all the objects do not share the same symbolic space, that there are different degrees of intensity – of emotional and aspirational investment – surrounding different objects. (Possessions, in other words, are not arranged within an abstract spatium.*) He remarks that all objects of one class (e.g. chairs) do not necessarily fulfil the same purposes (e.g. if a chair is an heirloom it is not just for sitting on but also serves to guarantee the continuity of family traditions, to conserve a living* sense *of family across the generations). He suggests that:*

> *In apartments one often notices that from the point of view of status, the configuration of the ensemble is not homogeneous – rarely are all objects of a single interior on the same wavelength. Do not certain objects connote a social membership, a factual status, while others a presumed status, a level of aspirations? Are there 'unrealistic objects', that is to say those which falsely register a contradiction of the real status, desperately*

testifying to an inaccessible standing (all else remaining equal, they are analogous to 'escapist' behaviour or to the utopian behaviours characteristic of critical phases of acculturation)? Conversely, are there 'witness objects' that, despite a socially mobile status, attest a fidelity to the original class and a tenacious acculturation?[45]

If Baudrillard's analysis of the apartment is transposed to my street and to Mr H.'s Thunderbird, where does it fit in Baudrillard's suggested scheme? It does not fit Baudrillard's category of the 'witness object' testifying against the owner's intentions to an earlier, occluded or suppressed social origin – unless we accept that Mr H. is downwardly mobile which in a limited, literal sense he probably is. He was once a small landowner in Cyprus and first arrived in London in the 1960s as a chauffeur before going on to work the nightshift for twenty years in a local bakery. But he was never been rich enough to properly afford the car he now owns and he was not brought up to expect ever to own such a car (although it is likely that in the culture into which he was born, the public display of material possessions was taken as a direct index to the owner's wealth and status). The Thunderbird perhaps corresponds more closely to Baudrillard's 'unrealistic object' testifying in a desperate fashion to a social standing which remains forever unattainable in 'real life'. It is 'escapist' and 'utopian'. However, these terms seem scarcely adequate either, because they suggest a flight from the real conditions of existence, a false consciousness – and the Thunderbird is real enough. It sits there, blinding passers-by as the sunlight bounces off its polished surfaces. 'Escapist', 'utopian': these terms are, in the context in which Baudrillard places them, purely negative and their negativity is predicated on Baudrillard's implicit conviction that the paramount realities are social class, occupational status, ownership of capital: that secular relations of power are all that matters. (This latter conviction survives Baudrillard's shift into nihilism, cynicism and 'fatalism'.) But is that really the case socially, existentially? Is that all life appears to be about?

I think it is better, then, to introduce another category and to call Mr H.'s car an 'impossible object'. It is impossible not because it encapsulates an unattainable dream of opulence – I don't really think that Mr H. craves to join the international jet set or to live inside an episode of Dallas. It is impossible because it serves so many different (symbolic) functions, supplies so many diverse needs – the need for recognition and respect, yes, but also the need for something to care for *and to care about, to bring up, cultivate, stand in awe of. It is impossible because it is a screen on to which so much inchoate yearning and desire are projected that putting them into words is impossible. That investment of energy, that projection of desire exceeds rational description – in a word, it is sublime. The car is also impossible because it is impossible to own, to use, or to protect properly given the circumstances in which Mr H. lives. It is impossible simply because he doesn't own a garage; impossible ultimately because he has to rely on faith in God – faith in people's good will – to protect the cherished possession from the carelessness, indifference and violence which threaten order of whatever kind wherever it's imposed. This is what makes it an impossible object.*

When I asked Mr H. how he felt about being kept awake by the post-punk musicians opposite, he said he felt unable to complain because they once threw a beer can at his car from one of the upstairs windows. If he complained he feared they would retaliate. Mr H. is frail and is not a fighter but he is no coward. He once threatened to kill a young man twice his size and less than half his age for allegedly 'bothering' his 13-year-old niece. It wasn't physical fear – fear for his person – which prevented his complaining. At least it wasn't only that. It is just that his love is too exposed. He couldn't afford to take the risk.

Mr H.'s relationship to his car is distinguished by a love as unreasonable, as inflated, as impractical as the love of Romeo for Juliet. It aspires to bring too much beauty into an imperfect world. The Thunderbird is an impossible object because it elicits an excess of feeling, an undecidable mix of proprietorial, paternal and filial emotions, of pleasure and fear. While no doubt rooted in the sensuous, in the erotic or quasi-erotic drives (the car, she: the beautiful madonna, inviolable, ever-virginal object – her hyman restored (magically like the hole in the windscreen) with every coat of wax), the exaggerated love Mr H. bears towards the Thunderbird involves a transubstantiation of the erotic, the libidinal into the spiritual. I don't think this is folly – either Mr H.'s exaggerated attachment to his car or my exaggerated description of that attachment. It is just that what we are talking about here is an act *of love and an act of love is always impossible, is always made against the odds. After all, what is an act of love but the attribution of ideal values to actual objects?*

In his famous essay on the work of art in the age of mechanical reproduction, Walter Benjamin suggested that the democratization of the media and of image-making would lead to the politicization of the aesthetic at the point when the desacralizing potential of the technologies of mass reproduction – film, photography, printing – was realized and the aura of the work of art – its uniqueness, authenticity, single authorship – was finally destroyed. How curious, then, that what I see in Mr H.'s agonized investments in an American car goes precisely against the secular grain of Benjamin's prediction. What Mr H. seems to have done is to confer upon an object the sacred aura denied it by the conditions and mode under which it was produced. There is no 'waning of affect' here but rather an amplification, an intensification, an excess of affect: a caring which is virtually palpable. Mr H. is humanizing and aestheticizing what is essentially blank, flat and given – an object which requires no creative expenditure on his part – a car made in a factory and sold on the market (though it does require technical mastery and driving skills to be used as a car). Through this humanization, this aestheticization, this act of love, he is giving value back, giving value (back) for money, turning a sign into an icon, a mass-produced commodity into a beautiful one-off. The words 'commodity fetishism' do not in my opinion do justice to the heroic transcendence of alienation, juvenile (post-punk) nihilism and virtual poverty which is encapsulated in Mr H.'s strange, hyperbolic, impossible relation to his beloved Thunderbird.

13

I have tried in this article to pose the question of aesthetics from a slightly different angle, challenging both the traditional Platonic and Kantian formulations and the bleaker aspects of the critical vision represented by some versions of postmodernism. I have none the less retained some characteristically 'Post' emphases, perceptions, foci, but I have attempted to move back against the Nietzschian grain which is built into that critical discourse. For it may be the case *intellectually* that, for certain kinds of cosmopolitan intellectual, the old explanatory and interpretative frameworks have collapsed, that the age-old need for a metaphysic, an ideal, an aesthetic which is capable of conferring value, meaning and direction on our experience has been thrown (again!) into question. But it is not the case ontologically, culturally, politically, existentially. So I have ended by returning home to the particular, to the concrete, to the culturalist, the ethnographic mode, in order to stress the primacy of that vital point where the individual and the biographical meet the collective and the historical, the point where lived culture – the experience of actual women and men – can intervene against the bleak perspectivism of certain currently fashionable kinds of crystal-ball gazing.

To those who would represent what is, after all, a welcome loosening of the old ties and constraints, a welcome opening-up to speech of different voices, different genders, different races as a global end-of-everything or a decentring 'anti-expressive' 'anti-aesthetic', I would say that 'anywhere' – the abstract 'anywhere' addressed in some postmodern descriptions – is quite simply nowhere. It does not exist because people do not occupy space in that way unless they are unfortunate enough to live in psychiatric hospitals. I would say, remember that no general tendency (no tendency to generalize) should be allowed to obscure the sense of the particular and the local – of *place* and *boundary* in the Heideggerian sense – which is the essential ground of a *sane* existence and which provides the lived and living ground upon which culture and politics are always made and remade. By starting from this universally felt need for place and boundary, from this nostalgia (in its most literal sense of 'homesickness') for the ideal made actual, we may perhaps be able to relocate and reassemble the components of a more open, more joyful and productive – that is more egalitarian – sense of what the aesthetic is and what it means. We may become sensitive once more to the liberatory potentials residing in that yearning for perfection and the possible which seems to be intrinsic, which seems to constitute what we might call the aesthetic imperative: that drive to go beyond the existent, beyond that which is 'already', to that which is ready to be brought forward into being. For in the end, *this* is the 'house of being' and all of us – intellectuals and non-intellectuals alike – will have to learn to live inside it because, as Nietzsche himself took such pains to point out, there is simply nowhere else to go.

14

One night I dreamt that Mr H.'s face appeared weeping at my window. His lips moved as if he were trying to speak but I couldn't hear the words. He lifted his arms as if to open the window but I saw he had no hands. The cuffs of his shirt were soaked in blood. His eyes were shining, blazing out against me and the darkness that threatened to engulf him. I knew – though I could scarcely acknowledge the fact – that it was I who had inflicted this injury upon him. To shut him out, I tugged at the curtains so sharply that I pulled them off the rail. I closed my eyes but when I'd opened them, Mr H. had flown and as soon as I had said this to myself, I heard a noise behind me: a feathery commotion as if a flock of birds were trapped inside the chimney. I turned round to see Mr H. suspended in the air hovering above the bed. Two huge red wings were spread out behind him like an oriental fan. They were twitching gently, brushing lightly against the ceiling and floor. (He had the measure of my house.) The air was filled with the sweet smell of honey, the thick musty odour of almonds. Without looking up into his face, I knew that Mr H.'s eyes were on me and I felt ashamed.

What was it I had taken from this man?

I saw that Mr H.'s feet were naked and I wanted to apologize for stealing his new shoes but as I looked up towards him, he threw his head back and laughed a booming laugh which reverberated off the walls, like thunder in a cave. The wings opened and closed in an arc over him and underneath him. Slowly, still laughing with his head thrown back, Mr H. flew across the room and through the wall. With the laughter still ringing in my ears, I followed him. I must explain. I must apologize. I tried in vain to find his face in the window and in the darkness beyond the window. In the space in the street reserved for Mr H.'s Thunderbird I saw a charred, deserted hulk, a mass of rust and tangled metal. The darkness grew suddenly deeper, heavier, and then as the lightning came to crack the darkness open, the rain began to fall and as it fell the rust formed bloody rivulets which gushed and churned and eddied round the metal shell. Somehow I knew the rain would never stop. The rivulets would form a stream, the stream would become a torrent, then a ruddy lake, at last a raging sea. This sea would swallow everything: these bits of twisted metal, this street, these houses, these words.

I looked up and saw the outline of a rose traced like a letter in the sky.

The rose was the promise in the wake of flight.

The bird had flown. The bird had found its wings.

NOTES

[1] See Hal Foster (ed.), *Postmodern Culture* (London: Pluto, 1985), published in the USA as *The Anti-Aesthetic* (Port Townsend, Washington: Bay Press, 1983).

[2] Raymond Williams, *Keywords* (London: Fontana, 1973).

110

[3] William Wordsworth, quoted in *ibid*.

[4] Raymond Williams, *Culture and Society 1790-1950* (Harmondsworth: Penguin, 1959).

[5] See Jean-François Lyotard, 'The sublime and the avant-garde', *Artforum* (April, 1984).

[6] Peter Fuller, 'Taste – you can't opt out', *Design 423* (March, 1984). See also Peter Fuller, *Aesthetics after Modernism* (London: Writers & Readers, 1983); Peter Fuller, *Art and Psychoanalysis* (London: Writers & Readers, 1980); Peter Fuller, *Beyond the Crisis in Art* (London: Writers & Readers, 1980).

[7] Clifford Geertz, 'Thick description', in *The Interpretation of Culture* (Basic Books, 1973).

[8] Roland Barthes, 'The goddess: the new Citroen', in his *Mythologies* (London: Cape, 1972).

[9] Tom Wolfe, *The Kandy-Kolored Tangerine-Flake Streamline Baby* (London: Bantam, 1964); Tom Wolfe, *The Pump House Gang* (London: Bantam, 1969).

[10] Vance Packard, *The Wastemakers* (Harmondsworth: Penguin, 1963); Vance Packard, *The Status Seekers* (Harmondsworth, Penguin, 1961). See also P. Willis, *Profane Culture* (London: Routledge & Kegan Paul, 1978).

[11] See 'The Private Life of the Ford Cortina' (directed by Nigel Finch), a TV documentary for the BBC arts series, *Arena*.

[12] For corroboration of this point, listen to 'Police officer', a satirical reggae lament by the young black British talk-over artist Smiley Culture. In the song, Smiley Culture enacts an imaginary dialogue between himself as a young black reggae star and a (white cockney) police officer who has stopped his car but who eventually agrees to let him go without a body search in return for an autograph. The song is peppered with Smiley's pleas delivered in a strong West Indian accent: 'Please officer, don't touch me ganja!', 'Please officer, don't give me no producer' (i.e. a demand to produce his driving licence for inspection at a specified police station within a specified period). The song points up the extent to which young black drivers are subject to routine harassment by the metropolitan police.

[13] Pierre Bourdieu, *Distinction: A Social Critique of the Judgement of Taste*, translated by Richard Nice (Cambridge, Mass.: Harvard University Press, and London: Routledge & Kegan Paul, 1984); originally published by Les Editions de Minuit (Paris, 1979). All Bourdieu quotes in this article are from this book unless otherwise indicated in a separate footnote.

[14] Richard Hoggart, *The Uses of Literacy* (Harmondsworth: Penguin, 1958).

[15] Bourdieu, *op.cit.*

[16] *Ibid.*

[17] Mikhail Bakhtin, *Rabelais and his World* (Cambridge, Mass.: MIT Press, 1968), published in Russian (1965).

[18] See, for instance, Dick Hebdige, *Subculture: The Meaning of Style* (London: Methuen, 1979); Dick Hebdige, *Hiding in the Light: On Images and Things* (London: Comedia, forthcoming); Willis, *op.cit.* 1978. For the use of Bakhtin see, for instance, Peter Wollen's introductory essay to the Komar and Melamid exhibition catalogue (MOMA) (Oxford, 1985); also Dick Hebdige, 'Some sons and their fathers', in *Ten. 8: Men in Camera*, 17 (1985).

[19] See, for instance, Pierre Bourdieu, *Outline of a Theory of Practice* (Cambridge: Cambridge University Press, 1977).

[20] Friedrich Nietzsche, 'Nietzsche contra Wagner', in Walter Kauffmann (ed.), *The Portable Nietzsche* (Chatto and Windus, 1971).

[21] 'The style of the book, whose long, complex sentences may offend – constructed as they are with a view to reconstituting the complexity of the social world in a language capable of holding together the most diverse things while setting them in rigorous perspective – stems partly from the endeavour to ... prevent the reading from slipping back into the simplicities of the smart essay or the political polemic': P. Bourdieu, preface to the English language edition of *Distinction*, *op.cit.*

[22] Roland Barthes, 'Change the object itself', in his *Image, Music, Text*, edited and translated by Stephen Heath (London: Fontana, 1977).

[23] See Wollen, *op.cit.*, 1985.

[24] See Jean-François Lyotard, *The Postmodern Condition: A Report on Knowledge* (Minneapolis: University of Minnesota Press, and Manchester: Manchester University Press, 1984) especially the essay 'What is postmodernism?' Also Lyotard, 'The sublime and the avant-garde' (April, 1984).

[25] Jean-François Lyotard, 'Defining the postmodern' in Lisa Appignanesi (ed.), *Postmodernism: ICA Documents 4* (London: Institute of Contemporary Arts, 1986).

[26] Jean-François Lyotard, 'Complexity and the sublime', in *ibid.*

[27] A more developed version of the argument presented in this section is available in an article entitled 'Postmodernism and "the other side" ' to be published in Hebdige, *Hiding in the Light*, forthcoming, and in *Journal of Communication Inquiry*, Summer 1985.

[28] *Les Immatériaux* was the title of an exhibition mounted by Jean-François Lyotard at the Pompidou Centre in 1984. The exhibition was designed to explore the new post-modern *sensorium* made available through simulation-technologies. See Jean-François Lyotard, 'Les Immateriaux', in *Art & Text 17: Expositionism* (1984).

[29] See Lyotard, *The Postmodern Condition*.

[30] Walter Benjamin, 'Theses on the philosophy of history', in his *Illuminations* (London: Fontana, 1973).

[31] Lyotard, 'Complexity and the sublime'.

[32] Kant cited *ibid.*

[33] *Ibid.*

[34] *Ibid.*

[35] Lyotard, 'Defining the postmodern'.

[36] Richard Rorty, 'Habermas and Lyotard on postmodernity', in Richard J. Bernstein (ed.), *Habermas and Modernity* (Oxford: Polity Press, Basil Blackwell, 1985).

[37] *Ibid.*

[38] Fredric Jameson, 'Postmodernism or the cultural logic of late capitalism', *New Left Review*, 146 (July-August, 1984).

[39] See Jean Baudrillard, *Simulations* and *In the Shadow of the Silent Majorities*, edited by Jim Fleming and Sylvere Lotringer, translated by Paul Foss, Paul Patton, Philip Beitchman, John Johnston (New York: Semiotext(e) Foreign

Agents Series, 1983). Also Baudrillard, 'The ecstasy of communication', in Foster (ed.), *op.cit.*

[40] Gilles Deleuze and Felix Guattari, *Anti-Oedipus* (New York: Viking Press, 1977).

[41] See Lyotard, *The Postmodern Condition.* The postmodern condition is defined here as an impossible tense – the 'future anterior' – post meaning 'after', modo meaning 'now'.

[42] For Nietzsche the final negation was the negation of negation: the (heroic) affirmation of what is.

[43] Jameson, *op.cit.*

[44] Jean Baudrillard, 'Sign function and class logic', in *For a Critique of the Political Economy of the Sign* (New York: Telos, 1981).

[45] *Ibid.*

Black Hair/Style Politics

Kobena Mercer

Some time ago Michael Jackson's hair caught fire when he was filming a television commercial. Perhaps the incident became newsworthy because it brought together two seemingly opposed news-values: fame and misfortune. But judging by the way it was reported in one black community newspaper, *The Black Voice*, Michael's unhappy accident took on a deeper significance for a cultural politics of beauty, style and fashion. In its feature article, 'Are we proud to be black?', beauty pageants, skin-bleaching cosmetics and the curly-perm hair-style epitomized by Jackson's image were interpreted as equivalent signs of a 'negative' black aesthetic. All three were roundly condemned for negating the 'natural' beauty of blackness and were seen as identical expressions of subjective enslavement to Eurocentric definitions of beauty, thus indicative of an 'inferiority complex'.[1]

The question of how ideologies of 'the beautiful' have been defined by, for and – for most of the time – against black people remains crucially important. But at the same time I want to take issue with the widespread argument that, because it involves straightening, the curly-perm hair-style represents either a wretched imitation of white people's hair or, what amounts to the same thing, a diseased state of black consciousness. I have a feeling that the equation between the curly-perm and skin-bleaching cremes is made to emphasize the potential health risk sometimes associated with the chemical contents of hair-straightening products. By exaggerating this marginal risk, a moral grounding is constructed for judgements which are then extrapolated to assumptions about mental health or illness. This conflation of moral and aesthetic judgement underpins the way the article also mentions, in horror and disgust, Jackson's alleged plastic surgery to make his features 'more European-looking'.

115

Reactions to the striking changes in Jackson's image have sparked off a range of everyday critiques on the cultural politics of 'race' and 'aesthetics'. The apparent transformation of his racial features through the glamorous violence of surgery has been read by some as the bizarre expression of a desire to achieve fame by 'becoming white' – a deracializing sell-out, the morbid symptom of a psychologically mutilated black consciousness. Hence, on this occasion, Michael's misfortune could be read as 'punishment' for the profane artificiality of his image; after all, it was the chemicals that caused his hair to catch afire.

The article did not prescribe hair-styles that would correspond to a 'positive' black self-image or a politically 'healthy' state of black subjectivity. But by reiterating the 1960s slogan – Black Is Beautiful – it implied that hair-styles which avoid artifice and look 'natural', such as the Afro or Dreadlocks, are the more authentically black hair-styles and thus more ideologically 'right-on'. But it is too late to simply repeat the slogans of a bygone era. That slogan no longer has the same cultural or political resonance as it once did; just as the Afro, popularized in the United States in the period of Black Power, has been displaced through the 1970s by a new range of black hair-styles, of which the curly-perm is just one of the most popular. Whether you care for the results or not, these changes have been registered by the stylistic mutations of Michael Jackson and surely his fame indicates something of a shift, a sign of the times, in the agendas of black cultural politics. How are we to interpret such changes? And what relation do changes in dress, style and fashion bear to the changed political, economic and social circumstances of black people in the 1980s?

To begin to explore these issues I feel we need to *de-psychologize* the question of hair-straightening and recognize hair-styling itself for what it is, a specifically cultural activity and practice. As such we require a historical perspective on how many different strands – economic, political, psychological – have been woven into the rich and complex texture of our nappy hair, such that issues of style are so highly charged as sensitive questions about our very 'identity'. As part of our modes of appearance in the everyday world, the ways we shape and style hair may be seen as both individual expressions of the self and as embodiments of society's norms, conventions and expectations. By taking both aspects into account and focusing on their interaction we find there is a question that arises prior to psychological considerations, namely: *why do we pour so much creative energy into our hair?*

In any black neighbourhood you cannot escape noticing the presence

BLACK HAIR/STYLE POLITICS

of so many barber-shops and hairdressing salons; so many hair-care products and so much advertising to help sell them all; and, among young people especially, so much skill and sheer fastidiousness that goes into the styles you can see on the street. Why so much time, money, energy and worry spent shaping our hair?

From a perspective informed by theoretical work on subcultures,[2] the question of style can be seen as a medium for expressing the aspirations of black people excluded from access to 'official' social institutions of representation and legitimation in the urban, industrialized societies of the capitalist First World. Here, black peoples of the African diaspora have developed distinct, if not unique, patterns of style across a range of practices from music, speech, dance, dress and even cookery, which are politically intelligible as creative responses to the experience of oppression and dispossession. Black hair-styling may thus be evaluated as a popular *art form* articulating a variety of aesthetic 'solutions' to a range of 'problems' created by ideologies of race and racism.

TANGLED ROOTS AND SPLIT ENDS: HAIR AS SYMBOLIC MATERIAL

As organic matter produced by physiological processes human hair seems to be a 'natural' aspect of the body. Yet hair is never a straighforward biological 'fact' because it is almost always groomed, prepared, cut, concealed and generally 'worked upon' by human hands. Such practices socialize hair, making it the medium of significant 'statements' about self and society and the codes of value that bind them, or don't. In this way hair is merely a raw material, constantly processed by cultural practices which thus invest it with 'meanings' and 'value'.

The symbolic value of hair is perhaps clearest in religious practices – shaving the head as a mark of worldly renunciation in Christianity or Buddhism, for example, or growing the hair as a sign of inner spiritual strength for Sikhs. Beliefs about gender are also evident in practices like the Muslim concealment of the woman's face and hair as a token of modesty.[3] Where race structures social relations of power, hair – as visible as skin colour, but also the most tangible sign of racial difference – takes on another forcefully symbolic dimension. If racism is conceived as an ideological code in which biological attributes are invested with societal values and meanings, then it is because our hair is

117

perceived within this framework that it is burdened with a range of 'negative' connotations. Classical ideologies of race established a classificatory symbolic system of colour with 'black' and 'white' as signifiers of a fundamental polarization of human worth – 'superiority/inferiority'. Distinctions of aesthetic value, 'beautiful/ ugly', have always been central to the way racism divides the world into binary oppositions in its adjudication of human worth.

Although dominant ideologies of race (and the way they dominate) have changed, the legacy of this biologizing and totalizing racism is traced as a presence in everyday comments made about our hair. 'Good hair', used to describe hair on a black person's head, means hair that looks 'European', straight, not too curly, not that kinky. And, more importantly, the given attributes of our hair are often referred to by descriptions such as 'woolly', 'tough', or, more to the point, just plain old 'nigger hair'. These terms crop up not only at the hairdresser's but more acutely when a baby is born and everyone is eager to inspect the baby's hair and predict how it will 'turn out'.[4] The pejorative precision of the salient expression, 'nigger hair', neatly spells out how, within racism's bipolar codification of human value, black people's hair has been historically devalued as the most visible stigma of blackness, second only to skin.

In discourses of 'scientific racism' in the seventeenth and eighteenth centuries, which developed in Europe alongside the slave trade, variations in pigmentation, skull and bone formation and hair texture among the species of 'man' were seized upon as signs to be identified, named, classified and ordered into a hierarchy of human worth. The ordering of differences constructed a 'regime of truth' that could validate the Enlightenment assumption of European 'superiority' and African 'inferiority'. In this process, racial differences – like the new scientific taxonomies of plants, animals and minerals – were named in Latin; thus was the world appropriated in the language of the 'west'. But whereas the proper name 'Negro' was coined to designate all that the west thought it was not, 'Caucasian' was the name chosen by the west's narcissistic delusion of 'superiority': 'Fredrich Bluembach introduced this word in 1795 to describe white Europeans in general, for he believed that the slopes of the Caucasus [mountains in eastern Europe] were the original home of the most beautiful European species.'[5] The very arbitrariness of this originary naming thus reveals how an *aesthetic* dimension, concerning blackness as the absolute negation or annulment of 'beauty', has always intertwined with the rationalization of racist sentiment.

The assumption that whiteness was the measure of true beauty, condemning Europe's Other to eternal ugliness, can also be seen in images articulated around race in nineteenth-century culture. In the stereotype of Sambo – and his British counterpart, the golliwog – the 'frizzy' hair of the character is an essential aspect of the iconography of 'inferiority'. In children's books and the minstrel shows of vaudeville, the 'woolly' hair is ridiculed, just as aspects of black people's speech were lampooned in both popular music-hall and the nineteenth-century novel as evidence of the 'quaint folkways' and 'cultural backwardness' of the slaves.

But the stigmatization of black people's hair did not gain its historical intransigence by being a mere idea: once we consider those New World societies created on the basis of the slave trade economy – the United States and the Caribbean especially – we can see that where 'race' is a constitutive element of social structure and social division, hair remains charged with symbolic currency. Plantation societies instituted a 'pigmentocracy'; that is, a division of labour based on 'racial' hierarchy where one's socio-economic position could be signified by one's skin colour. Fernando Henriques's account of family, class and colour in post-colonial Jamaica shows how this colour/class nexus continues to structure a plurality of horizontal ethnic categories into a vertical system of class stratification. His study draws attention to the ways in which the residual value-system of 'white bias' – the way ethnicities are valorized according to the tilt of whiteness – functions as the ideological basis for status ascription. In the sediment of this value-system, African elements – be they cultural or physical – are devalued as indices of low social status, while European elements are positively valorized as attributes enabling individual upward mobility.[6]

Stuart Hall in turn emphasizes the composite nature of white bias, which he refers to as the 'ethnic scale', as both physiological and cultural elements are intermixed in the symbolization of one's social status. Opportunities for social mobility are therefore determined by one's ranking on the ethnic scale and involve the negotiation not only of socio-economic factors such as wealth, income, education and marriage, but also of less easily changeable elements of status symbolism such as the shape of one's nose or the shade of one's blackness.[7] In the complexity of this social code, hair functions as a key 'ethnic signifier' because, compared with bodily shape or facial

119

features, it can be changed more easily by cultural practices such as straightening. Caught on the cusp between between self and society, nature and culture, the malleability of hair makes it a sensitive area of expression.

It is against this historical and sociological background that we must evaluate the personal and political economy of black hair-styles. Dominant ideologies such as white bias do not just dominate by 'universalizing' the values of hegemonic social/ethnic groups so that they become everywhere accepted as the 'norm'. Their hegemony and historical persistence is underwritten at a subjective level by the way ideologies construct positions from which individuals 'recognize' such values as a constituent element of their personal identity. Discourses of black nationalism, such as Marcus Garvey's, have always acknowledged that racism 'works' by encouraging the devaluation of blackness by black subjects themselves, and that a re-centring sense of pride is a prerequisite for a politics of resistance and reconstruction. But it was Frantz Fanon who first provided a systematic framework for the political analysis of racial hegemonies at the level of black subjectivity.[8] He regarded cultural preferences for all things white as symptomatic of psychic 'inferiorization' and thus might have agreed with Henrique's view of straightening as 'an active expression of the feeling that it tends to Europeanize a person'.

Such arguments gained influence in the 1960s when the Afro hair-style emerged as a symbol of Black Pride and Black Power. However, by regarding one's hair-style as directly 'expressive' of one's political awareness this sort of argument tends to prioritize self over society and ignore the mediated and often contradictory dialectic between the two. Cheryl Clarke's poem, 'Hair: a narrative', shows that the question of the relationship between self-image and hair-straightening is always shot through with emotional ambiguity. She describes her experience as implicating both pleasure and pain, shame and pride: the 'negative' aspects of the hot-lye and steel-comb method are held in counterpoint to the friendship and intimacy between herself and her hairdresser who 'against the war of tangles, against the burning metamorphosis ... taught me art, gave me good advice, gave me language, made me love something about myself'.[9] Another problem with prevailing anti-straightening arguments is that they rarely actually listen to what people think and feel about it.

Alternatively, I suggest that when hair-styling is critically evaluated as an aesthetic practice inscribed in everyday life, all black hair-styles are political in that they articulate responses to the panoply of historical forces which have invested this element of the ethnic signifier with both personal and political 'meaning' and significance.

With its organizing principles of biological determinism, racism first 'politicized' our hair by burdening it with a range of negative social and psychological 'meanings'. Devalorized as a 'problem', each of the many stylizing practices brought to bear on this element of ethnic differentiation articulates ever so many diverse 'solutions'. Through aesthetic stylization each black hair-style seeks to revalorize the ethnic signifier and the political significance of each rearticulation of value and meaning depends on the historical conditions under which each style emerges.

The historical importance of Afro and Dreadlocks hair-styles cannot be underestimated as marking a 'liberating' rupture or break with the dominance of white bias. But were they really that 'radical' as solutions to the ideological problematization of black people's hair? Yes: in their historical contexts, they counter-politicized the signifier of ethnic devalorization, redefining blackness as a positive attribute. But, on the other hand, perhaps not, because within a relatively short period both styles became rapidly *de*politicized and, with varying degrees of resistance, both were incorporated into mainstream fashions in the dominant culture. What is at stake, I believe, is the difference between two logics of black stylization – one emphasizing 'natural' looks, the other involving straightening to emphasize 'artifice'.

NATURE/CULTURE: SOME VAGARIES OF IMITATION AND DOMINATION

Our hair, like our skin, is a highly sensitive surface on which competing definitions of 'the beautiful' are played out in struggle. The racial over-determinations of this nature/culture ambivalence are inscribed in this description of hair-straightening by a Jamaican hairdresser:

> Next, apply hot oil, massaging the hair well which prepares it for a shampoo. You dry the hair, leaving a little moisture in it, and then apply grease. When the hair is completely dry you start *cultivating* it with a hot comb.... Now the hair is all straight. You can use the curling iron on it. Most people like it curled and waved, not just straight, not just dead straight.[10]

121

Her metaphor of 'cultivation' is telling because it makes sense in two contradictory ways. On the one hand, it recuperates the negative logic of white bias: to cultivate is to transform something found 'in the wild' into something of social use and value, like domesticating a forest into a field. It thus implies that in its 'natural' given state, black people's hair has no inherent aesthetic value: it must be worked upon before it can be 'beautiful'. But on the other hand, all human hair is 'cultivated' in this way in that it merely provides a raw material for practices, procedures and ritual techniques of cultural writing and social inscription. Moreover, in bringing out other aspects of the styling process which highlight its specificity as cultural practice – the skills of the hairdresser, the choices of the client – the ambiguous metaphor alerts us to the fact that nobody's hair is ever just natural but is always shaped or reshaped by social convention and symbolic intervention.

An appreciation of this delicate 'nature/culture' relation is crucial if we are to account both for the emergence of Dreadlocks and Afro as politicized statements of 'pride' *and* their eventual disappearance into the mainstream. To reconstruct the semiotic and political economy of these black hair-styles we need to examine their relation to other items of dress and the broader historical context in which ensembles of style emerged. An important clue with regard to the Afro in particular can be found in its names, as the Afro was also referred to as the 'natural'.

The interchangeability of its two names is important because both signified the embrace of a 'natural' aesthetic as an alternative ideological code of symbolic value. The 'naturalness' of the Afro consisted in its rejection both of straightened styles and of short haircuts: its distinguishing feature was the *length* of the hair. With the help of a 'pick' or Afro comb the hair was encouraged to grow upwards and outwards into its characteristic rounded shape. The three-dimensionality of its shape formed the signifying link with its status as a sign of Black Pride. Its morphology suggested a certain dignified body-posture, for to wear an Afro you have to hold your head up in pride, you cannot bow down in shame and still show off your 'natural' at the same time. As Flugel pointed out with regard to ceremonial head-dress and regal crowns, by virtue of their emphatic dimensions such items bestow a sense of presence, dignity and majesty on the wearer by magnifying apparent body-size and by shaping bodily movement accordingly so as to project stature and grace.[11] In a similar way, with the Afro we wore the crown, to the point where it could be assumed that the larger the Afro, the greater the degree of

122

black 'content' to one's consciousness.

In its 'naturalistic' logic the Afro sought a solution that went to the source of the problem. By emphasizing the length of hair when allowed to grow 'natural and free' the style counter-valorized attributes of curliness and kinkiness to convert stigmata of shame into emblematics of pride. Its name suggested a link between 'Africa' and 'nature' and this implied an oppositional stance against artificial techniques of any kind, as if any element of artificiality was imitative of Eurocentric, white-identified, aesthetic ideals. The oppositional economy of the Afro also depended on its connections with dress-styles adopted by various political movements of the time.

In contrast to the civil rights demand for racial equality within the given framework of society, the more radical and far-reaching objective of total 'liberation' and 'freedom' gained its leverage through identification and solidarity with anti-colonial and anti-imperial struggles of emergent Third World nations. And at one level, this 'other' political orientation of Black Power announced itself in the language of clothes.

The Black Panthers' 'urban guerrilla' attire – polo-necks, leather jackets, dark glasses and berets – encoded a uniform for protest and militancy by way of the connotations of the common denominator, the colour black. The Panthers' berets invoked solidarity with the often violent means of anti-imperialism, while the dark glasses, by concealing identity from the 'enemy', lent a certain political mystique and a romantic aura of dangerousness.

The Afro also featured in a range of ex-centric dress-styles associated with cultural nationalism, often influenced by the dress codes of Black Muslim organizations of the late 1950s. Here, elements of 'traditional' African dress – tunics or dashikis, head-wraps and skull-caps, elaborate beads and embroidery – all suggested that black people were 'contracting out' of westernness and identifying with all things African as a positive alternative. It may seem superficial to re-read these transformative political movements today in terms of style and dress: but we might also remember that as they filtered through mass media, such as television, these styles contributed to the increasing visibility of black people's struggles in the 1960s. As elements of everyday life, these black styles in hair and dress helped to underline massive shifts in popular aspirations among black people and participated in a populist logic of rupture.

As its name suggests, the Afro symbolized a reconstitutive link with

Africa, as part of a counter-hegemonic process helping to redefine a diasporean people not as Negro but as Afro-American. A similar upheaval was at work in the emergence of Dreadlocks. As the Afro's creole cousin, Dreadlocks spoke of pride and empowerment through their association with the radical discourse of Rastafari which, like Black Power in the United States, inaugurated a redirection of black consciousness in the Caribbean.[12] Within the strictures of Rastafari as doctrine, Dreadlocks embody an interpretation of a religious, biblical injunction that forbids the cutting of hair (along the lines of its rationale among Sikhs). However, once 'locks were popularized on a mass social scale – via the increasing militancy of reggae especially – their dread logic inscribed a beautification of blackness remarkably similar to the aesthetic logic of the Afro.

Dreadlocks also embrace the 'natural' in the way they celebrate the very materiality of black hair texture, for black people's is the only type of hair that can be 'matted' into such characteristic configurations. While the Afro's semiotics of pride depended on its rounded shape, 'locks counter-valorized nappy-headed blackness by way of this process of 'matting' which is an option not readily available to white people because their hair does not 'naturally' grow into such 'organic'-looking shapes and strands. And where the Afro suggested a link with Africa through its name and its association with radical political discourses, Dreadlocks similarly implied a symbolic link between their 'naturalistic' appearance and Africa by way of the reinterpretation of biblical narrative which identified Ethiopia as a 'Zion' or Promised Land. With varying degrees of emphasis both invoked 'nature' to inscribe 'Africa' as the symbol of personal and political opposition to the hegemony of the west over 'the rest'. Both championed an aesthetic of nature that opposed itself to any artifice as the sign of corrupting Eurocentric influence. But nature had nothing to do with it! Both these hair-styles were never just natural, waiting to be found: they were stylistically *cultivated* and politically *constructed* in a particular historical moment as part of a strategic contestation of white dominance and the cultural power of whiteness.

These styles sought to 'liberate' the materiality of black hair from the burdens bequeathed by racist ideology. But their respective logics of signification, positing links between the 'natural', Africa, and the goal of freedom, depended on what was only a *tactical inversion* of the chain of equivalences that structured the Eurocentric system of white bias. We saw how the biological determinism of classical racist ideology first 'politicized' our hair: its logic of devalorization of blackness radically devalued our hair, debarring it from access to dominant regimes of the 'truth of beauty'. The aesthetic de-negation 'logically' depended on prior relations of equivalence which posited the categories of 'Africa' and 'nature' as equally other to Europe's deluded self-image which sought to monopolize claims to beauty.

The equation between the two categories in Eurocentric thought rested on the assumption that Africans had no culture or civilization worthy of the name. Philosophers like Hume and Hegel validated such assumptions, legitimating the view that Africa was outside history in a savage and rude 'state of nature'. Yet, while certain Enlightenment reflections on aesthetics saw in the 'Negro' only the annulment of their ideas of beauty, Rousseau and later, in the eighteenth and nineteenth centuries, romanticism and realism, saw 'nature' on the other hand as the source of all that was good, true and beautiful. The Negro was none of these. But by inverting the symbolic order of racial polarity the aesthetic of 'nature' underpinning the Afro and Dreadlocks could negate the negation, turn white bias on its head and thus revalorize as positive all that had once been devalued as the annulment of aesthetics. In this way the black subject could accede – and only in the twentieth century, mind you – to that level of aesthetic idealization or self-valorization that had hitherto been denied as unthinkable. The radicality of the 1960s slogan, Black Is Beautiful, lay in the function of the logical copula 'is', as it marked the ontological affirmation of our nappy nigger hair, breaching the bar of negation signified in that utterance from the Song of Songs that Europe had rewritten (in the King James version of the Bible) as 'I am black *but* beautiful'.[13]

However radical this counter-move was, its tactical inversion of categories was limited. One reason why may be that the 'nature' invoked was not a neutral term but an ideologically loaded *idea* created by binary and dualistic logics from European culture. The 'nature' brought into play to signify a desire for 'liberation' and 'freedom' so effectively was also a western inheritance, sedimented with symbolic references by traditions of science, philosophy and art. Moreover, this ideological category had been fundamental to the hegemony of the west over 'the rest'; the nineteenth-century bourgeoisie sought to legitimate the imperial division of the world by way of mythologies which aimed to universalize, eternalize and hence 'naturalize' its power. The counter-hegemonic tactic of inversion appropriated a particularly romanticist version of 'nature' as a means of empowering the black subject; but by remaining in a dualistic logic of binary oppositionality (to Europe and artifice) the moment of rupture was delimited by the fact that it was only an imaginary 'Africa' that was put into play.

Clearly, this analysis is not to write off the openings and effective 'liberations' gained and made possible by inverting the order of aesthetic oppression; only to point out that the counter-hegemonic project inscribed by these hair-styles is not completed or closed and that this story of struggles over the same symbols continues. Nevertheless, the limitations underline the diasporean specificity of the Afro and Dreadlocks and ask us to examine, first, their conditions of commodification and, second, the question of their 'imaginary' relationship to Africa and African cultures as such.

Once commercialized in the market-place the Afro lost its specific signification as a 'black' cultural-political statement. Cut off from its original political contexts, it became just another fashion: with an Afro wig anyone could wear the style. Now the fact that it could be neutralized and incorporated so quickly suggests that the aesthetic interventions of the Afro operated on terrain already mapped out by the symbolic codes of the dominant white culture. The Afro not only echoed aspects of romanticism, but shared this in common with the 'counter-cultural' logic of long hair among white youth in the 1960s. From the Beatles' mop-tops to the hairy hippies of Woodstock, white subcultures of the 1960s expressed the idea that the longer you wore your hair, somehow the more 'radical' and 'right-on' your life-style or politics. This 'far-out' logic of long hair among the hippies may have sought to symbolize disaffection from western norms, but it was rapidly assimilated and dissimulated by commodity fetishism. The incorporation of long hair as the epitome of 'protest', via the fashion industry, advertising and other economies of capitalist mediation, culminated at one point in a Broadway musical that ran for years – *Hair*.

Like the Afghan coats and Kashmiri caftans worn by the hippy, the dashiki was reframed by dominant definitions of ethnic otherness as 'exotica': its connotations of cultural nationalism were clawed back as just another item of freakish exoticism for mass consumption. Consider also the inherent semiotic instability of militant chic. The black leather jackets and dark glasses of the Panthers were already inscribed as stylized synonyms for 'rebelliousness' in white male subcultures from the 1950s. There, via Marlon Brando and the metonymic association with macho and motor bikes, these elements encoded a youthful desire for 'freedom', in the image of the American highway and the open road, implying opposition to the domestic norms of their parent culture. Moreover, the colour black was not saturated by exclusively 'racial' connotations. Dark sombre colours (as well as the occasional French beret) featured in the downbeat dress statements of the 1950s boho-beatniks to suggest mystery, 'cool', outsider status, anything to 'alienate' the normative values of 'square society'.

The fact that these white subcultures themselves appropriated elements from black American culture (rock 'n' roll and bebop respectively) is as important as the fact that a portion of the semiotic effectiveness of the Panther's look derived from associations already 'embedded' by previous articulations of the same or similar elements of style. The movement back and forth indicates an underlying dynamic of struggle as different discourses compete for the same signs. It shows that for 'style' to be socially intelligible as an expression of conflicting values, each cultural nucleus or articulation of signs must share access to a common stock or resource of signifying elements. To make the point from another point of view would amount to saying that the Afro engaged in a critical 'dialogue' between black and white Americans, not one between black Americans and Africans. Even more so than Dreadlocks, there was nothing particularly African about the Afro at all. Neither style had a given reference point in existing African cultures, in which hair is rarely left to grow 'naturally'. Often it is plaited or braided, using 'weaving' techniques to produce a rich variety of sometimes highly elaborate styles that are reminiscent of the patternings of African cloth and the decorative designs of African ceramics, architecture and embroidery.[14] Underlying these practices is what might be termed an African aesthetic. In contrast to the separation of the aesthetic sphere in post-Kantian European thought, this is an aesthetic which incorporates practices of beautification in everyday life. Thus artifice is valued in its own right as a mark of both invention and tradition, and aesthetic skills are deployed within a complex economy of symbolic codes in which communal subjects recreate themselves collectively.[15]

Neither the Afro nor Dreadlocks operate within this aesthetic as such. In contemporary African societies, such styles would not signify Africanness ('locks in particular would be regarded as something 'alien', precisely the tactical objective of the Mau Mau in Kenya when they adopted such dread appearances in the 1950s); on the contrary, they would imply an identification with First World-ness. They are specifically diasporean. However strongly these styles expressed a desire to 'return to the roots' among black peoples in the diaspora, in Africa *as it is* they would speak of a 'modern' orientation, a modelling of oneself according to metropolitan images of blackness.

If there was nothing 'African' about these styles, this only goes to underline the point that neither style was as 'natural' as it claimed to be. Both presupposed quite artificial techniques to attain their characteristic shapes and hence political significance: the use of special combs in the case of the Afro, and the process of matting in the case of 'locks, often given a head-start by initially plaiting long strands of hair. In their rejection of artifice both styles embraced a 'naturalism' that owed much more to Europe than it did to Africa. The fate of the Afro in particular might best be understood by an analogy with what happened to the Harlem Renaissance in the 1920s.

There, complementing Garvey's call for repatriation to Africa, a generation of artists, poets, writers and dancers embraced all things African to renew and refashion a collective sense of black American identity. Yet when rich white patrons descended on Harlem seeking out the salubrious spectacle of the 'New Negro' it became clear – to Langston Hughes at least – that the Africa being evoked was not the real one but a mythological, imaginary 'Africa' of noble savagery and primitive grace. The creative upsurge in black American culture and politics marked a moment of rupture and a reconstruction of black subjectivity *en masse*, but it was done like the Afro through an inverted reinscription of the romanticist mythology created by Europe's Enlightenment. As Langston realized, 'I was only an American Negro – who had loved the surfaces of Africa and the rhythms of Africa – but I was not Africa.'[16] However strategically and historically important, such tactics of reversal remain unstable and contradictory because their assertion of difference so often hinges on what is only the inversion of the same.

STYLE AND FASHION: SEMIOTIC STRUGGLES IN THE FOREST OF SIGNS

Having alighted on a range of paradoxes of race and aesthetics via this brief excursion into the archaeology of the Afro, I want now to re-evaluate the political economy of straightening in the light of these contradictory relations between black and white cultures in diasporean societies. Having found no pre-existing referent for either style-statement in 'actually existing' African cultures it should be clear that what we are dealing with are New World creations of black people's culture which, in First World societies, bear markedly different relations with the dominant Euro-American culture from those that obtain in the Third World.

By ignoring these differences, arguments that hold straightened styles to be slavish 'imitations' of western norms are in fact complicit with an outmoded anthropological argument that once tried to explain dia-sporean black cultures as bastard products of unilateral 'acculturation'. By reversing the axes of traditional analysis we can see that in our era of cultural modernity it is white people who have been doing a great deal of the imitating while black people have done much of the innovating.

Refutations of the assumptions underpinning the racist myth of one-sided acculturation have often taken the form of 'discoveries', usually proclaimed by anthropologists, of 'africanisms' or the survival of African cultural traits across the middle passage to the New World; Melville Herskovits, for instance, made much of the retention of traditional African modes of hairdressing and covering among black Americans.[17] However, in the light of modern contradictions around 'inter-culturation', our attention must now be directed not so much to the retention of actual artefacts but to the reworking of what may be seen as a 'neo-African' approach to the aesthetic in disaporean cultural formations. The patterns and practices of aesthetic stylization developed by black cultures in First World societies may be seen as modalities of cultural practice *inscribed* in critical engagement with the dominant white culture and at the same time *expressive* of a 'neo-African' approach to the pleasures of beauty at the level of everyday life.

Black practices of aesthetic stylization are intelligible at one 'func-tional' level as dialogic responses to the racism of the dominant culture, but at another level involve acts of appropriation from that same 'master' culture through which 'syncretic' forms of diasporean culture have evolved. Syncretic strategies of black stylization, 'creolizing' found or given elements, are writ large in the black codes of modern music like jazz where elements such as scales, harmonies or even instruments like the piano or saxophone from western cultural traditions are radically transformed by this 'neo-African', improvisational approach to aes-thetic and cultural production. In addition there is another 'turn of the screw' in these modern relations of inter-culturation when these creolized cultural forms are made use of by other social groups and then, in turn, are all incorporated into mainstream 'mass' culture as comodities for consumption. Any analysis of black style, in hair or any other medium, must take this field of relationships into account.

Hair-styles such as the conk of the 1940s or the curly-perm of the 1980s are syncretic products of New World stylization. Refracting elements from both black and white cultures through this framework of exchange and appropriation, imitation and incorporation, such styles are characterized by the ambivalence of their 'meaning'. It is implausible to attempt a reading of this ambivalence in advance of an appreciation of the historical contexts in which they emerged alongside other stylized surfaces of syncretic inscription in speech, dance, music and dress.

As a way into this arena of ambiguity listen to this voice, as Malcolm X describes his own experience of hair-straightening. After recounting the physical pain of the hot-lye and steel-comb technology, he tells of pride and pleasure in the new, self-stylized image he has made for himself:

> My first view in the mirror blotted out the hurting. I'd seen some pretty conks, but when it's the first time, on your *own* head, the transformation, after a lifetimes of kinks, is staggering. The mirror reflected Shorty behind me. We were both grinning and sweating. On top of my head was this thick, smooth sheen of red hair – real red – as straight as any white man's.[18]

In his autobiographical narrative the voice then shifts immediately from past to present wherein Malcolm sees the conk as 'my first really big step towards self-degradation'. No attempt is made to address this mixture of feeling: pleasure and pride in the past, shame and self-denigration in the present. The narrative seems to 'forget' or exclude the whole life-style of which the conk hair-style was a part. By invoking the idea of 'imitation' Malcolm evades the ambiguity, his discourse cancels from the equation what his 'style' meant at that moment in front of the mirror.

In its context the conk was but one aspect of a modern style of black American life, forged in the subaltern social bloc of the northern ghettos by people who, like Malcolm Little, had migrated from southern systems of segregation only to find themselves locked into another, more modern, and equally violent, order of oppression. Shut out from access to illusions of 'making it', this marginalized urban formation of modern diasporean culture sponsored a sense of style that 'answered back' against these conditions of existence.

Between the years of economic depression and the Second World War, big bands like Duke Ellington's, Count Basie's and Lionel Hampton's (who played at the dance-hall where Malcolm worked as a shoeshine boy) accelerated on rhythm, seeking through 'speed' to pre-empt the possibility of white appropriations of jazz, as happened in the 1920s. In the 'underground' music scene incubated around Kansas City in the 1940s the accent on improvisation, which later flourished as bebop, articulated an 'escape' – simultaneously metaphysical and subterranean – from that system of socio-economic bondage, itself in the ruins of war. In the high-energy dance styles that might accompany the beat, the Lindy Hop and Jitter Bug traced another line of flight: through the catharsis of the dance a momentary 'release' might be obtained from all the pressures on mind and body accumulated under the ritual discriminations of racism. In speech and language, games like signifyin', playing the dozens and what became known as 'jive-talk', verbal style effected a discursive equivalent of jazz improvisation. The performative skills and sheer wit demanded by these speech-acts in black talk defied the idea that Black English was a degraded 'version' of the master language. These games refuted America's archetype of Sambo, all tongue-tied and dumb, muttering 'Yessa massa' in its miserable abjection. In the semantic play of verbal stylization, hep-cats of the cool world greeted each other as Man, systematically subverting the paternalistic interpellation – boy! – of the white master code, the voice of authority in the social text of the urban plantation.[19]

In this historical moment style was not a substitute for politics. But, in the absence of an organized direction of black political discourse and excluded from official 'democratic' channels of representation, the logic of style manifested across cultural surfaces of everyday life reinforced the terms of shared experience – blackness – and thus a sense of solidarity among a subaltern social bloc. Perhaps we can trace a fragile common thread running through these styles of the 1940s: they encoded a refusal of passivity by way of a creolizing accentuation and subtle inflection of given elements, codes and conventions.

The conk involved a violent technology of straightening, but this was only the initial stage in a process of creolizing stylization. The various waves, curls and lengths introduced by practical styling served to differentiate the conk from the conventional white hair-styles which supposedly constituted the 'models' from which this black hair-style was derived as imitation or 'copy'. No, the conk did not copy anything and certainly not any of the prevailing white male hair-styles of the day. Rather, the element of straightening suggested resemblance to white people's hair, but the nuances, inflections and accentuations introduced by artificial means of stylization emphasized difference. In this way the political economy of the conk rested on its ambiguity, the way it 'played' with the given outline shapes of convention only to 'disturb' the norm and hence invite a 'double take' demanding that you look twice.

Consider also the use of dye, red dye: why red? To assume that black men conked up *en masse* because they secretly wanted to become 'red-heads' would be way off the mark. In the chromatic scale of white bias, red is seen as a mild deviation from gendered norms which hold blonde hair as the colour of 'beauty' in women and brown hair among men. Far from an attempted simulation of whiteness I think the dye was used as a stylized means of defying the 'natural' colour codes of conventionality in order to highlight artificiality and hence exaggerate a sense of difference. Like the purple and green wigs worn by black women, which Malcolm mentions in disgust, the use of red dye seems trivial: but by flouting convention with varying degrees of artifice such techniques of black stylization participated in a defiant 'dandyism', fronting-out oppression by the artful manipulation of appearances. Such dandyism is a feature of the economy of style-statements in many subaltern class cultures where 'flashy' clothes are used in the art of impression-management to defy the assumption that to be poor one necessarily has to 'show' it. The strategic use of artifice in such stylized modes of self-presentation was written into the reat pleats of the zoot suit which, together with the conk, constituted the *de rigeur* hep-cat look in the black male 'hustler' life-styles of the 1940s ghettos. With its wide shoulders, tight waist and baggy pants – topped off with a wide-brimmed hat, and worn with slim Italian shoes and lots of gold jewels – the zoot suit projected stature, dignity and presence: it signified that the black man was 'important' in his own terrain and on his own terms.

The zoot suit is said to have originated among Latino males on the US west coast – whatever its source, it caused a 'race riot' in Los Angeles in 1943 as the amount of cloth implicated in its cut exceeded wartime rations, provoking ethnic resentment among white males. But perhaps the real historical importance of the zoot suit lies in the irony of its appropriation. By 1948 the American fashion industry had ripped it off and toned it down as the new post-war 'bold look' for the mainstream male. By being commodified within such a short period the zoot suit demonstrated a reversal in the flow of fashion-diffusion as now the style of the times emerged from social groups 'below', whereas previously regimes of taste had been set by the *haute couture* of the wealthy and then translated back down, via industrial reproduction, to the masses.[20] This is important because, as an aspect of inter-culturation, this story of black innovation/white imitation has been played out again and again in post-war popular culture, most markedly in music and, in so far as music has formed their nucleus, a whole procession of youth subcultures from Teddy boys to b-boys.

Once we re-contextualize the conk in this way we confront a series of 'style wars', skirmishes of appropriation and commodification played out around the semiotic economy of the ethnic signifier. The complexity of this force-field of inter-culturation ambushes any attempt to track down fixed meanings or finalized readings and opens out instead on to ambiguous relations of economic and aesthetic systems of valorization. On the one hand, the conk was conceived in a subaltern culture, dominated and hedged in by a capitalist master culture, yet operating in an 'underground' manner to subvert given elements by creolizing stylization. Style encoded political 'messages' to those in the know which were otherwise unintelligible to white society by virtue of their ambiguous accentuation and intonation. But, on the other hand, that dominant commodity culture appropriated bits and pieces from the otherness of ethnic differentiation in order to reproduce the 'new' and so, in turn, to strengthen its dominance and revalorize its own symbolic capital. Assessed in the light of these paradoxical relationships, the conk suggests a 'covert' logic of cultural struggle operating 'in and against' hegemonic cultural codes, a logic quite different from the overt oppositionality of the naturalistic Afro or Dreadlocks. At one level this only underlines the different historical conditions, but at another the emphasis on artifice and ambiguity rather than an inversion of equivalence strikes me as a particularly modern way in which cultural utterances may take on the force of 'political' statements. Syncretic practices of black stylization, such as the conk, zoot suit or jive-talk, recognize themselves self-consciously as products of a New World culture; that is, they incorporate an awareness of the contradictory conditions of inter-culturation. It is this self-consciousness that underscores their ambivalence and in turn marks them off and differentiates them as stylized signs of blackness. In jive-talk the very meanings of words are made uncertain and undecidable by self-conscious stylization which sends signifiers slipping and sliding over signifieds: bad means good, superbad means better. Because of the way blackness is recognized in such stratagems of creolizing intonation, inflection and accentuation, these practices of stylization exemplify 'modernist' interventions whose economy of political calculation might best be illustrated by the 'look' of someone like Malcolm X in the 1960s.

Malcolm always eschewed the ostentatious, overly symbolic dress code of the Muslims and wore 'respectable' suits and ties, but unlike the besuited civil rights leaders his appearance was always inflected by a certain 'sharpness', an accentuation of the hegemonic dress code of the corporate business suit. This intonation in his attire spelt out that he would talk to the polity on his terms, not theirs. This nuance in his public image echoed the 'intellectual' look adopted by jazz musicians in the 1950s, but then again, from another frame, Malcolm looked like a mod! And in the case of this particular 1960s subculture, white English youth had taken many of the 'found objects' of their stylistic bricolage from the diasporean cultural expression of black America and the Caribbean. Taking these relations of appropriation and counter-appropriation into account, it would be impossible to argue for any one 'authoritative' reading of either the conk in the past or the curly-perm today. Rather, the complexity of these violent relations of valorization, which loom so large over the popular experience of cultural modernity, demands that we ask instead: are there any laws that govern this 'semiotic guerrilla warfare' in the concrete jungle of the modern metropolis?

If, in the British context, 'we can watch, played out on the loaded surfaces of … working-class youth cultures, a phantom history of race relations since the war',[21] then any analysis of black hair-style in this territory of the diaspora must reckon with the contradictory terms of this accelerated inter-culturation around the ethnic signifier. Somewhere around 1967 or 1968 something very strange happened in the ethnic imaginary of Englishness as former mods assembled a new image out of their parents' work-clothes, creating a working-class youth culture that derived its name from their cropped hair-styles. Yet the skinhead hair-style was an imitation of the mid-1960s soulboy look where closely shaven haircuts provided one of the most 'classic' solutions to the problem of kinks and curls. Every black person (at least) recognizes the 'skinhead' as a political statement in its own right – but then how are we to understand the social or psychological bases for this post-imperial mode of mimicry, this ghost dance of white ethnicity? Like a photographic negative, the skinhead crop symbolized white power and white pride sure enough, but then *how* (like their love of ska and bluebeat) did this relate to their appropriation of Afro-Caribbean culture?

Similarly, we would have to confront the paradox whereby white appropriations seem to act both as a spur to further experimentation and as modified models to which black people themselves may conform. Once the Afro had been ingested, black Americans brought traditional braiding and plaiting styles out from under their wraps, introducing novel elements such as beads and feathers into cane-row patterns. No sooner said than done, by the mid-1970s the beaded cane-row style was appropriated by one-hit wonder Bo Derek. It also seemed that her success validated the style and encouraged more black people to cane-row their hair.

Moreover, if contemporary culture functions on the threshold of what has been called 'postmodernism', an analysis of this force-field of inter-culturation must surely figure in the forefront of any reconstructive rejoinder to debates which have so far marginalized popular culture and aesthetic practices in everyday life. If, as Fredric Jameson argues, postmodernity merely refers to the dominant cultural logic of late capitalism which 'now assigns an increasingly essential structural function to aesthetic innovation and experimentation', as a condition of commodity fetishism and higher rates of turn-over in mass consumption, then any attempt to account for the gradual dissolution of boundaries between 'high' and 'low' culture, 'taste' and 'style', must reckon with the dialogic interventions of diasporean, creolizing cultures.

As Angela McRobbie has noted, various postmodern stratagems of aesthetic critique have already been prefigured as dialogic, politicized interventions in popular culture. Scratching and rap in black music would be a good example of 'radical collage' engaged in popular culture or everyday life; like the bricoleur, the DJ appropriates and juxtaposes fragments from the arche-text of popular music history in a critical engagement or 'dialogue' with issues thrown up by the present.[22]

It is in the context of such critical bricolage that the question of the curly-perm today must be re-posed. One initial reading of this hair-style in the late 1970s, as symbol of black 'embourgeoisement', is undermined by the way that many wet-look styles retain the overall rounded shape of the Afro. Indeed, a point to notice about the present is that the curly-perm is not the 'one' uniformly popular black hair-style, but only one among many diverse configurations of 'post-liberated' black hair-styles that seem to revel in their allusions to an ever wider range of stylistic references. Relaxing cremes, gels, dyes and other new technologies have enabled a width of experimentation that suggests that hair-straightening does not 'mean' the same thing after as before the era of the Afro and Dreadlocks. Black practices of stylization today seem to exude confidence in their enthusiasm for combining elements from any source – black or white, past or present – into new configurations of cultural expression. Post-liberated black hair-styling emphasizes a 'pick 'n' mix' approach to aesthetic production, suggesting a different attitude to the past in its reckoning with modernity. The philly-cut on the hip-hop/go-go scene etches diagonalized lines across the head, refashioning a style from the 1940s where a parting would be shaved into the hair. Combinations of cane-row and curly-perm echo 'Egyptian' imagery; she looks like Nefertiti, but this is Neasden, nowhere near the Nile.

One particular style that fascinates me is a variant of the flat-top (popularized by Grace Jones, but also perhaps a long-distance echo of the wedge-cut of the 1960s) where, underneath a crest of miniaturized dreadlocks, the hair is cut really close at the back and the sides: naturalism is invented to accentuate artifice. The differential logics of ambivalence and equivalence are shown to be not necessarily exclusive as they interweave across each other: long 'locks are tied up in pony-tails, very practical, of course, but often done as aesthetic stylization (itself in subtle counterpoint to various 'new man' hair-styles that also involve the romanticist male dandyism of long hair). And perhaps the intertextual dimension of creolizing stylization is not so 'new'; after all, in the 1970s black people sometimes wore wild Afro wigs in bold pink and day-glo colours, prefiguring post-punk experimentation with anti-naturalistic, 'off' colours.

On top of all this, one cannot ignore how, alongside the commodification of hip-hop/electro, breakdancing and sportswear chic, some contemporary hair-styles among white youth maintain an ambiguous relationship with the stylizing practices of their black counterparts. Many use gels to effect sculptural forms and in some inner-city areas white kids use the relaxer creme technology marketed to black kids to simulate the 'wet-look'. So who, in this postmodern mêlée of semiotic appropriation and counter-creolization, is imitating whom?

Any attempt to make sense of these circuits of hyper-investment and over-expenditure around the symbolic economy of the ethnic signifier encounters issues that raise questions about race, power and modernity that go beyond those allowed by a static moral psychology of 'self-image'. I began with a polemic against one type of argument and have ended up in another: namely one that demands a critical analysis of the multi-faceted economy of black hair as a condition for appropriate aesthetic judgements. 'Only a fool does not judge by appearances,' Oscar Wilde said, and by the same token it would be foolish to assume that because somebody wears 'locks they are dealing in 'peace, love and unity'; Dennis Brown also reminded us to take the 'wolf in sheep's clothing' syndrome into account. There are no just black hair-styles, just black hair-styles. This article has prioritized the semiotic dimension in its readings to open up analyses of this polyvocal economy but there are other facets to be examined: such as the exploitative priorities of the black hairdressing industry as it affects consumers or workers under precarious market conditions, or the question of gendered differentiations (and similarities).

On the political horizon of postmodern popular culture I think the *diversity* of contemporary black hair-styles is something to be proud of. Because this variousness testifies to an inventive, improvisational aesthetic that should be valued as an aspect of Africa's 'gift' to modernity. And because, if there is the possibility of a 'unity in diversity' somewhere in this field of relations, then it challenges us to cherish plurality politically.[23]

NOTES

[1] *The Black Voice*, 15, 3 (June 1983) (paper of the Black Unity and Freedom Party, London SE15).
[2] See Tony Jefferson and Stuart Hall (eds), *Resistance through Rituals* (London: Hutchinson, 1975); and Dick Hebdige, *Subculture* (London: Methuen, 1979).
[3] See C.R. Hallpike, 'Social hair', in Ted Polhemus (ed.), *Social Aspects of the Human Body* (Harmondsworth: Penguin, 1978); on the veil see Frantz Fanon, 'Algeria unveiled', in *A Dying Colonialism* (Harmondsworth: Penguin, 1970).

[4] Such anxieties, I know, are intensified around the mixed-race subject:
'I still have to deal with people who go to touch my "soft" or "loose" or "wavy" hair as if in the touching something ... will be confirmed. Back then to the 60s it seems to me that my options ... were to keep it short and thereby less visible, or to have the living curl dragged out of it: *maybe then you'd look Italian ... or something.*' Derrick McClintock, 'Colour', *Ten.8*, 22 (1986).
[5] George Mosse, *Toward the Final Solution: a history of European racism* (London: Dent, 1978), 44.
[6] Fernando Henriques, *Family and Colour in Jamaica* (London: Secker & Warburg, 1953), 54-5.
[7] Stuart Hall, 'Pluralism, race and class in Caribbean society', in *Race and Class in Post-Colonial Society* (New York: UNESCO, 1977), 150-82.
[8] Frantz Fanon, *Black Skin, White Masks* (London: Pluto Press, 1986).
[9] Cheryl Clarke, *Narratives: poems in the tradition of black women* (New York: Kitchen Table/Women of Colour Press, 1982); see also *Hairpiece: A Film for Nappy-Headed People*, dir. Ayoka Chinzera, 1982.
[10] Henriques, *op.cit.*, 55.
[11] See John C. Flugel, *The Psychology of Clothes* (London: Hogarth Press, 1930).
[12] On connections between Black Power and Rastafari, see Walter Rodney, *The Groundings with my Brothers* (London: Bogle-L'Ouverture Publications, 1968), 32-3.
[13] On Africa as the 'annulment' of Eurocentric concepts of beauty see Christopher Miller, *Blank Darkness: Africanist discourse in French* (London and Chicago: University of Chicago Press, 1985). On systems of equivalence and difference in hegemonic struggles see Ernesto Laclau, 'Populist rupture and discourse', *Screen Education*, 34 (Spring 1980) and Ernesto Laclau and Chantal Mouffe, *Hegemony and Socialist Strategy* (London: Verso, 1985).
[14] Esi Sagay, *African Hairstyles* (London: Heinemann, 1983).
[15] See John Miller Chernoff, *African Rhythm and African Sensibility* (Chicago: University of Chicago Press, 1979); Victoria Ebin, *The Body Decorated* (London: Thames & Hudson, 1979) and Victor Turner, *The Forest of Symbols: aspects of Ndembu ritual* (Ithaca, NY: Cornell University Press, 1967).
[16] Langston Hughes, *The Big Sea* (London: Pluto Press, 1986); and see also Ralph Ellison, *Shadow and Act* (New York: Random House, 1964).
[17] Melville Herskovits, *The Myth of the Negro Past* (Boston, MA: Beacon Books, 1959). During the 1950s anthropologists influenced by the 'culture and personality' paradigm approached the ghetto as a domain of social pathology. Abrahams (mis)read the process rag hairdo, kept under a handkerchief until Saturday night, as 'an effeminate trait ... reminiscent of the handkerchief tying of Southern "mammies" ', a symptom of sex-role socialization gone wrong, cited in Charles Keil, *Urban Blues* (London and Chicago: University of Chicago Press, 1966), 26-7.
Alternative concepts of 'inter-culturation' and 'creolization' are developed by Edward K. Brathwaite, *Contradictory Omens: cultural diversity and integration in the Caribbean* (Mona, JA: Savacou Publications, 1974); see also Janheinz Jahn, *Muntu: an outline of Neo-African culture* (London: Faber, 1953).

BLACK HAIR/STYLE POLITICS

[18] *The Autobiography of Malcolm X* (Harmondsworth: Penguin, 1968), 134-9.
[19] On Afro-American stylization see Ben Sidran, *Black Talk* (London: Da Capo Press, 1973); Thomas Kochman, *Black and White Styles in Conflict* (London and Chicago: University of Chicago Press, 1981); and Henry Louis Gates Jr, 'The blackness of blackness: a critique of the sign and the signifying monkey', in Gates (ed.), *Black Literature and Literary Theory* (London and New York: Methuen, 1984).
[20] Steve Chibnall, 'Whistle and zoot: the changing meaning of a suit of clothes', *History Workshop Journal*, 20 (1985) and Stuart Cosgrove, 'The zoot suit and style warfare', *History Workshop Journal*, 18 (1984). See also J. Schwartz, 'Men's clothing and the Negro', in M.E. Roach and J.B. Eicher (eds), *Dress Adornment and the Social Order* (New York: Wiley, 1965).
[21] Hebdige, *op.cit.*, 45.
[22] Fredric Jameson, 'Postmodernism, or the cultural logic of late capitalism', *New Left Review*, 146 (July/August 1984), 56; and Angela McRobbie, 'Postmodernism and popular culture', *ICA Documents 4/5* (London: ICA, 1986).
[23] Sister Carol wears locks and wants a Black revolution
She tours with African dancers around the country
Sister Jenny has relaxed hair and wants a Black revolution
She paints scenes of oppression for an art gallery
Sister Sandra has an Afro and wants a Black revolution
She works at a women's collective in Brixton
Sister Angela wears braids and wants a Black revolution
She spreads love and harmony with her reggae song
All my sisters who want a Black revolution don't care
How they wear their hair. And they're all Beautiful.

Christabelle Peters, 'The politics of hair', Poets Corner, *The Voice* (15 March 1986).

I Want the Black One: Being Different

Is There a Place for Afro-American Culture in Commodity Culture?

Susan Willis

Adults, older girls, shops, magazines, newspapers, window signs – all the world had agreed that a blue-eyed, yellow-haired, pink-skinned doll was what every girl child treasured.

(Morrison, *The Bluest Eye*)

In her powerfully compressed first novel, *The Bluest Eye*, Toni Morrison scrutinizes the influence of the white-dominated culture industry on the lives and identities of black Americans. She tells the story of three young girls: Claudia and Frieda, who are sisters; and Pecola, who comes to stay with them during a period when her own brawling parents are cast out of their store-front home. The book's setting is a working-class urban black neighbourhood during the 1930s and 1940s, a time when it is already clear that American culture means white culture, and that this in turn is synonymous with mass media culture. Morrison singles out the apparently innocuous – or as Frieda and Pecola put it, 'cu-ute',[1] Shirley Temple, her dimpled face reproduced on cups, saucers, and baby dolls, to show how the icons of mass culture subtly and insidiously intervene in the daily lives of Afro-Americans.

Of the three girls, Claudia is the renegade. She hates Shirley Temple, and seethes with anger when she sees the blue-eyed, curly-haired child actress dancing alongside the culture hero that Claudia claims for herself: Bojangles. As she sees it, 'Bojangles is [her] friend, [her] uncle, [her] daddy, [and he] ought to have been soft-shoeing it and chuckling with [her]'.[2] Claudia's intractable hostility towards Shirley Temple

141

originates in her realization that in our society, she, like all racial 'others', participates in dominant culture as a consumer, but not as a producer. In rejecting Shirley Temple, and wanting to be the one dancing with Bojangles, Claudia refuses the two modes of accommodation that white culture holds out to black consumers. She neither accepts that white is somehow superior, thus enabling her to see Shirley Temple as a proper dancing partner for Bojangles, nor does she imagine herself miraculously translated into the body of Shirley Temple so as to live white experience vicariously as a negation of blackness. Instead, Claudia questions the basis for white cultural domination. This she does most dramatically by dismembering and tearing open the vapid blue-eyed baby dolls her parents and relatives give her for Christmas presents. Claudia's hostility is not blind, but motivated by the keen desire to get at the roots of white domination, 'to see of what it was made, to discover the dearness, to find the beauty, the desirability that had escaped [her], but only [her]'.[3]

Claudia's unmitigated rage against white culture, its dolls and movie stars, is equalled only by her realization that she could axe little white girls made of flesh and blood as readily as she rips open their plaster and sawdust replicas. The only thing that restrains Claudia from committing mayhem is her recognition that the acts of violence she imagines would be 'disinterested violence'.[4] This is an important point in Morrison's development of Claudia as the representation of a stance that Afro-Americans in general might take against white domination. By demonstrating that violence against whites runs the risk of being 'disinterested violence', Morrison suggests that white people are little more than abstractions. As the living embodiments of their culture, all white people partake of the Shirley Temple icon. To some extent, all are reified subjects, against whom it is impossible for blacks to mount passionate, self-affirming resistance or retaliation. In defining Claudia as someone who learns 'how repulsive disinterested violence [is]'[5] Morrison affirms the fullness of her character's humanity.

Morrison's treatment of Claudia explores the radical potential inherent in the position of being 'other' to dominant society. The critical nature of *The Bluest Eye* may be best appreciated when apprehended in relation to efforts by Edward Said and Frantz Fanon to expose the emotionally crippling aspects of colonialism. Morrison's genius as a writer of fiction is to develop the experience of 'otherness' and its denunciation in ways that were not open to either Said in *Orientalism* or Fanon in *Black Skin, White Masks*. This is because

142

Morrison's fictional characters, while they articulate history, are not themselves bound by historical events and social structures as were Fanon's patients whose case histories are the narrative raw material of his book. Morrison's portrayal of Pecola is the most horrifying example of the mental distortion produced by being 'other' to white culture. She transforms the Fanonian model of a little black girl caught behind a white mask into a little black girl whose white mask becomes her face. Pecola's dialectical antithesis is, then, Claudia who tears to shreds the white mask society wants her to wear.

However, Claudia's critical reversal of 'otherness' is short-lived. Indeed, she later learned to 'worship' [6] Shirley Temple, knowing even as she did 'that the change was adjustment without improvement'.[7] In this, Morrison suggests that white cultural domination is far too complex to be addressed only in a retaliatory manner. A simple, straightforward response to cultural domination cannot be mounted, let alone imagined, because domination is bound up with the media, and this with commodity gratification. Claudia's desire to dance with Bojangles raises a question so crucial as to put all of American culture to the test. That is, can we conceive of mass culture as black culture? Or is mass culture by its very definition white culture with a few blacks in it? Can we even begin to imagine the media as capable of expressing Afro-American cultural identity?

Morrison addresses these questions by way of a parable. She tells the story of how Claudia and her sister plant a bed of marigolds and believe that the health and vigour of their seeds will ensure the health and vigour of their friend's incestuously conceived child. Morrison makes the parallel explicit: 'We had dropped our seeds in our own little plot of black dirt just as Pecola's father had dropped his seeds in his own plot of black dirt.'[8] But there were no marigolds. The seeds 'shriveled and died'[9] as did Pecola's baby. The parable of the flower garden resonates with more meaning than the mere procreation and survival of black people. In its fullest sense, the parable asks if we can conceive of an Afro-American cultural garden capable of bringing all its people to fruition. In the absence of a whole and sustaining Afro-American culture, Morrison shows black people making 'adjustments' to mass white culture. Claudia preserves more integrity than her sister, Frieda; but both finally learn to love the white icon. Pecola magically attains the bluest eyes and with them the madness of assimilation to the white icon. Maureen, the 'high-yellow dream child with long brown hair',[10] mimics the white icon with rich displays of fashion: 'patent-leather shoes with buckles',[11] coloured knee socks',[12] and a 'brown velvet coat trimmed in white rabbit fur and a matching muff'.[13] Taken together, the four young girls represent varying degrees of distortion and denial of self produced in relation to a culture they and their parents do not make, but cannot help but consume. Can we, then, conceive of an Afro-American culture capable of sustaining all four young girls, individually and collectively? And can such a culture take a mass form? To open up these questions, I want to move into the present, out of literature and into advertising, where mass media culture has made black its 'other' most frequently viewed population, as compared to the less visible Asian-Americans and all but invisible Hispanics.

SHOP TILL YOU DROP

> I don't want to know! I just want that magical moment when I go into a store and get what I want with my credit card. I don't even want to know I'll have to pay for it. (Comment made by a white male student when I explained that commodity fetishism denies knowledge of the work that goes into the things we buy.)

There is a photograph by Barbara Kruger that devastatingly sums up the abstraction of self and reality in consumer society. The photograph shows no more than a white hand whose thumb and forefinger grasp what looks like a red credit card, whose motto reads 'I Shop Therefore I Am'.[14] Kruger's photo captures the double nature of commodity fetishism as it informs both self and activity. The reduction of being to consumption coincides with the abstraction of shopping. This is because 'using plastic' represents a deepening of the already abstract character of exchange based on money as the general equivalent.

If shopping equals mere existence, then the purchase of brand names is the individual's means for designating a specific identity. Consumer society has produced a population of corporate logo-wearers: 'Esprit', 'Benetton', 'Calvin Klein', 'Jordache', and the latest on the fashion scene, McDonalds 'McKids'. The stitched or printed logo is a visible detail of fashion not unlike the sticker on a banana peel. In the eyes of the corporate fashion industry, our function is to bring advertising into our daily lives. We may well ask if we are any different from the old-time sandwich-board advertisers who once patrolled city streets with signs recommending 'Eat at Joe's'.

I WANT THE BLACK ONE

Until recently it was clear in the way fashion featured white models that buying a brand-name designer label meant buying a white identity. The workers who produce brand-name clothing today are predominantly Chinese, Filipino, and Mexican; or, closer to home, they are Hispanics and Asian Americans; but the corporations are as white as the interests and culture of the ruling class they maintain. The introduction of black fashion models in major fashion magazines like *Vogue, Harper's Bazaar,* and *Glamour* may have at one time represented a potential loosening of white cultural hegemony. But this was never fully realized because high fashion circumscribes ethnic and racial identity by portraying people of colour as exotic. Today, blacks appear in all forms of advertising, most often as deracinated, decultured black integers in a white equation. This is even true in many of the ads one finds in such black magazines as *Ebony* and *Essence*, where the format, models, and slogans are black mirror images of the same ads one sees month by month in the white magazines. For instance, in February 1988, Virginia Slims ran a magazine and billboard ad that featured a white model in a red and black flamenco dancing-dress. Black magazines and billboards in black neighbourhoods ran the same ad, same dress. The only difference was the black model inside the dress.

The question of whether or not black people can affirm identity by way of a brand name is nowhere more acutely posed than by Michael Jordan's association with 'Air Nike'. Michael Jordan *is* 'Air Nike'. He is not just shown wearing the shoes as some other champion might be shown eating 'the breakfast of champions'. Rather, his name and the brand name form a single unified logo-refrain. No other sports star, white or black, has ever attained such an intimate relationship between self and commodity. However, the personal connection between product and star does not suggest a more personalized product, rather it speaks for the commodification of Jordan himself. Moreover, the intimate oneness between the black basketball player and the white sneaker does not represent an inroad on the white corporation, but it does ensure that thousands of black youths from 16 to 25 will have a good reason for wanting hundred-dollar shoes.

A decade before Michael Jordan made black synonymous with a brand name, Toni Morrison used another of her novels to demonstrate the futility of affirming blackness with a white label. In *Song of Solomon*, Morrison depicts the anguish of Hagar, who wakes one morning to the realization that the reason for her boyfriend's lack of

145

interest is her looks. 'Look at how I look. I look awful. No wonder he didn't want me . I look terrible.'[15] Hagar's 'look' is black urban, northern, working-class, with a still strong attachment to the rural south. What little connection she has to the larger white culture has been fashioned out of her mother's sweepstakes prizes and her grandmother's impulse purchases. There is nothing contrived or premeditated about Hagar and the way she spontaneously defines herself and her love for Milkman. Her boyfriend, on the other hand, is the progeny of the urban black middle class whose forebears conquered the professions and gained access to private property. Not as fully assimilated to the brand name as Michael Jordan, Milkman, nevertheless, is a walking collection of commodities from his 'cordovan leather' shoes to his 'Good cut of suit'.[16]

In rationalizing her boyfriend's rejection of her as a fault of her 'looks'. Hagar assimilates race to style. She had previously been devastated by Milkman's flirtation with a woman with 'penny-colored hair' and 'lemon-colored skin',[17] and decides that in order to hold on to her boyfriend she must make herself into a less black woman. What Hagar doesn't grasp is that Milkman's uncaring regard for her is an expression of his primary sexism as well as his acceptance of the larger society's racist measure of blacks in terms of how closely an individual's skin and hair approximate the white model. Hagar lives her rejection as a personal affront and turns to the only means our society holds out to individuals to improve their lot and solve their problems: consumption. Hagar embodies all the pain and anxiety produced when racism and sexism permeate an intimate relationship; and she is the living articulation of consumer society's solution to racism and sexism. That is: buy a new you. Transform yourself by piling on as many brand-name styles and scents as your pocket-book will allow. The solution to a racist society is a 'pretty little black skinned girl',[18] 'who dresses herself up in the white-with-a-band-of-color skirt and matching bolero, the Maidenform brassiere, the Fruit of the Loom panties, the no color hose, the Playtex garter belt and the Joyce con brios';[19] who does her face in 'sunny-glo' and 'mango-tango'; and who puts 'baby clear sky light to outwit the day light on her eyelids'.[20]

Morrison reveals her sensitive understanding of how commodity consumption mutilates black personhood when she has Hagar appear before her mother and grandmother newly decked out in the clothes and cosmetics she hauled home through a driving rainstorm: her 'wet ripped hose, the soiled white dress, the sticky, lumpy face powder, the streaked rouge, and the wild wet shoals of hair'.[21] If Hagar had indeed achieved the 'look' she so desperately sought, she would have been only a black mimicry of a white cultural model. Instead, as the sodden, pitiful child who finally sees how grotesque she has made herself look, Hagar is the sublime manifestation of the contradiction between the ideology of consumer society that would have everyone believe that we all trade equally in commodities, and the reality of all marginalized people for whom translation into the dominant white model is impossible.

Morrison's condemnation of commodity consumption as a hollow solution to the problems of race, class, and gender is as final and absolute as are Hagar's subsequent delirium and death. Unable to find, let alone affirm, herself; unable to bridge the contradiction in her life by way of a shopping spree and a Cinderella transformation, Hagar falls into a fever and eventually perishes.

If consumer society were to erect a tombstone for Hagar, it would read 'Shop till you drop'. This is clearly the ugliest expression ever coined by shopping mall publicity people. Yet it is currently proclaimed with pride and glee by compulsive shoppers from coast to coast. Emblazoned on T-shirts, bumper stickers, and flashy advertising layouts, 'Shop till you drop' attests the ultimate degradation of the consumer. How often have you heard a young woman remark, such as the one I saw on *The Newlywed Game*, 'Whenever I feel low, I just shop till I drop!'? This is exactly what Hagar did. The difference between Morrison's portrayal of Hagar, and the relish with which the *Newlywed* contestant characterizes her shopping orgies, is Morrison's incisive revelation of the victimization and dehumanization inherent in mass consumption. 'Shop till you drop' is a message aimed at and accepted largely by women. (I have yet to hear a male shopper characterize himself in such a way.) The extreme sexism of the retail and advertising industries could not be more abusively stated. However, the victimization, the sexism, the degradation and dehumanization – all go unnoticed because the notion of consumption is synonymous with gratification. To demonstrate the fundamental impossibility of realizing gratification in commodity consumption, we have only to shift the focus from consumption to production. Now I ask you, would anyone wear a T-shirt proclaiming 'Work till you drop'? The cold fact of capitalism is that much of the workforce is expendable. Are we to assume that a fair number of consumers are also expendable provided they set high consumption standards on the way out?

FROM BLACK REPLICANTS TO MICHAEL JACKSON

Toni Morrison's strong condemnation of the fetishizing quality of white-dominated commodity culture is by no means unique to the tradition of black women writers. In her novel *Meridian*, Alice Walker creates a caricature of the reification of white society that is even more grotesque than Morrison's frozen-faced white baby dolls. This is the dead white woman whose mummified body is carted about from town to town and displayed as a side-show attraction by her money-grubbing husband. In death, as was probably the case in her life, the white woman's labour power is the basis for her husband's livelihood. As a dead body, she is literally the embodiment of the congealed labour that exemplifies the commodity form. What Morrison and Walker are documenting in their portrayals of reified white characters is the consequence of the longer and deeper association with the commodity form that whites in our society have had as opposed to racial minorities. In reacting so strongly against the fetishizing power of the commodity, contemporary black women's fiction stands aghast at the level of commodity consumption that Hagar attempts in *Song of Solomon*, and suggests that total immersion in commodities is a fairly recent historical phenomenon for the broad mass of Afro-Americans. Indeed, one way to read *Song of Solomon* is as a parable of black people's integration with the commodity form that is depicted across the book's three female generations, from Pilate who trades and barters for daily needs and very seldom makes a commodity purchase; to her daughter, Reba, who gets and gives a vast array of commodities that she wins rather than purchases; to Hagar, who desperately yearns for and dies because of commodities. The larger implications of Morrison's parable suggest that while the commodity form has been dominant throughout the twentieth century, daily life economics may have been only partially commodified owing to the many social groups who, until recently, did not fully participate as consumers.

While Morrison rejects out of hand the possibility of creating a positive, affirming black cultural identity out of 'sunny-glo' and 'mango-tango', Kobena Mercer, the British film and art critic, dramatically affirms the contrary. In considering the politics of black hair-styles, Mercer defines an approach to consumer society that sees commodities giving new forms of access to black people's self-expression.[22] Mercer contrasts the social meanings associated with the Afro, a hair-style popular amongst black radicals in the 1960s, and the general cultural movement that promoted 'Black is beautiful' on into the 1970s, with the conk, a hair-style contrived during the late 1930s and early 1940s by urban black males. Mercer sees the popular interpretation of these two hair-styles as wholly influenced by the way western culture, ever since romanticism, has validated the natural as opposed to the artificial. The 'Fro' was read culturally as making a strong positive statement because it was taken to represent the natural. Then, because western mythology equates the natural with the primitive – and primitive with Africa – the 'Fro' was seen as truly African, hence, the most valid form of Afro-American cultural expression. Mercer deflates these myths by pointing out that the 'Fro' was not natural but had to be specially cut and combed with a pik to produce the uniform rounded look. Moreover, the cultural map of African hair-styles reveals a complex geography of complicated plaits and cuts that are anything but natural. Mercer's final point is that if the 'Fro' was seen as natural, it was defined as such by dominant white society for whom the longer hair-styles of the late 1960s meant Hippies and their version of a communal back-to-nature movement. In this way, dominant white culture assimilated the 'Fro' to its meanings – including its counter-cultural meanings.

By comparison, Mercer sees the conk as allowing a form of Afro-American cultural expression that was not possible with the 'Fro' precisely because the conk was seen as artificial. At the time of its popularity and even on into the present, the conk has been condemned as an attempt by black men to 'whiten' their appearance. Mercer gives the prevailing line of thought by citing Malcolm X on his own first conk: 'on top of my head was this thick, smooth sheen of red hair – real red – as straight as any white man's ... [the conk was] my first really big step towards self-degradation.'[23] In contrast, Mercer's opinion of the conk is very different. As he sees it, if black men were trying to make themselves look more white and more acceptable to white ideals of style, they would not have chosen the conk. The hair was straightened by what he calls a 'violent technology' and treated to produce a tight cap of glistening red to orange hair. For its artificiality, the conk made a radical cultural statement that cannot be inscribed in dominant racialized interpretations of culture.

Far from an attempted simulation of whiteness I think the dye was used as a stylized means of defying the 'natural' colour codes of conventionality in order to highlight artificiality and hence exaggerate a sense of difference. Like the purple and green wigs worn by black women, which Malcolm X mentions in disgust, the use of red dye seems trivial: but by flouting convention with varying degrees of artifice such techniques of black stylization participated in a defiant 'dandyism', fronting-out oppression by the artful manipulation of appearances.[24]

Mercer's point is finally that black culture has at its disposal and can manipulate all the signs and artefacts produced by the larger culture. The fact that these are already inscribed with meanings inherited through centuries of domination does not inhibit the production of viable cultural statements, even though it influences the way such statements are read. The readings may vary depending on the historical period as well as the class, race, and gender of the reader. Mercer's own reading of the conk is facilitated by current theories in popular culture that see the commodity form as the raw material for the meanings that people produce. From this point of view, the most recognizable commodity (what's seen as wholly 'artificial') is somehow freer of past associations and more capable of giving access to alternative meanings.

There is, however, an important consideration that is not addressed either by Morrison in her condemnation of commodity culture or by Mercer in his delight over the possibilities of manipulating cultural meanings. This is the way the dominant white culture industry produces consumable images of blacks. Considerable effort in Afro-American criticism has been devoted towards revealing racism in the images of blacks on TV and in film, but little has been written about more mundane areas such as advertising and the mass toy market. I want to suggest a hypothesis that will help us understand consumer society in a more complex way than to simply point out its racism. That is: in mass culture many of the social contradictions of capitalism appear to us as if those very contradictions had been resolved. The mass cultural object articulates the social contradiction and its imaginary resolution in commodity form. Witness the way mass culture suggests the resolution of racism.

In contrast to Morrison's Claudia, who in *circa* 1940 was made to play with white baby dolls, black mothers in the late 1960s could buy their little girls Barbie's black equivalent: Christie. Mattel marketed Christie as Barbie's friend; and in so doing, cashed in on the civil rights movement and black upward social mobility. With Christie, Mattel also set an important precedent in the toy industry for the creation of black replicants of white cultural models. The invention of Christie is not wholly unlike the inception of a black Shirley Temple doll. If the notion of a black simulacrum of Shirley Temple is difficult to imagine, this is because only recent trends in mass marketing have taught us to accept black replicants as 'separate but equal' expressions of the white world. In the 1930s a black Shirley Temple would not have been possible, but if she were a 5-year-old dancing princess today, Mattel would make a doll of her in black and in white and no one would consider it strange. I say this because as soon as we started to see those grotesque, sunken-chinned white 'Cabbage Patch' dolls, we started to see black ones as well. Similarly, the more appealing but curiously furry-skinned 'My Child' dolls are now available in black or white, and in boy and girl models. Clearly, in the 1990s race and gender have become equal integers on the toy store shelf. I know many white girls who own mass-marketed black baby dolls such as these, but I have yet to see a single little black girl with a black 'Cabbage Patch' doll. What these dolls mean to little girls, both black and white, is a problem no adult should presume to fully understand, particularly as the dolls raise questions of mothering and adoption along with race. I mention these dolls because they sum up for me the crucial question of whether it is possible to give egalitarian expression to cultural diversity in a society where the white middle class is the norm against which all else is judged. This is another way to focus the problem I raised earlier when I asked whether it is possible for Afro-American culture to find expression in a mass cultural form.

In an essay inaugurating the new magazine *Zeta*, bell hooks develops the important distinction between white supremacy and older forms of racism. Hooks sees white supremacy as 'the most useful term to denote exploitation of people of color in this society'[25] both in relation to liberal politics and liberal feminism. I would add that white supremacy is the only way to begin to understand the exploitation of black people as consumers. In contrast to racism, which bars people of colour from dominant modes of production and consumption, white supremacy suggests the equalization of the races at the level of consumption. This is possible only because all the models are white. As replicants, black versions of white cultural models are of necessity secondary and devoid of cultural integrity. The black replicant ensures rather than subverts domination. The notion of 'otherness', or unassimilable marginality, is in the replicant attenuated by its mirroring of the white model. Finally the proliferation of black replicants in toys, fashion and advertising smothers the possibility for creating black cultural alternatives.

While the production of blacks as replicants of whites has been the dominant mass-market strategy for some twenty years, there are indications that this formula is itself in the process of being replaced by a newer mode of representation that in turn suggests a different approach to racism in society. I am referring to the look of racial homogeneity that is currently prevalent in high fashion marketing. Such a look depicts race as no more meaningful than a blend of paint. For example, the March 1988 issue of *Elle* magazine featured a beige woman on its cover. Many more fashion magazines have since followed suit in marketing what's now called 'the new ethnicity'. The ethnic model who appeared in *Elle* is clearly not 'a high-yellow dream child', Morrison's version of a black approximation to whiteness *circa* 1940. Rather, she is a woman whose features, skin tone, and hair suggest no one race, or even the fusion of social contraries. She is, instead, all races in one. A perusal of *Elle*'s fashion pages reveals more beige women and a greater number of white women who have been photographed in beige tones. The use of beige fashion models is the industry's metaphor for the magical erasure of race as a problem in our society. It underscores white supremacy without directly invoking the dominant race. To understand how this is achieved we have only to compare the look of racial homogeneity to the look of gender homogeneity. For some time now the fashion industry has suggested that all women, whether they are photographed in Maidenform or denim, whether they are 12 years old or 45, are equally gendered. Dominant male-defined notions about female gender, such as appear in fashion advertising, have inured many women to the possibility of gender heterogeneity. Now, the suggestion is that women with the proper 'look' are equally 'raced'. Such a look denies the possibility for articulating cultural diversity precisely because it demonstrates that difference is only a matter of fashion. It is the new autumn colours, the latest style, and the corporate logo or label, a discrete emblematic representation of the otherwise invisible white corporate godfather.

I mention *Elle*'s beige women because the fashion industry's portrayal of racial homogeneity provides an initial means for interpreting Michael Jackson who in this context emerges as the quintessential mass cultural commodity. Nowhere do we see so many apparent resolutions of social contradiction as we apprehend in Michael Jackson. If youth culture and expanding youth markets belie a society whose senior members are growing more numerous, more impoverished, more marginal, then Michael Jackson as the ageless child of 30 represents a solution to ageing. If ours is a sexist society, then Michael Jackson, who expresses both femininity and masculinity but fails to generate the threat or fear generally associated with androgyny, supplies a resolution to society's sexual inequality. If ours is a racist society, then Michael Jackson, who articulates whiteness and blackness as surgical rather than cultural identities, offers an easy solution to racial conflict.

Recently I was struck when Benson, on the television show by the same name, remarked that Michael Jackson looked like Diana Ross. The show confirmed what popular opinion has been saying for some time. The comparison of Michael Jackson to Diana Ross is particularly astute when we see Jackson both as a 'look' and as a music statement. Rather than defining Michael Jackson in relation to the black male music tradition, I think it makes more sense to evaluate his music with respect to black women singers – and to go much further back than Diana Ross to the great blues singers like 'Ma' Rainey, Bessie Smith, and Ethel Waters. Diana Ross and the Motown sound is in many ways the mass cultural cancellation of the threatening remembrance of 'ladies who really did sing the blues'. In a path-breaking essay on the sexual politics of the blues, Hazel Carby shows how the black women blues singers attacked patriarchy by affirming women's right to mobility and sexual independence.[26] Getting out of town and out from under a misbehaving man, refusing to be cooped up in the house and taking the initiative in sexual relations – these are the oft-repeated themes of the black female blues tradition. By comparison, the incessant chant style developed by 'Diana Ross and the Supremes' features refrains aimed at the containment of women's desire and the acceptance of victimization. Background percussion that delivers a chain-like sound reminiscent of slavery is an apt instrumental metaphor for lyrics such as 'My world is empty without you, Babe', 'I need your love, Oh, how I need your love'. By physically transforming himself into a Diana Ross look-alike, Michael Jackson situates himself in the tradition of black women's blues. The thematic concerns of his music often take up the question and consequences of being sexually renegade, i.e. 'bad'; however, Jackson ultimately represents the black male reversal of all that was threatening to patriarchy in black women's blues music. Where the black women singers affirmed the right to self-determination, both economically and sexually, Jackson taunts that he is 'bad' but asks for punishment. Jackson toys with the hostility associated with sexual oppression, but, rather than unleashing it, he calls for the reassertion of a patriarchal form of authority.

This does not, however, exhaust the question of Michael Jackson. As the most successful Afro-American in the mass culture industry, Jackson begs us to consider whether he represents a successful expression of Afro-American culture in mass form. To begin to answer this question we need to go back to the notion of the commodity and recognize that above all else Michael Jackson is the consummate expression of the commodity form. Fredric Jameson offers one way of understanding Michael Jackson as a commodity when he defines the contradictory function of repetition.[27] On the one hand, repetition evokes the endlessly reproducible and degraded commodity form itself. Jameson demonstrates how mass culture, through the production of numerous genres, forms, and styles, attempts to create the notion of newness, uniqueness, or originality. What's contradictory about repetition is that while we shun it for the haunting reminder of commodity seriality, we also seek it out. This, Jameson sees, is especially the case in popular music, where a single piece of music hardly means anything to us the first time we hear it, but comes to be associated with enjoyment and to take on personal meanings through subsequent listenings. This is because 'the pop single, by means of repetition, insensibly becomes part of the existential fabric of our own lives, so that what we listen to is ourselves, our own previous auditions'.[28]

From this point of view, we might be tempted to interpret Michael Jackson's numerous physical transformations as analogous to Ford's yearly production of its 'new' models. Jackson produces a new version of himself for each concert tour or album release. The notion of a 'new identity' is certainly not original with Jackson. However, the mode of his transformations and its implications define a striking difference between Michael Jackson and any previous performer's use of identity change. This is particularly true with respect to David Bowie, whose transformations from Ziggy Stardust to The Thin White Duke were enacted as artifice. Concocted out of make-up and fashion, Bowie's identities enjoyed the precarious reality of mask and costume. The insubstantial nature of Bowie's identities, coupled with their

154

theatricality, were, then, the bases for generating disconcerting social commentary. For Jackson, on the other hand, each new identity is the result of surgical technology. Rather than a progressively developing and maturing public figure who erupts into the social fabric newly made up to make a new statement, Jackson produces each new Jackson as a simulacrum of himself whose moment of appearance signals the immediate denial of the previous Michael Jackson. Rather than making a social statement, Jackson states himself as a commodity. As a final observation, and this is in line with Jameson's thoughts on repetition, I would say that the 'original' Michael Jackson, the small boy who sang with the 'Jackson Five', also becomes a commodified identity with respect to the subsequent Michael Jacksons. In Jameson's words, 'the first time event is by definition not a repetition of anything: it is then reconverted into repetition the second time around'.[29] The Michael Jackson of the 'Jackson Five' becomes 'retroactively'[30] a simulacrum once the chain of Jackson simulacra comes into being. Such a reading is a devastating cancellation of the desire for black expression in mass culture that Toni Morrison set in motion when she asked us to imagine Claudia dancing in the movies with Bojangles. This interpretation sees the commodity form as the denial of difference. All moments and modes are merely incorporated in its infinite seriality.

Commodity seriality negates the explosive potential inherent in transformation, but transformation, as it is represented culturally, need not only be seen as an expression of commodity seriality. In the black American entertainment tradition, the original metaphor for transformation, which is also a source for Michael Jackson's use of identity change, is the blackface worn by nineteenth-century minstrel performers. When, in 1829, Thomas Dartmouth Rice, a white man, blacked his face and jumped 'Jim Crow' for the first time, he set in motion one of the most popular entertainment forms of the nineteenth century. By the late 1840s, the Christy Minstrels had defined many of the standard routines and characters, including the cake walk and the Tambo and Bones figures that are synonymous with minstrelsy. In the 1850s and 1860s hundreds of minstrel troupes were touring the American states, generally on a New York-Ohio axis. Some even journeyed to London where they were equally successful. By the 1880s and 1890s there were far fewer troupes, but the shows put on by the few remaining companies expanded into mammoth extravaganzas, such as those mounted by the Mastodon Minstrels.

Broadly speaking, the minstrel shows portrayed blacks as the 'folk', a population wholly formed under a paternalistic southern plantation system. They were shown to be backward and downright simple-minded; they were lazy, fun-loving, and foolish; given to philandering, gambling, and dancing; they were victimized, made the brunt of slapstick humour and lewd jokes. The men were 'pussy whipped' and the women were liars, cheats, and flirts. No wonder the minstrel shows have been so roundly condemned by Afro-American intellectuals, including Nathan Huggins for whom the most crippling aspect of minstrelsy is the way its popularity prevented the formation of an alternative 'Negro ethnic theater'.[31] Nevertheless, a few critics have advanced the notion that minstrelsy represents a nascent form of people's culture, whose oblique – albeit distorted – reference to real plantation culture cannot be denied.[32] What's interesting is that neither position in this debate seems adequate to explain why blacks performed in minstrel shows; and why, when they did so, they too blacked their faces with burnt cork and exaggerated the shape of their lips and eyes. If the shows promoted the debasement of blacks, can black participation in them be explained by their immense popularity, or the opportunity the shows provided to blacks in entertainment, or the money a performer might make? If the shows were an early form of people's theatre, was it, then, necessary for blacks in them to reiterate the racist stereotyping that blackface signified?

An initial response to these questions is provided by Burt Williams, one of the most famous black actors in this century, who joined the Ziegfeld Follies against the protests of the entire white cast. Williams proved incredibly successful, earning up to $2,500 a week. Nevertheless, he chose throughout his career to perform in blackface. In their anthology of black theatre, James Hatch and Ted Shine suggest that blackface was for Burt Williams 'a badge of his trade, a disguise from which to work, and a positive reminder to his audience that he was a black man'.[33] These explanations get at the motives behind Burt Williams's choice, but I suggest that we consider blackface as something more than a disguise or mask, and apprehend it, instead, as a metaphor that functions in two systems of meanings. On the one hand, it is the overt embodiment of the southern racist stereotyping of blacks; but as a theatrical form, blackface is a metaphor of the commodity. It is the sign of what people paid to see. It is the image consumed and it is the site of the actor's estrangement from self into role. Blackface is a trademark and as such it can be either full or empty of meaning.

156

In his comprehensive study on minstrelsy, Eric Lott interprets blackface in terms of race and gender relations.[34] He describes it as the site where all sorts of dissimulations and transformations take place that have their origin in social tensions. In blackface, white men portrayed black men. Black men portrayed white men portraying black men; and men, both black and white, became female impersonators and acted the 'wench'. Audiences enjoyed flirting with the notion of actually seeing a black man on stage, when such was generally not allowed. And they enjoyed the implications of seeing men put themselves in the bodies of women so as to enact sexual affairs with other men. Blackface allowed the transgression of sexual roles and gender definitions even while it disavowed its occurrence. As Eric Lott points out, minstrelsy was highly inflected with the desire to assume the power of the 'other', even while such power is being denigrated and denied. As he puts it, minstrelsy was 'a derisive celebration of the power of blacks' (and I would add, women, too) which is contained within the authority of the white male performer. So, on the one hand, blackface is heavily laden with overt racist and sexist messages; but, on the other hand, it is hollowed of social meanings and restraints. This makes blackface a site where the fear of miscegenation can be both expressed and managed, where misogyny can be affirmed and denied, and where race and gender can be stereotyped and transgressed.

The contradictory meanings of minstrelsy offer another way of looking at Michael Jackson who from this perspective emerges as the embodiment of blackface. His physical transformations are his trademark – a means for bringing all the sexual tensions and social contradictions present in blackface into a contemporary form. From this perspective, Jackson's artistic antecedent is not Diana Ross or even Burt Williams, but the great black dancer Juba, who electrified white audiences with a kinetic skill that had people seeing his body turned back to front, his legs turned left to right. While Juba performed in blackface, his body was for him yet a more personal means for generating parody and ironic self-dissimulation. Juba's 'Imitation Dance' offered his highly perfected rendition of each of the blackfaced white actors who had defined a particular breakdown dance, as well as an imitation of himself dancing his own consummate version of breakdown. This is the tradition that best defines Michael Jackson's 1989 feature-length video, *Moonwalker*. Here, Jackson includes video versions of himself as a child singing and dancing the Motown equivalent of breakdown; then ricochets this 'real' image of himself off the image of a contemporary child impersonator who imitates Jackson in dress, face, song, and dance; and, finally, bounces these versions off a dozen or so other memorable Jackson images – his teen years, Captain EO – which are preserved on video and appear like so many Jackson personae or masks. In fading from one version of Jackson to the next, or splicing one Jackson against another, *Moonwalker* represents transformation as formalized content. Not surprisingly, most of the stories on the video are about transformation – a theme stunningly aided by the magic of every cinematic special effect currently available.

In opening her analysis of the sambo and minstrel figures, Sylvia Wynter states that the 'imperative task' of black culture is 'transformation'.[35] Wynter's optimistic account of the power of stigmatized black and popular culture to create a system of subversive counter-meanings leads her to see minstrelsy as the place where black culture 'began the cultural subversion of the normative bourgeois American reality'.[36] Michael Jackson's *Moonwalker* opens with the desire for equally sweeping social change. The initial piece, 'Man in the Mirror', surveys the faces of the world's disinherited, vanquished, and famished people, along with their often martyred benefactors – Gandhi, Mother Teresa, the Kennedy brothers, Martin Luther King, – against whom are counterposed the images of fascist oppressors from Hitler to the Klan. The message of the song, hammered home to the beat of the refrain, is if you want to change the world, begin with the 'Man in the Mirror'. That the desire for social change is deflected into multitudinous self-transformations is to varying degrees the substance of all the video narratives assembled in *Moonwalker*. Two of these specifically demonstrate how blackface is redefined in the rubric of contemporary commodity culture.

In 'Smooth Criminal', the grease and burnt cork that turned the minstrel artist into 'Jim Crow' or 'Zip Coon' are replaced by the metallic shell and electronic circuitry that turn Michael Jackson into a larger than life transformer robot. The story has Michael Jackson pitted against a depraved white drug lord bent on taking over the world by turning all young children (white, black; boys and girls) into addicts. The drug lord is aided by an army of gestapo-style troops, reminiscent of the storm-troopers from *Star Wars*. At the story's climactic moment, the army encircles Jackson, trapping him in the depths of their drug factory hide-away. Writhing on the floor under a relentless spotlight, completely surrounded by the faceless army,

158

Michael Jackson is caught in a setting that dramatically summons up a parallel image: the rock star, alone on the stage in an immense stadium where he is besieged by a wall of faceless fans. The emblematic similarity between the story of persecution and subjugation and the experience of rock stardom establishes a connection to the minstrel tradition where the theatre was the site for enacting the forms of domination and their potential transformation.

Jackson's submission to the forces of domination is broken when the drug lord begins to beat a little girl whom he has kidnapped and whose cries push Jackson to the brink of superhuman action. Suddenly, Jackson's face, already tightly stretched over surgically sculpted bones, becomes even more taut; indeed, metallic. His eyes lose their pupils, glow, and become lasers. Jackson rises and a control box pops out of his stomach. His feet and arms sprout weapons. Michael Jackson is a robot. The transformation makes a stunning commentary on all Jackson's real-life physical transformations that *Moonwalker* cites; and suggests that robotics is the logical next step in medical technology's reshaping of the human body.

However, the most powerful implication of Jackson's transformation – one that every child will grasp – is that Michael Jackson has made himself into a commodity. He is not a generic robot, but specifically a transformer. This, Jackson demonstrates when he subsequently transforms himself from robot warrior into an armed space vehicle. In this shape, he ultimately vanquishes the drug lord. Jackson's assimilation to transformer includes the erasure of gender traits simultaneous with the assumption of absolute male sexual potency. The transformer represents industrial technology in commodity form. If in this country, industry and the market are controlled by a largely white male hierarchy, then Jackson's transformation figurally raises the question of social power relationships. The question is whether Jackson, in becoming a transformer, appropriates an image associated with white male economic and sexual domination, or whether he has been assimilated to the image. Is this a case of usurping power; or has Jackson, as 'other', merely been absorbed? Another way to look at this question is to ask if the appropriation of the commodity form is in any way analogous to previous instances where blacks have appropriated white cultural forms. We might substitute religion for the commodity and ask some of the same questions. Has religion, commencing with colonization and the slave trade, functioned as an ideological arm of white domination; or does the appropriation of religion by the black church represent the reverse of colonization where blacks denied salvation claimed God for their own? We are back to the dilemma that I initially posed with reference to Toni Morrison, who might well argue that the transformer represents a form of colonization even more dehumanizing than that embodied by the blue-eyed Pecola because in it race and gender are wholly erased. In contrast, Kobena Mercer might be tempted to see the transformer as today's equivalent of the conk.

As if in response, and to consider the commodity from yet another angle, Michael Jackson enacts another parable of transformation. In 'Speed Demon', the video wizards employ the magic of claymation to turn Michael Jackson into a Brer Rabbit figure, whose invisible popular culture referent is, of course, Gumby. 'He was once a little green blob of clay, but you should see what Gumby can do today.' This is a refrain familiar to childhood TV audiences of the early 1970s. The song is about transformation from blob of clay to boy, making Gumby a proto-transformer. Indeed, Gumby's boyish degendering corresponds with the erasure of gender traits that we see in the transformers. His body absolutely smooth and malleable, Gumby's only noticeable features are his big eyes and rubbery mouth. If gender is de-emphasized, Gumby's green hue suggests possible racial otherness. Bear in mind that Gumby coincides with the advent of *Sesame Street* where multiracial and multicultural neighbourhoods are depicted by collections of multicoloured humans, monsters, and animals. Purple, yellow, green, and blue are the colours of *Sesame Street*'s Rainbow Coalition.

'Speed Demon' reworks the themes of pursuit and entrapment in a theatrical setting that parallels, although in a more light-hearted way, the portrayal of these themes in the transformer script. In this case Michael Jackson is pursued by overly zealous fans, who, during the course of a movie studio tour, recognize Michael Jackson and chase him through various lots and sound stages. The fans are grotesquely depicted as clay animations with horribly gesticulating faces and lumpy bodies. At one point Jackson appears to be cornered by a host of frenzied fans, but manages to slip into a vast wardrobe building where he discovers a full head mask of a rather goofy but sly-looking rabbit. At this point, Jackson undergoes claymation transformation. This completely redefines the terms of his relationship to his pursuers. Claymation turns Michael Jackson into a motor-cycle-riding Brer Rabbit, the trickster of the Afro-American folk tradition who toys with the oppressors, outsmarts them, outmanoeuvres them – and with glee! The Speed Demon is Gumby, he is Brer Rabbit, and he is also most definitely Michael Jackson, whose 'wet curl' look caps the clay head of the rabbit, and whose trademark dance, the 'moonwalk', is the rabbit's particular forte.

At the tale's conclusion, Michael, having eluded his pursuers, greets the sunrise in the Californian desert. Here he removes the rabbit disguise, which at this point is not the claymation body double but a simple mask and costume that Jackson unzips and steps out of. But lo and behold, the discarded costume takes on a life of its own and becomes a man-sized, moonwalking rabbit who challenges Jackson to a dancing duel. In a video rife with transformations and doublings, this is the defining instance. In dance, the vernacular of black cultural expression, the conflict between the artist and his exaggerated, folksy, blackface *alter ego* is enacted.[37] Like Juba dancing an imitation of himself, Michael Jackson separates himself from his blackface and out-moonwalks the commodity form of himself.

In posing transformation as the site where the desire for black cultural autonomy coincides with the fetishization of commodity capitalism, *Moonwalker* denies commodity seriality. Instead, it defines the commodity form in the tradition of blackface as the nexus of struggle. The cultural commodity is not neutral, but instead defines a zone of contention where the terms of cultural definition have been largely determined by the white male dominated system of capitalist production, and reified by the fetishizing nature of the commodity itself.

In my accounts of 'Smooth Criminal' and 'Speed Demon', I suggest that some commodity manifestations provide more room for counter-statements than others. The transformers are so closely associated with high-tech capitalism that they offer little opening other than the ambiguity of over-appropriation versus assimilation. By comparison, the complex relationship between Gumby, Brer Rabbit, and Michael Jackson creates a space where the collision between black vernacular and mass media forms suggests the subversion of domination. 'Speed Demon' deconstructs the commodity form; and with it, Michael Jackson as well, who by the end of the video emerges as a multiple subject reflected back from a dozen commodified mirror images. *Moonwalker* engages commodity fetishism and opens up the commodity form, but does it provide a platform for the emergence of what Stuart Hall calls the 'concrete historical subject'?[38] Is there a

Meridian in this text, capable of discovering a self out of the social fragments and conflicts? Can anything approaching the autonomous subject be discerned in this text? *Moonwalker* suggests a split between contemporary black women's fiction, which strives to create images of social wholeness based on the rejection of commodity capitalism, and what seems to be a black male position which sees the commodity as something that can be played with and enjoyed or subverted. Where Michael Jackson tricks the commodity form, and is able to do so precisely because its meanings are fetishized and therefore not culturally specific, Alice Walker refuses commodity fetishism and, in *The Color Purple*, imagines a form of cottage industry that has Celie organizing the collective production of customized pants for her extended community of family and friends. Jackson reaches back into the culture industry to minstrelsy and seizes blackface, updates it in contemporary forms, and unites himself with the history of black male actors who were made and unmade by their relationship to the commodity. Contrarywise, Alice Walker looks back upon commodity production, sees its earliest manifestation in the 'slops' produced for slaves,[39] its continuation in the fashion industry that destroyed Morrison's Hagar, and summarily denies the possibility of the mass-produced commodity as having anything to offer Afro-Americans.

MINSTRELS: THE DISNEY VERSION

If, as a cultural commodity, Michael Jackson occasionally opens the commodity form to reveal its contradictory subtexts, this is not necessarily the case in the culture industry as a whole. Indeed, it is a rarity. Most often, the commodity effaces contradiction by compressing its varied and potentially contradictory subtexts into a single homogenized and ahistorical form. To demonstrate what I mean, and to underscore the potentially radical discontinuities that Michael Jackson articulates in *Moonwalker*, I want to cite another figure from mass culture who is even more popular than Michael Jackson and who embodies the compression of contradiction in commodity form. I am referring to Mickey Mouse. The scandalous point I want to make is that Mickey Mouse is black; indeed, a minstrel performer. Of course, at the same time, he is quite simply Mickey Mouse, the most famous cultural icon, born of Walt Disney's entrepreneurial genius and, as a commodity, laundered of all possible social and historical associations. Nevertheless, the original Mickey Mouse was often portrayed dancing an erratic jig: animation's version of what it must have been like to jump 'Jim Crow'. Then too, the escapades and narrow escapes that typify Mickey's early cartoons closely resemble those found in the 'pickaninny' cartoons from the same and a somewhat later period. In fact, Mickey's physical features – scrawny black body, big head, big mouth – differ from those of the 'pickaninny' only in the substitution of big ears for kinky hair. The 'pickaninny' cartoons invariably showed a black baby being chased and swallowed by alligators, hippos, lions, and other beasts with cavernous mouths. These are the sight gags that Mickey Mouse reverses in his debut film, *Steamboat Willie*. Instead of being swallowed, Mickey beats a tune out of a cow's teeth and twangs a goat's tongue. Significantly, the tune is 'Turkey in the Straw', a melody originally sung by George Washington Dixon, an early blackface performer.

The fact that I can tease out references to minstrels in *Steamboat Willie* and establish comparisons between Mickey, whose black body is not stated as a signifier of race, and the 'pickaninnies', whose black bodies signified race, testifies to the partial iconographic commodification of the 1929 version of Mickey Mouse. I doubt any of these buried referents can be brought out of the bland, big-cheeked Mickey of the 1960s, whose morphological development from rat to baby-faced mouse is the subject of an interesting essay by the popular science writer, Stephen J. Gould.[40] Nevertheless, submerged references to minstrelsy were evoked as late as the 1950s by two other cartoon figures: Heckle and Jeckle, a pair of magpies whose plumes are the naturalized equivalent of the black tail-feathers that Burt Williams wore to emphasize racist stereotyping. There is yet another buried minstrel subtext in the depiction of Heckle and Jeckle. In their particular magpie loquaciousness, the way the birds practise verbal one-upmanship, Heckle and Jeckle re-create two stock minstrel figures: Mr Tambo and Mr Bones. Where Heckle and Jeckle are invariably shown perched on a branch and 'signifying' at each other, Tambo and Bones stood at opposite ends of the minstrel line of players. From these positions, they bantered back and forth through the straw dog mediator: the 'interlocutor'. By its very nature, the commodity form – and particularly the mass media commodity as compared to earlier forms of commodified entertainment – reduces the historical specificity of its referential material and combines a tremendous array of cultural sources. Besides being minstrel players, Heckle and Jeckle are also Jekyll and Hyde. And finally, they are simply Heckle and Jeckle, two magpies invented by Terry Toons.

The advent of cultural icons such as Mickey Mouse and Heckle and Jeckle signals the moment when it is no longer possible to distinguish the historical subtexts at the point of consumption. Mickey Mouse came to the screen some twenty to thirty years after the height of the minstrel tradition. Indeed, as a cultural commodity, Mickey Mouse is finally not black. He is precisely the cancellation of the black cultural subtext, and quite possibly the 'retroactive' eradication of the original minstrel performer who jumped 'Jim Crow' to the tune of 'Turkey in the Straw'. This first-time event, now apprehended from the cultural moment defined by Mickey Mouse, is, then redefined as a simulacrum of the Disney tradition.

We might unwrap and unpack all our homogenized commodity icons as I have done with Mickey Mouse in order to reveal how each and every one compresses and negates social contradictions. However, the deconstruction of commodities is not a transformation of the social and economic inequalities inherent in commodity capitalism. Or, like Toni Morrison and Alice Walker, we might reject the commodity for its reification of human qualities and cancellation of cultural difference; and attempt, as they do in their novels, to imagine Utopian social relationships. Such a strategy has the potential to estrange the racism and sexism that are internalized in relationships, so that these can be apprehended critically. However, this approach risks essentializing, if not blackness, then a rural over an urban experience or a prior historical period such as the 1930s or 1940s over the present. Or, like Michael Jackson, we might fully assume the commodity and, with every act of cultural statement, stake the risk of absolute reification against the possibility of generating transcendent cultural images. This approach fully relinquishes a connection to the social for the sake of developing control over the image as a commodity. All these strategies are partialities, and can only be so, in a system where the totalizing factor is the commodity form.

NOTES

1 T. Morrison, *The Bluest Eye* (Washington Square Press, 1970), 19.
2 *Ibid.*, 1.
3 *Ibid.*, 20.
4 *Ibid.*, 22.

[5] *Ibid.*

[6] *Ibid.*

[7] *Ibid.*

[8] *Ibid.*, 9.

[9] *Ibid.*

[10] *Ibid.*, 52.

[11] *Ibid.*

[12] *Ibid.*, 53.

[13] *Ibid.*

[14] B. Kruger, *Untitled* (1987).

[15] T. Morrison, *Song of Solomon* (New American Library, 1977), 12.

[16] *Ibid.*, 256.

[17] *Ibid.*, 319.

[18] *Ibid.*, 310.

[19] *Ibid.*, 318.

[20] *Ibid.*

[21] *Ibid.*

[22] K. Mercer, 'Black hair/style politics', *New Formations*, 3 (Winter 1987), 33-54.

[23] *Ibid.*

[24] *Ibid.*, 49.

[25] b. hooks, 'Overcoming white supremacy', *Zeta* (January 1988), 24.

[26] H. Carby, 'Sometimes it jus bes dat way', *Radical America*, 20, 4 (June/July 1986), 9-22.

[27] F. Jameson, 'Reification and Utopia in mass culture', *Social Text*, 1 (Winter 1979), 135-48.

[28] *Ibid.*, 138.

[29] *Ibid.*, 137.

[30] *Ibid.*

[31] N. I. Huggins, *Harlem Renaissance* (Oxford University Press, 1971), 286.

[32] E. Lott, 'Blackface and blackness: politics of early minstrelsy', American Studies Association Convention, Miami 1988.

[33] J. V. Hatch (ed.) and T. Shine (consultant), *Black Theater USA* (Macmillan, 1974), 618.

[34] Lott, *op. cit.*

[35] S. Wynter, 149.

[36] *Ibid.*, 155.

[37] Dick Hebdige develops the cultural politics of black vernacular with reference to Jamaican music in *Cut 'n Mix* (Routledge, Chapman & Hall, 1987).

[38] S. Hall, 'On postmodernism and articulation', *Journal of Communication Inquiry*, 1, 2 (Summer 1986), 45-60.

[39] S. Ewen and E. Ewen, *Channels of Desire* (McGraw-Hill, 1982), 167.

[40] S. J. Gould, *The Panda's Thumb* (Norton, 1982).

The Vicissitudes of 'Progressive Television'

Ien Ang

If there is ever to be an American television industry that aims to do something different, to challenge us rather than hook us and fawn on us and condescend to us, it would have to come because publics organize to insist on it, in part at least out of a felt need and desire to create a public domain where citizens can feel empowered to transact public affairs.[1]

This is part of how Todd Gitlin rounds off his *Inside Prime Time*, a celebrated study of the inside world of American network television. The quote reveals the position from which Gitlin has approached the industry: on the one hand, that of the critical outsider (the networks are 'them'), on the other hand, that of the representative of 'us', those who are hooked, fawned on and condescended to. Gitlin's tone is an indignant, albeit somewhat tired one. Like so many progressives, he demonstrates an intense discontent with the social and cultural outcome of the greedy commercialism of American television and opts for another, different television – one that is at least 'more intelligent, complicated, true, beautiful, or public-spirited'.[2] The ideal, then, is a television that tries 'to stimulate us to thought, or inspire us to belief, or remind us of what it is to be human and live on the earth late in the twentieth century'.[3]

Although Gitlin leaves no doubt that the American commercial model of television production cannot possibly meet his ideal of progressive television – *Inside Prime Time* gives us an almost cynical account of the networks' endless, obsessive attempts to 'hook' – it remains less clear how alternatives should be brought about. In the end, Gitlin can do nothing else but resort to the image of (and hope for) a better audience, that will act as 'publics [who] organize to insist on it'. Typically, *Inside Prime Time*'s very last sentence is a rather rueful quote from Walt Whitman: 'To have great poets there must be great audiences, too'.[4] In other words, it is the absence of an active and engaged public life that, in Gitlin's vision, is the ultimate background of the deplorable state of American television culture. But the diagnosis can also be extended to a more international plane. According to Gitlin, another economic and institutional set-up of broadcast television does not suffice:

> By itself, the formal structure of a noncommercial television system along European lines wouldn't accomplish all that much; the mass-marketing mentality pervades much of noncommercial television to almost the same degree as in America, though without the compulsion of the profit motive.[5]

So it is up to 'us': only by our refusing a positioning as television consumers and by our taking up the role of active, committed citizens could an ideal, progressive television begin to be developed. This is a rather bold appeal and also, I would add, an amazingly awkward one. For who is this amorphous 'we' Gitlin is speaking for? And how are 'we' supposed to attain the energy and motivation to perform the task, if the very condition for it (a lively public sphere) is lacking? It is the voluntarism implied in the appeal that makes it sound so awesome and daunting.

In this article, I will try to unravel some of the dilemmas and difficulties of the project of 'progressive television', to which Gitlin bears witness. By the project of 'progressive television' I mean all those critical concerns and pursuits, in theory and practice, that aim at changing television as a cultural form and political apparatus, based upon a shared rejection of dominant or mainstream television as conservative to all intents and purposes.[6] I will restrict myself here to the case of broadcast television, that hegemonic institutional organization of television that is characterized, in the words of Raymond Williams, by centralized transmission and privatized reception.[7] Many attempts to create 'progressive television' are of course made outside the parameters of broadcasting, but it seems to me that these should be analysed and evaluated in a different context – they do not pose a challenge to the large-scale practices of broadcast television. It is the limits of the broadcasting model that will be at issue here.

Of course, it would not be fair to consider Gitlin's formulations as a fully-fledged proposal for the arrangement of a 'progressive television'. After all, this was not his ambition in *Inside Prime Time* at all.[8] But the very awkwardness of the book's epilogue – from which the quotes above have been taken – reveals the more general unease that confronts critical observers who not only want to analyse and criticize the television we have, but also aim to construct visions of a television we could have. As with every utopian perspective, the precise substance of this other television remains elusive. It is mostly defined in negative terms, by what it should *not* be. Thus, whereas, according to Gitlin, 'weightless images' reign supreme in American commercial television, most critics would agree that 'progressive television' should amount to something, that it should have some wider social, political and cultural relevance. *Inside Prime Time*'s epilogue should perhaps be read, therefore, less as a contribution to the outlining of the substance of a 'progressive television', than as a narrative which is not only one motivated by desire for a television whose functioning is totally different from dominant television, but also one whose narrator seems to claim to speak on behalf and for the benefit of the whole audience, 'all of us'. If I understand Gitlin correctly, his ideal is a television that would not only result in the production and transmission of entirely different programmes, but one which would also culminate in a completely altered positioning of the audience: as subject rather than object, as publics rather than consumers.

A rather peculiar model for a politics of 'progressive television' emerges here. It is 'revolutionary' in that it is based upon a radical opposition between 'dominant television' and 'progressive television', upon an absolute certainty that commercial television will always ultimately be condescending, and, what's more, reproduce bourgeois hegemony.[9] From this point of view, a politics of 'progressive television' can be conceptualized in no other way than from a 'vanguardist' position. Particularly striking is the missionary and teleological character of its aims: it seeks to transgress the boundaries of dominant television by proposing a wholly new constellation of television production and consumption.[10]

A totalizing vision characterizes this conceptualization of 'progressive television'. It is premised upon the assumption that universal standards are possible according to which a new television culture could be designed. It is driven by an ethos of emancipation, democratic participation, 'civilization'.

It is clear that such a comprehensive 'cultural revolution' is hard to imagine, let alone realize. What does it mean, for example, to expect television to stimulate thought and inspire belief, thereby contributing to the strengthening and enlivening of the public sphere, as Gitlin would have it? How might 'progressive television' help realize this Habermas-orientated social utopia? In relation to this, I would suggest, the position of the audience becomes a central issue. As there seems to be no doubt that the 'we' that would be prepared to take up the challenge will be only a rather small section of the population, must it be 'our' task to convince 'the others' to join the project? In other words, should television viewers be educated to become the 'great audiences' Whitman pondered about? Should they learn to resist being hooked, fawned on and condescended to?

I may have pushed Gitlin's notes too far. I have done this, however, in order to get a clearer picture of the implicit scheme that is often at work in critiques of dominant, commercial television. A perfect future alternative is evoked before which the television we have loses all lustre. A complete rupture between ideal and reality is therefore created -- a typical case of utopian thinking.

But whereas such a distant, utopian stance could easily be maintained when one remains in the position of the critical outsider, it is far more problematical to conceive it as a basis for concrete action. To confront the existing arrangement of television culture, a politics of progressive television cannot indulge in utopianism. It has to intervene in the structures in which that culture is currently produced. For one thing, broadcast television is a highly institutionalized practice and change does not seem to be possible outside some institutional context. But which one? Although there is a widely shared antipathy towards commercialism among progressives, the defence of public broadcasting is also fraught with problems.[11] As Gitlin has already noted, many public broadcasting organizations are only non-commercial in a formal sense, and are actually prone to the same preoccupation to hook as the American networks. The question, then, cannot be resolved within the debate on public versus commercial broadcasting. More important, I would suggest, is to evaluate how the ideas of 'progressive television' can be pursued within the present cultural conjuncture – a conjuncture in which the dominance of (American) commercial television, and its popularity, is ever expanding. Under these circumstances, 'progressive television' can be nothing else but a 'counter-television'. What role could utopian ideals play in this?

It is not my intention to tackle this issue in the abstract. Instead, I will be drawing upon a specific historical case that in many ways is in accordance with Gitlin's voluntaristic appeal indicated above: the setting-up of institutions by progressives themselves, who would earnestly set themselves the task of establishing 'progressive television' in some way or other.[12] I am speaking of an internationally little-known case of self-proclaimed 'progressive television', embodied by the Dutch Socialist broadcasting organization VARA. Within the general framework of Dutch public broadcasting, VARA constitutes a broadcasting practice that is more specifically set up to represent the interests and preferences of the democratic socialist current within the Dutch nation.[13] Although the position of VARA in the Dutch national context is a very specific one, which I will not go into here, more general conclusions can be drawn from its experiences. Of course, VARA's politics cannot be seen as a perfect incarnation of the utopian project outlined above. Inscribed in its aims and ideals, however, is the very rhetoric of emancipation and universalism that I find characteristic of the project. By exploring the problems VARA is confronted with in its attempts to perform its task, I hope to assess the general entanglements of this 'utopianism in practice'. As will become clear, a central issue is the very definition of the politics of 'progressive television'. It is utopian reasoning itself, I would suggest, that turns the idealized practice of 'progressive television' against itself.

INSTITUTIONALIZED PROGRESSIVISM

Throughout the sixty years of its existence, the Dutch Socialist broadcasting network VARA has been dedicated to the ideal of producing and transmitting 'progressive television' for a committed, working-class audience. VARA is one of the five oldest and largest networks within the Dutch public broadcasting system. Founded in 1925, the organization has traditionally had formal ties with the social democratic movement, such as the Labour Party and the social democratic trade unions. These ties were transformed into informal ones in the late 1960s.[14] As a consequence, VARA's basis of 'progressiveness' could no longer be considered self-evident, something that can be simply conjured up by referring to formal institutional associations with other, ideologically 'correct', political

171

organizations. VARA is now left to its own will and devices to give an expression to its self-proclaimed 'progressiveness'. It persists in its official aspiration to be a 'cultural and political instrument for progressive Netherlands'.[15] But how can this aim be accomplished? VARA has become preoccupied with the question of how to fulfil its 'mission' – to express it in VARA language. Thus, the profuse policy debates within VARA in the past fifteen years can be interpreted as resulting from heated controversies over what it means to make 'progressive television'.[16]

For example, in the early 1970s one group of VARA workers and sympathizers, mostly belonging to related leftist circles, opted for a radical socialist VARA, with a commitment to class struggle and to the strengthening of working-class consciousness, solidarity and political activism.[17] VARA programmes produced by adherents to this group typically reflected its philosophy: these were mostly radical populist documentaries in which the exploitation of the working class and other oppressed groups in capitalist society was shown and condemned.[18] Implicit in this conception of 'progressive television' is the assumption that television as a medium could be utilized as a tool for political mobilization – a hypothesis that was borrowed from Enzensberger's theory of 'emancipatory media'.[19] This option, however, criticized within VARA for its crude obtrusiveness and its consequent lack of popular appeal, was soon superseded by a more moderate current. It also called itself 'socialist', but its version of socialism was less a political than a moral one. Not class struggle, but the cultural and ethical emancipation – that is, elevation – of the people is its central aim. According to one representative of this current, it should be the task of VARA to spread Enlightenment ideals such as rationality, tolerance and human dignity among the people (working class or otherwise).[20] In connection with this goes a more modest assessment of the political potential of the television medium. Television cannot be used as an instigator for political action and social change, so it is said, it can only signal social discontents and inform the public about them. Furthermore, it is stated that VARA should perform this task by transmitting programmes that are accessible and appealing to a large audience. To make full use of the potential of broadcast television as a *mass* medium it should not only be progressive, but also popular. From this point of view, VARA's role is that of public mentor, of popular educator. It should help to endow the people with the right mentality; only then can a better, more just society be brought within reach. We need not quarrel about the ideological and political pros and cons of this formulation of the aim of 'progressive television' here; suffice it to say that it is this philosophy that still informs VARA's self-conception today.

Of course, carrying out this project is not without difficulties. But these are mostly conceived of as practical ones, having to do with the concrete pressures brought to bear upon the institution. In the last few years, for instance, VARA has opted for programming that is heavily spiced with spectacular quiz shows and popular comedies, to attract a large audience. Critics have slashed this policy with the argument that VARA has now betrayed its own 'progressive' aims and surrendered to the despised logic of the ratings. In reaction, VARA officials defend the policy by referring to its delicate position in relation to the 'commercial' networks.[21] Popular programmes are deemed necessary to beat them with their own weapons. Besides, it is argued that VARA can only be genuinely progressive if and when it manages to speak to the bulk of the common people. Giving them popular entertainment is seen as one way to increase their support for the organization, and as a first step to draw their attention to the progressive messages that are communicated in, for example, the current affairs programme. It is denied that such a strategy would pose a threat to VARA's 'progressiveness': 'It is our popularity, not our [progressive] identity that is the problem.'[22] In other words, what is at stake is VARA's survival (for which a large following is necessary), not its ideological stance.

Whatever the conflicts over the specific content given to the notion of 'progressive television' may be, the consensus over VARA's *raison d'être* as an independent broadcasting organization that should be loyal to progressive politics (however defined[23]) has never been challenged. On the contrary, this ideological commitment is a precondition for the functioning of VARA. In other words, 'progressiveness' is the key marker by which VARA attempts to construct its identity. It is used both epistemologically and rhetorically to legitimize its own existence and support. At the same time, 'progressiveness' also functions as a signifier of VARA's difference, of the way in which VARA presents itself as distinct from other broadcasting companies. The stress on difference is all the more important, as noted above, in the light of VARA's need to compete with other popular, commercially orientated networks whose programming is directed at the same sections of the audience. After all,

173

VARA wants to be progressive, and popular too. Or conversely, VARA wants to be popular, but in a progressive manner. It needs a 'progressive identity' to differentiate itself from the 'merely popular'. This is why VARA clings, at least in principle, to its self-definition as a 'leftwing popular network'.[24]

VARA, then, represents a broadcasting practice for which 'progressiveness' is its ideological 'essence'. Located within a firm institutional framework, the project of 'progressive television' seems here to possess a principally safeguarded setting, a committed custodian. In this sense, VARA could be considered as one courageous representative of 'us', actually adopting the undertaking Gitlin dreams about. However, as I have already indicated, the practical outcome is far from untroubled by ambivalences. It is hardly surprising, for instance, that the emphasis on popular entertainment in this version of 'progressive television' is so controversial. Exactly these ambivalences, however, could be seen as symptomatic of the more general problems and limits of the project. Should VARA's policy be interpreted as another surrender to the mass-marketing mentality, which according to Gitlin pervades European public broadcasting? The problem, however, is more complex and structural than this question suggests. VARA's programming dilemmas are not so much the result of pressing external forces (such as the aggressiveness of commercial competitors) or internal weaknesses (such as lack of dedication to its own aims), but should first and foremost be associated with the very definition of the project. With VARA, the utopian project of 'progressive television' has become institutionalized. Paradoxically, this 'institutional progressivism' tends to impede and inhibit the development of a fruitful conception and practice of 'progressive television'.

VICISSITUDES

For an organization like VARA, its identity/difference as a popular leftwing network constitutes its ultimate sure truth. Whatever its actual accomplishments, its intentions are 'progressive' – nobody is allowed to cast doubt upon that. As a result, progressiveness for VARA is taken for granted; it serves as imaginary source and self-defined justification for all its activities. But 'progressive television' can never be the automatic result of 'progressive' intentions. It needs much effort to construct it. Nor is VARA unaware of this. However, its self-image as 'a network with a mission' logically leads to a conception of broadcasting practice as an ideally linear process in which a pre-existent commitment is to be expressed in programming choices and decisions. The making of progressive television then tends to be defined as merely a problem of translation: a certain progressive essence, located in the intentions of the institution, has to be reflected, in some way or other, in concrete television programmes. This is a rather mechanistic conception of the production of 'progressive television', and it inevitably leads to tremendous difficulties for the institution in determining what kinds of programmes should be broadcast.[25]

Programming as instrumental to an a priori ideological substance: this is the fate of the politics of 'progressive television' when it is cast within the framework of institutionalized progressivism. Not surprisingly, the problem is most easily solved where the translation process appears to be most transparent: in the area of the journalistic. As a result, for VARA informative programmes about themes that are readily recognized as relevant for the left (Third World politics or nuclear disarmament, for example) are the ideological pointers of its programming strategy. Hence, genres like current affairs, documentaries and, in some sense, talk shows are seen to be VARA's so-called 'identity carriers' – it is in these programmes that the progressive identity of the institution is alleged to be most clearly displayed. But what about other genres? How are they conceptualized? To be sure, a large number of VARA's programmes are entertainment, but these are not seen as 'identity carriers'. They are not, in VARA's philosophy, suitable vehicles for progressive meanings – how is a progressive quiz show to be distinguished from others? These programmes are in the schedule solely to boost VARA's popularity. Entertainment is not seen as politically meaningful in itself, but as a means to get in touch with the mass audience.[26] The gap between 'identity' and 'non-identity' is resolved here by the principle that entertainment programmes should at least not be *in conflict* with VARA's identity. In selecting foreign fiction series, for example, VARA generally shuns American commercial products – somehow it is considered obvious that serials like *Dallas* would not fit VARA's identity – in favour of British and Italian serials with a more 'arty' status.[27]

In other words, VARA programmes can have two functions: they are either assigned the role of strengthening its institutional identity, or are principally designed to reach a large audience. Progressiveness and popularity are conceived as fixed entities external to each other. Both are seen as equally important for the institution, and one of the problems that preoccupies the network is finding a balance between them – a rather irksome task, which has provoked many quarrels and disputes. I don't want to go into the details of VARA's programming politics here. More important is the way that this quite 'schizophrenic' conception of television programming reveals VARA's own view of its relationship to the audience.

This relationship is characterized by a troubled fusion of paternalism and populism – an apparently contradictory attitude which indicates less a case of 'mistaken identity' than a fundamental problem inherent in institutionalized progressivism.

Like any other broadcasting network, a progressive organization needs a sense of being successful in order to be able to continue its activities. Commercial networks pragmatically defined 'success' in terms of ratings and profit. For an institution like VARA, however, notions of success must be spelled out in a more qualitative, idealistic manner: the institution's ambition to perform a 'progressive' role in society demands the belief and the presupposition that its practice will achieve something beyond the maintenance of its own position. In order to remain true to its own identity, it must thus assume a surplus of effectivity – and this effectivity cannot but be located in the specific practice concerned: broadcasting. Its programmes must be watched by the audience, but, in contrast to commercial television, this in itself is not enough. In principle, watching television is seen here as merely a means towards a larger politico-ideological end. Success, in other words, is specified as the persuasive communication of ideas, values and tastes which the institution has designated as belonging to some 'progressive world-view'. This success, of course, is a rather elusive matter, but it must always be somehow presumed and imagined in the operations of the institution. One former VARA chairman has made the issue very clear:

> Roughly speaking, we can distinguish between two sorts of networks. The first sees radio and television solely as a means of satisfying the needs of the mass audience, no matter what needs. Its highest aspiration is to please the largest common denominator of the public, without demanding any effort ... The other type of network tries to achieve specific effects with its audience. It is not satisfaction of manifest needs that is the most important, but change of patterns of needs, cultivation of discrimination, orientation towards values that go further than the

satisfaction of needs. All this demands effort.[28]

Whose effort, we could ask, and to what effect? If 'progressive television' is to be considered as an 'art of effects',[29] its target is the television audience. To put it disrespectfully, whereas commercial television delivers audiences to advertisers, 'progressive television', at least when it is constructed within the context of institutional progressivism, aims to deliver audiences to the institution's stated ideals. The difference is, of course, that for commercial networks 'any other purpose is subordinated to the larger design of keeping a sufficient number of people tuned in', as Gitlin cynically remarks,[30] whereas a 'network with a mission' (progressive or otherwise) needs to keep a sufficient number of people tuned in for it to be sufficiently effective in its idealistic, public purpose. And it is this problem, brought about by the very arrangement of the broadcasting model, that has to be solved. After all, the broadcasting situation confronts the institution with a heterogeneous, anonymous 'mass' of potential viewers, whose readiness to pay attention to the institution's mission cannot possibly be guaranteed. Thus, what comes to the fore as a central problematic here is the need to overcome the contrast between two opposing modes of addressing viewers: on the one hand, they are to be imagined as a political and moral category, a *public* to be instructed and enlightened, on the other hand, they will also inevitably be constructed as an *audience*, a category instrumental to the interests (i.e. survival) of the institution itself.[31]

Within VARA, the purport of this contradiction is expressed in its evocation of the 'ordinary people' as its target group. The 'ordinary people' is a key term in VARA discourse in that it magically resolves the ambivalences in VARA's pretensions. It serves as a statistical measure: it delimits the broad, quantitative range of the 'mass' to be reached. After all, there are so many 'ordinary people' ... These are the people that are sociologically defined as those with low income and little schooling – that is, according to VARA's wilfully optimistic calculations, 40 per cent of the Dutch population! VARA wants to work for all these people. At the same time, the 'ordinary people' are also positioned as those whom VARA wants to protect: 'the socially vulnerable' who are most susceptible to the seductions of commercial television. Of course, VARA cannot do very much, and says it does not wish to, against their watching 'violent scuffles and relationships in the lives of oil magnates'.[32] Nevertheless, it does see its ethical task as rescuing the 'ordinary people' from the threat of ongoing cultural 'proletarization' that commercial television represents. As an imaginary construct, then, the 'ordinary people' performs a magnificent reconciliatory role. It enables VARA to solve the conflict between its public mission and its need for an audience – at least on a discursive level.

Practically, however, this same construct tends to produce the mode of addressing viewers which I characterize as a blend of paternalism and populism. Paternalism is the inevitable result of VARA's pedagogic approach to viewers. Such an approach goes hand in hand with any project of 'progressive television' that starts out with a fixed idea of what is right and wrong, and VARA feels justified, obliged even, to broadcast this to the public at large. Populism, on the other hand, stems from the realization that the audience it addresses is often resistant to its pedagogic appeals. Populism, in other words, is the result of a paternalism gone astray. It is the anxious reaction of the teacher facing unwilling pupils. Populism, then, is a didactic tactic by which VARA attempts to win viewers over, to gain their sympathy, in order to be more effective in its overall pedagogic mission. Hence, VARA's chairman Marcel van Dam passionately defends its very popular, but critically scorned, comedy series *Zeg's AAA*, not only by contending that 'ordinary people' have a right to have a good laugh, but also that the programme could pull viewers into the more serious one following it.[33] This is the typical reasoning behind the sandwich formula for television scheduling.

VARA's programming dilemmas are fundamentally connected with the difficulty of keeping the two approaches in balance: too much paternalism will drive the audience off, too much populism will endanger the network's identity/difference. However it may be, though, both paternalism and populism are marked by an equally distant stance towards viewers. Both attitudes are informed by an awareness that a profound chasm has to be bridged. It would seem, then, that the relationship between television institution and viewers will necessarily tend to take on the form of an opposition between 'us' and 'them', 'them' and 'us'. So, one programme-maker gave vent to his concern about VARA's dilemma in these impassioned words:

> It is necessary for us to speak a language they understand, but with the content we deem important. We should not water down [our message] more and more until [they] are prepared to watch and listen to our

programmes; we should have the courage to be consistently educative, simple in tone and sincere in content, until even they will want us.[34]

What is painfully expressed here is a troubled mixture of self-righteousness and regret. A desired future is projected in which the opposition between 'them' and 'us' will no longer exist because all will then be part of one great community, though under one coalition: it will be under the banner of 'us'. But sadly enough this honourable utopian project encounters resistance. Eventually, the image of the 'obstinate audience'[35] looms up – an audience that does not seem to watch television 'properly', an audience that does not live up to its desired positioning of public to be enlightened, an audience that stubbornly refuses to listen to the good, 'progressive' message. Here lies the ultimate irony of institutionalized progressivism. Its aspiration to educate viewers into an enlightened public becomes conflated with an urge to transform them into a 'better audience' – better according to the institution's own standards. Motivated by its self-asserted ethical purpose, in short, the institution ends up striving for control over the television viewing practices of the people 'out there'.

At this point, the import of the mass-marketing mentality that is said to pervade the practices of European public broadcasting can be clarified. It is not just an institutional error or weakness that could be overturned by principle or choice ('our' choice). It is, I would argue, a general drift of broadcast television as such, in so far as it necessarily implies a notion of viewers as an audience whose attention has to be attracted, whose interest has to be whetted, whose favour has to be gained. The notion of audience-as-object, which is the core of marketing philosophy, can be found operating, in some way or other, in every television network, even if advanced marketing techniques are not always as widely used as in America.[36] Here, the claim to produce 'progressive television' for a public is confronted with the structural limits of broadcast television.

To repeat Raymond Williams's phrase, broadcasting formally consists of centralized transmission and privatized reception[37] – a constellation of power reminiscent of the Panopticon described by Foucault in *Discipline and Punish*. The panoptic structuring of power enables a central gaze to monitor those subjected to it, constantly forcing the latter into the position of compulsory visibility. In a similar but curiously reversed way, broadcast television is arranged in such a way as to direct attention to itself by placing itself in the privileged

179

position of permanent visibility, and complementary to this, it manoeuvres people into the position of 'compulsory' viewers, of audience. If panoptic power is exercised by making the subjects be permanently seen, broadcast television enacts a form of power based upon the principle of impelling the subjects to see, to look, to watch.[38] Considered from this perspective, the practices of television networks as agents of centralized transmission, could be seen as disciplinary methods to stimulate the watching of television according to their rules, their interests. In this light, the practice of audience measurement can be seen as a method for looking at people looking – watching subjects objectified. What is at stake, then, is the pressure towards the organization of reception. It is a *conditio sine qua non* for the arrangement of broadcast television as such: transmission presupposes a will to be received. Of course, this is by no means limited to the operations of commercial television. It is not the economic pursuit of profit that primarily conditions networks to hunt for ways of channelling viewers' behaviour; no broadcasting instance can logically escape this predicament. Thus all broadcasting systems are necessarily 'authoritarian', in so far as they are bound to strive for the management and regulation of reception.

In a sense, institutionalized progressivism is even more 'authoritarian' than a commercial network, as it doubly objectifies viewers. First, by turning them into audience, a necessary attribute for the continued existence of the institution itself. Second, because it is an 'authoritarian system with a conscience',[39] by treating viewers as pawns, as it were, to satisfy its own conscience. It is ironic, then, that the aim of mobilizing viewers for some utopian ideal ends up in a desire for audiences who are not only sympathetic, but also loyal and 'obedient'. VARA's 'ordinary people' are locked into this positioning. In other words, if the commercial context is based on the premiss of seduction to consume, the progressivist context as discussed here tends to be unsatisfied with consumption *per se*. It strives for more than that. Paradoxically, we could say that it is not just consumption but a sort of *passive* consumption that characterizes its imagined ideal viewer. Semiologically speaking, 'passive consumption' is generated when viewer decodings take place within the dominant code; that is, when the communicator's calculated message is read 'correctly'.[40] And this is exactly what the 'progressive' institution is seeking. Ideally, its ideological messages should come across undamaged and undistorted. Its effect should be persuasion, consent, affirmation. As a result, its textual politics tends to be guided by a privileging of 'closed texts', texts in which the messages (the connections between signifier and signified) are fixed and definitive, texts that leave as little space as possible open to differentiated readings.[41] This is the manipulation of the reception process taken to an extreme.

It would seem that institutionalized progressivism is trapped in a muddle of structural contradictions, which it cannot easily escape, no matter how sincere and earnest its stated aims. In its assiduous desire to realize another television, a television that would contribute to the emancipation of the people and their active participation in public life, it is finally led to construct an image of the audience – and consequently, a conception of programming – that tends to deprive it of its autonomy. In its zealous attempt to mobilize viewers, it finds itself in a field of struggle in which the politics of consumption is at stake: tragically, an original act of – perhaps sentimental but certainly well-intended – solidarity has turned into a structural antagonism, disrupting the 'progressive project' right from the inside.

BEYOND UTOPIANISM

Does all this mean that the idea of 'progressive television' is by definition doomed to failure? Not necessarily so. The case of institutionalized progressivism however, clarifies what a 'progressive' politics of television should try to circumvent.

First of all, it should take leave of a transcendental, utopian definition of 'progressiveness' – the presumption that there exists an ontological and universal progressive essence, which is seen as the dialectical negation of the 'commercial', the conservative, the hegemonic. As I have tried to show, such a starting-point of eternal truth can only lead to an obsessive preoccupation with the strengthening of the identity/difference of the originator of the project, to which all its practices are ultimately subordinated. 'Progressive television' is reduced here to an instrumental status: its task is to prove the legitimacy and effectivity of the project itself, its force is evaluated in terms of the way in which it confirms the preferred, objectifying relationship between institution and viewers. Because of its function as relay for fixed progressive values and ideas, it remains locked within 'the prison of message and meaning'.[42]

This brings us to another major drawback of institutionalized progressivism. It is all but inevitable that its commitment to the

181

institution's existential identity would conduce towards what we could call a productivist view of 'progressive television'. What it holds to be decisive is the *production* of television programmes that bear 'progressive' messages and meanings. The moments of circulation and consumption are thus not only seen as chronologically secondary, but also, ideally, as formal derivatives of the vanguard position taken up by the productive apparatus – if the project is to be pursued successfully. Here again, we see how the idea of an 'obedient' audience becomes an indispensable imperative for institutionalized progressivism. An autonomous politics of reception and consumption is beyond its scope.[43]

To escape this circular mechanism, an entirely different conception of 'progressive television' needs to be developed. This would drop the utopian search for a definite, substantial guarantee of what constitutes 'progressive television'. It would accept that 'the progressive' can never be a given ideal that transcends time and place, but is something that has to be constructed again and again, under ever-changing circumstances. A context-dependent and conjunctural notion of 'progressive television' could then be elaborated. 'Progressive television' should not be situated in a fixed, formal opposition against dominant television, but has to be seen as a temporary and local politico-cultural effect, the dynamic and overdetermined result of a specific confrontation between television and viewers, often unpredictable and seemingly accidental. A 'progressive' moment in that confrontation can take on the form of contestation, but also affirmation; resistance, but also empowerment; angry protest, but also joyful disengagement. It is difficult and probably undesirable to slot these effects, always historically specific and therefore transitory, into reassuringly all-encompassing and permanent categories such as emancipation and education. Defining 'progressive television' in this way would make it possible to take account of the specificity of broadcasting as a cultural practice: it is within the parameters of centralized transmission and privatized reception itself that moments of breakdown of hegemony should be traced.

What I am proposing is a vision of 'progressiveness' stripped of high-flown utopian connotations and, as a result, all the more sensitive, not only to the limitations, but also to the unexpected potentialities of the broadcasting framework. For instance, who can tell in advance what happens when 'the images of women constructed in glossy US soap operas collide with those daily enforced by the rituals of southern Italian catholicism'?[44] It would be absurd to expect some direct, feminist consciousness-raising here, but in some cases, under certain conditions, that collision might help to articulate female objections to traditional constructions of femininity. 'Progressive' effects such as these cannot be planned, and they will always be temporary and lost again, but that does not make them any less worthwhile.

If anything, this conception of 'progressive television' would lead us to challenge the representative certainty of universal dichotomies posed by more vanguardist definitions of pregressivism. We all get hooked by television, commercial or otherwise, we may all be fawned on, but there is no absolute dividing line between the condescending and the stimulating – as Gitlin would have it.

This does not mean that the outcome of institutionalized progressivism can never be 'progressive'. It can be, but if it is, then the role of the institution will only be an enabling rather than a determining one. As a context for production, a broadcasting institution is never more than one moment in the whole process in which a 'progressive' effect may be produced. And perhaps the 'progressive effect' will be most likely in those instances where straightforward 'progressive intentions' seem least at stake.

Let me finish with an apparently anecdotal example. In 1985, VARA had a semi-satirical programme called *Pisa*. Critics were dissatisfied: the programme's satire was, to their mind, not serious enough, too simplistic, too rude to be intelligent. In the spring of 1985, *Pisa* launched the character of Popie Jopie, a playful parody of the Pope. Week after week, Popie Jopie was shown in the most compromising and ridiculous situations – in particular, his woeful failure to bring his visit to that strange country called Holland to a dignified conclusion because of his lack of familiarity with Dutch folklore. By the time the real Pope came to visit the Netherlands (a visit that was accompanied by a grandiose amount of official attention and protection), Popie Jopie had become so popular that it played a major part in the articulation of popular discontent with the visit. The Popie Jopie song could be heard everywhere. It would be too ambitious to claim that the programme was responsible for the visit's proving to be politically less successful than hoped for and anticipated, but it certainly helped make it lose much of its haughty aura. For a short moment, the 'great audiences' were there after all.

AFTERWORD

By 1995, VARA's institutional status as a 'progressive' broadcasting organization has come increasingly under threat. In the past ten years Dutch television has, as anywhere else in the world, irrevocably changed as a result of accelarated processes of commercialization, transnationalization and fragmentation. Cable and satellite now provide audiences with a multiplicity of channels from which to choose. Consequently, the all-embracing, totalizing and comprehensive vision of 'progressiveness' which VARA claimed to embody has become increasingly difficult to sustain, if it is not obsolete. It is not at all certain whether VARA will still exist by the year 2000, given the current overall crisis of the Dutch public broadcasting system. In this sense, the demise of VARA can be seen as an instance of the slow unravelling of the great European tradition of that branch of the modernist left which sought to transform 'society' through large-scale institutional reform and intervention. In the age of global, postmodern capitalism, the possibility of realizing idealist change seems more remote than ever.

NOTES

This article was presented as a paper to the 1986 International Television Studies Conference, organized by the British Film Institute in co-operation with the Institute of Education of the University of London (London: July 1986).
[1] Todd Gitlin, *Inside Prime Time* (New York: Pantheon Books, 1985), 334.
[2] *Ibid.*
[3] *Ibid.*
[4] *Ibid.*, 335.
[5] *Ibid.*, 334-5.
[6] I use the term 'progressive' rather loosely here to refer to a politico-cultural attitude that is characterized by a leftist opposition to the dominant state of affairs in society. Terms intimately connected with 'progressive' are critical, alternative, radical, and so on. The substantial differences between these terms are not relevant here.
[7] Raymond Williams, *Television: technology and cultural form* (London: Fontana/Collins, 1974), 30.
[8] Gitlin, *op.cit.*, 334.
[9] Gitlin's Marxist background is more explicitly disclosed in some of his other work. See, for example, Todd Gitlin, 'Television's screens: hegemony in transition', in Michael W. Apple (ed.), *Cultural and Economic Reproduction in Education* (London: Routledge & Kegan Paul, 1982), 202-46.
[10] I would like to stress at this point that the politics of 'progressive television'

discussed in this article is principally directed at the institutional context of the project. It is interesting to note that the question of institutional structures has largely been absent in debates on 'progressiveness' generated in film studies in the 1970s, in which a preoccupation with the (theoretical) construction of the 'progressive text' predominated. Concerned almost entirely with the formal features of the cinematic text and the way in which the spectator is positioned by the text, 'progressiveness' was generally identified in terms of a modernist and anti-realist aesthetic. See, for a useful summary and critique of the 'progressive text' debate, Barbara Klinger, 'Cinema/ideology/criticism revisited: the progressive text', in *Screen*, 25, 1 (January/February 1984), 30-44. In the field of television, the terms of the 'progressive text' problematic can be found in the debate over Ken Loach's drama series *Days of Hope* in *Screen*. See especially the contributions of Colin Mcarthur, Colin MacCabe and John Caughie to this debate, all reprinted in Tony Bennett *et al.* (eds), *Popular Television and Film* (London: British Film Institute, 1981), 302-52. One could see the rather one-sided preoccupation of 'textual progressiveness' as the formalistic equivalence of the fetishization of institutional structures (what I will be calling 'institutionalized progressivism') I shall be criticizing here.

[11] See, for example, Nicholas Garnham, 'Public service versus the market', in *Screen*, 24, 1 (January/February 1983), 6-27; and Ian Connell, 'Commercial broadcasting and the British left', in *Screen*, 24, 6 (November/December 1983), 70-80.

[12] The setting-up of the British Channel Four could be seen as a recent example of this.

[13] I cannot go into the complicated structure and history of the Dutch broadcasting system here. See, for instance, Ien Ang, 'The battle between television and its audiences: the politics of watching television', in Philip Drummond and Richard Paterson (eds), *Television in Transition* (London: British Film Institute, 1985), esp. 258-63.

[14] I would like to stress that it is not my intention to give a complete account of VARA's history. This history could be reconstructed from many different angles and perspectives, and it would be impossible to do justice to it here. In this article, my emphasis lies in the ways in which VARA has attempted to construct its self-proclaimed 'progressiveness', particularly throughout the 1970s and early 1980s. A more comprehensive analysis of the role of VARA in social democratic cultural politics and in Dutch broadcasting history is given in Ien Ang, Paul Pennings and Ido Weijers, 'De progressieve cocktail. De VARA en sociaal-democratische identiteiten 1955-1985' (unpublished manuscript).

[15] André Kloos in a speech for the Council of the Association of VARA, 10 November 1978. In official VARA discourse, especially exemplified in internal policy notes and the like, the idea of 'progressiveness' is marked out by the extensive use of focal concepts such as 'progressive', 'democratic', 'socialist', 'emancipatory', 'solidarity', 'tolerance' and 'cultural vanguard'.

[16] Of course, television is not VARA's only field of action; it has also a radio department and it produces its own TV Guide. However, as television is seen as 'the most important mass medium', the most vehement discussions within VARA generally revolve around the issue of what to do with television.

[17] This current within VARA was organized within the Werkgroep Socialistische VARA, which was most active in the period of 1975-6.

[18] The most famous programme is *Van Onderen*, a series of radical documentaries on the world of industrial labour in contemporary capitalism, produced and transmitted between 1972 and 1974. Militant in ideological intent, overtly didactic in its mode of address and, for that matter, not very popular with the audience groups the programme was aimed at, this series became the subject of controversy over the 'correct' definition of 'progressive television' within VARA.

[19] See Hans Magnus Enzensberger, 'Constituents of a theory of the media', in Horace Newcomb (ed.), *Television: the critical view* (New York and Oxford: Oxford University Press, 1979), 462-93.

[20] See Milo Anstadt, *Op zoek naar een mentaliteit* (In search of a mentality) (Amsterdam: Wetenschappelijke Uitgeverij, 1973).

[21] See, for an account of the rise and success of popular, commercially orientated networks within the Dutch broadcasting system, Ang, 'The battle....'

[22] *De VARA in perspectief, 1984-1989* (August 1984), 23.

[23] VARA's inherited engagement with the Labour Party has meant that the social democratic version of leftwing politics and culture has remained dominant in VARA's progressivist orientation. For example, VARA's present chairman, Marcel van Dam, was Member of Parliament for the Labour Party before he accepted the new position. Furthermore, VARA's relationship with the radical left such as the Communist Party has always been a troubled and difficult one; even more so the relationship with new social movements such as feminism and the squatter's movement.

[24] The stress on popularity as asserted by VARA management is not uncontested within the organization. Some contend that striving for popularity would necessarily be incompatible with being progressive.

[25] This interpretation of VARA's programming conceptions is constructed out of a reading of several internal policy and planning statements and reports. I should like to thank the VARA administration for allowing me to peruse them.

[26] See, for example, 'Tweestromenland' (Land of two streams), an internal note of the Section for Television Variety Programmes (November 1982).

[27] According to Trees Te Nuyl, head of the Film Division until 1985, 'quality' is the most important criterion for selecting foreign films and series to be broadcast by VARA. What is quality? 'A good story, good writing, good acting', says Te Nuyl in the VARA Annual Report (1984, 60). Furthermore, she mentions several things which must be absent from chosen programmes, such as hard violence, discrimination, anti-feminism and the celebration of the right-wing establishment. All well and good, but how is one to decide whether a programme – say, *Dallas* – is anti-feminist or celebrates the rightwing establishment? It is certain that questions of textual politics are not seriously discussed within VARA. Judgements are mostly made according to received standards of 'good taste'. Among the British TV series that have been selected by Te Nuyl are *The Forsyte Saga, The Onedin Line, Man about the House, George and Mildred, Reilly – Ace of Spies* and *Jewel in the Crown*. VARA has also always been proud of having given *Coronation Street* to the ordinary people in

the early 1970s, a soap opera which, according to Te Nuyl, fits perfectly in VARA's profile as a result of its 'realism', contrary to the American soap *Peyton Place*. Still, VARA did broadcast some American shows too, such as *Macmillan and Wife, MacCloud* and *Love Boat*. The choice of the latter comedy series was heavily criticized by television critics, who contend that such American trash runs counter to VARA's identity as a progressive network.

[28] André Kloos, quoted in *Zorg om de cultuur* (Hilversum: VARA, 1983), 12.

[29] Michel Foucault, *Discipline and Punish* (Harmondsworth: Penguin, 1979), 93.

[30] Gitlin, *Inside Prime Time*, 56.

[31] See, for the distinction between 'audience' and 'public', Andrew Turow, 'Pressure groups and television entertainment', in Willard D. Rowland Jr and Bruce Watkins (eds), *Interpreting Television* (London and Beverly Hills: Sage, 1984), 142-62.

[32] *Het Totaalplan* (June 1983), 56.

[33] During a public meeting on cultural programming for television, Paradiso, Amsterdam, March 1986.

[34] Taken from a letter from one of VARA's leading programme-makers to his colleagues.

[35] The term is borrowed from Raymond A. Bauer, 'The obstinate audience: the influence process from the point of view of social communication', in Wilbur Schramm and Donald F. Brooks (eds), *The Process and Effects of Mass Communication* (Urbana Ill.: University of Illinois Press, 1971), 326-46.

[36] Cf. Denis McQuail, 'Uncertainty about the audience and the organization of mass communications', in Paul Halmos (ed.), *The Sociology of Mass Communicators* (Keele: The University of Keele, 1969), 75-84.

[37] Williams, *op.cit.*, 30.

[38] Cf. Foucault, *op.cit.* Compare also John Ellis, *Visible Fictions* (London: Routledge & Kegan Paul, 1982).

[39] Raymond Williams, *Communications* (Harmondsworth: Penguin, 1976), 131.

[40] Cf. Stuart Hall, 'Encoding/decoding', in Stuart Hall *et al.* (eds), *Culture, Media, Language* (London: Hutchinson, 1980), 128-38.

[41] Cf. Umberto Eco, *The Role of the Reader* (London: Hutchinson, 1979).

[42] Colin Mercer, 'A poverty of desire: pleasure and popular politics', in *Formations of Pleasure* (London: Routledge & Kegan Paul, 1983), 86.

[43] Cf. Hal Foster, 'For a concept of the political in contemporary art', in Hal Foster, *Recodings: art, spectacle, cultural politics* (Port Townshend, WA: Bay Press, 1985), 142.

[44] Ian Connell and Lidia Curti, 'Popular broadcasting in Italy and Britain: some issues and problems', in Drummond and Paterson, *op.cit.*, 110.

Satellite Dishes and the Landscapes of Taste

Charlotte Brunsdon

INTRODUCTION

This chapter was originally written for an interdisciplinary conference on the study of the audience held at the University of Illinois (Urbana-Champaign). In that context, where the disciplinary origins of my contribution would be seen as part of a 'Cultural Studies' grouping – as opposed to, for example, Psychology of Mass Communication, I wanted to use an analysis of a particular, historical 'taste war' to pose questions about the relation of individual audience practices to a wider social. This was, by implication, to raise questions about how we understand the 'new' small scale ethnographic studies which are coming out of research projects influenced by Cultural Studies.[1] These were not questions about the generalizability of the findings traditionally posed to this type of research, but questions about the very constitution of the social at a theoretical level. Methodologically, as Ang and Hermes (1991) point out, this is partly a problem of the construction of interpretative categories, such as class or gender, 'whose impact as a structuring principle for experience can only be conceptualized within the concrete historical context in which it is articulated' (p314).

The way I address the issue is partly through a kind of pun about the social and British public space which enables me to argue that there is a spatialization of debates about British broadcasting policy apparent in the seemingly minor public spats about the siting of satellite dishes. Focusing on an audience practice, the erection of satellite dish aerials, and the ensuing taste wars, also allows me to move away from a concentration on the verbal.

However, it is also clear that the paradigm I am using is most familiar from cultural studies sub-cultural work of the 1970s, 'resistance through rituals'.[2] This work, with its stress on the transforming agency of members of subcultures – or audiences, in its media studies incarnation – has, despite appearances, a strongly formalist element, a certain insouciance about 'content'. At a time when the expansion of satellite broadcasting has dramatized many of the issues constituting the crisis in European public service broadcasting, these paradigms for the analysis of sub-cultures fit very uneasily with debates about policy. It is this uneasy fit which retrospectively seems the most urgent subject for debate.

PART I

> 'I like to like what's better to like'.
>
> Billie (Judy Holliday) in *Born Yesterday*
> (George Cukor, 1950)

This case-study of the newspaper coverage of the erection of satellite dishes in Britain in 1989-90 offers a series of more and less implicit points of theoretical engagement with current research into the television audience. I try to show the way in which the personal tastes and preferences experienced and articulated in the domestic context to which ethnography gives us some access, while always being *personal* are always also profoundly *social*. While this issue is an acknowledged focus of ethnographic concern, it is not usually discussed in the way in which I wish to address it, but more commonly forms a site for a recognition of a certain kind of trouble for the ethnographer.[3]

Ellen Seiter (1990) discusses this lucidly in her reflection on the Tübingen/Volkswagen project 'Case study of a troubling interview'. She points to the way in which the different social statuses of those involved in the interview, as well as their contrasted approach to, and desires for, the occasion structures the interaction, and indeed could be considered the substance of the interview. Basically, the two interviewees involved do not want to offer detailed textual readings of television programmes to two university professors because of their attitudes to television in general, and their sense of what it is appropriate to discuss with professors. These views, to Seiter and Borchers' discomfort, they are happy to expound. Seiter's account directly addresses and reads this trouble in the interview, this failure to gain the data envisaged in the original research design. It is these failures, these gaps, these pauses – the moments when an interviewee changes tack in the middle of a sentence with which I am initially concerned, for these seem to me moments in which we can locate the often unconscious recognition and negotiation of cultural power, in that we see here the struggle of an individual to locate themselves in relation to already circulating discourses of taste. In Billie's words, 'to like what's better to like'.

Ang (1985) addresses this directly in her *Dallas* study, and it leads her to her formulation of the 'Ideology of Mass Culture'. It is thus that she designates the cultural attitudes with which her respondents have to negotiate when recounting the experience of watching *Dallas*. She had actively solicited this self referential reflection in the formulation of her original advertisement: 'I like watching the TV serial *Dallas* but often get odd reactions to it', and offers a sophisticated analysis of the different discursive strategies whereby her respondents' incorporate the recognition that the object of their pleasure is not culturally prestigious. As her respondents sometimes repudiate and disavow any pleasure, Ang also touches on the very complex relation of conscious and unconscious desire, something which has hardly been touched in empirical audience studies.

Janice Radway becomes concerned with the issue of readers' understanding of the cultural value of their pleasure in her 1984 study, *Reading the Romance* when she investigates the connotations of reading 'to escape' for her readers. Although they recognize that this is what they do, Radway insists: 'if given another comparable choice that does not carry the connotations of disparagement, they will choose the more favourable sounding explanation'.[4] Later she continues:

> In an effort to combat both the resentment of others and their own feelings of shame about their 'hedonist' behavior, the women have worked out a complex rationalization for romance reading that not only asserts their equal right to pleasure but also legitimates the books by linking them with values more widely approved within American culture. (90)

Although it is not her central concern, Radway gives clear accounts of the way in which romance reading is legitimated through recourse to less controversial benefits like 'learning about other countries'.

In what might be taken to be a quite similar case, the reactions of fans to *Gone with the Wind*, we find rather less tortuous work done by the women to justify and explain their pleasures. Helen Taylor (1989)

191

points to the way in which the celebrated 'legendary' status and commercial success of GWTW functions partly to legitimate her correspondents' pleasure to themselves, as well as to her. So 'what's better to like' is not generically given, although there clearly has been a historical association of feminine genres like the novel, melodrama, soap opera and romance with the downside of taste. But, as in the case of GWTW, a certain kind of success can lead to a change of category, just as different media – the novel, cinema, television – have all in their time been seen to seduce the (non-masculine) feeble-minded (Lovell 1987).

Andrew Ross (1989), in his reading of contemporary US responses to the Rosenberg letters points to a related process, when the cultural legitimacy – or otherwise – of tastes and vocabularies determines their reading so thoroughly that it can be quite invisible to researchers and commentators. He compares the relative failure of the published letters to gain the Rosenbergs any support from the erstwhile left intelligentsia with the later reception of George Jackson's letters. He argues, most persuasively, that the revelation of the intimate sensibilities of the Rosenbergs, their quotidian middle-brow tastes, and specifically, the fluctuating expressive register of Ethel Rosenberg's style, which mobilizes all her 'ordinary' cultural resources to write these (public) private letters, were profoundly embarrassing for the more mandarin tastes of (anti-Stalinist) intellectuals. The letters – indeed the lives of the Rosenbergs – were too centrally formed within a petit bourgeois aesthetic to be readable as authentic by legitimate intellectuals – unlike the authenticity incarnate of Jackson's 'otherness'. Ross's reading of the letters attempts to address what is specific to these letters, rather than what they are not, and argues for their continuing capacity 'to compromise every possible canon of "legitimate" taste' (29). Ross concludes this part of his research by arguing that it is the 'untidy problematic of lower-middle class culture' which is most neglected in cultural studies.

My case-study is the erection and reception, in England in 1989/90 of dish aerials to receive satellite television. Available figures suggest that these dishes have been overwhelmingly bought and rented by those in social classes C1 (19.3 per cent), C2 (35.3 per cent) and D (20.3 per cent).[5] The dishes, which are about 2ft across, first easily became available to the private purchaser in 1988, shortly before the launch of Rupert Murdoch's Sky television in February 1989. Cabling is the exception rather than the rule in Britain, and a different dish (the squarial) was necessary to receive British Satellite Broadcasting (BSB), the more upmarket satellite channel, which started broadcasting in May 1990.[6] There has been a certain amount of public discussion about satellite dishes, and it is on this, mainly as reported in newspapers, which I wish to concentrate. I want to argue that in this one example we see condensed a complex set of issues, including a conflict of taste codes which is illustrative of the history and status of different taste formations in Britain. The argument about who has the right to put satellite dishes where provides, if you like, a *mise-en-abyme* of current conflict about broadcasting policy in Britain (Brunsdon 1990a). More germanely for this context, it provides a site within which we can trace the vocabulary and discursive contours of 'television tastes', within which individuals experience and articulate their own preferences, which in their turn redefine, extend and reinforce the conflicting fields and their relation to each other.

Like channel selection, or programme watching, but unlike giving an account of either of these two activities, erecting a satellite dish is not necessarily a verbal activity. Buying or renting a dish can I think legitimately be read as an act which signals a desire, a connection with something that these dishes are understood to mean, or connote, or promise.[7] However, unlike channel selection, or programme watching, which are activities performed in the privacy of the home, erecting a satellite dish is done outside the home. This audience practice is, among other things, a non-verbal signifier of taste and choice – or, as an article in the *London Evening Standard* put it:

> So far in London, take-up of Sky has been slow. If, however, you actually welcome the round-the-clock rubbish being beamed out the problem is that you can't watch it discreetly.
>
> Under normal circumstances if your tastes extend no further than Neighbours, Capital Radio and Dynasty at least you can indulge yourself without the whole street knowing about it.
>
> Mark Edmonds, 'Fright on the Tiles' (12 July 1989), 23

This passage uses a structure common in discussion of taste, one which is present in the negotiations with the researchers in work I have cited earlier. This is a distinction between a private and a public taste, an indoors slippers and dressing gown and a Sunday Best of taste. The invocation of a known hierarchy of 'what's better to like', from which ordinary mortals fall away. For this writer, the problem for those who like 'round-the-clock' rubbish from space is that they can no longer indulge secretly.

However, this private/public distinction can work more than one way with satellite dishes – people can have quite different attitudes to acknowledged hierarchies of taste. Ondina Fachel Leal (1990) uses the idea of the television 'entourage' to discuss the customary decoration of the television set in Brazilian homes. In fact, as her work shows, the notion of the entourage – the doilies, plastic flowers, photographs of loved ones carefully arranged on the television set – is appropriate only in the case of lower-class homes. The upper classes, instead of decorating and celebrating the television, enshrining it as the centre of family life, often give it a room of its own, and always leave it unembellished in its techno-austerity. The case of satellite dishes, and the question of their siting, has similarities with the creation, or not, of a television entourage, but also substantial differences. Leal demonstrates that the television in working-class homes must be placed in such a way that passers-by can see that the family possesses a television, so the difference between the two is not simply that the entourage is in the home, while the satellite dish is outside it, although, at the same time, the public siting of the dish is exactly what is at issue, and it is this which I wish to explore.

PART II

> 'It's a nice extra, like a jacuzzi, that I'm sure would interest a lot of people.'
>
> Mark Goldberg, Hamptons Estate Agents, quoted in
> *The Evening Standard* (12 July 1989), 23

Press coverage of satellite dishes in Britain can be divided into three categories, if we exclude the trade press and advertising features generated by Sky television and BSB themselves. This distinction is not always easy to maintain, as can be seen by investigating the first category, business/industrial coverage of satellite television. This necessarily, and properly, entails the reporting of satellite television within discussions of Rupert Murdoch's communications empire, as well as smaller scale coverage of employment in dish-making factories, and individual entrepreneurs of the dish revolution, like Liz Stewart, 'a bubbly brunette from Fife', who, reports the *Sunday Express*, designed a system which 'dishes out a blow to satellite giants' (16 October 1988,

25). However, in early 1989, it was noticeable that it is the Murdoch owned papers, *The Times* and the *Sun* which carried news reports about the increased demand for satellite dishes. For example, the *Sun* reported in January, shortly before Sky opened, that there were 'THOUSANDS IN DASH FOR SATELLITE TELLY DISHES', and quoted a spokesman ostensibly from Dixons, an electrical goods retailer, saying: 'The fantastic range of programmes being offered by the Sky station has really caused a stir' (5 January 1989, 5). Similarly, in February *The Times* reported that 'Sky launch boosts demand for dishes' (4 February 1989, 3) and a couple of days later, 'Satellite dish firm expanding' (7 February 1989, 2). The earlier of these two articles, which includes a statement from the Council for the Protection of Rural England, offers an early formulation of 'satellite dishes as a threat to the environment' with which I will be centrally concerned in my third category. Thus although there is a certain fuzziness, particularly in some newspapers, about this category, we can still legitimately distinguish it from the other two, 'consumer guides' and 'dish-siting controversy'. However, it should be noted that it is the *Independent* which has given most prominent coverage to the latter controversy which has been covered almost exclusively by non-Murdoch titles.

The consumer guides are fairly self-explanatory and were mainly a feature of the immediate pre- and post-Sky launch period. For our purposes what is significant is the way in which the choice of what to buy or rent is presented solely as an individual consumer purchase – a private, domestic matter which is treated appropriately by different newspapers with their different images of the type of consumers their readers are. Thus *Today* (4 February 1989) makes no mention of BSB and addresses '[t]he big question facing viewers keen to wire up to satellite television [which is] whether to rent or buy' (22), while the *Independent* (1 February 1989), in an article called 'The cost to the viewer' consults a range of experts and mentions BSB and W.H. Smith Television (Astra). Here, the reader is regarded not as a potentially 'keen' viewer, but as more distanced – 'curious' – as in 'For the curious consumer, the message seems to be: tread carefully' (13). There are no mentions in any papers of planning restrictions – or indeed of the fact that these dishes will be put on the outside of houses. It is only in the third category of coverage that this private consumer choice is seen to have public consequences. It is the formulations of these consequences that are of interest to us here, articulating as they do a range of oppositions:

private: public
consumer: citizen
entertainment: culture
supranational: national
future (innovation): history (conservation)

The controversy about the siting of satellite dishes, peculiarly resonant as it is in 1990 against a decade of 'heritage enterprise' in Britain, also reworks and re-presents founding historical conflicts about broadcasting, some of which have simultaneously been articulated in the debates over the quality threshold in the 1990 Broadcasting Bill. Indeed, the BSB/Media Education pack aimed at those taking GCSE Media Studies draws attention to the hostility in some quarters which greeted changes in broadcasting from the 1920s through the juxtaposition of a series of (unattributed) hostile quotations from 1922 to 1982, asking, 'Knowing when these comments were made, and the ways in which all of the developments referred to are now part of everyday life, how far do you think people are justified in criticising satellite television?' (Wall and Chater, undated, 12). The false ingenuousness of this question is to some extent redeemed if we consider the most obvious historical parallel to the satellite dish, the television aerial in the 1950s.[8] Oral history and historical ethnographic research such as O'Sullivan's (1991) confirm that there was public controversy about the erection of television aerials in the 1950s, although there is no trace of this controversy in the standard histories of the BBC and Independent Television (Briggs 1985; Sendall 1982), nor in standard text books on planning such as Cullingworth (1964/1988) or histories of planning such as Punter (1985) or Cullingworth (1979). The traces of this history can be found in repetitions, such as the fact that many of the places that have banned satellite dishes, like the Joseph Rowntree Trust village, New Earswick in Yorkshire, also have bans on outdoor aerials,[9] or the inclusion of television aerials within the strict national restrictions on any alterations to Grade I and II listed buildings. New towns like Milton Keynes, built in the 1960s were cabled throughout, partly to avoid exterior television aerials. It is noteworthy that the public debate about aerials in the 1950s coincides with the more general debates about the Americanization and commercialization of British culture of the period which are particularly focused by the opening of commercial television in 1955. Tim O'Sullivan (1991), conducting interviews with people about their memories of first getting television, shows the way in which to some the television aerial symbolized a proud stake in modernity. As Charles Barr (1986) and John Hill (1986) have shown, in British cinema of the 1950s and early 1960s, commercial television functions metaphorically to condense a set of attitudes to the commercial, the American, the mass produced. Raymond Williams, in his 1960 essay about advertising, dates the battle for the skyline much earlier, to the 1890s 'with "taste" and "the needs of commerce" as adversaries' (Williams 1980, 177). The point about history repeating itself in this way, now that television aerials have, in the main, become accepted as part of the urban landscape, or as the BSB pamphlet puts it, 'part of everyday life', is partly the significant differences (Sky television, rather than television as such, etc.). But it is also the way in which the similarities of some of the debates and discursive figures, encrusting/constituting a new object, the satellite dish, reveal that new ideas don't drop from the sky, but indeed, as others have argued about the television set itself, are constructed as meaningful within networks of relationships and discourses which pre-exist the technological innovation (Lull 1988, 1990; Morley 1986; Gray 1987).

Thus much of James Lull's work has been concerned to explore the way in which the television set is used within the familial domestic context. He uses the concept of extension to conceptualize the relationship between the set and the already existing dynamics of interaction within the family. In a 1988 piece he argues that McCluhan's original notion of the mass media extending the human senses through technological capability can be revamped to allow us to classify extension at three levels, the personal, the familial and the cultural. I have some reservations about a certain uncontradictory quality of this concept, but would here wish to propose that satellite dishes, as well as being literally extensions, also condense familial and cultural extensions. The several instances of men erecting, and indeed inventing their own dishes, further suggest that this new technology may have a particular place in the gendered division of labour – and personal extension.[10] Recent ethnographic work offers specific instances of the mapping of gender and generation across and through domestic technology (Morley and Silverstone 1990; Gray 1991; Seiter et al 1989). Thus Tim O'Sullivan (1991) finds that the final decision to buy a television set in the 1950s often rested with the man of the household, who frequently also installed the aerial, and sometimes retained a residual proprietorial power over the on/off switch. Moores

(1990) maps the fluctuating gender/generational conflicts around satellite television, in which different family members occupy different positions at different times to different others in relation to the 'same' equipment. For example, a woman unhappy with her spouse's purchase of satellite television defending that same purchase to her parents. These fluctuating identifications should make us cautious about ascribing essential qualities to technology and technology use, while still being alert to the patternings of power in specific historical divisions of labour, use and attitude. Here it is useful to recall Ang and Hermes' theorization of the interplay of gender and generation in the Meier household recorded by Bausinger (Ang and Hermes 1991; Bausinger 1984). Ang and Hermes observe, at the beginning of their article:

> Mr Meier, the male football fan, ends up not watching his favourite team's game on television, while his wife, who doesn't care for sports, finds herself seating herself in front of the TV set the very moment the sports programme is on. Gender is obviously not a reliable predictor of viewing behaviour here. (p307)

They proceed to argue for a postmodern feminist understanding of gender, in which the concept of articulation is central. They conclude, 'We must accept contingency as posing the utter limit for our understanding, and historical specificity as the only ground on which continuities and discontinuities in the ongoing but unpredictable articulation of gender in media consumption can be traced'. Ang and Hermes include within the logic of their argument about gender a similar critique of the way in which class (and race/ethnicity, although this is not developed) can be used within ethnographic accounts, as pre-constituted and pre-emptive explanatory factors.

The public debate in Britain in 1989-90 about the siting of satellite dishes offers us a particular, national, historical example of a conflict of values, which, because it is staged on the skyline gives us some access to non-verbal audience practice. Working as I do here from one source, national newspapers, will obviously provide only one kind of outline of this debate. I think it offers an account of some of the discourses in play. How individuals position themselves in relation to these differentially available circulating discourses at particular times and in particular contexts cannot be deduced, and can only be investigated through particular ethnographies of the type that Ang and

Hermes advocate. However researchers cannot do anything with these particular local knowledges unless there is also an attempt to apprehend a wider discursive field. To 'place practices of media consumption firmly within their complex and contradictory social contexts' (Ang and Hermes) requires some mapping or constitution of these contexts.[11]

It is in relation to this argument that I wish to place a discussion of the third category of press coverage of satellite dishes, 'controversy about siting'. Working from a corrupt and rather random corpus – national, non-specialist newspaper coverage of rows about the siting of dishes, certain patterns emerge with striking clarity.

Firstly, there is the question of who speaks. Two categories of persons appear in these reports, 'Anti-dishers' and 'Dish-erectors'. Coverage is overwhelmingly dominated by anti-dishers who are always professional – graphic designers, professors etc. – and nearly always *representative* – councillors, spokespeople for Trusts or Estates, Residents Associations. Often of course, they will have initiated the news item as part of their campaign to get a dish removed, but for our purposes what is significant is the way in which they never represent themselves as speaking on their own behalf. Anti-dishers, who in Bourdieu's terms, are the possessors of, indeed propagandists for legitimate cultural capital, act and speak at a general social level about a matter of public concern (Bourdieu, 1984).

Dish erectors, on the other hand, are always particular individuals; for example, the Radford family of Norton-sub-Hamdon, in Somerset, who won a dish in July 1989. I quote:

> John Radford, a building worker, pinned it proudly and prominently to the wall of his little cottage, a Grade II listed dwelling and settled back with his wife Jean, a cheese packer, to watch Mr Murdoch's old movies dropping in from outer space.
>
> 'Sky dish is the limit for listed village', the *Independent* (25 October 1989), 3

Here we have a construction worker and a cheese packer. In February 1989 we had Steven Davenport, a forty-two-year-old unemployed disabled man:

> A disabled TV viewer has been ordered by town hall planners to take down his rooftop satellite dish in a test case which could affect the future

of satellite broadcasting in Britain.
Steven Davenport was stunned by the council decision....
'Satellite TV dish banned as "eyesore" ' *Sunday Express*
(19 February 1989), 17

Most interesting, though, is the case of dish-erector Maggie Brown, who is also the media editor of the national newspaper, the *Independent*. Unlike all other reported dish erectors she is a well-paid professional with access to the media, a profile more common in anti-dishers. Furthermore, despite her designation of her own house as 'undistinguished', given that it is administered by Dulwich College, it must certainly be within reach of the most desirable areas of south London. Reported dish controversies have taken place either within villages, where there may still be local working-class occupancy of desirable cottages, or in areas of terraced urban housing. The erection of dishes on secluded detached houses has aroused no comment.[12] Similarly the extensive dishing of the river frontage of luxury dockland apartments on the north Thames bank also appears to be uncontroversial. Although as Muthesius (1982) traces, the terraced house, in England, was built for, and is occupied by all classes of society, it is not in the very prestigious terraces, of, for example, Bath, Brighton and Leamington Spa that there has been dish controversy. Nor in the inner city, where there is usually a mixture of terraced housing and newer council blocks, despite the fact that the satellite dish has come to signify the conspicuous consumption of a certain kind of poverty, as in this commentary on a Gallup poll for *Moneywise* which voted Nottingham the most desirable place to live: 'There is relatively little difference between rich and poor in Nottingham; the way to tell the middle-class area from the council estate is that the council houses all have satellite dishes' (Leith 1990). The controversies have taken place in areas which have a more mixed occupancy, where what section 4 of the 1971 Town and Country Planning Act refers to as 'the essential character of the area' is a matter of continuous everyday struggle. The character of the docklands development is in some ways perfectly homologous with the character of the satellite dish. Thus although Maggie Brown has many characteristics of the anti-disher, she, for professional reasons – and she is careful to point out the professional necessity of having a dish – is a dish erector, and her case-study, 'My dish did not go down well' (the *Independent*, 8 May

1990, 14) conforms to the individuated format of all dish erectors, which is particularly interesting given that she has written it herself.

The very contradictoriness of 'My dish did not go down well' allows us to outline the contours of anti-dish discourse, which is remarkably uniform. Dish-erectors, in contrast, are normally marooned in the personal, specific and concrete.

i) Anti-dishers generally make no reference to television programmes. Brown, who we could describe as an anti-disher with a dish, illuminates this point because she wants to have both BSB and Sky. Generally though, anti-dishers discuss dishes quite formally as alien protruberances perversely attached to the outside of houses by untutored DIYers.

ii) Reference is always made to architectural provenance – often with some precision, 'perfectly good late Victorian terraced house' (*Independent*, 14 July 1989); 'villages built of lovely honey-coloured hamstone' (*Independent*, 25 October 1989); 'terraced Edwardian House' (*Daily Telegraph*, 7 October 1989) or, in Maggie Brown's case, 'the front of my Victorian house'.

The contrasted repertoires of knowledge, television versus architecture, are, evidently, contrasts between less and more culturally legitimate forms.

iii) Some knowledge of the relevant environmental regulation and town planning acts is often displayed. Anti-dishers often express regret at the lack of legal restriction, particularly for unlisted buildings. Thus, of Queen's Park, London:

> A classic late-Victorian suburb, the district is supposedly a protected area of 'special architectural or historic interest', a place where the writ of the home-improvement brigade should not run unchecked; where picture windows, stone cladding and television dishes are outlawed. Does it work? 'This may have been declared a conservation area' but my answer is 'so what?'
>
> 'Battle against blots on the townscape', *Independent* (14 July 1989)

The law, for anti-dishers, is not in these matters strong enough and is not enforced satisfactorily.

iv) Certain evaluative phrases reoccur. The favoured written adjective is 'unsightly' which is such a normative word that it does not exist in the positive 'sightly'. 'Eyesores', 'Blight/Blot on the landscape' are also favoured, often as a headline (see above). This phrase in particular has been offered to me quite unsolicited by many passers-by when I have been out photographing houses with dishes, and was also volunteered by the lab which develops my films.

v) Value. Apart from the estate agent who provided my opening epigraph, which, with its comparison of satellite dishes to jacuzzis, items of conspicuous consumption of a very particular provenance, sees dishes as potentially valuable home-improvements, the consensus among the anti-dishers, the worry which underlies the articulated, public spirited architectural concern for the integrity of the buildings is one about value. This is not necessarily simply house prices, but for example in villages is to do with a more generalized 'heritage' value. Thus of Norton-sub-Hamdon:

> A council spokesman said: 'We'd be asolutely appalled if this became widespread. Somerset's value as a tourist venue relies on the character of its historic buildings and villages …
>
> *Independent* (25 October 1989), 3

In London, though, things are harsher:

> And apart from the effects on the skyline, who knows what will happen to house prices once dishes start sprouting in earnest from our roofs and walls?
>
> Mark Edmonds, 'Fright on the tiles', *Evening Standard* (12 July 1989)

> Mr Tyler believes most householders appreciate the benefits of following the rules. House prices in a conservation area can be significantly raised.
>
> 'People who buy houses round here tend to have regard to the ambience of the area as a whole …'
>
> Michael Durham, 'Battle against …', *Independent* (14 July 1989)

> The dishes have to face south, and a view of a south-facing facade with satellite receivers along part of it is not going to make a house on the opposite side of the street easier to sell.
>
> Tim Rowland, 'The blight of the satellite dish', *Daily Telegraph* (1 October 1989)

It is, in the end, not what the dishes look like that matters – it is what they mean. And what they mean is both very simple and very complex. It is not necessary to be reductive, to say, well it's all about house prices really, because this move is made so spontaneously by the anti-dishers themselves. It is not made by all of them, and I'm sure most would protest if this was offered, say by an audience researcher, as a primary motivation. Sometimes, indeed, mention of house prices figures as a rhetorical last resort, an attempt to speak the language of philistines – or to recognize the values most endorsed in Britain in the last twelve years. Furthermore, financial gain does not have to be a primary motivation, if we follow Bourdieu's arguments about the disinterestedness of the inheritors of legitimate culture, for financial reward to result. There is a vision inspiring many of the anti-dishers, a vision of a particular England, as Patrick Wright (1985) puts it, of an old country. This harmonious, orderly community is self policing because of its shared values and assumptions, vigilant against the autodidacts of the environment. To continue the quotation I began above:

> 'People who buy houses round here tend to have regard to the ambience of the area as a whole,' he said. 'By and large they are not the kind of do-it-yourselfers who think it's the bee's knees to put in a mock Georgian frontage, or go down to a DIY superstore to pick up a timber cladding front porch. They tend to stick to traditional styles, though we still have to be vigilant – there are exceptions.'
>
> Mr Tyler, quoted in Durham, 'Battle against ...' *Independent* (14 July 1989)

The shifts in this speech, 'People who buy houses round here ...' 'They' ... 'We' ... trace the fragility of this community of natural taste, the way in which it is made through vigilance as well as born. There is here a particular characterizing of the relationship between the public and the private, which, as I argued earlier, is a significant division within discourses of taste. Judy Attfield (1989) provides a fascinating example of conflict over this distinction in her account of the net curtain war between tenants and architects in Harlow New Town in the 1950s. In this, in some ways analogous, public conflict the architects repeatedly complain that tenants ruin their open plan picture window dwellings in a quest for cosiness pursued through the obstructive placing of furniture, heavy curtaining and nets. Attfield observes, 'Through the appropriation of privacy by the concealment of the interior from the uninvited gaze, people took control of their own interior space and at the same time made a public declaration of their variance from the architects' design' (228). This example provides another indication of the way in which public and private are constructed spaces, perceived differentially and differently accessible to different persons. Mr Tyler's speech above is the discourse of the unselfconscious inheritors of public space who accept external uniformity in the absolute confidence of internal, private uniqueness. This vision of Britain has to be set against the aggressively downmarket image of Sky. As Mark Edmonds put it nearly a year before:

> But unless Sky changes tack and goes for a more upmarket audience, a satellite dish protruding from the front wall will do about as much for your standing in the neighbourhood as a visit from a rat-catcher.
>
> Edmonds, 'Fright on the tiles', *Evening Standard* (12 July 1989)

Dish erectors defend themselves with considerable resignation, in vocabularies of the personal, which hint at other meanings for dishes. Thus Mr Bolton, of New Earswick:

> 'The village is beautifully kept and a much more desirable place to live than most council estates, but the people who have a big say in our lives tend to be old folk with old-fashioned ideas. Like it or not, satellite TV is here to stay and it's frustrating to be denied it.'
>
> 'TV dish ban in "Quaker" village', *Daily Mail* (4 December 1989), 15

or Mrs Kidd of the same village, quoted in another newspaper:

> 'We saved up £130 to buy the dish. We have three kiddies who love the films.'
>
> 'Village bans TV satellite dishes', *The Guardian* (4 December 1989)

Or the Radfords' son, Colin:

> 'I know all my friends would like one. I also know what they're saying about spoiling the village. For me it's rather *boring*.'
>
> 'Sky dish is the limit....' *Independent* (25 October 1989)

The dissatisfactions which leak out of these plain statements, the half expressed desire for another order, one more modern, or more fun for the kiddies, less *boring* are of a quite different type to the confident, regulatory public spirited complaints of the anti-dishers. Dishes are a

DIY chance of a better environment of satisfaction. In the classic privatized consumer transaction, you pays your money and you takes your choice. The fact that the choice itself may be less than anticipated, or that the quality of what is available may be disappointing is another matter. The discursive context within which this choice is made, the double jeopardy of satellite television in the terms of legitimate culture, militates against elaborated defence or critique. The *Daily Telegraph* (13 April 1989, 23) epitomized this point in heading an article about a man who made a dish from a dustbin lid, 'The man who cannot complain about trash on TV'. For the anti-dishers though, each 60cm platter, 'scarring rows of houses at exactly the level where their uniformity remains most intact' (Rowland), signals an opting out of, an impediment to a certain public vision. And it is this, as I have argued, which is the hegemonic taste code, this which constitutes dish-discourse, which frames the terms and reporting of dish conflict, and will therefore also provide one of the contexts in which dish erectors articulate their defences. It is thus that the non-verbal aspects of the practice become sigificant. We could say actions speak louder than words. Certainly at a general level the dishes can be approached as conspicuous consumption, and classically, conspicuous leisure consumption. But the erection of a dish is also historically specific, a particular act, a concrete and visible sign of a consumer who has bought into the supranational entertainment space, who will not necessarily be available for the ritual, citizen-making moments of national broadcasting (Scannell 1988; Chaney 1979). Who is abandoning the local citizenry and the national landscape of heritage and preservation (Morley and Robins 1989). Erecting a satellite dish on the front of your house is partly a declaration of not being bothered 'to like what's better to like'.

APPENDIX

In discussion at Champaign I argued that one hypothesis that could be advanced from the research for this paper was that British Satellite Broadcasting (BSB), the 'quality' satellite station broadcasting to Britain was unlikely to survive because its target audience was precisely the people who, for the reasons outlined below, would feel most reluctant to erect satellite dishes on their homes.[13] Since then, on 2 November 1990, British Satellite Broadcasting (owned by a consortium of mainly British media interests, including Pearson,

Granada, Chargeur and Reed International) has been merged very suddenly with Sky (News International) to form British Sky Broadcasting. Despite the retention of the BSB acronym, most commentators, including, for example, Anthony Simonds-Gooding, the head of BSB, regarded the deal as a Sky coup which finally gave Murdoch (a non-EC citizen and a British newspaper owner) an (unregulated) place in (regulated) British television.[14] Murdoch's other media interests were incompatible with this in terms of the 1990 Broadcasting Bill, a problem evaded in the use of the older Astra (Sky) satellite which is regarded as Luxembourgian not British. Certainly, the nationwide posters which herald the merger at present (November 1990), read: SKY AND BSB MERGE, THE BEST OF BOTH WORLDS – SKY, and two of the five BSB channels have now stopped broadcasting. It is not clear yet whether there will be any intervention by the Office of Fair Trading or the Independent Broadcasting Authority.

Of course, the reasons for the failure of BSB are complex, and must be seen alongside the massive losses sustained by Sky since inception. Satellite television in Britain is not yet profitable for anyone.[15] However, in all the retrospective discussion of investment levels, multi-media support etc., I would still argue for the significance of the taste codes discussed below as one element in the final outcome. My argument above is exclusively concerned with the erection of Sky dishes. This is partly because Sky started broadcasting earlier than BSB, so all press coverage was initially about Sky and satellite dishes meant Sky. It is also because there are very many more Sky dishes easily visible.[16] This fact is not in and of itself an explanation of why Sky survives. It is a fact which also needs explaining. This I hope the paper makes some moves towards.

ACKNOWLEDGEMENTS

The first version of this paper was presented to the Interdisciplinary Conference on *Audience* organized by Larry Grossberg, James Hey and Ellen Wartella in September 1990 at the University of Illinois, Champaign-Urbana, and I should like to thank the organizers for inviting me. A later version of the paper was presented to the International Television Studies Conference in London, 1991.

SATELLITE DISHES AND THE LANDSCAPES OF TASTE

This article originally appeared with images; however, due to pressures on space the editors have omitted all illustrations from this collection. The editors apologise to both authors and readers for this omission.

NOTES

References to newspaper articles are given in full in the text or footnotes.

[1] See for example, Gray 1987; Seiter *et al.* 1989; Tullock 1989; Morley and Silverstone 1990; Moores 1990.
[2] The key titles here are Hall and Jefferson 1976 and Hebdige 1978. However, it is the media studies take-up of these paradigms, rather than the initial sub-cultural formulations which are more indifferent to content.
[3] My argument should be understood, if I may phrase it this way, as 'post-Clifford and Marcus' (1986). That is I am not pointing out that power is always inscribed within the ethnographic enterprise etc. etc., and would here follow Geertz (1988) in his response to post-colonial and epistemological critiques: 'The moral assymetries across which ethnography works and the discursive complexity within which it works make any attempt to portray it as anything more than the representation of one sort of life in the categories of another impossible to defend' (144). Within this recognition, he does, however, strongly defend the ethnographic enterprise. I am concerned with how, if you like, cultural power is spoken and circumscribes speech.
[4] Radway 1984, 89. See also the review of this book, Ien Ang (1988) 'Feminist Desire and Female Pleasure'.
[5] BARB figures, Socio Economic Breakdown of Satellite Viewers, week ending 10 June 1990. Published in *Broadcast* (11 August 1990), 10-11.
[6] The merger of BSB with Sky was announced on 2 November 1990 with little warning. See appendix for comment.
[7] Thorstein Veblen's classic notion of 'conspicuous consumption' provides one obvious possible approach to the acquisition of satellite dishes (Veblen 1899). Another is offered by Alfred Gell who discusses the (hard-earned) purchase of television sets by Catholic Sri-Lankan fishermen. He argues that for these poor hardworking people the (electrically unconnected) television set functions like a work of art to negate/transcend the real world. He argues that this is 'adventurous consumerism' 'which struggles against the limits of the known world', rather than dull unimaginative consumerism which reiterates the class habitus. Attractive as this argument is, and it would obviously form one direction for future research, I think it would be more tenable in the case of satellite dishes if they did not in fact receive satellite television. Alfred Gell (1983), 'Newcomers to the world of goods: consumption among the Muria Gonds'. The Algerian film, *From Hollywood to Tamanrasset* (directed by Mahmoud Zemmori, 1990), a comedy of dish-passion in Algiers, posits the anarchy of satellite reception against the staid state channel.
[8] Television ownership and rental increased very rapidly in Britain in the 1950s. Calculated from the number of sound and TV licences issued, the

increase was from 763,941 in 1951 to 9,255, 422 in 1959. Figures from John Montgomery *The Fifties* (London: George Allen & Unwin, 1965).

[9] 'The elected representatives of the villagers say they do not want these unsightly dishes everywhere,' he said. 'It is not that they dislike satellite television. We already have a strict rule of indoor aerials only' (Mr Cedric Dennis, director of housing, New Earswick, Yorkshire, *Daily Telegraph* (4 December 1989), 5.

[10] A *Daily Telegraph* story, 'Camouflage designed to hide eyesore dishes' featured Mr Peter Plaskett, photographed painting a dish in a leafy pattern. Mr Plaskett is marketing individually designed dishes and 'said he was being kept busy by people who are concerned about the neighbourhoods' (8 December 1989, 9). Another *Daily Telegraph* story, with a guest writer from *Electronics Weekly*, Leon Clifford, featured a similarly posed 'man and dish' photograph of Mr Stan Bacon who has made a satellite receiver from a dustbin lid. The Sky spokesperson commented that this method was used for reception of Superchannel in Poland (13 April 1989, 23).

[11] It is this I understand John Fiske (1990) to be specifying in his use of the langue/parole distinction in a discussion of taste, or Lull (1988) in his notion of cultural extension.

[12] John Wyver made a feature for the Channel Four arts programme, *Without Walls* (tx. 17 October 1990) which had several wonderful examples of satellite dishes in secluded spots.

[13] In the letters to the national press following the merger, Dr Michael Ward commented, 'My family's decision to buy a "squarial" was a considered one because we believed the quality and variety of the programmes on offer to be appropriate to our viewing needs. We had no wish to receive Sky transmission as we felt the programmes to be largely inane' (letter to the *Independent*, 5 November 1990). The following day Mr Warren Newman wrote, 'Above all, we will miss the high quality of digital stereo sound and picture from the MAC satellite. We will miss the compact aerials which will have to be replaced by ASTRA monsters' (letter to the *Independent*, 6 November 1990). Apart from the intriguing unanimity of the 'we' of each letter from a paterfamilias, we see here also the uphill struggle of 'quality' television taste. On this see Brunsdon 1990.

[14] See, for example, Anthony Simonds-Gooding, 'When the Sky fell in', 'My Week' feature in the *Independent* (14 November 1990); Maggie Brown, 'Murdoch takes his revenge', the *Independent* (7 November 1990); Georgina Henry, 'A deal that dishes the law-makers', *The Guardian* (5 November 1990). The report in *The Times* the day after the merger maintains a 50-50 interpretation ('Bitter battle ends as Sky and BSB become one', 3 November 1990), while *Today*, which greeted the news with a front page headline, TV THRILLER, scrupulously points out that News International owns *Today* as well as Sky.

[15] Immediately after the merger, shares rose for BSB backers, Granada Group, Pearson and Reed International, as well as for News International and News Corporation (*Financial Times*, Share Index, Tuesday, 6 November 1990). Bronwen Maddox of Kleinwort Benson Securities estimated that Sky had lost £95m in the year to June 1990, while BSB would lose more than £330m this year. Maddox was quoted with (approximately) these figures in all the quality

press on 3 November 1990. I have taken the conservative estimate of BSB's losses quoted by the *Independent, The Times* quoted £400m for 1990.
[16] At the time of the merger, Sky claimed reception in 1.5m homes (including Eire), while BSB 600,000 (Nisse and Fagan, 'BSB to merge with Sky', the *Independent*, 3 November 1990).

REFERENCES

References to newspaper articles are given in full in the text or footnotes.

Ang, Ien (1985), *Watching Dallas*, London: Methuen.
Ang, Ien (1988), 'Feminist Desire and Female Pleasure: On Janice Radway's *Reading the Romance*', *Camera Obscura*, 16 (January), 179-92.
Ang, Ien and Hermes, Joke (1991), 'Gender and/in media consumption', in James Curran and Michael Gurevitch (eds), *Mass Communication and Society*, London: Edward Arnold, 307-28.
Attfield, Judy (1989), 'Inside Pram Town: A Case Study of Harlow House Interiors, 1951-1961', in Attfield and Kirkham (1989) 215-38.
Attfield, Judy and Kirkham, Pat (1989), *A View from the Interior*, London: Virago.
Barr, Charles (1986), 'Broadcasting and Cinema: 2: Screens within Screens', in Charles Barr (ed.), *All Our Yesterdays*, London: British Film Institute, 206-24.
Bausinger, Hemann (1984), 'Media, Technology and Daily Life', *Media, Culture and Society*, 6, 4, 343-51.
Bourdieu, Pierre (1984), *Distinction*, trans. Richard Nice, London: Routledge & Kegan Paul.
Briggs, Asa (1985), *The BBC: The First Fifty Years*, Oxford: Oxford University Press.
Brunsdon, Charlotte (1990), 'Television: Aesthetics and Audiences', in Patricia Mellencamp (ed.), *Logics of Television*, Bloomington and London: Indiana University Press and the British Film Institute, 59-72.
Brunsdon, Charlotte (1990a), 'Problems with Quality', *Screen* 31, 1, 67-90.
Chaney, David (1979), *Fictions and Ceremonies*, London: Edward Arnold.
Clifford, James and Marcus, George E. (1986), *Writing Culture: the poetics and politics of ethnography*, Berkeley: University of California Press.
Corner, John (1991), *Popular Television in Britain*, London: British Film Institute.
Cullingworth, J.B. (1964), Tenth edition: 1988, *Town and Country Planning in Britain*, London: Unwin.
Cullingworth, J.B. (1979), *Peacetime History of Environmental Planning* Vol 111, *1939-1969, New Towns Policy*, London: HMSO.
Fiske, John (1990), 'Ethnosemiotics: some personal and theoretical reflections', *Cultural Studies* 4, 1, 85-99.
Geertz, Clifford (1988), *Works and Lives: the anthropologist as author*, Cambridge: Polity Press.
Gell, Alfred (1988), 'Newcomers to the world of goods: consumption among the Muria Gonds', in A. Appachurai (ed.), *The Social Life of Things*,

Cambridge; Cambridge University Press, 110-19.

Gray, Ann (1987), 'Behind Closed Doors: Video Recorders in the Home', in Helen Baehr and Gillian Dyer (eds), *Boxed In: Women and Television*, London: Pandora, 38-54.

Gray, Ann (1991), *Video Playtime: The Gendering of a Communications Technology*, London: Comedia/Routledge.

Hall, Stuart and Jefferson, Tony (eds) (1976), *Resistance through Rituals*, London: Hutchinson.

Hebdige, Dick (1978), *Subculture: the meaning of style*, London: Methuen.

Hill, John (1986), *Sex, Class and Realism*, London, British Film Institute.

Leal, Ondina Fachel (1990), 'Popular Taste and Erudite Repertoire: the place and space of television in Brazil', *Cultural Studies* 4, 1 (January), 19-29.

Leith, William (1990), 'Life is not so bad and that's the bottom line', *Independent on Sunday* (26 August 1990), 3.

Lovell, Terry (1987), *Consuming Fiction*, London: Verso.

Lull, James (1988), 'Constructing Rituals of Extension Through Family Television Viewing', in Lull (ed.), *World Families Watch Television*, Newbury Park: Sage.

Lull, James (1990), *Inside Family Viewing: Ethnographic Research on Television's Audiences*, London: Routledge/Comedia.

Montgomery, John (1965), *The Fifties*, London: George Allen & Unwin.

Moores, Shaun (1990), 'Dishes and Domestic Cultures: Satellite TV as Household Technology', unpublished paper, Polytechnic of Wales.

Morley, David (1986), *Family Television: Cultural Power and Domestic Leisure*, London: Comedia.

Morley, David and Robins, Kevin (1989), 'Spaces of Identity: Communications Technologies and the Reconfiguration of Europe', *Screen* 30, 4, 10-34.

Morley, David and Silverstone, Roger (1990), 'Domestic Communications: Technologies and Meanings', *Media, Culture and Society*, 12, 1, 31-55.

Muthesius, Stefan (1982), *The English Terraced House*, New Haven and London: Yale University Press.

O'Sullivan, Tim (1991), 'Television Memories and Cultures of Viewing 1950-1960', in Corner (ed.) (1991, 159-81).

Punter, John (1984 and 1985), *A History of Aesthetic Control I: The control of the external appearance of development in England and Wales* 1909-1947 (1984); 1947-1985 (1985), Reading: Dept. of Land Management, University of Reading.

Radway, Janice (1984), *Reading the Romance*, Chapel Hill: University of North Carolina Press.

Ross, Andrew (1989), *No Respect: Intellectuals and Popular Culture*, New York: Routledge.

Scannell, Paddy (1988), 'Radio Times', in Drummond and R. Paterson (eds), *Television and its Audience*, London: British Film Institute.

Seiter, Ellen (1990), 'Making Distinctions in TV Audience Research: Case Study of a Troubling Interview', *Cultural Studies*, 4, 1 (January), 61-84.

Seiter, Ellen *et al.* (ed.) (1989), *Remote Control*, London: Routledge.

Taylor, Helen (1989), *Scarlett's Women*: Gone with the Wind *and its Female*

Fans, London: Virago.

Tulloch, John (1989), 'Approaching the Audience: the Elderly', in Seiter *et al.* (eds) (1989), 180-203.

Veblen, Thorstein (1899), *The Theory of the Leisure Class*, New York: Macmillan.

Wall, Ian and Chater, Louise (undated, c. 1990), *British Satellite Broadcasting: Study Material*, London: BSB and Media Education.

Williams, Raymond (1960), 'Advertising: the Magic System', reprinted in *Problems of Materialism and Culture*, London: Verso, 1980, 170-95.

Wright, Patrick (1985), *On Living in an Old Country*, London: Verso.

C. Democracy and Difference

Us and Them

On the Philosophical Bases of Political Criticism

Satya P. Mohanty

This article is an attempt to identify, define, and criticize what I see as an unexamined philosophical position latent in contemporary political-critical practice – cultural or historical relativism. Relativism appears less as an idea than as a practical and theoretical bias, and leads, I believe, to a certain amount of historical simplification and political naivety.

My specific contention is that a relativist position does not allow for a complex understanding of social and cultural phenomena since the vagueness of its definition of rationality precludes a serious analysis of historical agency. In outlining the claims of two versions of relativism, an extreme and a more sophisticated kind, I intend to show why we need a more precise definition of rationality than either offers. I suggest that the need for a basic definition of human agency, and the conception of rationality it implies, should be faced directly by political criticism.

FRAMING THE ISSUES: CONTEXTS AND DEFINITIONS

Even though it took definite shape in the course of the nineteenth century, relativism has its origins in the late-eighteenth-century reaction to the universalist claims of Enlightenment thought. Stressing not merely the presence of historical variety but also the constitutional differences evident in human languages, communities, and societies, writers such as J.G. Herder urged that we recognize the changeability of human 'nature'. Their arguments pointed up the inability of any single faculty, such as what the Enlightenment thinkers called Reason, to comprehend the diverse manifestations of human culture and history. Herder emphasized the creativity of the human mind, and

215

argued that we understand its individual creations only by situating them in their particular social and cultural contexts. The development of relativism as a powerful intellectual presence is best seen as a post-Herderian phenomenon that draws on nineteenth-century German idealist philosophy, with Fichte, Hegel, and ultimately Dilthey as the convenient individual signposts of this intellectual-historical narrative.[1] Very generally understood, this development underscored the need to define the claims of difference over identity, historical novelty and variety over methodological monism. Against the Enlightenment's emphasis on a singular rationality underlying and comprehending all human activities, relativism pursued the possibilities of change, variety, and difference, and began thereby to pose the question of otherness.

It is this question that becomes a basic political gesture in the context of contemporary literary theory and criticism. To situate and illustrate this politics, let me cite three quotations from fairly influential and representative sources that suggest both the dominant political-critical climate these days and a possible basis for relativist arguments. These passages are representative of a general tendency in contemporary criticism emphasising discontinuity, the celebration of difference and heterogeneity, and the assertion of plurality as opposed to reductive unities.

> [The] epistemological mutation is not yet complete. But it is not of recent origin either, since its first phase can no doubt be traced back to Marx. But it took a long time to have much effect. Even now – and this is especially true in the case of the history of thought – it has been neither registered nor reflected upon, while other, more recent transformations – those of linguistics, for example – have been. It is as if it was particularly difficult, in the history in which men retrace their own ideas and their own knowledge, to formulate a general theory of discontinuity; of series, of limits, unities, specific orders, and differentiated autonomies and dependencies. As if, in that field where we had become used to seeking origins, to pushing back further and further the line of antecedents, to reconstituting traditions, to following evolutive curves, to projecting teleologies, and to having constant recourse to metaphors of life, we felt a particular repugnance to conceiving of difference, to describing separations and dispersions, to dissociating the reassuring form of the identical ... As if we were afraid to conceive of the *Other* in the time of our own thought.

In the beginning are our differences. The new love dares for the other, wants the other, makes dizzying, precipitous flights between knowledge and invention. The woman arriving over and over again does not stand still; she's everywhere, she exchanges, she is the desire-that-gives ... Wherever history unfolds as the history of death, she does not tread. Opposition, hierarchizing exchange, the struggle for mastery ... all that comes from a period in time governed by phallocentric values. The fact that this period extends into the present doesn't prevent woman from starting the history of life somewhere else. Elsewhere, she gives ... This is an 'economy' that can no longer be put in economic terms. Wherever she loves, all the old concepts of management are left behind. At the end of a more or less conscious computation, she finds not her sum but her differences ... When I write, it's everything that we don't know we can be that is written out of me ... Heterogeneous, yes ... the erotogeneity of the heterogeneous.

What is now in crisis is a whole conception of socialism which rests upon the ontological centrality of the working class, upon the role of Revolution, with a capital 'r', as the founding moment in the transition from one type of society to another, and upon the illusory prospect of a perfectly unitary and homogeneous collective will that will render pointless the moment of politics. The plural and multifarious character of contemporary social struggles has finally dissolved the last foundation for that political imaginary: Peopled with 'universal' subjects and conceptually built around History in the singular, it has postulated 'society' as an intelligible structure that could be intellectually mastered on the basis of certain class positions and reconstituted, as a rational, transparent order, through a founding act of a political character. Today the Left is witnessing the final act of the dissolution of that Jacobin imaginary.[2]

Common to all three passages is the idea that something of significance has been repressed or left unarticulated in our traditional conceptual frameworks. Though what is left out is variously formulated and named, the political force of these passages derives from a recognition that crucial social interests might be at stake in these absences or repressions, and the challenge for a critical discourse is to create the possibility for their (self-)representation. At the very least these passages urge us to respect the difference between the terms of the dominant framework and those the absent or repressed might use for its self-presentation. What the passages urge us to do is radicalize the idea of difference itself – the other is not us, they insist, and is quite possibly not even *like* us. Herein lies the challenge: how do we conceive the other, indeed the Other, outside of our inherited concepts and beliefs so as not to replicate the patterns of repression and subjugation we notice in the traditional conceptual frameworks?

Now, there are large and very difficult issues implied by this question, and much of our understanding of what is crucial to a poststructuralist political and critical climate depends on how we define and specify these issues. More than any synoptic or comprehensive view of poststructuralism, what we need today is greater clarity about what is presupposed, implied, or entailed by our formulation of questions of the 'other', which would in effect be an interrogation of proposed agendas through the process of seeking precise definitions. It is with this in view that I would like to ask whether one of the possible extreme implications of these passages – that it is necessary to conceive the Other as a radically separable and separate entity in order for it to command our respect – is a useful idea. Just how other, we need to force ourselves to specify, is the Other? In literary criticism such a question arises whenever we discuss unequal relations among groups of people, among languages, and canons with their institutionally sanctioned definitions of value, coherence, unity, and intelligibility. In all these instances, the crucial problems arise when we encounter other canons (or the non-canonical), other languages and values – in short, when we encounter competing claims and are forced to adjudicate. It is then that relativism becomes a viable philosophical option.

Relativism, as a methodological and substantive thesis, appears in various forms in various disciplinary contexts, but the most immediate context from which contemporary criticism learns to specify its discussion of cultural otherness is anthropology. The institutional history of anthropology is tied to European colonial expansion in the latter part of the nineteenth century. Naturally, the decline of the formal empires of Europe and the rise of anti-colonial movements and independent national states of the 'Third World' can be said to have encouraged a greater self-consciousness among anthropologists – from both the international 'metropoles' and the 'peripheral' countries – about the politics of studying other cultures. Thus if it was possible to see anthropological description and interpretation of Third World cultures during the heyday of imperialism as largely complicitous with the exercise of power and the discursive mapping and manipulation of powerless others, the self-criticism of western anthropology needs to be understood not simply as the natural maturation and intellectual coming of age of a discipline, but rather as the result of both political challenges presented by these others and the related demystification of the west's recent history by its own progressive intellectuals. In this context, it is possible to see in the debates within, say, social anthropology in Britain in the last four decades or so, a heightened concern with methodological politics, an awareness of the historically entrenched nature of scholarly representations. Unselfconscious – and interested – misreadings of Third World societies and their values, texts, and practices, were, it was found, made possible not so much because of overt and explicitly stated racism (although there was a good dose of that in scholarly literature for anyone interested in looking), but primarily because of uncritical application and extension of the very ideas with which the west has defined its enlightenment and its modernity – Reason, Progress, Civilization.[3]

In this general context the relativist thesis initially becomes a valuable political weapon. Opposing the imperial arrogance of the scholar who interprets aspects of other cultures in terms of the inflexible norms and categories of the scholar's own, the relativist insists on the fundamentally sound idea that individual elements of a given culture must be interpreted primarily in terms of that culture, relative, that is, to that system of meanings and values. Thus there is a clear political lesson that relativism teaches: it cautions us against ethnocentrist explanations of other communities and cultures. Drawing on the example of ethnology, the relativist will tell us that texts (or events or values) can be significantly *misunderstood* if they are not seen in relation to their particular contexts; that interpretation and understanding have historically been tied to political activities, and that 'strong' and 'meaningful' interpretations have often been acts of discursive domination. Instead, relativism urges care and attentiveness to the specificities of context; it emphasizes the differences between and among us rather than pointing to shared spaces.

RELATIVISM IN ANTHROPOLOGY:
AN INSTRUCTIVE EXCHANGE

I shall be arguing that relativism is an untenable – and indeed rather dangerous – philosophical ally for political criticism. But let me first identify the larger scope and potential ambiguity of the issues involved by focusing on two essays, by Ernest Gellner and Talal Asad respectively. Gellner's is a classic essay, first published in 1951 and canonized by its inclusion in undergraduate textbooks in Britain to this day; Asad's critique appeared in a recent collection of essays by anthropologists critical of the politics of their own inherited tradition.[4] Gellner attacks the relativist thesis in anthropological theory, associating it with a confused and 'excessively charitable' intellectual and political attitude. Asad, in his critique of Gellner's essay, does not so much defend relativism as outline one serious way in which Gellner's attack is misconceived. In Asad's view, the emphasis should be placed on the practices and institutions of anthropological 'cultural translation', existing as they do in a matrix of unequal languages and asymmetrical access to the institutions of discourse and power.

One of the main points Gellner wishes to make in his essay concerns our attitude towards what we might consider 'illogical' or 'incoherent' ideas in the culture being studied. If the relativist claim remains that all cultural ideas are to be adequately understood only in their own contexts, is the interpreter necessarily committed to always finding meaning and coherence and giving up all capacity to judge ideas in other cultures as incoherent and meaningless? The contextualist-relativist, says Gellner, errs in adopting this attitude of unwarranted 'charity'. For often in fact we *need* to grasp the internal incoherence of ideas as they operate within a culture in order to understand their precise function and valence. Thus even though the contextual interpretation claims to be giving us the 'real' interpretation of something by situating it in its surrounding world of beliefs and practices, Gellner would argue that in many cases the acontextual evaluation of it (i.e. of a statement, proposition, or belief) is necessary if we are to provide deeper accounts of it as a cultural phenomenon. What Gellner calls interpretive 'charity' is thus more a kind of sentimental liberalism: it dehistoricizes in the name of contextual analysis, and ends up ignoring the deep structural bases of the other culture.

After identifying the extreme form of the contextualist position, which would argue that all ideas are to be interpreted solely in terms internal to the context in which they are produced and used, Gellner insists on the need for a strong evaluative interpretation. Building on his claim that 'sympathetic, positive interpretations of indigenous assertions are not the result of a sophisticated appreciation of context', and that in fact it may be that 'the manner in which the context is invoked, the amount and kind of context and the way the context itself is interpreted, depends on prior tacit determination concerning the kind of interpretation one wishes to find' (33), Gellner introduces a series of more specific claims. He argues that: 'the logical assessment' of an idea we have identified in the other culture is absolutely necessary for interpretation of the idea; an adequate interpretation of an idea in an unfamiliar culture involves a close translation into the 'language' of the familiar – i.e. the anthropologist's – culture. If Gellner is right, we need to worry more about the internal coherence or logic of the idea in isolation *before* we begin to determine what the appropriate context for interpreting it might be.

We evaluate an idea encountered in another culture by apprehending it as an 'assertion', for which we then seek an equivalent assertion in our own language. And just as we judge assertions in our own language as either 'Good' or 'Bad' we need also to evaluate the assertion/idea in the other culture. However, the 'tolerance-engendering contextual interpretation' evades this rigorous process of 'logical assessment' by assuming in advance that all assertions we encounter in the other culture are 'Good', i.e. meaningful and coherent. For Gellner, this makes a mockery of the interpretive process itself, which must build on the logical assessment of (isolated) assertions.

The crucial assumption here is that 'logical assessment' of assertions can be made only to the extent that we define them in isolation, and we isolate assertions in their (unfamiliar) language exactly the way we do in our (familiar) one. It would seem that for Gellner the identification of an assertion is an unproblematical activity. It is this naive atomism, difficult enough to sustain when we are studying elements *within* our own culture and obviously more complicated and arrogant when we are approaching another, on which Gellner's argument seems to be based. Despite the occasional appearance of terms like 'interpretation' and 'hermeneutics', the essay exists in the bliss of pre-hermeneutical positivist confidence, obscuring the most significant issues involved in anthropological interpretation in several ways. Talal Asad identifies one of these quite well.

Since Asad's critique of Gellner might have significant bearing on contemporary literary-critical theory and practice, it would be instructive to look at it in some detail. The most basic consideration Asad wishes to introduce into the discussion is simply that of the context of anthropological interpretation itself. For what Gellner is able to ignore in his entire essay is the existence of institutionally sanctioned power relations between interpreter and the interpreted that determine the politics of meaning in the first place. That the following reminder is necessary is itself embarrassing, and it might indeed point up the ambiguity of any critique of relativism, including the one I am making in this article. But Asad, let us remember, is not interested in defending the version of contextual-relativism Gellner attacks; rather, he is at pains to lay out the basic contextual terms with which any anthropological interpretive practice that sees itself performing 'cultural translation' must engage:

> The relevant question ... is not how tolerant an attitude the translator ought to display toward the original author (an abstract ethical dilemma), but how she can test the tolerance of her own language for assuming unaccustomed forms ... The matter is largely something the translator cannot determine by individual activity (any more than the individual speaker can affect the evolution of his or her language) – that it is governed by institutionally governed power relations between the languages/modes of life concerned. To put it crudely: because the languages of Third World societies – including, of course, the societies that social anthropologists have traditionally studied – are 'weaker' in relation to Western languages ... they are more likely to submit to forcible transformation in the translation process than the other way around. The reason for this is, first, that in their political-economic relations with Third World countries, Western nations have the greater ability to manipulate ... And, second, Western languages produce and deploy desired knowledge more readily than Third World languages do.
>
> (157-8)

There are two closely related questions Asad raises here to contest Gellner's abstract approach. The first wonders about the adequacy of Gellner's formulation of the problem of interpretation in terms of logical 'charity' or 'tolerance'. The second question deals with the fundamental model of 'translation' itself. Gellner's formulation of anthropological interpretation in terms of 'charity' is a convenient abstraction that obscures the practice of western anthropologists studying other cultures particularly in colonial and postcolonial contexts, since it ignores the basic hermeneutic question about the adequacy of the anthropologist's own cultural language (i.e. its capacity for 'tolerance' of new and unfamiliar meanings). The *possibility* that the interpreter and her analytical apparatus might be fundamentally challenged and changed by the material she (and it) are attempting to 'assess' is one that Gellner's account of the interpretive process ignores. Whether this account and others like it are naively positivist or whether they trail clouds of ideology and a specifiable political motive is something that needs analysis on its own terms. It may well be that 'decolonizing' anthropology will involve writing the discipline's prehistory in the process of developing such analyses, situating these glaring political blindnesses in the context of what may be their limited and skewed intellectual insights.[5]

In our obsessive fear that the typical western anthropologist might be guilty of excessive interpretive charity, we ignore the more significant fact that in our particular historical contexts the anthropologist, in order to be able to interpret at all, needs to educate herself through cultural and political 'sympathy'. Indeed, if we deepen our analysis we realize that the model of cultural translation is itself a misleading one: 'the anthropologist's translation is not merely a matter of matching sentences in the abstract, but of *learning to live another form of life*' (Asad, 149). The echo of Wittgenstein raises the important question about the limits of conception of anthropological interpretation as a translation from one language to another. It suggests that 'languages' are not merely 'texts' if by that we mean that 'translations' can be considered '*essentially* a matter of verbal representation' (160). Anthropological interpretation can be conceived as translation only if we recognize that a successful translation may potentially change our very language. By extension, these latter include our institutional contexts of interpretation, our 'disciplines' and their regimes of truth and scientificity, and the organization of power relations within the global system. An adequte anthropological interpretation must then include not only 'translation' but also an account of 'how power enters into the process of "cultural translation" [which must be] seen both as a discursive and as a non-discursive practice' (163). An instance of this *discursive* power – and the non-discursive power it banks on – is Gellner's very influential formulation of the interpretive process. The model of language and writing here serves to blind us to an entire history that is embedded in the processes of 'logical assessment' and decoding meaning. Gellner arrogates to himself the 'privileged position' of the interpreter in the very extent that he wishes, as anthropologist, not to interrogate his very real control of the entire operation of this translation, 'from field notes to printed ethnography'.

Gellner's 'logic' encompasses the entire space of the globe and its meanings; complexity of contextual function and meaning in every conceivable other space is granted only a limited autonomy since its essential terms remain formulated by the terms of Gellner's discursive world.

THE POLITICAL IMPLICATIONS OF RELATIVISM

Reacting sharply to the ahistorical vision underlying Gellner's Whiggery, the extreme relativist would point to the necessity of restoring to our critical perspective the presence of a plurality of spaces and values, the plurality of criteria of judgement and rationality implicit in the different cultural and historical contexts. Gellner's narrow conception of rationality, it would be easy to argue, is predicated on a false and reductive view of modern history as unproblematically One: guided by Reason, obeying the logic of progress and modernization. Gellner's model of history is one that should belong to the prehistory of a critical anthropology. For in our 'postmodern' world, history is no longer feasible; what we need to talk about, to pay attention to, are histories – in the plural. This position builds on the pervasive feeling in the human sciences these days that the grand narrative of history seems a little embarrassing. What we need to reclaim instead, as is often pointed out in cultural criticism and theory, is the plurality of our heterogeneous lives, the darker and unspoken densities of past and present that are lived, fought, and imagined as various communities and peoples seek to retrace and reweave the historical text. In the history of criticism, encountering for the first time the challenge of alternative canons defined by feminist, black, Third World scholars and others, this is initially not only a valuable critical idea but also the basis for an energizing critical-political project. After all, we have just been learning to speak of feminisms, instead of the singular form that implicitly hid the varied experiences of women's struggles along different racial and class vectors under the hegemonic self-image of the heterosexual white middle-class movement; we have learned to write 'marxism' without captalizing the 'm', thereby pointing to the need to reconceive the relationship to some unitary originary source; we have, in effect, taught ourselves that if history was available to us, it was always as a *text*, i.e. to be read and reread dialogically, and to be rewritten in a form other than that of a monologue, no matter how consoling or noble the latter's tone or import.

Plurality is thus a political ideal as much as it is a methodological slogan. But the issue of competing rationalities raises a nagging question: how do we negotiate between my history and yours? How would it be possible for us to recover our commonality, not the ambiguous imperial-humanist myth of our shared human attributes, which are supposed to distinguish us all from animals, but, more significantly, the imbrication of our various pasts and presents, the ineluctable relationships of shared and contested meanings, values, material resources? It is necessary to assert our dense particularities, our lived and imagined differences; but could we afford to leave untheorized the question of how our differences are intertwined and, indeed, hierarchically organized? Could we, in other words, afford to have *entirely* different histories, to see ourselves as living – and having lived – in entirely heterogeneous and discrete spaces?

It will not do to formulate the issue of competing rationalities and histories in the rather simplistic terms of merely *different* rationalities and histories. For the extreme relativist position, despite its initial attraction, seems to be philosophically and politically confused. This kind of relativism is easily refutable: if the relativist position is that there can be nothing other than context-specific truth-claims, that the 'truth' of every cultural or historical text is purely immanent to its immediate context, then on what grounds should I believe the relativist? If the relativist says that everything is entirely context-specific, claiming that we cannot adjudicate among contexts or texts on the basis of larger evaluative or interpretative criteria, then why should I bother to take seriously *that very relativist claim*? The point is that one cannot both claim to hold the relativist position and expect really to convince anyone who does not already believe the position. There is a self-refutation built into the argument, and it renders relativism less a significant philosophical position than a pious – though not ineffectual – political wish.

The problem is, however, that a refutation of this sort is not quite relevant for the way relativist ideas operate in contemporary critical circles. It is rarely as an explicit and reasoned position that relativism appears; instead it is embedded in our critical gestures, in the kinds of questions we ask or refuse to raise.[6] The more significant challenge would be to see whether there are political implications of the relativist position that the relativist would be interested in *not* bringing in with her in her baggage. And I think there is at least one rather serious

225

problem in what relativism entails: to believe that you have your space and I mine; to believe, further, that there can be no responsible way in which I can adjudicate between your space – cultural and historical – and mine by developing a set of general criteria that would have interpretive validity in both contexts (because there can be no interpretation that is not simultaneously an evaluation), is to assert something quite substantial. Quite simply, it is to assert that *all spaces are equivalent*: that they have equal value, that since the lowest common principle of evaluation is all that I can invoke, I cannot – and consequently need not – think about how your space impinges on mine, or how my history is defined together with yours. If that is the case, I may have started by declaring a pious political wish, but I end by denying that I need to take you seriously. Plurality instead of a single homogeneous space, yes. But also, unfortunately, debilitatingly insular spaces. Thus what needs to be emphasized is that this extreme relativist position is in no way a feasible theoretical basis of politically motivated criticism. It is in fact a dangerous philosophical ally, since it is built on, at best, naive and sentimental reasoning. To the extent that our initial interest in relativism was motivated by a political respect for other selves, other spaces, other contexts, relativism seems now to be an unacceptable theoretical position. For it might encourage a greater sensitivity to the contexts of production of cultural ideas, but it will not, given the terms of its formulation, enable a 'genuine dialogue' between anthropologist and native, the ex-colonizer and the ex-colonized.

A genuine dialogue of the kind Asad envisions would become possible only when we admit that crucial aspects of the non-western culture may have a great degree of coherence as part of a larger web of ideas, beliefs and practices, and moreover that *some* of these aspects may be untranslatable to the language of the western anthropologist's culture in terms of its historically sedimented and institutionally determined practices of knowing. The classic example ecountered by anthropologists in this context is the practice of 'magic' and ritual. From the point of view of the modern west, of course, these practices might be seen as coherent and of a piece with an entire form of life, but interpreted more rigorously they could reveal a 'primitive' system of belief and an 'irrational' practice. Magical rites are patently 'unscientific' when the primitive culture pursues them despite the lack of observable or tabulatable evidence that they do have the effects they are supposed to have. Rituals surrounding the planting of crops, for instance, may be practised because of the belief that they bring about the right kind of weather and, if this were observed to be true, the practice of such rituals would have at least *an* intelligible basis in reason. But what if, as the anthropologist may well note in instance after instance, the practice of this ritual continues despite the absence of any correlation between it and the weather? In that case should the practitioners not be considered irrational in their practice of at least this ritual, and quite possibly unscientific in their use of magic and ritual generally?

The philosopher Peter Winch argues in his famous essay 'Understanding a primitive society' that it would be wrong to come to even this conclusion.[7] Conducting a debate with Alasdair MacIntyre, who argues something like the above concerning the practices of the Azande, Winch points out how important it is to specify with greater care the details of the context. For it may be that the Zande practice of magic and ritual can go hand in hand with a clear working distinction between practices and knowledges that are technical and those that are magical. In this case – and indeed this is the case according to the anthropological account of the Azande by Evans-Pritchard, which both Winch and MacIntyre are discussing – Zande magic cannot be subsumed into the western category of the 'unscientific'. Since Zande practices exist in a larger web constituted in part by the magical-technical opposition, Zande magic could be considered (merely) unscientific only if the Azande *confused* it with their technical practices. In the case where a clear distinction exists between magical and technical practices, a one-to-one translation across cultures that ignores the intention of the practitioners becomes either misleading or at least grossly reductionist. According to Winch, the significant hermeneutical problem in this context can be raised through a kind of dialogue between the western web of beliefs and practices and the Zande one. Thus he considers it important to recognize 'that *we* do not initially have a category that looks at all like the Zande category of magic' (102). This is the source of the difficulty but also the beginning of an answer: 'Since it is we who want to understand the Zande category, it appears that the onus is on us to extend our understanding so as to make room for the Zande category; rather than to insist on seeing it in terms of our own ready-made distinction between science and non-science' (102). The reason this would constitute the beginning of a *dialogue* is that 'we' are forced to extend our understanding by interrogating its limits in terms of Zande categories of self-understanding. This dialogue marks the true hermeneutical moment rather than the explanation – or, worse yet, the 'logical assessment' (Gellner) – of a discursive object.

Two systems of understanding encounter each other to the very extent that both are contextualized as forms of life; this encounter leaves open the possibility of a fundamental change in both. If we recall the basic issues raised by the passages I quoted at the beginning of this essay, it will be clear how this kind of hermeneutical encounter provides at least one solution to the problem posed by the Other.

Winch's achievement consists in showing us that we need to respect other cultures not as insular and impenetrable wholes but rather as complex webs of beliefs and actions. He does this by emphasizing that notions of rationality cannot be unproblematically applied across cultures precisely because there are different – and *competing* – rationalities, and one must acknowledge this fact in order to appreciate the specific modalities of actions and beliefs in a given culture. The relationship between cause and effect in cultural practices, for instance, can be understood at different levels. Here is the way Winch explains the idea of different orders, i.e. different levels of human practice:

> A man's sense of the importance of something to him shows itself in all sorts of ways; not merely in precautions to safeguard that thing. He may want to come to terms with its importance to him in quite a different way: to contemplate it, to gain some sense of his life in relation to it. He may wish thereby, in a certain sense, to *free* himself from dependence on it. I do not mean by making sure that it does not let him down, because the point is that, *whatever* he does, he may still be let down. The important thing is that he should understand *that* and come to terms with it, though perhaps it is a necessary condition for so doing, for a man may equally well be transfixed and terrorized by the contemplation of such a possibility. He must see that he can still go on even if he is let down by what is vitally important to him; and he must so order his life that he still *can* go on in such circumstances.
>
> (103-4; emphases in the original)

The terms with which Winch formulates the discussion in this rich passage make clear that to conceive magical rites as complex practices not reducible to the rational-irrational or scientific-unscientific polarities of the west involves a deeper conception of human practices in general – i.e. in all societies – as complex in their modalities of intention and meaning. As suggested earlier, the notion of cause and effect is itself one that needs to be interpreted according to its specific modalities. Not to acknowledge these differences is simply – as we say in contemporary criticism – to 'read' badly. Thus, the most useful lesson that the sophisticated relativist teaches us is that we cannot understand complex cultural acts by reducing them hastily to their propositional content; indeed the reduction often involves basic kinds of misreading and misidentification. And to the extent that we define 'rationality' on the basis of such terms as logical consistency or the pragmatic choice of means for our technical ends, Winch's arguments as I have presented them would challenge this most fundamental of our concepts.

CULTURE, RATIONALITY AND HUMAN AGENCY: THE LIMITS OF OTHERNESS

The key issue is, of course, whether there can be more to the idea of rationality – or culture – than this. For even though he discusses the ways in which different cultures can learn from one another, Winch does not quite face up to the question inherent in his own idea of *competing* rationalities. Difference teaches us not merely new technical possibilities, Winch tells us, but also new and possible forms of life. And he is right in emphasizing this. Criteria of rationality are connected to what we call 'culture', the larger moral and imaginative patterns through which we deal with our world. However, content as he is with definitions of rationality and cultural practices at the most general level, seeing cultures only as coherent systems, Winch underestimates the complexity of the question of evaluative comparison among these rationalities and cultures. (The absence of emphasis on evaluative comparison is, we recall, what makes a theoretical position ultimately a relativist one.) But such a comparison would necessarily be more rigorously interpretive, involving specification of the various elements and levels which constitute cultures as *articulated* wholes. Winch's cross-cultural comparison of 'forms of life' is pitched at such a high level of generality that his versions of human culture and rationality cannot register and include significant moral and imaginative practices and choices. If it is to constitute a relevant political interrogation, I would argue, the dialogue across cultures that we envision anthropological interpretation at its best to be conducting must in principle be able to include the levels of ordinary, everyday activity. For this to be possible, we need a minimal conception of rationality that will help us understand human activities – both the grand and the humbler ones – as the actions of agents.

For Peter Winch, the common point of all human cultures is the presence of a few 'limiting notions' – fundamental ideas that determine the 'ethical space' of all cultures, the space 'within which the possibilities of good and evil ... can be exercised' (107). The three such notions Winch specifies are birth, sexuality, and death. Together they map the limits of possibility that define our lives for us, and consequently outline our ethical universe. According to Winch, then, it is in this universe that rationality has its moorings. I wonder, however, if we do not lose as much as we gain if we pitch the issues on this high a level. We are, according to Winch, rational creatures and can engage in a dialogue with those who are significantly different from us, but this difference is negotiated at such a level of generality that significant aspects of human life such as, for instance, the conditions in which we work, our struggles to forge political communities, or our varying conceptions of cultural identity and selfhood, remain unarticulated and indeed invisible. Winch's human cultures are individually rational, and they are capable of communicating with one another in a process of hermeneutical self-critique and interrogation. But the 'rationality' they share is not defined in terms specific enough to register and include a great deal of what we usually consider to be our significant practices and beliefs: it is defined merely as the overall *coherence* of the *whole*, the most general systematicity revealed in the way a culture's actions, beliefs, and intellectual judgements all hang together. Given such a broad definition, *most* of what constitutes our historical life, our humbler acts as social agents and thinkers, remains closed to transcultural dialogue – to the very extent that these acts are not ultimately subsumable to birth, death, and sexuality, not registered in the systematicity of the whole. Winch's version of rationality – as inevitably tied in this way to the large cultural schemes by which we define and live our lives – has gained in moral suppleness over the positivist or the ethnocentric ones, but it seems to have forfeited much of its capacity to judge and interpret.

A more specific commonality than the one Winch's definition would posit for all human cultures and societies is the one that is implicit in the very definition of 'culture' as social practice. The perspective of 'practice', as it has been proposed in several recent developments in social theory across disciplines and methodological approaches,[8] does not necessarily involve the notion of a unitary and self-sufficient Subject as the author of its actions. The basic claims would include the following: humans make their world; they make their world in conditions they inherit and that are not all within their control;

theoretically understanding this 'making' involves redefining social structures and cultural institutions as not simply given but *constituted*, and hence containing the possibility of being changed. Moreover, in this conception, humans are seen as individual and collective *agents* in their world; and their practices can be specified for analysis without a necessary reduction to their subjective beliefs and intentions. Of course, the agents' intentions and beliefs about their practices are not irrelevant (since they can be aware of their purposes and actions); but these beliefs cannot be considered the *sole* determinant of meaning. 'Culture' is thus best appreciated as defining the realm of human choices in (potentially) definable contexts, choices of individuals and collectives as potentially self-aware agents; it is constituted *in* (and *as*) history. It is the significance of this kind of agency that Winch's related definitions of culture and rationality fail to register adequately. One specification we need to make in literary and cultural criticism, I would argue, is through the conception of *agency* as a basic capacity shared by all humans *across cultures*. And in understanding the divide between 'us' and 'them', it is this common space we all share that needs to be elaborated and defined.

In literary and cultural criticism, developments associated with structuralism and poststructuralism in particular have made us aware of the way language and cultural and semiotic systems, seen as systems, determine both meanings and subject-positions. The political agendas of these movements have been tied to a genealogical analysis of European humanism, and a great deal of attention has been paid to the deconstruction of one of the hallmarks of modern European history – the Subject, an effect of specific discursive and institutional forces masquerading as universal Man. In this archaeological critical climate, instances of positive elaboration of the human have been noticeably absent. This is due to a salutary caution: we are all familiar with accounts of 'the human' that are patently speculative and serve sexist, racist, and imperialist programmes. We are also aware of how historical knowledge can be used selectively to construct such accounts, and how these definitions can be made to serve dangerous political ends. But the larger question that a philosophical anthropology pursues regarding the capacities, tasks, and limits that might comprise a specifically human existence will not go away, quite simply because our analyses of social and cultural phenomena often involve acknowledged or implicit answers to this and related questions. To the extent that criticism deals with 'culture', i.e. it engages in the interpretation of texts and contexts in the light of what people – individually and collectively – do, think, and

231

make of their lives, these questions regarding the *subject* of cultural practices will remain to be dealt with explicitly. A thoroughgoing deconstruction of 'humanism' and its self-authorizing Subject is less an avoidance of this issue than, first and foremost, a clearing of the ground for reconsidering the problems involved.

It is in the context of political criticism that the need for a minimal account of the human, defining a commonality we all share, becomes immediate and clear. Donald Davidson has shown us in a series of recent essays the extent to which an interpretation of the Other is dependent on an acknowledgement of common ground. Arguing against the general idea of radical untranslatability (between conceptual schemes, cultures, rationalities, etc.) that an extreme relativist position assumes, Davidson has stressed that we appreciate differences to the very extent that we acknowledge our pool of shared words, thoughts, and ideas.[9] Indeed, 'we *improve* the clarity and bite of our declarations of difference ... by *enlarging* the basis of shared (translatable) language or of shared opinion' (197; emphases added). Davidson concludes by saying that there is no 'intelligible' basis for the position that all cultures, rationalities, and languages are so radically different that we cannot translate any portion of one to the other at all; at the same time, the fond belief that all humankind shares 'a common scheme and ontology' (198) is one that is not – yet – convincing either. Winch's 'rationalities' are homologous to what Davidson calls 'schemes' here, and I think it would be important to recognize the ways in which the competition among rationalities must be conceived, beyond Winch's own account, *by specifying and elaborating shared terms, ideas, and spaces*. The shared ground helps us situate and specify difference, understand where its deepest resonances might originate. If we are to deal seriously with other cultures and not reduce them to insignificance or irrelevance, we need to begin by positing the following minimal commonality between us and them: the capacity to act purposefully, to be capable of agency and the basic rationality that the human agent must in principle possess.

But what exactly does a specifically *human* agency imply? What, by our most careful contemporary philosophical accounts, distinguishes us from animals is that we possess the capacity for a certain kind of second-degree thought, i.e. not merely the capacity to act purposefully but also to *evaluate* actions and purposes in terms of larger ideas we might hold about, say, our political and moral world, or our sense of beauty or form. It is this capacity for a second-order understanding and evaluation which enables us to be critically and cumulatively self-aware in relation to our actions, that defines human agency and makes possible the sociality and the historicality of human existence. It is this theoretical ability in effect to possess a meaningful history that we cannot afford to deny to the cultural Other if we are to interpret it.

To return to our discussion of relativism, then, we can see why it is important to go beyond a simple recognition of *differences* across cultures. For 'they' do ultimately what 'we' do, since they share with us a capacity for self-aware historical agency. If their terms, categories, and solutions are fundamentally different from ours, we have identified not merely a difference but what Charles Taylor calls an 'incommensurability'. Incommensurable activities are different, according to Taylor's useful distinction, but 'they somehow occupy the same space'; 'The real challenge is to see the incommensurability, to come to understand how their range of possible activities, that is, the way in which they identify and distinguish activities, differs from ours.'[10] The 'range of possible activities' outlines the space of 'culture'. The centrality of practice in this understanding of culture, emphasizing the social actions of individuals and collectives in definable situations, enriches our notion of difference by historicizing it. Only when we have defined our commonality in this way can the why-question, about the reason underlying different practices and different choices, become not only intelligible but also *necessary*. For given this essential common space, otherness appears not in the form of insularity or in a relationship of mere contiguity, but as a complex historical phenomenon, available to us only through a process of hermeneutical comparison and specification. Mere difference leads to a sentimental charity, for there is nothing in its logic that necessitates our attention to the other. Winch's sophisticated relativism emphasizes the ethical dimension, but to the extent that it too remains underspecified in its conception of rationality, its political implications are at best vague. The rationality that a political cultural criticism cannot afford to ignore is one that is implicit in the very definition of human agency sketched above, as the capacity that all human 'persons' and 'cultures' in principle possess to understand their actions and evaluate them in terms of their (social and historical) significance for them. It is this issue that relativism, in both the extreme and the sophisticated formulations I have discussed, obscures.

I do not see how political criticism (poststructuralist or otherwise) can afford to deny this minimal rationality that is implicit in human agency or avoid theorizing what it entails.[11] Consideration of the question of rationality is unnecessarily complicated if we confuse the kinds of basic definitional issues I have been outlining here with the philosophical search for large schemes we have traditionally called Reason. Whether in any of its positivist garbs, or as the more dialectical 'communicative rationality' that Habermas has been seeking. Reason formulated as the grand foundational structure that would subtend (and hence explain) all human capacities and ground all knowledge is now probably best seen as a noble but failed dream. But that does not mean either that there is no rational component to human actions, or – more crucially – that we can afford to (philosophically) ignore this rationality. My attempt in this paper has been to explain why it would be debilitating at the present moment to confuse the claims of an ideal and comprehensive Reason with the basic capacities we can identify and define only in terms of the minimal rationalities they involve.

Moreover, once we understand that human rationality need not simply be a formal matter, as positivists insist, but is instead a fundamental capacity for articulation that underlies our social actions and enables us to be historical creatures, we can begin to realize what else is at stake in all this for political criticism. So long as we base our political analyses of culture on relativist grounds, avoiding the challenge posed by the competing claims of various (cultural) rationalities, we will surrender complex historical knowledge of Others to sentimental ethical gestures in their direction. We might remain wary of ethnocentric evaluation of alterity, but there is a basic evaluation involved in positing connections, perceiving similarities and differences, organizing complex bodies of information into provisionally intelligible wholes. Central to this process of evaluative judgement, with its minimal tasks of ordering and creating hierarchies of significance, is the understanding of humans across cultural and historical divides as capable of the minimal rationality implicit in agency. This cross-cultural commonality is one limit our contemporary political notions of difference and otherness need to acknowledge and theorize.

There are immediate practical considerations involved in all of this. In criticism, for instance, the call for respect for alternative canons can be made on the basis of a purely liberal respect for other literatures and experiences, but that will not necessarily comprise a challenge to the dominant order to the very extent that alternative canons are seen simply as coexisting peacefully in a pluralistic academy. If what I have

234

said about the inadequacy of a logic of difference is convincing, the charity evident in institutional pluralism may in fact hide a more fundamental indifference. For in the study of modern literatures, the most crucial political question that arises concerns a history 'we' all share, a history whose very terms and definitions are now being openly contested and formulated. When pluralist arguments are used to support the proliferation of various minority canons and discourses, the question of historical imbrication, indeed the question of this unequal history itself, is obscured by a narrowly pragmatic logic. The study of minority literatures, for instance, can be defended on the ground that an adequate definition of literature must include all of 'its' variant forms and all the various human experiences they represent. The difficulty with this formulation is that its *vagueness* leaves it open to all kinds of ironic recuperation. Thus when the Moroccan-French writer Tahar Ben Jelloun won France's prestigious Goncourt Prize, that President Mitterrand found it possible to describe the event as further evidence of the universality of the French language. Ben Jelloun, the first North African writer to win this prize, writes in both French and Arabic and has remained a critic of both the Moroccan regime and the racist practices of the French against North African immigrants. To read – and teach – his works as evidence of the universality of the French language, or even of the rich diversity of the human experience, is precisely to erase the specificity of the postcolonial immigrant writer, ambivalently situated in the belly of the imperial beast.[12] Ignoring the history of colonialism by merely celebrating God's literary plenty, the pluralist critic would be no different here from the socialist President in containing the potential significance of any otherness. One way for criticism to battle such historical amnesia would be to stress the complex agencies of both the colonizers and the colonized that are evident in cultural production and consumption. In fact, it is in the imbrication of these agencies that cultural configurations of colonial histories, of patterns of domination and the resistances to them, can be traced and understood.[13] The academy's eager acceptance of alternative canons – defined often as dehistoricized, formal constructs – suggests the urgent need to go beyond purely *literary*-historical reformulations.[14]

One function of political criticism is to identify the social interests that the reading and writing of literature serve. These interests can be variously oppressive or liberating; and there is nothing inherent in the texts themselves that can control and limit the uses to which they are put or the meanings and values they are made to deploy. We cannot understand the interests of different social groups or different political visions of the world, however, without historical specification; a general rhetoric of alterity reveals structures and systems, not the terms and conditions through which individual and collective experiences can be identified. Our formulation of such terms and conditions is dependent on a positive elaboration of the varieties of cultural and political practice, and on a theoretical understanding of human agency. For despite the mystifications of the numerous ideologies of the Subject it would be a little too soon to conclude that humans have not acted, believed, and attempted to make and remake their worlds. This has happened in the Third World as much as in the First. To the extent that we specify the common terms on the level of human practice, and seek to articulate and understand our contexts, goals, and possibilities, we consider human history potentially intelligible, and the individual and collective actions of humans open to rational analysis. Notwithstanding our contemporary slogans of otherness, and our fervent denunciations of Reason and the Subject, there is an unavoidable conception of rational action, enquiry, and dialogue inherent in this political-critical project, and if we deny or obscure it we ought at least to know at what cost.

NOTES

This is an abridged version of an article that originally appeared in *Yale Journal of Criticism*, Spring 1989. I develop the arguments presented here in 'The Epistemic Status of Cultural Identity: On *Beloved* and the Postcolonial Condition', *Cultural Critique* 1993, and 'Colonial Legacies, Multicultural Futures: Relativism. Objectivity, and the Challenge of Otherness', *PMLA* 1995, as well as in my book *Literary Theory and the Claims of History: Postmodernism, Objectivity, Politics*, forthcoming from Cornell University Press.

[1] Patrick Gardiner, 'German philosophy and the rise of relativism', *The Monist* 64 (April 1981), 138-54. Useful recent discussions of relativism, with good bibliographies, can be found in Martin Hollis and Steven Lukes (eds), *Rationality and Relativism* (Oxford: Blackwell, 1982) and M. Krausz and J. Meiland (eds), *Relativism: Cognitive and moral* (Notre Dame, Ind.: University of Notre Dame Press, 1982). See also the earlier publication, Bryan Wilson (ed.), *Rationality* (Oxford: Blackwell, 1970; rpt 1985).
[2] The quotations are taken from: Michel Foucault, *The Archaeology of Knowledge*, trans. A.M. Sheridan Smith (London: Tavistock, 1972), 11-12;

Hélène Cixous, 'The laugh of the Medusa', in Elaine Marks and Isabelle de Courtivron (eds), *New French Feminisms* (New York: Shocken Books, 1981), 263-4, 260; Ernesto Laclau and Chantal Mouffe, *Hegemony and Socialist Strategy: Towards a radical democratic politics*, trans. Winston Moore and Paul Cammack (London: Verso, 1985), 2.

[3] Useful studies of this phenomenon include: Talal Asad (ed.), *Anthropology and the Colonial Encounter* (London: Ithaca Press, 1973); George E. Marcus and Michael M.J. Fischer, *Anthropology as Cultural Critique: An experimental moment in the human sciences* (Chicago and London: University of Chicago Press, 1986); James Clifford and George E. Marcus (eds), *Writing Culture: The poetics and politics of ethnography* (Berkeley, Calif.: University of California Press, 1986); George W. Stocking, Jnr, *Victorian Anthropology* (London: Collier Macmillan, 1987), esp. c. 7; Douglas A. Lorimer, 'Theoretical racism in late-Victorian anthropology 1870-1900', *Victorian Studies* 31, 3 (Spring 1988), 405-30; and, of course, for a more general account, Edward Said, *Orientalism* (London: Routledge & Kegan Paul, 1978). For a feminist critique of some of the dominant anthropological categories, see Felicity Eldhom, Olivia Harris, and Kate Young, 'Conceptualising women', *Critique of Anthropology*, 3, 9/10 (1977); and for a productive encounter between anthropological concepts and a global materialist history, Eric R. Wolf, *Europe and the People without History* (Berkeley, Calif.: University of California Press, 1982). For an analysis of politically motivated scholarship about the Third World which unselfconsciously reproduces larger patterns of discursive colonization, see Chandra Talpade Mohanty, 'Under western eyes: feminist scholarship and colonial discourses', *Boundary* 2, 12, 3/13, 1; revised version in *Feminist Review*, 30 (1988).

[4] Ernest Gellner, 'Concepts and society', in Wilson, *Rationality*, 18-49; Talal Asad, 'The concept of cultural translation', in Clifford and Marcus, *Writing Culture*, 141-64. Further page references given in the text.

[5] 'Decolonizing anthropology' necessarily suggests a collective and historically specific project. I borrow the term from the special session held at the 1987 convention of the American Anthropological Association.

[6] One well-known instance might suffice here. The need to base political criticism in a space that is itself an articulation of several, of at least the dominant and the marginal, is what Myra Jehlen emphasizes in her valuable essay, 'Archimedes and the paradox of feminist criticism', *Signs*, 6, 4 (Summer 1981), 575-601. Jehlen uses her central metaphor of an Archimedean point for criticism to argue 'that a terrestrial fulcrum, a standpoint from which we can see our conceptual universe whole but which nonetheless rests firmly on male ground, is what feminists really need' (576). However, the fact that she does not examine further the problems of the relativist position she would seem to be attacking here leads to a strange vagueness. Thus, although in her conclusion she talks about 'points of contradiction as the places where we can see the whole structure of our world most clearly', she is able to see this as implying 'the immanent relativity of all perception and knowledge' (600, 601). If Jehlen means by this that comparative perspectives and analyses reveal the extent to which the different structures of perception and knowledge are produced in specific contexts, and are thus in part understandable in terms

237

relative to these contexts, she has a point, but she seems to want to *suggest* more. For in the very next sentence she sees much larger consequences following from the above point: 'Thus, what appears first as a methodological contradiction, then becomes a subject in itself, seems finally to be shaping something like a new epistemology' (601). Accepting the legitimate relativist-contextualist insight about the significance of context helps us fight, say, andro- or ethnocentrism, but since that does not necessarily involve or entail changing the very ways in which we conceive of knowledge and the process of knowing, i.e. seeking a new *epistemology*, I am not sure what Jehlen's suggestion means here. Since she argues an anti-separatist or anti-relativist position throughout the essay, I see this suggestion at the end as a confusing vagueness rather than a contradiction in her argument; but it is at least evidence that her position would be clearer and stronger if she thought through the issue of relativism and what it entails.

It might be that cultural criticism is, at least at the present moment, particularly unconcerned about relativism as a problematic position. It would be illuminating to contrast Jehlen's essay with Sandra Harding's recent discussion of the implications of feminism for the social sciences: 'Introduction: is there a feminist method?' in *Feminism and Methodology*, ed. Sandra Harding (Bloomington, Ind.: Indiana University Press, 1987), 1-14. Harding's strictures on relativists include a pertinent political diagnosis: 'Historically, relativism appears as an intellectual possibility, and as a "problem", only for dominating groups at the point where the hegemony (the universality) of their views is being challenged. As a modern intellectual position, it emerged in the belated recognition by nineteenth-century Europeans that the apparently bizarre beliefs and behaviors of non-Europeans had a rationality or logic of their own. Perhaps the preferred Western beliefs might not be the only reasonable ones. The point here is that relativism is not a problem originating in, or justifiable in terms of, women's experiences or feminist agendas. It is fundamentally a sexist response that attempts to preserve the legitimacy of androcentric claims in the face of contrary evidence' (10).
[7] Peter Winch, 'Understanding a primitive society', in Wilson, *Rationality*, 78-111. Page references given in the text.
[8] For an excellent summary and discussion, see R.W. Connell, *Gender and Power* (Cambridge: Polity Press, 1987). The most original and ambitious work with this focus is Pierre Bourdieu's; see especially *Outline of a Theory of Practice* (Cambridge: Cambridge University Press, 1977) and, for a succinct formulation of his theory, *Distinction: A social critique of the judgement of taste* (London: Routledge & Kegan Paul, 1984). On the idea that social actions are 'recursive', i.e. never entirely original and always a form of revision of existing social meanings, see Anthony Giddens, *The Constitution of Society: Outline of the theory of structuration* (Cambridge: Polity Press, 1984).
[9] Donald Davidson, 'On the very idea of a conceptual scheme', in his *Inquiries into Truth and Interpretation* (Oxford: Oxford University Press, 1984), 183-98.
[10] The useful distinction between 'difference' and 'incommensurability' is developed in Taylor's essay, 'Rationality', in his *Philosophy and the Human Sciences: Philosophical Papers*, Volume 2 (Cambridge: Cambridge University

Press, 1985), 134-51, which contains a good discussion of Winch and one of the best accounts of what I have been calling a minimal conception of rationality (the quotations are from p145). Taylor considers our capacity for 'articulation' or laying things out 'in perspicuous order' the basic component of human rationality, although it is not quite clear whether he would consider this to be a historically or culturally universal phenomenon. There is a good account of the issues involved in conceiving a post-positivist rationality in Hilary Putnam, *Reason, Truth and History* (Cambridge: Cambridge University Press, 1981), and the essay 'Beyond historicism' in his *Realism and Reason: Philosophical Papers*, Volume 3 (Cambridge: Cambridge University Press, 1983), 287-303. Many of these questions have been debated fruitfully by historians and philosophers of science.

[11] See Christopher Cherniak, *Minimal Rationality* (Cambridge, Mass.: MIT Press, 1986), 20.

[12] The ambivalent relationship between contemporary minority writers and their 'metropolitan' audiences is highlighted in the context of Europe's new immigrant populations. At what may have been the first American conference on this subject, 'Europe's New Minority Cultures' (Cornell, February 1988), the issue of cultural appropriation and a critical pedagogy which would prevent that became a central issue in both the papers and the discussions which followed. I would like to mention in particular the presentations by Ted Chamberlain on 'Britain's new poetry' and Samia Mehrez on 'The Francophone North African cultural presence in France'.

[13] Indeed, developments in the historiography of colonialism (e.g. New World slavery or colonial formations such as British India) as well as of post-colonial societies (focusing in particular on the roles of the peasantry and of women) suggest the extent to which the 'imbrication' of the agencies of the colonizers and the colonized is itself an image that demands further specification. Thus, it forces historians of anti-colonial struggles to go beyond the visible and institutionally organized nationalism of the middle classes in order to trace patterns of resistance in peasant movements and revolts, a kind of resistance colonial historians had been content to characterize as criminal acts or at best unselfconscious and inchoate upsurges of powerful feeling. In the context of South Asia, see Sumit Sarkar, *Modern Indian History: 1895-1947* (New Delhi: Macmillan, 1983), for a useful survey of the 'history from below' approach. The ongoing work on the role of the peasantry in Indian nationalist struggles can be followed in the pages of such journals as *Economic and Political Weekly* (Bombay), the *Journal of Peasant Studies* (London), *Modern Asian Studies* (Cambridge), as well as in the series of volumes titled *Subaltern Studies*, ed. R. Guha, published by Oxford University Press, Delhi. Questions of gender in the historiography of colonial India, and the difficult methodological issues raised by other uncoded practices of resistance, are dealt with cogently by Rosalind O'Hanlon in her recent review essay 'Recovering the subject: *Subaltern Studies* and histories of resistance in colonial South Asia', *Modern Asian Studies*, 22, 1 (1988), 189-224. For the most detailed recent study of 'everyday' resistance, which extends our understanding of historical agency by focusing on non-insurrectionary practices, see James C. Scott, *Weapons of the Weak: Everyday forms of peasant resistance* (New Haven, Conn. and London:

Yale University Press, 1985). All these analyses of the historically imbricated agencies of the 'oppressed' and the 'oppressor' owe much to Eugene Genovese's path-breaking studies of North American slavery, especially *The World the Slaveholders Made* (1969) and *Roll Jordan Roll: The World the Slaves Made* (1974).

The most basic lesson of such historiographical developments for a colonial and post-colonial *cultural* studies is at the very least that we need to be wary of too easily distinguishing 'culture' from 'history'. Even more clearly than in contemporary analyses of metropolitan societies, the challenge for students of the Third World is to suspend the traditional notion of culture as a realm apart of sweetness and light. The rueful joke that the west possesses a history and a sociology, the Third World merely an anthropology, does have a point, especially about the racial-ideological biases inherent in modern disciplinary demarcations and territories. But we might do well to be wary of the convenient reaction to these biases which would consist in investing Third World societies with 'culture' in the traditional western mould (after all, that was what both the Orientalists and the early nationalists, in their own ways, tried to do), and be more ready to specify and re-examine notions of 'history' and 'culture' together. (For an account of 'race' as a historical process evidenced in cultural practices and tendencies, see my 'Kipling's children and the colour line', *Race and Class* (1989). For an analysis of 'agency' on a very different register in the context of a contemporary poet who is often read as a 'postmodernist', see S.P. Mohanty and Jonathan Monroe, 'John Ashbery and the articulation of the social', *Diacritics* 17, 3.)

[14] For an astute discussion of such issues, especially in the context of possible institutional appropriation of minority discourses, see Cornel West, 'Minority discourse and the pitfalls of canon formation', *Yale Journal of Criticism* 1, 1 (Fall 1987), 193-201.

Pluralism and Modern Democracy: Around Carl Schmitt

Chantal Mouffe

Does the downfall of Communism signify the end of history, as Fukuyama proclaims, or the beginning of a new era for the democratic project, now at last freed of the burden with which the image of 'real existing socialism' loaded it down? We have, in fact, to acknowledge that the victory of liberal democracy is due more to the collapse of its enemy than to its own successes. Far from being in excellent health, there is growing disaffection with political life in the Western democracies and clear signs of a dangerous erosion of democratic values. The rise of the extreme Right, the rebirth of fundamentalism and the creeping marginalization of vast sectors of the population are there to remind us that the situation is far from satisfactory in our own countries.

As Norberto Bobbio points out, the crisis of communism now presents the affluent democracies with a real challenge. Will they be capable of solving the problems to which that system proved incapable of providing solutions? In his view, it would be very dangerous to imagine that the defeat of Communism has put an end to poverty and the longing for justice. 'Democracy', he writes, 'has admittedly come out on top in the battle with historical communism. But what resources and ideals does it possess with which to confront those problems that gave rise to the Communist challenge?'[1] I believe it is important to provide an answer to this question and that the moment has come to engage in some uncompromising thinking on the nature of liberal democratic societies. The disappearance of the spectre of totalitarianism should allow us to come at such an enquiry from a

241

different angle. The point is no longer to provide an apologia for democracy but to analyse its principles, examine its operation, discover its limitations and bring out its potentialities.

To do this, we must grasp the specificity of pluralist liberal democracy as a *political* form of society, as a new regime (*politeia*), the nature of which, far from consisting in the articulation of democracy and capitalism, as some claim, is to be sought exclusively on the level of the political.

To mark out the broad outlines for a thoroughgoing study of the liberal democratic regime, its nature and the possibilities it offers, I propose to take as my starting point the work of one of its most brilliant and intransigent opponents, Carl Schmitt. Though they were developed at the beginning of the century Schmitt's criticisms are, in fact, still pertinent and it would be superficial to believe that the writer's subsequent membership of the National Socialist Party means that we can simply ignore them. On the contrary, I believe it is by facing up to the challenge posed by such a rigorous and perspicacious opponent that we shall succeed in grasping the weak points in the dominant conception of modern democracy, in order that these may be remedied.

Schmitt takes the view that the articulation of liberalism and democracy, which occurred in the nineteenth century, gave birth to a hybrid regime characterized by the union of two absolutely heterogeneous political principles. As he sees it, parliamentary democracy brings about a situation in which the principle of identity proper to the democratic form co-exists with the principle of representation specific to monarchy. In *The Crisis of Parliamentary Democracy*, he declares that, contrary to the normally accepted view, the principle of parliamentarism, as pre-eminence of the legislative over the executive, does not belong to the universe of thought of democracy, but to that of liberalism. Unlike many political theorists, Schmitt sees that it was not for reasons of scale – the argument that size would have made the exercise of direct democracy impossible – that representative democracy was instituted. He rightly points out that if it had been for reasons of practical expediency that representatives were entrusted with decision-making on behalf of the people, this could just as easily have been used to justify anti-parliamentary Caesarism.[2] It is not, therefore, in his view, to the democratic principle of identity that we should look for the *ratio* of the parliamentary system, but to the universe of liberal thought. Hence the importance of grasping the coherence of liberalism as an overall metaphysical system. Schmitt argues that the basic liberal principle around which all the rest revolves is that truth can be arrived at through the unfettered conflict of opinions. For liberalism, there is no final truth, and truth becomes, in that theory, 'a mere function of the eternal competition of opinions'.[3] This, says Schmitt, throws a new light on the nature of parliamentarism, the *raison d'être* of which must be sought in its constituting a process of confrontation of opinions, from which the political will is supposed to emerge. Consequently, what is essential in the parliament is 'public deliberation of argument and counter-argument, public debate and public discussions, parley, and all this without taking democracy into account'.[4] It is Schmitt's view that the representative element constitutes a non-democratic aspect of parliamentary democracy insofar as it renders impossible that identity between government and governed inherent in the logic of democracy. There is therefore, as he sees it, a contradiction at the heart of the liberal form of government which means that liberalism denies democracy and democracy denies liberalism. This becomes clearly visible with the crisis of the parliamentary system we find in modern mass democracy. In that system, public discussion, with its dialectical interplay of opinions, has been replaced by partisan negotiation and the calculation of interests; the parties have become pressure groups, 'calculating their mutual interests and opportunities for power, and they actually agree compromises and coalitions on this basis'.[5]

In his view, this came about in the following way. The liberal parliamentary order required that a whole series of disruptive questions concerning morality, religion and the economy be confined to the private sphere. This was a necessary pre-condition if parliament was to be able to present itself as the place where individuals, distanced from the conflictual interests which separated them, could discuss and arrive at a rational consensus. In this way, the homogeneity was created which, in Schmitt's view, is required for any democracy to function. The development of modern mass democracy was, however, to lead to the appearance of the 'total state', which would be forced to intervene in an increasing range of fields as a result of democratic pressure for the extension of rights. The phenomenon of 'neutralization' which characterized the previous phase was, then, to give way to an opposite movement of 'politicization' of the various forms of social relations. The consequences of the development of that 'total state' for the parliament were incalculable. Not only did it see its influence diminish, since many decisions, including some of the most important, began to be made in other ways; it also became the arena where antagonistic interests came into conflict. Schmitt's conclusion was that the parliamentary system had lost all credibility since no one could believe any longer in the principles on which it was based. As a result, parliamentary democracy found itself bereft of its intellectual foundations. And in 1926, in the preface to the second edition of his critique of parliamentarism, he wrote these words, which should give us reason to pause:

> Even if Bolshevism is suppressed and Fascism held at bay, the crisis of contemporary parliamentarism would not be overcome in the least. For it has not appeared as a result of the appearance of those two opponents; it was there before them and will persist after them. Rather the crisis springs from the consequences of modern mass democracy and, in the last analysis, from the contradiction of a liberal individualism burdened by a moral pathos and a democratic sentiment governed essentially by political ideals ... It is, in its depths, the inescapable contradiction of liberal individualism and democratic homogeneity.[6]

THE NATURE OF MODERN DEMOCRACY

While not accepting the consequences Schmitt draws, we can nevertheless acknowledge that he has to be taken seriously when he points up the deficiencies of liberal parliamentary democracy. To the extent that its institutions are perceived as mere instrumental techniques, it is improbable that it can be assured of the type of adherence which would guarantee effective participation. The 'political virtue' Montesquieu regarded as indispensable to democracy and which he identified with 'the love of laws and the fatherland' cannot develop in such a context. Now, nothing has occurred since the beginning of the century to remedy this absence of a satisfactory elaboration of what might be called the 'political principles' of representative democracy. On the contrary, it is actually the case that all attempts to provide ethical and philosophical arguments for it have been abandoned. With the development of what C. B. Macpherson has described as the 'equilibrium model', democracy became purely a mechanism for choosing and empowering governments and it has been reduced to a competition between elites. As for the citizens, they are treated as consumers in the political marketplace. Hence there is nothing surprising about the low level of participation in the democratic process which is found in many Western societies today. How, then, is liberal democracy to be given those 'intellectual foundations' without which it is unable to command solid support: this is the challenge Schmitt's work poses for contemporary political philosophy.

To perform such an undertaking, it is important first to grasp the specificity of modern democracy and the central role played in it by pluralism. By this I mean the recognition of individual freedom, that freedom which John Stuart Mill defends in his essay, 'On Liberty', as the only freedom worthy of the name, and which he defines as the possibility for every individual to pursue happiness as he sees fit, to set his own goals and attempt to achieve them in his own way. Pluralism is therefore linked to the abandonment of a substantive and unique vision of the common good and of the *eudaemonia* which is constitutive of modernity. It is at the centre of the vision of the world that might be termed 'liberal' and that is why what characterizes modern democracy as a political form of society is the articulation between liberalism and democracy. Unlike many liberals, Schmitt clearly sees that such a regime presupposes that the idea of absolute truth be put in question. Some liberals, on account of their rationalism, in fact imagine that they can retain the idea of a truth that is discoverable by everyone, so long as they are capable of leaving aside their own interests and judging solely from the viewpoint of reason. Now, for Schmitt, in relation to truth, liberalism implies 'renouncing a definite result'.[7] It is precisely for this reason that he denounces the articulation which gave rise to liberal democracy. It is indeed clear in his critique of parliamentary democracy that it is not democracy that Schmitt opposes. Democracy, which he defines as a logic of identity between government and governed, between the law and the popular will, is, in his view, perfectly compatible with an authoritarian form of government. Thus he declares that 'Bolshevism and Fascism ... are, like all dictatorships, certainly antiliberal but not necessarily antidemocratic.'[8] Admittedly, many will find such an assertion offensive, but it would be wrong to reject it in the name of the 'true' sense of democracy. What it ought to show us is the extent to which what most of us understand by democracy is determined by its modern, liberal form.

If Schmitt can help us to understand the nature of modern democracy, it is, paradoxically, because he must himself remain blind to it. And there is a very simple reason for this: for him, modernity has never come into being. In *Political Theology*, he declares that 'All significant concepts of the modern theory of the State are secularized theological concepts'.[9] What appears as modern politics is merely a secularization of theology, a transformation of theological concepts and attitudes for non-religious ends. There can therefore be no break, nothing new, no previously unknown form of legitimacy can emerge.

The idea that, since the democratic revolution, we are on wholly different ground, in another mode of instituting the social, which demands that we conceive democracy in a modern way, making room for pluralism, is, for Schmitt, strictly unthinkable. There is no possibility, within the scope of his thinking, for liberal democracy as a new and legitimate form of government. I believe that the 'unthinkability' this represents for Schmitt is extremely instructive and that it provides us with a key to the totalitarian phenomenon as consisting in wishing to think of democracy in the modern period without liberalism. In my view, it is incorrect to assert, as some do, that Schmitt's thinking was imbued with Nazism before his turnabout of 1933 and his espousal of Hitler's movement. There is, however, no doubt that it was his deep hostility to liberalism which made possible, or which did not prevent, his joining the Nazis.

Reflecting upon the case of Schmitt may thus help us to understand the perils present in certain forms of rejection of liberal democracy, even when those rejections are, like the projects for 'participatory democracy' inspired by the New Left of the sixties, profoundly anti-totalitarian. Such projects often see liberalism merely as a façade behind which the class divisions of capitalist society are concealed. For them, as for Schmitt, parties and the parliamentary system are obstacles to the achievement of a true democratic homogeneity. Similar resonances can be found in the critique levelled at liberalism by the so-called 'communitarian', writers. They too reject pluralism and dream of an organic community.[10] In all these endeavours, which, it should be said in passing, are often well-intentioned and very far from Schmitt's conservative and authoritarian positions, we find the same lack of understanding of modern democracy. In societies where democratic revolutions have taken place and which are, by that token, exposed to what Claude Lefort refers to as 'the dissolution of the markers of certainty',[11] it is necessary to rethink democratic politics in such a way that space is allowed for pluralism and individual freedom. The democratic logic of the identity of government and governed cannot alone guarantee respect for human rights. In conditions where one can no longer speak of the people as if it were a unified and homogenous entity with a single general will, it is only by virtue of its articulation of political liberalism that the logic of popular sovereignty can avoid descending into tyranny.

LIBERALISM AND POLITICS

If, against Schmitt's view, we restore the legitimacy of the liberal democratic regime, we may begin to enquire into its political principles. Up to this point, he has helped us – in spite of himself – to grasp the importance of the articulation of the democratic logic of identity and the pluralist logic of liberalism. We now have to examine the liberal problematic in order to determine which of its different elements must be defended and which rejected if the aim is to provide the liberal democratic regime with an ethical and philosophical content. Here again, Schmitt may, by his criticisms, indicate how we should proceed. His challenging of liberal individualism which, in his view, is incapable of grasping the nature of the phenomenon of politics is, in my view, most important. In *The Concept of the Political*, he writes:

> liberal thought evades or ignores state and politics and moves instead in a typical always recurring polarity of two heterogenous spheres, namely ethics and economics, intellect and trade, education and property. The critical distrust of state and politics is easily explained by the principles of a system whereby the individual must remain *terminus a quo* and *terminus ad quem*.[12]

Liberal thinking necessarily finds itself blocked on the question of the political, since its individualism prevents it from understanding the formation of collective identities. Now, for Schmitt, the criterion of the political, its *differentia specifica* is the friend-enemy relation; this involves the creation of a 'we' which stands in opposition to a 'them', and it is located, from the outset, in the realm of collective identifications. The political always has to do with conflicts and antagonisms and cannot but be beyond liberal rationalism since it is precisely the case that it indicates the limits to any rational consensus and reveals that any consensus is based on acts of exclusion. The liberal belief that the general interest is a product of the free play of private interests and that a rational universal consensus can be arrived at on the basis of free discussion must necessarily render liberalism blind to the political phenomenon. In Schmitt's view, that phenomenon can be understood 'only in the context of the ever present possibility of the friend-and-enemy grouping, regardless of the aspects which this possibility implies for morality, aesthetics, and economics'.[13] Liberalism imagines that, by relegating disruptive questions to the private sphere, an agreement on the rules of procedure should be sufficient to administer the plurality of interests which exist in society. However, in Schmitt's view, this attempt to annihilate the political is doomed to failure since the political cannot be domesticated, as it derives its energy from the most diverse sources and 'every religious, moral, economic, ethical or other antithesis transforms into a political one if it is sufficiently strong to group human beings effectively according to friend and enemy'[14]

To defend liberalism whilst at the same time accepting the criticisms Schmitt makes of individualism and rationalism, we must separate what constitutes liberal thinking's fundamental contribution to democratic modernity – namely, pluralism and the whole range of institutions characteristic of political liberalism – from the other discourses which are often presented as forming an integral part of liberal doctrine. Here the perspective developed by Hans Blumenberg is particularly helpful.

In his book, *The Legitimacy of the Modern Age*, he discusses the secularization thesis as formulated by Schmitt and Karl Löwith among others.[15] Unlike these writers, he defends the idea that the modern age possesses a truly novel quality in the form of the idea of 'self-assertion'. This emerges as a response to the situation created by scholastic theology's decline into 'theological absolutism', which for him means a set of ideas associated with belief in an omnipotent and completely free God. In his view, in the face of this 'theological absolutism', which made the world seem completely contingent, the only solution was the affirmation of human reason (science, art, philosophy, etc.) as a measure of order and source of value in the world. There is, then, a genuine break, but it co-exists with a certain continuity. That continuity is, however, a continuity of problems, not of solutions, and of questions, not of answers. It is around this question that Blumenberg introduces one of his most interesting concepts, that of 'reoccupation':

> What mainly occurred in the process that is interpreted as secularization
> ... should be described not as the *transposition* of authentically

248

theological contents into secularized alienation from their origin, but rather as the *reoccupation* of answer positions that had become vacant and whose corresponding questions could not be eliminated.[16]

On this basis, we may then distinguish, as Blumenberg does, between what is truly modern – the idea of self-assertion – and what, like the idea of necessary and inevitable progress, is merely the reoccupation of a medieval position, an attempt to give a modern answer to a pre-modern question instead of abandoning it, as a rationality conscious of its limits would have done. Rationalism may thus be seen, not as something essential to the idea of human self-assertion, to which the defence of individual liberty and pluralism are linked, but as a hangover from the absolutist medieval problematic. This illusion of providing itself with its own foundations, which accompanied the labour of liberation from theology carried out by the Enlightenment, may therefore be recognized as such without calling into question the other aspect – which is constitutive of modernity – namely, self-assertion. It is when it acknowledges its limitations and when it completely comes to terms with pluralism and accepts the impossibility of total control and final harmony that modern reason frees itself from its pre-modern heritage and the idea of cosmos. This is why, as liberals like Isaiah Berlin have understood, a coherent liberalism cannot but abandon rationalism.

We must, therefore, detach ethical pluralism and political liberalism from the discourse of rationalism in order to reformulate modernity's ideal of 'self assertion' without recourse to what present themselves as the universal dictates of reason. In this way, it will be possible to detach a crucial notion for modern democracy like that of the individual from the problematic of individualism and re-think it in a wholly other domain.

THE QUESTION OF THE NEUTRALITY OF THE STATE

In order to bring out the ethico-political dimension of the liberal democratic regime and provide it with principles of legitimacy, the liberal doctrine of the neutrality of the state must be challenged. It is linked to a fundamental idea of liberalism, that of 'limited government', and also to the distinction between public and private and the affirmation of pluralism. There are, however, various ways of defending the neutrality thesis and some of these have negative consequences.

Some liberals take the view that, in order fully to respect pluralism and not to interfere with the freedom of individuals to choose their own goals, it is necessary to deny any authority to the State insofar as the possibility of promoting or encouraging a particular conception of the good life is concerned: the State is under an obligation to be absolutely neutral in this sphere. Recently, Charles Larmore even went so far as to declare that 'if liberals are to follow fully the spirit of liberalism, they must also devise a *neutral justification of political neutrality*'.[17] This means that, in advocating liberalism, they should refrain from using arguments such as those advanced by John Stuart Mill or by Kant, which imply the assertion of certain values such as plurality or autonomy.

For the defenders of 'neutrality', any reference to ethical values can only give rise to disagreements and it is seen as important to avoid the trap of 'perfectionism', i.e. the philosophical *démarche* which aims to identify forms of life that are superior and to make these the goal to be realized by political life. They see in this a profoundly anti-liberal theory and one that is incompatible with pluralism. While opposing perfectionism, Ronald Dworkin none the less attempts to distance himself from the idea of an absolute neutrality. In his view, there is a certain conception of equality at the very heart of liberalism. It is because it must treat all its members as equal that the liberal State must be neutral. Thus he writes,

> Since the citizens of a society differ in their conceptions [of the good life], the government does not treat them as equals if it prefers one conception to another, either because the officials believe that one is intrinsically superior, or because one is held by the more numerous or more powerful groups.[18]

Dworkin takes the view that a justification of the neutrality of the State must not seek to be neutral and that it has to be recognized that liberalism is based on a constitutive morality. As he sees it, 'Liberalism cannot be based on scepticism. Its constitutive morality provides that human beings must be treated as equals by their government, not because there is no right or wrong in political morality, but because that is what is right'.[19] In order to prove this thesis, Dworkin has recourse to natural law and the existence of rights 'that are *natural* in the sense that they are not the product of any legislation, or convention, or hypothetical contract'.[20] It is, moreover, in this sense that he interprets the theory of justice of John Rawls, of which he has been a solid advocate since its earliest formulation. In Dworkin's view,

> justice as fairness rests on the assumption of a natural right of all men and women to equality of concern and respect, a right they possess not by virtue of birth or characteristics or merit or excellence but simply as human beings with the capacity to make plans and give justice.[21]

For this reason, he disagrees with the interpretation Rawls has now begun to make of his own theory. Rawls is now, in fact, proposing a more historicist version which emphasizes the place that the values specific to our liberal democratic tradition occupy within it; he even asserts that he never had the intention of establishing a theory of justice that would be valid for all societies.[22] Yet this is precisely what Dworkin recommends, believing that a theory of justice must call on 'general ... principles' and its objective must be to 'try to find some inclusive formula that can be used to measure social justice in any society'.[23]

The problem with a perspective like Dworkin's is that it is a form of liberalism which has not broken with rationalism and which can only think the ethical aspect of the political in terms of an application of the principles of a universalist morality to that field. Under cover of a political philosophy, what he offers us is in fact a 'public morality', i.e. something of the order of moral philosophy, which is of little assistance when the task is to elaborate the political principles of the liberal democratic regime.

What is, in my view, a much more interesting approach to the question of the neutrality of the State is that of Joseph Raz in his book *The Morality of Freedom*. Unlike most liberals, Raz adopts a perfectionist point of view, since he believes the State must take up a position as regards the various possible forms of life: it must promote some forms and forbid others. In his view, the State cannot therefore be neutral and must have the character of an 'ethical State'. The form of perfectionism he defends, however, is not incompatible with liberalism since it also includes pluralism. But the limits of that pluralism are given by what, in his view, constitutes the basic value that must prevail in a liberal and democratic State: personal autonomy or 'self-creation'. The central thesis of his book is that personal freedom, when it is understood as implying a pluralism of values and as having its form of expression in personal autonomy, should be encouraged by political action. Raz is very close to John Stuart Mill, whose 'harm principle' he takes over in a reinterpreted form. For him, this principle refers to the way the State has an obligation to respect certain limits in the promotion of its ideals. In effect,

> given that people should live autonomous lives, the state cannot force them to be moral. All it can do is to provide the conditions of autonomy. Using coercion invades autonomy and thus defeats the purpose of promoting it, unless it is done to promote autonomy by preventing harm.[24]

Autonomy is therefore to serve as a criterion for deciding which institutions and social practices should be fostered by a liberal democratic State.

In spite of my reservations about the appropriateness of subscribing to the cause of perfectionism – even when the 'sting' is taken out of it by pluralism – rather than rejecting the neutrality versus perfectionism dichotomy, I consider Raz's approach to be potentially one of the most fruitful in contemporary liberal thought, since it enables us to put the ethical dimension back at the heart of the political and to establish limits for State intervention without postulating the State's neutrality.

Another aspect deserving of attention is that the liberalism defended by Raz is one that rejects individualism and defends a conception of the subject close to some communitarian writers, such as Charles Taylor. He thus recognizes that autonomy is not an attribute of individuals independently of their insertion in history, that it is the product of an evolution and that it requires specific institutions and practices. If this value is central for us, this is because it is constitutive of our liberal democratic tradition. He is very far from subscribing to the idea of a political philosophy pursuing objective truth and claiming to establish eternal verities.

Because it combines the fundamental contribution of liberalism – the defence of pluralism and of individual freedom – with a conception of the subject which avoids the dangers of individualism, Raz's conception may help us to advance our thinking on the nature of liberal democratic politics. It seems to me, however, that the way in which he conceives pluralism is ultimately unsatisfactory. As in all liberal thinking, what we find here is a pluralism without antagonism.

Raz does, admittedly, leave room for competition and he recognizes that not all modes of life are realizable at the same time but, like Rawls and all the other liberals, he has nothing to contribute on what, for Schmitt, constitutes the criterion of the political, namely the friend-enemy relation. No doubt some will object at this point that the contribution of pluralism is precisely that it enables us to transcend such an opposition, but I believe this to be a dangerous liberal illusion which renders us incapable of grasping the phenomenon of politics. The limits to pluralism are not only empirical limits; they also have to do with the fact that some modes of life and some values are by definition incompatible with others and that it is this very exclusion which constitutes them. We have to take Nietzsche's idea of the 'war of the gods' seriously and accept that, if there is no creation of an 'us' without de-limiting a 'them', this relation may at any time become the site of an antagonism and the other may come to be perceived as an enemy. Once we have abandoned the rationalist idea that a formula can be found through which men's different ends might be harmonized, we have to come to terms with the fact that a society from which antagonism has been eliminated is radically impossible. This is why we have to accept with Schmitt, that 'the phenomenon of the political can be understood only in the context of the ever present possibility of the friend-and-enemy grouping ...'[25]

DEMOCRACY AS SUBSTANCE OR AS PROCEDURE

There is, in contemporary thinking on liberal democracy another theme which connects with that of the neutrality of the State, which also needs to be rethought. This is the idea that democracy merely consists of a set of procedures. This conception – which is very much in vogue today – is far from new and even at the beginning of the century Hans Kelsen, the legal philosopher who was Schmitt's most important intellectual opponent, referred to it to justify the parliamentary system. According to Kelsen, it was not the possibility of arriving at truth through discussion that was at the origin of parliamentary democracy, but rather the awareness that there was no possible truth. If liberal democracy has recourse to political parties and parliament as instruments of the general will, it is because it recognizes that a substantial homogeneity can never be achieved. He concludes from this that we have to renounce 'ideal' democracy in favour of 'real' democracy and that a realist vision of politics must conceive modern democracy as being defined by a certain number of procedures among which parliament and parties play a central role.[26]

To Schmitt's vision of democracy as substance, Kelsen therefore opposes a view of democracy which stresses its procedural character and puts the emphasis on its functioning. Whereas Schmitt conceives true democracy as being based on homogeneity, Kelsen presents parties and parliament as the necessary instruments for the formation of the will of the State. For Schmitt, such a conception is contradictory since he believes that in democracy such a will has to be pre-given at the outset and cannot be the product of discussion. The people must be able to express their political unity directly and without mediations. It is on these grounds that he criticizes the idea of the 'social contract' since, he says, either unanimity is pre-given or it is not pre-given; where it does not exist, a contract will not bring it into being and where it does exist, there is no point in a contract.[27] Have we then no alternative but a choice between democracy as substance, with all the dangers that implies, and democracy as procedure, with the impoverishment of the concept thereby entailed? I do not believe so and I think there are correct and useful elements in the writings of both Kelsen and Schmitt, but that they need to be reinterpreted.

Kelsen is right to insist on the need for procedures which enable agreement to be achieved in conditions where a single and homogeneous general will is not possible. He is, however, wrong to reduce democracy to a mere question of procedures. On the other hand, in a certain sense, Schmitt is right when he asserts that, without homogeneity, there can be no democracy. Everything depends on the way this homogeneity is conceived. In his *Verfassungslehre*, he relates it to the notion of equality and declares that the political form specific to democracy must be linked to a substantial concept of equality. This equality must be conceived as political equality and it cannot be based on making no distinction between persons, but must be grounded in the fact of belonging to a determinate political community. That community can, however, be defined by different criteria: race, religion, physical or moral qualities, destiny or tradition. Since the nineteenth century, says Schmitt, it has been membership of a determinate nation that has constituted the substance of democratic equality.[28] For Schmitt, the basic problem is one of political unity for, without such unity, there can be no State. This unity must be provided by a common substance, in which the citizens share, which will enable them to be treated as equals in a democracy. What renders his conception extremely questionable and potentially totalitarian is that he presents this homogeneity as being substantial in nature, leaving no place for pluralism. Yet it seems to me that, while accepting this need for homogeneity, one could interpret that homogeneity as being constituted by agreement on a certain number of political principles. It is identification with these principles which would provide the common substance required for democratic citizenship.

One finds a similar view in Hermann Heller who, in his critique of Schmitt's *The Concept of the Political*, acknowledges that a certain degree of social homogeneity and shared political values is necessary if democratic unity is to be achieved, but argues that this does not imply the elimination of social antagonisms. So far as parliamentarism is concerned, his reply to Schmitt is that the intellectual bases for this are to be found 'not in the belief in public discussion as such, but in the belief that a common basis for discussion exists and in the idea of fairness to the opponent, with whom one wishes to arrive at an agreement in conditions which exclude the use of brute force.'[29]

What I am proposing is that adherence to the political principles of the liberal democratic regime should be considered as the basis of homogeneity required for democratic equality. The principles in question are those of liberty and equality and it is clear that they can give rise to multiple interpretations and that no-one can pretend to possess the 'correct' interpretation of them. It is, therefore, essential to establish a certain number of mechanisms and procedures for arriving at decisions and for determining the will of the State within the framework of a debate on the interpretation of these principles. We thus find ourselves partially in agreement with both Schmitt and Kelsen, with the former because procedures are not seen as sufficient for creating the political unity of a democracy and a more substantial homogeneity is required, and with the latter because we recognize that the general will can never be immediately pre-given without the mediation of a certain number of procedures.

Such a solution would, of course, be unacceptable to Schmitt who believes in the existence of absolute truth. Nor would it satisfy Kelsen since it runs counter to his 'pure theory' of law. It implies that, in the field of politics and law, one is always in the domain of power-relations and that no consensus could be established as an outcome of a process of pure reasoning. Where there is power, force and violence cannot be completely eliminated, even though these may only take the form of 'force of argument' or 'symbolic violence'.

To defend political liberalism and pluralism in a perspective which is not rationalist, we have to see parliament not as the place where one accedes to truth, but as the place where it ought to be possible to arrive at an agreement on a reasonable solution through argument and persuasion. Hence the importance of re-creating the connection, in politics, with the great tradition of rhetoric, as suggested by Chaim Perelman.[30]

To accord parliament and parties a crucial role in modern democracy, in a manner that runs counter to Schmitt's critique, in no sense amounts to defending these institutions as they currently function. It is beyond doubt that they leave a great deal to be desired and that many of the defects exposed by Schmitt have since become more acute. A healthy democratic system requires a whole range of conditions, both political and economic, that are increasingly difficult to find in our societies, dominated as they are by large corporate bodies. What has to be challenged, however, is not pluralist democracy as such, as Schmitt would have it, but its limitations. And it ought to be possible to find a remedy for these. It is the central thesis of this article that the whole question of modern democracy revolves around pluralism. Up to this point, Schmitt has served us as an 'indicator', showing both the force of attraction that unity-based thinking exerts and the dangers inherent in it. He may, however, also serve to put us on our guard against the excesses of a certain type of pluralism. In his discussion of Anglo-Saxon pluralist theories, he does in fact provide a series of arguments of great importance. According to pluralists like Harold Laski or G.D.H. Cole, each individual is a member of many communities and associations, none of which may have priority over the others. They thus conceive the State as an association of the same type as religious societies or professional groupings, and see individuals as having no overriding obligations to it. For Schmitt, this is a conception typical of liberal individualism, which always attributes the key role in the resolution of conflict to the individual. For his part, he takes the view that 'Only as long as the essence of the political is not comprehended or not taken into consideration is it possible to place a political association pluralistically on the same level with religious, cultural, economic, or other associations and permit it to compete with these'.[31]

Schmitt is right to insist on the specificity of political associations and I believe we must not be led by the defence of pluralism to argue that our participation in the State as a political community is on the same level as our other forms of social integration. Any thinking on the political needs to recognize the limits of pluralism. Antagonistic principles of legitimacy cannot coexist within the same political association; there cannot be pluralism at that level without the political reality of the State automatically disappearing. But in a liberal democratic regime, this does not exclude there being cultural, religious and moral pluralism at another level, as well as a plurality of different parties. However, this pluralism requires allegiance to the State as an 'ethical State' which crystallizes the institutions and principles proper to the mode of collective existence that is modern democracy. Here we may take up again Schmitt's idea of an 'ethics laid down by the State as autonomous ethical subject, an ethics emanating from it',[32] on condition that we formulate it in terms of that new Regime characterized by the articulation of democracy and liberalism.

Those who conceive the pluralism of modern democracy as a total pluralism, with the only restriction on this being an agreement on procedures, forget that such 'regulative' rules only have meaning in relation to 'constitutive' rules which are necessarily of another order. Far from being bound up with a 'relativist' vision of the world, as some writers have it, modern democracy requires the affirmation of a certain number of 'values' which, like equality and freedom constitute its 'political principles'. It establishes a form of human co-existence which requires a distinction between the public and the private, the separation of church and State, and of civil and religious law. These are some of the basic achievements of the democratic revolution and it is that revolution that makes the existence of pluralism possible. One cannot therefore call these distinctions into question in the name of pluralism. Hence the problem posed by the integration of a religion like Islam, which does not accept these distinctions. Recent events surrounding the Rushdie affair show that there is a problem here which will not be easily solved. We find ourselves faced now with a real challenge: how are we to defend the greatest possible degree of pluralism while not yielding over what constitutes the essence of modern democracy? How are we to make the distinction between those values and customs in our 'public morality' that are specific to Christianity and which we therefore cannot justly impose on everyone in what has become an objectively multi-ethnic and multi-cultural society, and those values and customs that are an expression of principles without which pluralist democracy could not continue to exist? This is far from easy and doubtless there is no clear and simple answer to such a question, but it is one which must be taken into consideration in our thinking.

To understand the specificity of the liberal democratic regime as a form of society is also to grasp its historical character. Far from being an irreversible event, the democratic revolution may come under threat and has to be defended. The rise of various forms of religious fundamentalism of Christian origin in the USA and the resurgence of Catholic integrism in France indicate that the danger does not come solely from outside but also from our own tradition. The relegation of religion to the private sphere, which we now have to make Muslims accept, was only imposed with great difficulty upon the Christian church and is still not completely accomplished. And, from a different angle, individual freedom is in a distinctly precarious position when wealth and power are concentrated in the hands of groups that are increasingly outside the control of the democratic process.

Isn't the creation of a true democratic pluralism a project which could infuse a little enthusiasm into our societies where scepticism and apathy shade into despair and revolt? To achieve this, however, a difficult balance has to be struck between, on the one hand, democracy understood as a set of procedures required to cope with plurality, and on the other, democracy as adherence to values which inform a particular mode of co-existence. Any attempt to give one aspect precedence over the other runs the risk of depriving us of the most precious element of this new regime.

It is true that there is something paradoxical about modern democracy and Schmitt helps us to see this, though he also fails to understand its real significance. For him, pluralist democracy is a contradictory combination of irreconcilable principles; whereas democracy is a logic of identity and equivalence, its complete realization is rendered impossible by the logic of pluralism which constitutes an obstacle to a total system of identification. It cannot be denied that, through the articulation of liberalism and democracy, the democratic logic of equivalence has been linked with the liberal logic of difference, which tends to construe every identity as positivity, thus establishing a pluralism which subverts every attempt at totalization. These two logics are, therefore, ultimately incompatible, but this in no way means that liberal democracy is a non-viable regime as Schmitt declares. I believe, on the contrary, that it is the existence of this tension between the logic of identity and the logic of difference that defines the essence of pluralist democracy and makes it particularly

PLURALISM AND MODERN DEMOCRACY

well-suited to the undecidable character of modern politics. Far from bewailing this tension, we should be thankful for it and see it as something to be defended, not eliminated. It is this tension, in fact, which also shows up as a tension between our identities as individuals and as citizens or between the principles of freedom and equality, which constitutes the best guarantee that the project of modern democracy is alive and inhabited by pluralism. The desire to resolve it could lead only to the elimination of the political and the destruction of democracy.

Translated by Chris Turner

NOTES

1 Norberto Bobbio, *La Stampa*, 9 June 1989.
2 Carl Schmitt, *The Crisis of Parliamentary Democracy*, trans. E. Kennedy (Cambridge, Mass./London, 1985), 34.
3 *Ibid.*, 35.
4 *Ibid.*, 34-5
5 *Ibid.*, 6.
6 *Ibid.*, 17.
7 *Ibid.*, 35.
8 *Ibid.*, 16.
9 Carl Schmitt, *Political Theology*, Trans. George Schwab, (Cambridge, Mass./London, 1985), 36.
10 On this point, see my article, 'Le libéralisme américain et ses critiques', *Esprit*, March 1987.
11 Claude Lefort, *Democracy and Political Theory*, trans. D. Macey (Cambridge, 1988) 19.
12 Carl Schmitt, *The Concept of the Political*, trans. George Schwab (New Brunswick, 1976), 70-1.
13 *Ibid.*, 35.
14 *Ibid.*, 37.
15 Hans Blumenberg, *The Legitimacy of the Modern Age*, (Cambridge, Mass., 1983).
16 *Ibid.*, 65.
17 Charles E. Larmore, *Patterns of Moral Complexity*, (Cambridge, 1987), 53.
18 Ronald Dworkin, 'Liberalism' in Stuart Hampshire, (ed.), *Public and Private Morality* (Cambridge, 1978), 127.
19 *Ibid.*, 142.
20 Ronald Dworkin, *Taking Rights Seriously* (Cambridge, Mass., 1977), 176.
21 *Ibid.*, 182.
22 I examine this development in Rawls's work in 'Rawls: Political Philosophy without Politics', *The Return of the Political*, London: Verso 1993.
23 Ronald Dworkin, *New York Review of Books*, 17 April 1983.

259

[24] Joseph Raz, *The Morality of Freedom* (Oxford, 1986), 420.
[25] Schmitt, *The Concept of the Political*, 35.
[26] Kelsen's work is very extensive and highly specialized. On the subject that concerns us here, *What is Justice? Justice, law and politics in the mirror of science* (Berkeley, 1957).
[27] Schmitt, *The Crisis of Parliamentary Democracy*, p 14.
[28] Schmitt, *Verfassungslehre* (Munich/Leipzig, 1928). This work has not been translated into English.
[29] Hermann Heller, 'Politische Demokratie und soziale Homogenität', *Gesammelte Schriften*, vol 2, (Leyden, 1971) 427. This is referred to by Ellen Kennedy in her introduction to Schmitt, *The Crisis of Parliamentary Democracy*, pxlix.
[30] For Chaim Perelman's work, see particularly *Le Champ de l'Argumentation* (Brussels, 1970); *Justice et Raison* (Brussels, 1972); *L'Empire rhétorique* (Paris, 1977).
[31] Schmitt, *The Concept of the Political*, p45.
[32] Schmitt, 'Ethique de l'Etat et l'état pluraliste', in *Parlementarisme et démocratie* (Paris, 1988), 148.

The Legacy of the Enlightenment: Foucault and Lacan

Mladen Dolar

My objective is to try to show how the Foucauldian project on one hand and the Lacanian on the other – two major theoretical endeavours of our time – situate themselves in relation to modernity and to the legacy of the Enlightenment. The problem is obviously too large to be tackled in a single article and, apart from that, it is formulated in terms which are too vague or ambiguous, given the rather wild debates going on about (post)modernism where those terms are used in such a variety of ways that they have almost lost any meaning – or, rather, they have become privileged empty signifiers which are the very locus of the battle, the field of a campaign to include them in different competing discourses.[1] So I propose to narrow down the question and to concentrate on one single issue, on the reading of one text – the text that Foucault himself singled out as essential to the very idea of modernity: a short paper by Kant, written in 1784, which bears the title 'What is Enlightenment?' This was meant to be a programmatic text and Foucault himself takes it as 'emblematic', as he says, and in many ways decisive for an outline of the fundamental attitude of modernity. I will try to show what implications Foucault draws from it and how those implications match the assessment that Lacan made of Kant's position – which he views, as does Foucault, as essential for the modern condition and for the very discovery of psychoanalysis (Lacan goes even so far as to imply that there would be no psychoanalysis without the Kantian turn).

I will start, however, with some general considerations. Both psychoanalysis and Foucault have a strong and at the same time largely ambiguous link with modernity. For psychoanalysis, this link seems to be evident enough on the three levels of epistemological, artistic and political modernity.

On the first level, the connection manifests itself in Freud's relentless commitment to the Enlightenment ideals of scientificity, the universality of science against any kind of irrationalism. He saw himself as a warrior at the outpost of science, in those obscure regions not yet clarified by the light of reason: those small marginal phenomena of dreams, slips of the tongue, symptoms etc. which could be seen as an emergence of the contingent not accounted for by sufficient reason, that Leibnizian core of scientific explanation. They presented the realm of the rest, the left-over beyond the limit of scientific rationality. Yet Freud never considered giving up the Enlightenment attitude in favour of some kind of mythical or para-scientific knowledge; he proposed instead to extend it beyond that limit.[2] This extension immediately raised the question, not only of whether psychoanalysis was really a science (scientists tend to remain largely sceptical), but also the question of the very nature of scientificity as such and its underlying assumptions.

On the second level, that of aesthetic modernism, this to a greater or smaller extent embraced psychoanalysis as the theory of its own artistic practice. One need only think of the first Surrealist Manifesto, where Breton hailed Freud as the hero of the imagination against rationalist civilization, the rebel fighting in the name of that which reason had to suppress. Whereas Freud saw himself as a rigorous man of science, a large part of the aesthetic avant-garde greeted psychoanalysis as an anti-rationalist endeavour, which opened the way to unconscious productivity. Freud, rather a conservative in his artistic taste, remained largely sceptical and saw the whole thing as a misunderstanding. His own analyses of art rather point to the assumption that, for him, 'traditional' art was better placed to demonstrate the mechanisms of the unconscious than modernist practice, with its attempt to relay those mechanisms immediately and directly.

In the third respect as well, the political one, the position of psychoanalysis was highly ambiguous. It clearly had subversive effects; it corroded authoritarian practices and brought to light an astonishing amount of material repressed by social domination. In this sense, it seemed to join hands with left movements, demanding the liberation of desire etc. In 1968, psychoanalysis massively walked the streets of Paris. But there was, on the other hand, a deep mark of pessimism, a profound scepticism about the notion of progress and the possibilities of liberation, which made it difficult to range psychoanalysis unproblematically on the side of the struggle for democratic progress and produced an uneasiness about taking psychoanalysis for a trustworthy ally in left-wing politics: it rather seems to imply a limit to the progress of democracy.

So in all three respects, psychoanalysis seems to be deeply ambivalent in its relation to modernity, being both its vanguard and its counterpoint. But perhaps one could argue that the ambiguous position of psychoanalysis is actually a symptom of a deep ambiguity within modernity itself – the ambiguity which was embedded all the time in modernity from the very outset and which psychoanalysis merely highlighted in a particularly telling way. The adherence to the ideas of the Enlightenment – the universality of reason, scientific rationality, liberation, as well as the type of subjectivity that goes along with these – was constantly accompanied by a critique of those ideas presented powerfully not only by writers from Nietzsche, Heidegger, Horkheimer and Adorno to the (post)structuralists,[3] but, less obviously, already by Kant and Hegel. So one could argue that modernity was from the outset caught in a contradiction between the claims of the universality of reason and its internal limit; or, to put it simply, that modernity from the very beginning included or implied a post-modernity. If there is a sense to all the massive amount of talk about postmodernism, it is perhaps best tackled not as a rejection of modernity or a going beyond it, but as maintaining the contradiction inherent in modernity itself. Psychoanalysis offers perhaps the best way of doing this. (In Lacanian theory, one can present the issue in perhaps the simplest and most revealing terms. To put it in a simple slogan: psychoanalysis combines in the same gesture the modern concept of the subject – $ – with a postmodern concept of the object – what Lacan calles *objet a*.)

For Foucault too, modernity is a highly problematic project. One could see all his work as an endeavour to show, through different and very convincing examples, how the universal principles of reason and freedom were underpinned by their very opposite – a tightly knit system of discipline and control, a microcosmos of domination, a disciplinary institutional network based on the models of the asylum, prison, clinic etc. Foucault placed himself in the counter-Enlightenment tradition as a disciple of Nietzsche (and also of

Horkheimer and Adorno, as he somewhat surprisingly pointed out in some of his last interviews). But what I am interested in here is what could be called his 'rehabilitation' of the Enlightenment in his later writings (a step which has particularly rejoiced Habermas, cf. 1985, 126 ff.), especially in the two lectures published just before his death (Foucault 1984a and 1984b).[4] One could say that it is only here that he appears not only as a critic of the Enlightenment, but as its heir. The issue for him is no longer simply to critique new forms of enlightened slavery, but to disseminate a positive message that we must hold on to; that he can see himself not merely as a disciple of Nietzsche, but of Kant as well, and that the Enlightenment can be assessed not only as a disease – because of its profound complicity with the disciplinary system – but also as a remedy. There is in the Enlightenment itself perhaps the best antidote to the disease of the Enlightenment.

So both the psychoanalytic and the Foucauldian view pinpoint an essential ambivalence within the Enlightenment. Yet at the very point where these two perspectives seem to converge most closely, they are perhaps at their furthest apart. The key question around which their difference circulates, is this: what kind of subjectivity belongs to modernity?

For Foucault, the rehabilitation of the Enlightenment depends on the possibility of not taking the Enlightenment *en bloc*, wholesale; that is, not falling into the trap of choosing between alternatives: *either* the defence of the principles of reason, progress, freedom etc., *or* their rejection as insufficient, the highlighting of their hidden repressive character etc. The first of these alternatives has been defended by various proponents of scientific and political progress, the other promoted in various ways by a series of thinkers from Nietzsche to, finally, Foucault himself. But to accept this alternative, Foucault points out now, would mean to be subject to a certain 'blackmail' by the Enlightenment (Foucault 1984b, 42-3): one is pushed against the wall to be either for it or against it. Even those who questioned and criticized it have themselves fallen into the trap of believing the Enlightenment's myth about its own nature as a coherent, unitary project, which can only be either accepted, or questioned *in toto*. The dividing line is for Foucault now quite different: it is drawn inside the Enlightenment itself. Kant is thus, according to Foucault, at the source of two different traditions which can both be seen as the legitimate heirs of the Enlightenment (Foucault 1984a, 39): on the one hand, what Foucault calls '*the analytique of truth*' – the analysis of the conditions of any knowledge which has pretensions to truth, an analysis aiming at an identification of the transhistorical, transcendental conditions of knowledge (most of so-called analytic philosophy, for instance, could be put into this category); and on the other hand, the type of questioning which Foucault sums up as *'the ontology of the present'* – the questioning of who we are and of the nature of this historic moment that we belong to (since we 'are' only through our belonging to a privileged historic moment). This second type of questioning, in opposition to the first, results in a historicizing of all universal claims – the historical conditioning of every universality. In this second sense, the critics of the Enlightenment belong to the Enlightenment in a perhaps more fundamental sense – and it is of this line that Foucault sees himself as the inheritor.[5]

The posing of the question 'what are we and what is this historic moment that we belong to?' is for Foucault the novelty of the Enlightenment. Not that that question was not raised before in certain ways (from Plato and Augustine to Descartes and Vico, to quote Foucault's examples), but the Enlightenment does it in a new and unprecedented way. The present appears for the first time as a philosophical event. First of all, the Enlightenment is a historic period which invents its own name: the Enlightenment calls itself Enlightenment, it perceives itself as the Enlightenment (Foucault 1984a, 36), it defines itself as a privileged moment in history, as a way out of immaturity into adulthood, as Kant will put it, as a coming of age – an adulthood which implies the use of reason without an outside authority to rely on. It situates itself towards a past and a future by determining its present duty. It is out of this historical concern that spring the three Kantian critiques: 'it is precisely at this moment that critique is necessary' to determine 'the conditions under which the use of reason is legitimate – in order to know what can be known, what must be done and what may be hoped for' (Foucault 1984b, 38). So the 'transhistorical' endeavour of Kant – his drive to determine the universal conditions of knowledge and action – springs out of an historic choice, or rather, a choice of history, of an attitude towards that privileged moment of history when humanity will put its own reason to use. It is because of the emergence of historicity that seemingly transhistorical questions have to be raised. Thus 'the analytique of truth' is ultimately derivative of 'the ontology of the present'.

It follows that the Enlightenment is defined, not so much by an adherence to a certain ideal or a doctrine, but by the choice of an ethical attitude. Foucault illustrates this with the example of what Baudelaire called 'the heroism of modern life': the choice of a certain way of life, the style of a dandy, of a *flâneur*, an 'aesthetics of existence', finding 'eternity in the passing moment' etc. What makes this attitude typical of modernity is the constant reconstruction and reinvention of the present which goes along with the reconstruction and the reinvention of the self. Both elements – the subject and the present it belongs to – have no 'objective' status; they have to be perpetually (re)constructed, and their status is purely 'ethical'. So modernity essentially results in an ethics of self-construction.

It is no coincidence that Foucault here uses concepts derived from his analysis of the ethics of antiquity (Foucault 1984c and 1984d), which he elaborated in parallel to his reassessment of the Enlightenment. One could say, in a somewhat simplified way, that the ethical mission of modernity in a certain historical period – the period after the decline of Christianity as the universal basis of legitimation – is ultimately to accomplish what the subject of Antiquity achieved in relation to its own age – to invent a new form of 'self-construction', 'self-relation', 'a stylistic of existence', 'a technique of the self', 'enkrateia' etc. It is here, for Foucault, that the essential source of subjectivation has to be situated: in the production of a precarious balance of self-construction which deals with the essential discord of the human being. There is no natural balance one can rely on and no fixed rules to follow: every balance has always to be constructed anew, the rules are self-imposed and have no claim to be the Law. Once the Greek order of Antiquity had crumbled, Christianity introduced the heteronomy of a universal Law imposed from the outside, to replace the precarious 'universality without law' (Foucault 1984d, 215) which was the happy privilege of Antiquity.[6] Yet Christianity was based on a Law one could never measure up to; thus one was by definition a sinful being which had constantly to undergo the rituals of confession and repentance and which was subject to a permanent watchfulness. The heteronomy of a Law revealed only by an external instance goes together with the inherent depravity of human beings. (Hence Foucault's in many ways brilliant and detailed analyses of the techniques of Christianity, the very idea of a confession etc.)[7]

For Foucault, the Enlightenment presents anew the possibility of an ethics based on self-construction (along with a new awareness of the simultaneous construction of one's own historical epoch). Foucault is, of course, very well aware that there is no going back to Greek ethics; nevertheless, he maintains, an analogous ethical gesture has to be made – 'a bit, no doubt, like what the Greeks called an *ethos*' (Foucault 1984b, 39 – but how much is a bit?). Yet the Enlightenment does see the emergence of a new form of subjectivity which goes hand in hand with the emergence of historicity. Thus in one and the same gesture, modernity combines ethics, epistemology and aesthetics.

If we take a closer look at Kant's text on the Enlightenment,[8] we soon stumble upon a manifest paradox (and one also identified by Foucault). Kant begins, in militant programmatic mode, with the slogan of the Enlightenment: *Sapere aude!* Dare to know! Have the courage to use your own reason against any kind of imposed or external authority – this is what summarizes the endeavour of the Enlightenment. But a few pages on he adds, in what appears to be the most flagrant self-contradiction: '*Reason* as much as you want and on what you want, *but obey*!' (Kant 1912, 165). So the truth of *Sapere aude* is ultimately 'Use your own reason freely – provided that you obey!' This paradox (if such it be) is, for Kant, constitutive of the Enlightenment itself. Freedom and obedience form a pattern, they belong together.

How then to reconcile this paradox? Kant resolves the contradiction by placing the freedom of reasoning and obedience in two different spheres, the public and the private. His point is however not, 'Think what you wish in private, as long as you obey in public', but exactly the opposite: the use of reason belongs in the public sphere – the whole success of the Enlightenment depends on there being no limits to the public use of reason – while obedience is a private affair. The sphere of the private, somewhat astonishingly, consists for Kant of what Althusser would later call the repressive and the ideological state apparatuses – Kant repeatedly gives the examples of the Church and the Army, just as Freud will do in his 'Group Psychology'. The state apparatuses belong to the realm of the private because they are valid in a limited sphere, and appeal to a limited public: as a clergyman, I address my parish, as a captain, I address a certain corps, as a civil servant, I serve the state – always within a particular and limited domain of use and validity. As a man of reason however, a universal human being – in short, as a Man – I can freely and publicly address a universal audience, Mankind (the big Other, in other words, since the public itself is still conceived as immature), purely on the basis of rational arguments. Kant thus tries here to establish as a basic mechanism of the Enlightenment the following: that private obedience is the inner condition of the public freedom of reasoning. To put this another way: there is a mutual limitation between power and knowledge, and that limitation is the inner condition of universality. (Surprisingly enough, Foucault, who was best placed to reflect upon this, stops at the very point where Kant's text gets really intriguing!) The division power/knowledge traverses both terms: power must admit its limit and entirely give up its jurisdiction in matters of reason, whereas reason can be universal only by admitting limited sovereignty to a power which is itself not grounded in reason.

This division public/private, power (as private)/knowledge (as public) is actually drawn inside every individual. As an army officer, for example, I have to obey orders which are ultimately not based in reason; but being at the same time a man of reason, I can make a public appeal that questions the whole military organization. If the use of reason is public and unlimited, then there is a chance that my proposals will gain public support and eventually be put into practice. This is the point of the whole mechanism: it is Kant's optimistic conviction that if reason gets a hearing, it will necessarily gain the upper hand. This victory will however not bring an end to division; it does not do away with the scission splitting each individual – indeed it ultimately makes it deeper. The subject of the Enlightenment, for Kant, is a split subject and can only remain free as long as it accepts this split. The persistent split is indeed the place of freedom, not something to be overcome. Thus it is not appropriate to criticize the universal claims of Enlightenment, at least as far as Kant is concerned, by pointing out that they dissimulate a split, for example, the class division of society. Kant not only admits a division reason/power, but he actually takes it as the very matrix of the Enlightenment: for to admit the split as constitutive is the best way to deal with the unreason of power.[9]

This division power/knowledge is thus paradigmatically present in the internal division of knowledge itself. It emerges most clearly in the problematic organization of the institution which takes care of the universality of knowledge – appropriately called the University. Kant tackles this in an afterword, a sort of lengthy PS to the Enlightenment paper, *The Contest of Faculties* (1794) (the text is also referred to by Foucault, though he again leaves out the best bits). If in the first paper Kant addressed the Church and the Army as model institutions, then he became even more Althusserian in the second paper, by identifying the school as the fundamental ideological state apparatus of the modern age. The structure of the University precisely duplicated the internalized division power/knowledge. Reason is not master even in its own house. The University is divided into higher and lower faculties, the higher ones being theology, law and medicine, while the lower one is the faculty of philosophy. The higher faculties are higher only because they are closer to power – they actually provide the staff for the ideological state apparatuses – they are charged with the education of clergymen, lawyers and physicians. Their foundations are what Kant calls the 'statutes', certain written regulations, prescriptions, laws, 'based in the arbitrariness of a superior power (in themselves not originating in reason)', in 'the order of an external legislator' (Kant 1912, 566). Those 'statutes' are the Bible, the Law, medical regulations etc. Thus the higher faculties are found in a scripture, a writing, a letter independent of reason. The lower faculty, meanwhile, pursues only knowledge and truth, regardless of any other considerations. It obeys only the autonomy of reason, but can do so only at a price: by being cut off from any exercise of power. It can take care of knowledge only by giving up any claim to power.

The whole edifice is thus constructed on the basis of an underlying supposition that reason is powerless and that power is not based in reason. The law is valid, but not true.[10] Of course Kant's point is precisely to get the voice of reason heard, to expose power to the criticism of knowledge. There is here a kind of contradictory mutual agreement: reason gives up all claims to power in order to be able to exert its influence; power, meanwhile, provides the place for reason to be heard and so limits itself; it exposes itself to the control and criticism of a none the less powerless reason. This mutual recognition is moreover only possible on the supposition of a radical split between the two. Kant is deeply ambiguous about this: he often speaks of the possibility ultimately of founding the law in reason – of bridging the gap sometime in the future, or at least diminishing it in a constant approximation of the two into infinity. But, on the other hand, the approximation must remain approximation, it must never reach its end. It is an endless task in which the split is constantly reproduced – for, should it reach its end, both sides would dissolve. It seems that they only have consistence in division. Thus, apart from Kant's general teleological view of human history and its ultimate progress, he also makes some rather gloomy predictions[11] for the University: the higher faculties will never give up their 'passion for domination' (Kant 1912, 580), so the best one can hope for is a coexistence of a *concordia discors*, *discordia concors* (p. 582). Hence the endeavour to make provision for the interminable 'contest of faculties' referenced in Kant's title.

How then should one treat their inevitable conflicts? Kant proposes a parliamentary route, quite literally, where the higher faculties will occupy 'the benches of the Government' (Kant was a great admirer of the English Constitution), and the lower one, the faculty of philosophy, the benches of the opposition – 'the left side', as he adds in brackets (p. 581). So philosophy is predestined to be the left opposition (note the self-evident assumption that the left is by its very nature in opposition). The assumption is based on Kant's belief that the left side is weaker by its very nature. He gives a number of examples in the same text, in the part dealing with medicine. In an incredible footnote, he raises the question: why is it that in the army one has to start marching with the left leg? Kant's answer: it is to give swing to the right leg! (p. 662). Just as one needs two legs to march, one needs the two sides of the division – power and knowledge, the Government and the opposition. The division is basic and irreducible (cf. Derrida 1984).

A translation of the above into Lacanian terms allows one to describe it in the most economical and minimal way. There is in Kant an ultimate division between S_1 and S_2, the 'master-signifier' and the chain of knowledge, where the 'statute', the law, the letter on which the power is based is not reducible to its determination by reason, by the series of S_2. The law is itself not founded in sufficient reason.

It seems that what Kant tries to achieve in delineating this mechanism of the Enlightenment is to establish a paradoxical place for freedom. His strategy is based on the assumption that *limitation liberates*. Reason can be universal only as long as it admits an exception; its universality indeed calls for an exception. Should reason and freedom encompass totality, they would evaporate. (One could take the point in reverse and draw the conclusion that the danger of 'totalitarianism', to use a modern word, lies in its demand for the amalgamation of law and reason, power and knowledge, S_1 and S_2: its claim that the social totality should be based simply on the rule of reason.)

In a way, then, Kant, at the peak of the Enlightenment, seems to turn the Enlightenment project upside down. Let me indicate in passing (though this issue demands a much longer development) that the 'statute', the 'letter' of power which cannot be determined by the foundations of truth and knowledge, is correlative to the Hegelian

270

gesture of putting the Monarch in the place of 'the highest category'. The Hegelian Monarch is precisely the S_1 that is irreducible to the chain of S_2. All subjects are what they make themselves into – by their social activity, their abilities and merits etc. The Monarch by contrast is what he is by his very nature, both as a moment of nature in the midst of society (the blood affiliation etc.) and as a pure name, an empty signifier (the only function of the Monarch being, for Hegel, to put his signature on decisions made by other people). So the Monarch is the purely formal peak of power; he does not possess any actual power, since, being in this exceptional, excluded, non-social place of S_1, his actual function is simply to hold society together. It is only through the exception that a rational society can be conceived (cf. Žižek 1988, 43-6). Thus both Kant and Hegel insist on the Lacanian thesis that totality and universality are always based in exclusion.

As we have seen, the 'statute', the law, is for Kant situated in an exceptional place not vouched for by sufficient reason. But of course this exception to reason does not mean that we have to put up with an irrational law, or to treat the law as something sacred. Quite the contrary: the admission in advance of its unfoundedness actually entails a kind of degradation of the law. The law demands obedience, but only as external compliance, not as conviction or belief. This Kantian law does not need ideology as necessarily produced false consciousness or as an 'internalization of external demands'. To admit the authority of the law actually deprives the law of its internal authority; at the same time, it clears a place for 'real' authority to be established: the authority of reason and truth. That is why power appears in the Kantian system as something particular and private, opposed to universality.

This attitude, emerging at the peak of the Enlightenment, actually opens a new dimension in conceptions of the law. The law it envisions is not based in an inherent rationality, neither is it supported by any transcendent guarantee – God, the supreme right of the monarch etc. The traditional, pre-modern attitude endowed the law with a transcendent authority, whereas for Kant, it is simply given, but nevertheless unsurmountable (cf. Žižek 1989, 80). For Kant, there is no problem in leaving to God what belongs to God and to Caesar what belongs to Caesar, provided that both secular and religious power leave to philosophy what belongs to philosophy. Philosophy is thus situated at the very core of the 'political': it has radical political implications precisely by virtue of its renunciation of any kind of political concerns. Kant proposes a political strategy for philosophy, a certain 'politics of knowledge': his point is not that the philosopher should get involved in the tedious business of power (though s/he can do this as well), but that there is a political dimension in the theoretical as such – it is a space which is itself devoid of power, but which sets the limit to every form of power and thus makes apparent the element of arbitrariness, or contingency, implied within it. The renunciation of power is the source of the power of philosophy; its powerless appeal is its strongest weapon. Its appeal is always 'I have no power over you', but this is what makes it invincible. The law which commands, prohibits and threatens appears powerless compared to this weak voice.

Does Foucault espouse this strategy? He seems to be fascinated by it, but he stops short of drawing out its most interesting implications and he ultimately deems it insufficient (which it certainly is if we judge it on historical grounds – it does not give an adequate description of what actually happened in the Enlightenment – Foucault 1984b, 37). He tends to disregard certain of the solutions proposed by Kant in favour of a discussion of the attitude from which they can be made: the attitude of responsibility to the historical moment to which we belong, the construction of modernity. The point where Foucault's conclusions stop is however only the beginning of the Lacanian reading.

The point of the Kantian mechanism of Enlightenment outlined above was not, as it might seem, merely to separate sharply the realm of external obedience to an arbitrary law from the realm of the internal autonomy of reason. That would still leave intact the idea of a pure interiority as the domain of universality, autonomy and reason: a domain which would remain immaculate at the price of its limitation. But the argument must be taken further if we are to grasp the Kantian point for it is only by liberating the autonomy of its heteronomous elements (placing them under the jurisdiction of an external arbitrary power) that internal Law can come to hold sway. Thus, at the very centre of autonomy, there exists a moral law, as a traumatic internal kernel which actually disrupts autonomy from the inside. The significant opposition, for Kant, is thus ultimately not between the heteronomy of external law and the autonomy of reason, but between two different kinds of law: submission to external law (on which power is based and society is built) is opposed by the Law of categorical imperative, the autonomous imposition of duty. The very

272

element that was supposed to secure inner autonomy is ultimately what disrupts it; autonomy imposed internal heteronomy as its traumatic core.

Kant conceives the Enlightenment in an analogous way to moral Law. Just as moral Law must be rid of any heteronomous source – of an origin in what Kant calls the pathological: pleasure, gain, interest, fear, counting on future reward etc. – if it is to be reduced to pure universalization (acts based on the maxim of the will as universal law), so in the same way the heteronomous moment of submission must be confined to external arbitrary law, and it is this delimitation that opens the space of the Law. The first law makes me obey, for example by observing religious rituals, paying taxes etc.; but it is only moral Law that constitutes me as a subject: for it is the Law that the subject imposes 'from within' that destroys the illusion of an autonomous subject. It is only in this pure autonomy that the subject has the experience of not being master in his/her house. The Law requires the sacrifice of any particularity, any pursuit of the pleasure principle; yet in so doing, it precisely opens up a space for the emergence of the Kantian subject. It is impossible for the subject to measure up to internal Law; there is always something more that s/he would have to give up, a left-over, a pathological rest of particularity that is impossible to universalize. At the same time, this impossible is, precisely, the subject.

So, for Lacan, the Kantian problem is ultimately not that social law is not based in reason, but that reason itself is ultimately based on a traumatic Law. Social laws both constitute and guarantee social reality, but moral Law presents us with the dimension of the Real, which emerges into and disrupts purified autonomous internal space. The remedy that Kant proposes turns out to be much worse than the disease. The very principle of autonomy seems to be immediately precipitated into the intrusion of Otherness, the other place of the Law – the Law that cannot be reflexively appropriated or reduced to the subject's self-determination. It opens an internal crack which is the actual place of the Kantian subject.

It is here that Foucault's and Lacan's routes diverge radically. For Lacan, in establishing his project of an *Ethics of Psychoanalysis*, Kant is the turning point, the presupposition of psychoanalytic discovery – precisely because his work reveals the inner impossibility of an autonomous subject. Kantian ethics is a rigorous consequence of the stance of the Enlightenment. In a well-known popular formula, Kant has been labelled 'the Newton of morals', the implication being that it was he who first perceived the radical consequences of the universality of scientific rationality for the domain of practical philosophy.[12] What moral Law demands is nothing less than the imposition of universality on all human action: the demand that every action be considered in view of its universalisability. This is a simple and radical idea, and for Lacan, it is precisely in its simplicity that it produces the rest, the bit of the Real; that it implies *jouissance* as a limit, the limit to universality, that which cannot be universalized.

One can trace Lacan's argument on three levels. First, *jouissance* is conceived as the residue of particularity which guarantees that the subject can never measure up to the Law. Even if the subject gives up all his/her inclinations as pathological, there is always more that s/he should give up: this is why Kant has to conceive the categorical imperative as an infinite task. But on the second level (and here begins Lacan's criticism of Kant), the rest is seen not simply as a left-over, but as the product of the universal form itself: the paradoxical *jouissance* that emerges from renunciation, from renouncing pathological pleasure. This demonstrates in the simplest way the opposition between pleasure and *jouissance*. Renunciation is itself the source of *jouissance*; it itself produces the rest that it pretends to get rid of. This is what Lacan calls *le plus de jouir*, the surplus *jouissance*, the only *jouissance* accessible to the human being subjected to the Law.

And third (here Lacan's critique gets even harsher), the very formality and universality of the Law has an obscene side to it (in this sense, it can be seen as analogous to the Freudian Superego). It is endowed with a malevolent neutrality with regard to the subject's good: the neutrality with which it inexorably demands just doing one's duty regardless of the consequences. It is further comparable with the Superego in terms of the impossibility of satisfying its demands. Lacan's thesis is that the obscene edge implied in Kantian Law came manifestly to light in Kant's great contemporary, the Marquis de Sade (cf. Lacan 1986, 93 ff., 221 ff., 363 ff. and *passim*).[13] What makes de Sade's characters perverse is the fact that they always speak in the name of universal law; they justify themselves quite scientifically, appealing to the laws governing history and human nature etc. More than this, they are willing to subject their position (the position of a 'will to *jouissance*') to the Kantian test of universalizability. Hence all the paradoxes of including *jouissance*, the right to *jouissance*, into the newly proclaimed declaration of human rights – 'Frenchmen, one more effort' – one more extension of human rights in order to include *jouissance*, that which cannot be universalized and which will forever haunt universality.'

In conclusion: I have tried to show how Foucault and Lacan derive quite opposing conclusions from the same Kantian premises, though both claim that the Kantian turn is essential to modernity. For Foucault, Kant's most significant invention is his new attitude: his notion of the essential 'ontological' belonging of the subject to the present, the ethical attitude in which he constructs himself as well as the age he belongs to. This for Foucault is the legacy of the Enlightenment. In this perspective, Kant also represents a turning point insofar as, after centuries of Christianity and its heteronomy, he returned, in a new and radical way, to the subject as the self-construction.[14] To arrive at this reading of Kant, Foucault has seriously to reconsider and reconstruct his own theoretical position: he has to introduce the notion of the subject (the relation to the self, the construction of the self) as the third, and even the most fundamental, axis of his work – after the axis of knowledge (the relation to things) and the axis of power (the relation to others).[15] 'Thus it is not power, but the subject', we are now surprised to learn, 'which is the general theme of my research' (Foucault 1982, 209). Foucault's claim, in other words, is that there was a dimension of subjectivity implicit all along in his analyses of knowledge and power, even if it emerged only at the end of his life's work, as an oblique and surprising restoration of the 'autonomous subject' (a virtually proscribed notion in the heyday of structuralism).

But it is here, I think, that Foucault fails to acknowledge the real novelty of Kant's radical position. He reduces the subject of the Enlightenment – which emerges at the peak of the Enlightenment as the Kantian subject of moral Law – to squeeze it back into the framework of a pre-Kantian subjectivity.

For Lacan, on the other hand, Kant proves a very different point: the inner impossibility of an autonomous subject. There is a kernel of the Real which prevents self-construction from the inside and disrupts any delicate balance in the relation to the self, the traumatic point around which the subjectivity is constituted. It is paradoxically from there, from this emergence of an inner limit in the project of the Enlightenment, that psychoanalysis raises its claim to the legacy of the Enlightenment.

275

NOTES

This paper presents a modified version of a lecture given at Essex and Sussex Universities in January 1990.

[1] Cf. Laclau and Mouffe (1985), p. 112-13 and *passim*.

[2] Lacan as well, in the programmatic text on the cover of *Écrits*, describes his work as the continuation of 'a single debate, always the same, which ... recognizes itself as the debate of the Enlightenment' (Lacan 1966).

[3] Aesthetic modernism as a whole can be seen as a counterpoint to the self-transparent and unitary subject implied in the Enlightenment: a fragmented and mutilated subjectivity which has lost its unity and transparence as the result of the progress of the universality of reason.

[4] The French and the English version, while treating the same topic and making largely the same points, differ in many important respects.

[5] 'This form of philosophy (sc. a critical thought taking the form of an ontology of ourselves, an ontology of the actuality), from Hegel to the Frankfurt School, passing through Nietzsche and Max Weber, has founded a form of reflection in which I have tried to situate my work' (Foucault 1984a, 39).

[6] The question of what particularly determines the precarious position of stoicism is the object of Foucault's close scrutiny (in 1984d). Stoicism presents the paradox of producing practically all the elements of the Christian moral code (the inclusion of women and slaves, equal moral obligations for men and women, virginity before marriage, rejection of homosexuality etc.), yet its position of enunciation is different. So the transition to Christianity had to accomplish both a smaller and a greater step than it appears.

[7] Particularly in his unfortunately yet unpublished lectures on Collège de France (which I had the privilege to attend in 1980/81).

[8] Kant's text was written as a response to a public question put forward by a magazine, *Berlinische Monatsschrift*, which was in itself a typical Enlightenment set-up.

[9] Of course it is not difficult to show Kant's bias in detail. His autonomous public, for example, turns out on closer scrutiny to consist only of *artifices* (in Marxist terms, the owners of the means of production, since only they can be considered as independent) and not of *operarii* (those who merely sell their labour). To take one of Kant's own examples: the barber is not an autonomous subject, since he merely sells his services, but the wigmaker is, although they both perform operations which are 'to a hair' alike.

[10] Kant seems to echo here almost literally the famous dictum from Kafka's *Trial*.

[11] 'A doctor humoured his patients from day to day with the hope of an imminent recovery: he said to one that his pulse was getting better, the other that his stool, the third one that his perspiration promised an improvement. When visited by one of his friends, he first asked: "How is your health?" "How could it be? *I am dying of getting better all the time!*" ' (Kant 1912, 647). Kant concludes with this joke the part of the paper dealing with the

question whether the humankind is making constant progress. This is perhaps not a bad definition of progress: dying of getting better all the time.

[12]'Kantian ethics emerges at the moment when the disorientating effect of physics becomes apparent, physics in the form of Newtonian physics, having reached independence in relation to *das Ding*/the Thing/, the human *das Ding*. It was Newtonian physics that forced Kant into a radical revision of the function of reason as pure, and it is explicitly out of his questioning of scientific origin that Kant derives the morals whose rigorous framework could never be imagined up to then – the morals which are expressly detached from any reference to any object of affection, any reference to what Kant calls *pathologisches Objekt*, a pathological object ...' (Lacan 1986, 93).

[13] Lacan's main paper on the topic actually bears the title 'Kant avec Sade' (Lacan 1966, 765 ff.). It is too complex to be tackled in this present paper.

[14] Foucault's assessment of Kant is very different here from the analysis he made in *Les Mots et les classes* (Foucault 1966, 329ff), where Kant, with his positing of the limitations of finitude as the transcendental conditions of an infinite progress of knowledge, was taken as a paradigm of the pitfalls of modern knowledge, of the emergence of the science of man etc. Cf. Habermas's opinion: 'Here (in the last lecture) we do not find the Kant we were familiar with from *Les Mots et les choses*, the critic of knowledge who with his analytics of finitude opens the gate of the era of anthropological thought and human sciences; in this lecture, we find *another* Kant – Kant as the predecessor of young Hegelians, who was the first to break seriously with the metaphysical legacy, who turns philosophy away from truth and the eternal being to concentrate on what had so far, among philosophers, passed for non-conceptual and not being, the contingent and the passing.' Habermas 1985, 127.

[15] In the most explicit way in the short paper attached as an Afterword to the famous book by Dreyfuss and Rabinow.

REFERENCES

Derrida, Jacques (1984), 'Mochlos ou le conflit des facultés', *Philosophie*, no. 2, Paris: Minuit.
Foucault, Michel (1966), *Les Mots et les choses*, Paris: Gallimard.
Foucault, Michel (1980), *Power/Knowledge*, ed. Colin Gordon, Brighton: Harvester Press.
Foucault, Michel (1982), 'The subject and power', Afterword in Hubert L. Dreyfuss and Paul Rabinow, *Michel Foucault: Beyond structuralism and hermeneutics*, Brighton: Harvester Press.
Foucault, Michel (1984a). 'Un cours inédit', *Magazine littéraire*, no. 207 (mai 1984).
Foucault, Michel (1984b), 'What is Enlightenment?', in, Paul Rabinow (ed.), *The Foucault Reader*, London: Penguin.
Foucault, Michel (1984c), *L'Usage des plaisirs*, Paris: Gallimard.
Foucault, Michel (1984d), *Le Souci de soi*, Paris: Gallimard.
Habermas, Jürgen (1985), *Die Nueue Unübersichtlichkeit*, Frankfurt: Suhrkamp.

Kant, Immanuel (1912), *Vermischte Schriften*, Leipzig: Inselverlag.
Lacan, Jacques (1966), *Écrits*, Paris: Seuil.
Lacan, Jacques (1986), *L'Éthique de la psychanalyse, Le Séminaire, Livre VII* (texte établi par J.-A. Miller), Paris: Seuil.
Laclau, Ernesto and Mouffe, Chantal (1985), *Hegemony and Socialist Strategy. Towards a radical democratic politics*, London: Verso.
Žižek, Slavoj (1988), *Les plus sublime des hystériques. Hegel passe*, Paris: Point Hors Ligne.
Žižek, Slavoj (1989), *The Sublime Object of Ideology*, London: Verso.

The *Unvermögender* Other: Hysteria and Democracy in America

Joan Copjec

THE TEFLON TOTEM

You don't have to know the plan of a building in order to bang your head against its walls; as a matter of fact, it is precisely through your ignorance that you *guarantee* such accidents. I couldn't help recalling Lacan's observation – a kind of ironic re-echoing of Dr Johnson's refutation of Bishop Berkeley – as I watched the various episodes of television's comically repeated battle with what it called the 'Teflon President'. Every idiotic blunder, every bold-faced lie that was caught by the cameras was played and replayed on the nightly news, juxtaposed to an image which directly contradicted, and thus exposed the falsity of the President's words. But though by this means it could decisively refute one statement after another, the medium could not – by its own incredulously tendered admission – menace the position of the President himself. Ronald Reagan emerged virtually unscathed by all these proofs of the incompetence and mendacity of his speech. It was as though America had acquired its own Shroud of Turin, immune to all the doubts produced by fibre analysis.

Let's not stoop to lazy name-calling by noting merely that it was television which proved the bigger imbecile here; analysis is doomed unless one can name the precise failing involved. In this case we must point out (more precisely) that it was its own '*realist* imbecility' which television ended up exposing.[1] This malady received its clinical designation in 'The Seminar on "The Purloined Letter"', where Lacan used it to explain the police's failure to locate the object of its methodically misdirected search: the Queen's stolen letter. Why

279

couldn't the police find this object so obviously displayed? Because they were looking for it in the wrong place. The only time something can be hidden in plain sight (which is where, in fact, the letter was hidden) is when its invisibility is a psychical condition, and not merely a physical one. The police comb geographic space and neglect completely the 'intersubjective'[2] or signifying space, which is where the letter remains unobserved. The realist imbecility, then, is just this sort of error committed in the service of a 'referential plenitude'. As Barthes describes it in his essay on 'The realistic effect', this imbecility results from a tampering with the 'tripartite nature of the sign', a sacrificing of the signified – the dimension of intersubjective truth – in favour of the referent.[3] This sacrifice of the signified is, moreover, strictly dependent on the effacement of a statement's marks of enunciation. In other words, the particularity of the enunciator must be abolished for the 'referential illusion' to take hold, for it to become possible to believe that it is the referent alone which determines the truth value of a statement. The reign, since the nineteenth century, of 'objective' history is a consequence of this belief, of this effacement of the signifying trace of the authorial voice. Reality thus appears to be free-standing, to be independent of and prior to any statements one can make about it. History, then, follows reality; it emerges from the fact that something happened then, something existed there. The sole function of history is to tell the tale of what once has been.

Barthes, who wrote his essay on the 'reality effect' in 1968, cites the then-current success of the Tutankhamun exhibit to illustrate the way this 'having-been-there' quality which history attributes to things continues to induce the most massive response, the way it continues to structure our world and dictate our actions. His excellent example of the modern rage for the referent lacks only the properly ludicrous dimension of a more recent example, again provided by American television. Toward the end of December 1989, major and local television networks all at once dispatched their camera crews and news staffs to Aspen, Colorado. What was the purpose of this not insignificant expenditure of time and money? In each case it was to obtain one very specific image: that of the now-empty spot in front of Bonnie's restaurant where Ivana had confronted Donald Trump. Now, it is precisely this imbecilic devotion to the referent which made television news the dupes in their battle with Reagan. So absorbed were the news staffs in pinning down the President's lies and errors – his referential failures, let us call them – that they neglected to consider the intersubjective dimension of the whole affair; they forgot to take account of the strength of the American audience's *love* for Reagan. If you know anything about love, then you perforce know something about Lacan; you know what he means when he says that love is giving what you do not have. He means that what one loves in another is something more than the other, some unnameable thing that exceeds any of the other's manifestations, anything he has to give. We accept someone's gifts and ministrations because we love him, we do not love him because he gives us these gifts. And since it is that something beyond the gifts that we love and not the gifts themselves, it is possible to dislike the gifts, to find fault with all the other's manifestations, and still love the other – as the behaviour of the hysteric makes clear. The unnameable excess, the exorbitant thing that is loved is what Lacan calls the object (a), and so we might say that television didn't have to know anything of Lacanian theory in order to bang its head against this object. What television attacked was the President's statements, what it left intact was the object (a), the instance of enunciation – that very thing which the 'realist imbecility' always and necessarily (as the condition of its possibility) disregards. It is this object which allowed Reagan to be Reagan; it was in this object – and obviously not in his statements – that his consistency was to be found. America didn't love Reagan for what he said, but simply because he was Reagan.

It is important not to confuse the object (a) with some poetical or essentialist notion of the subject. This object does not precede the statement, but is instead its retroactive effect, the surplus that overruns what is said and that 'always comes back to the same place', always designates the same thing – again, retroactively – no matter how self-contradictory the statements that produce it. This is why it cannot be dispersed by any simple appeal to the referent, by any refutation of the subject's speech – because it posits a subject which is the same without being self-identical.

Counterbalancing America's love for Reagan was its often noted lack of regard for the news media. It has also been noted that 'liberal bourgeois states' (states with long-standing democracies), such as Britain, France, and America do not regard the police very favourably.[4] These observations may not be unrelated for it might be supposed that it is precisely because the news *acts* like the police that it meets with such disfavour. Of course, just what it means to 'act like the police' is not immediately apparent and so we refer to a certain type of fiction – produced first, and primarily, in Britain, France, and

America[5] – which has always been intent on clarifying this for us: it is called detective fiction. This fiction systematically differentiates the law of the police from the law of the detective in order to valorize the latter. My hypothesis is that *detective fiction is a product of modern democracy* and thus I will argue that the law of the detective is that which subtends democracy and that it is shown to be jeopardized by the law of the police, that is, by the law of scientific realism.

There are, of course, some who continue to insist on tracing detective fiction back to Greek drama, but most critics are willing to acknowledge that detection is a historically specific form of fiction that only began in the 1840s, with writers such as Edgar Allan Poe. Those who hold to the former belief, however, usually argue that the genre is occasioned by the rise of scientific reason and the establishment of the laws of evidence. They then propose that detective fiction is a celebration of scientific reason, that the detective is an exemplar of positivist thought. What proponents of this argument ignore is the fact that scientific reason is only there in detective fiction to be ridiculed and subverted. What they remain blind to is the 'symbolic mutation' in which detection participates, a mutation otherwise referred to as the democratic revolution.[6] This is not to say, however, that there is no relation between the scientific and the social revolutions, for, indeed, there is.

To understand this relation – and the subtlety of the difference between the two terms – let us return to the phenomenon of the 'Teflon President'. It is possible to conceive a different argument than the one we proposed. One might have supposed instead that by continuing to believe in the President even as it grew more and more suspicious of the President's statements, the American television audience was repeating – in a peculiar, twentieth-century way – the gesture of a late seventeenth-century philosopher: René Descartes. For what, in fact, did Descartes do if not reveal that there is an instance (which we have been calling, according to linguistic theory, the enunciating instance) which exceeds all the enunciations, or statements, a subject may make? The cogito is nothing but this enunciating instance and its isolation by Descartes is what allowed him to make his remarkable, historically consequential argument: even if every thought one thinks, every statement one utters can be doubted, can be shown to be guilty of some error or deception, the *instance* of doubt – of thought or speech – *cannot* be doubted; it remains innocent of all charges of error.

This would not be the first time Americans were suspected of Cartesian sympathies. At the beginning of Part II of *Democracy in America*, for example, Alexis de Tocqueville declares Cartesianism to be the natural mode of thought in democracies.[7] Rather than relying on the authority of others, on a tradition of knowledge established by ancestor-scholars, de Tocqueville claims, democratic peoples prefer to base their thinking on common sense, on those clear and distinct ideas which are, in principle, available to anyone who will submit his thinking to radical doubt, who will purge himself of all subjective particulars. What is, of course, precipitated out by this radical operation is a pure mode of the subject, denatured, universal, the subject, in short, of modern science. Some might object that there is, on the contrary, a good deal of *un*scientific hocus-pocus in Descartes, that he uses God as a gimmick to cheat science, but this is to misunderstand that his God is merely the principle that the Other is just like you and that this is the very same principle – that of the possibility of total consensus – upon which modern science is founded.

But not only science. This principle also unleashed the great democratic revolutions of the eighteenth century, making Descartes the father not only of science, but of the American revolution as well. For no one would have thought of fighting for the rights of a universal subject – a subject whose value is not determined by race, creed, colour, sex, or station in life – no one would have thought of waging a war on behalf of liberty and justice for *all* subjects if Descartes had not already isolated that abstract instance in whose name the war would be waged: the democratic subject, devoid of characteristics.[8]

America's sense of its own 'radical innocence' has its most profound origins in this belief that there is a basic humanity unaltered by the diversity of the citizens who share in it. Democracy is the universal quantifier by which America – the 'melting pot', the 'nation of immigrants' – constitutes itself as a nation. If *all* our citizens can be said to be Americans, this is not because we share any positive characteristics, but rather because we have all been given the right to *shed* these characteristics, to present ourselves as disembodied before the law. I divest myself of positive identity, therefore I am a citizen. This is the peculiar logic of democracy. It is also a logic that can be used to explain the phenomenon of the Teflon President. An American public made sentimental about the flag, redoubled its belief in the fundamental democratic principle for which it stands. Reagan, who was largely responsible for stirring up this sentiment, became the

283

emblematic repository, the most visible beneficiary of this increase of belief that beyond all its diverse and dubious statements there exists a precious, universal, 'innocent', instance in which we can all recognize ourselves.

We now have, then, two different explanations for the same phenomenon. In both cases we claimed that the charges against Reagan did not stick because they were aimed exclusively at the concrete man – his class-belonging and alliances (the Bloomingdale's friends), his professional background as an actor, his 'psychological make-up' (the unwillingness to 'meddle' in administrative affairs, the inability or unwillingness to recall details), and so on. But by establishing these parallels between the object (a) and the cogito, the psychoanalytic and the philosophical explanations, have we not invited the reiteration of one of the most common charges against psychoanalysis: that it is ahistorical, that it disregards the concrete individual in favour of an abstract, universal subject? How much of *this* charge can be made to stick?

One must first recall that the concept of the universal subject is not itself ahistorical; introduced, as we have said, by Descartes only at the end of the seventeenth century, it must instead be acknowledged as a modern, historically-specific concept – and one without which psychoanalysis would have been unthinkable. For psychoanalysis, too, addresses itself to a non-concrete subject; it founds itself on the denial of the nominalist claim that all one encounters in everyday reality are particular, determinate individuals. The subject is never fully determinate according to psychoanalysis, which treats this indeterminacy as a real feature of the subject. This is why the historicist response to the psychoanalytic concept of the subject is so misguided. The response – which characterizes much of contemporary theory – approaches the universal subject as a vague concept that can, with more or less effort and a better knowledge of history, be given more precise attributes. This hasty historicism fails to understand that the universal subject is not a *vague* concept but, in Charles S. Pierce's sense of the term, a *general* one. That is, the concept does not poorly or wrongly describe a subject whose structure is actually determinate, but precisely indicates a subject which is in some sense *objectively indeterminate*. Against the faddish critique of the universal subject, psychoanalysis insists on this concept's political importance.

But even while admitting the similarity between the psychoanalytic and Cartesian notions of the subject, we have already begun to

284

underline their differences. For if both subjects proclaim themselves to be devoid of substantial, determinate existence, only the psychoanalytic subject can properly be described as *in*determinate. The cogito, on the contrary, is an instance of certainty. What is it that accounts for this difference? The love of the Other. The cogito is the object (a) under the aspect of love.

Let us cite the Lacanian formula once again: love is giving what one does not have, but let us this time put the formula in perspective by reviewing the distinctions between need, demand, and desire. On the level of need the subject can be satisfied by some *thing* which is in the possession of the Other. A hungry child will be satisfied by food – but only by food. If the mother, mistaking the meaning of her child's cry, proffers, instead, a blanket, she will, of course, fail to satisfy the child. Need requires for its satisfaction a *particular* object, nourishment, for example, *or* warmth; it is not a matter of indifference which, one cannot be substituted for another. It is on the next level, that of demand, that love is situated. Whether one gives a child whose cry expresses a demand for love a blanket, or food, or even a scolding matters little. The particularity of the object is here annulled, almost any will satisfy – as long as it comes from the one to whom the demand is addressed. Unlike need, which is particular, demand is, in other words, absolute, universalizing. The indifferent objects are all received as signs of the Other's love. But what does this mean? It means that the objects come to represent something more than themselves, that the Other now appears to give something more than just these objects. What is this 'something more' and what, then, is love? The something more is the indeterminate part of its being (in Lacanian terms the object (a) which the Other (or subject) *is* but does not *have*. And therefore cannot give. Love's deception, however, is that the object (a) can be given, that the Other can surrender the indeterminate part of its being to the subject who thus becomes the Other's sole satisfaction, its reason to be. This relation is reciprocal, with the subject also surrendering that which *it* lacks to the Other. Finally, there is desire. On this level the Other retains what it does not have and does not surrender it to that subject. The subject's desire is aimed, then, at a *particular absolute, absolute* in the sense that, like demand, it aims beyond particular objects to the 'something more' which exceeds them, *particular* in that the refusal to surrender it means that it remains unique to the Other – it is nontransferable.

Let us return to our discussion: the cogito's certainty derives from the love of the Other. In addition to the cogito's certainty, this logic of love explains the curious fact that while Descartes began by placing his certainty with the cogito and doubting all the cogito's thoughts, he (and the historicism he enabled) ended up by allowing the cogito to disappear beneath the truth of its thoughts and statements. As long as these indifferent, doubtable objects come from the cogito, they are received as the signifiers of the Other's love, of the communicability and truth which unites one cogito with another.

The situation in America is somewhat altered. Here we make a point of resisting the universalizing that belongs to the order of the cogito in order to celebrate difference, particularity. This does not mean that we have given up loving our leaders; unfortunately we still continue to participate in love's deception that the Other will give us what it cannot possibly give. We continue, in short, to demand a master, but one that is significantly different from the Other that sustains the cogito, since we require *this* master to accredit our singularity rather than our commonality. Yet in posing this demand to its elected leaders, Americans are confronted by a dilemma: every sign of accreditation cancels the difference to which it is supposed to bear witness, for it is precisely by bearing witness, by making difference communicable to another, that any sign automatically universalizes what it represents and thereby abolishes its singularity; how, then, to maintain simultaneously one's relation to a master and one's uniqueness?

America's solution is, in analytic terms, hysterical: one elects a master who is demonstrably fallible – even, in some cases, incompetent. What may first appear to be a stumbling block turns out on closer inspection to be a solution: Americans love their masters not simply in spite of their frailties, but because of them. We can put it this way: the pluralism that characterizes American democracy depends on our devotion to an *unvermögender* Other.[8] If everything this Other says or does *fails* to deliver the accreditation we seek, if all the Other's responses prove inadequate, then our difference is saved, it survives intact, as undiminished as our devotion – which is lodged, like our demands, with the Other and not with the Other's responses. It is, in fact, the differential between demand and response, the very vanity of our hopes, which sustains them. Unlike the relation to the cogito, in which all its statements are taken for truths, the relation to the *unvermögender* Other insures that its statements will be taken for lies.

Television news, then – to conclude our consideration of the teflon totem – by pointing out the errors in Reagan's statements, was not, as

286

we had originally assumed, simply attempting to discredit the President. Rather, by discrediting him, it sought to sustain our appeals to him. Like Dora, who dedicated herself to procuring for her invalid father, the news dedicated itself to hysterical, televisual displays designed to keep the American demand for a master alive.

THE HYSTERICIZED SUBJECT

It must be made clear, however, that the paradox which supports the peculiarly American relation to its masters is, in some sense, specific to democracy *as such*. Democracy hystericizes the subject. This observation can be sustained by reference to a number of ineliminable paradoxes, but we will cite only one, that provided by the practice of universal suffrage. According to the terms of this stated right, every citizen is given the opportunity to express his or her individual will, every citizen is given a vote that counts. The paradox is that it only counts as one, as an abstract statistic. The individual's particularity is thus annulled by the very act of its expression.[9] If one's difference is, by definition, that which escapes recognition, then any recognition of it will always seem to miss the mark, to leave something unremarked. The subject of democracy is thus constantly hystericized, divided between the signifiers that seek to name it and the enigma that refuses to be named.

The problem with the American *form* of democracy is that however visibly it decries the actions of the Other, it still continues to believe in the Other's power to sanction the vast array of differences to which its citizens lay claim. This belief encourages that 'narcissism of small differences' against which Freud and all the other critics of 'bourgeois individualism' have for so long warned us. This narcissism fuels the single-minded and dangerous defence of difference which so totally isolates us from our neighbours. And yet this belief in the Other-who-authorizes convinces us (despite every indication to the contrary) that this isolation can, in principle, be peacefully maintained, that the Other presides over a nonconflictual space in which all differences can harmoniously coexist.

Lacan's systematic assault on American ego psychology and, beyond this, the 'American way of life' is mounted in defence of a different notion of difference. Not one that demands to be attended to *now*, recognized *now*, but one that waits to be exfoliated in time and through a relation to others. This other difference will only emerge

287

once our appeals to the Other have been abandoned, once we accept the fact that there is 'no Other of the Other'. Nothing guarantees the Other's certainty, consistency, or completeness. The Other possesses nothing that we want, nothing to validate our existence.

That the time for understanding this notion of difference has not arrived in America is everywhere apparent, from local phenomena like that of the Reagan/news relation to our basic conception of the role of the law. In America it is assumed that the law of democracy is one that withdraws, that recedes as far as possible, intervenes as little as possible in order to allow the individuality of each subject to flourish unhampered. Big government is urged to retreat, to assert itself merely as the neutral agent overseeing the protection of the individual. To illustrate this principle let me recall for you the way America has been, to a large extent, spatially disposed. With the Land Ordinance of 1785, Thomas Jefferson (another 'father of democracy') decreed that the western territories would be laid out according to a grid plan adapted from several important eastern cities. This was a Cartesian gesture if ever there was one, for the grid disregarded all characteristics of topography and submitted America to an abstract law. The argument made for the plan, and the reason it was so widely accepted, was that it was thought to be the least obtrusive, most neutral way of legislating the carving up of space. The grid does not rule in advance the sort of building, city, or whatever that will come to occupy any particular quadrant; it was perceived to be a plan without a programme.

Supporting this conception of the law is a belief in a protective (against what we shall soon see), consistent Other which can, in principle, accommodate all the demands of its citizens. The psychoanalytic notion of the law is not like this; rather than being merely 'neutral', this law comports a certain exceptional violence. There is within the law itself something lawless. Let us call it, with reference to our image of the grid: Broadway. Lacan's critique of the 'American way of life' is directed, we might say, at our suppression of 'Broadway'. As opposed to the American conception, which believes that justice has only to be distributed, this psychoanalytic conception believes justice must be created.

MODERN POWER

> Above the race of men stands an immense and tutelary power ... that
> power is absolute, minute, regular, provident and mild ... it provides for

288

[the] security [of its citizens], foresees and supplies their necessities, manages their principal concerns, directs their industry ... I have always thought that servitude of the regular, quiet and gentle kind which I have just described might be combined more easily than is commonly believed with some outward forms of freedom and that it might even establish itself under the wing of the sovereignty of the people.[10]

It is de Tocqueville who is the author of this, one of the best-known passages from *Democracy in America*. It may, nevertheless, strike some of us as a bit uncanny. For since the dramatic opening of *Discipline and Punish*, in which we witnessed the wholesale displacement of a repressive form of power by one which sought to provide for the welfare of its subjects, we have become more familiar with Foucault's analysis of the paradoxical effects of this brand new 'mild and provident' form of law. But this comparison obliges us to observe an important and unsettling difference: when de Tocqueville wrote his book, in 1835, the new form of despotism whose emergence he feared had not yet come into existence; when Foucault wrote, however, fascism and a whole list of other despotic horrors had already been unleashed by totalitarian regimes. How is it, then, that Foucault continued to speak of *the* modern form of power, as though there were only one? What I wish to criticize is not only his historical blindness, but (since it is more fundamental, the very source of this blindness) his conception of disciplinary power itself. Foucault presents it as though it were a permanently viable form of power, as though its prolonged continuance did not lead inexorably to its own subversion by totalitarianism. The strength of the argument advanced by de Tocqueville is that it understands the tutelary form of democracy as an unstable form which must either be overthrown in favour of new freedoms or taken over entirely by a new despotism.

What is the basic argument – shared not only by de Tocqueville and Foucault, but by others as well – regarding this modern form of power? It is a power enabled by the historic overthrow of monarchy. At this point power ceases to be incorporated in the body of the king or in any other source. All connections to the old order of society – to its traditions, knowledges, heirlooms, as well as its fathers – are radically severed; the new order is structured around their disappearance. But if it is no longer incorporated in a source, if no authority wields it, what is it that legitimates the modern exercise of power? With no external support, it appears that it legitimates itself.

Power is simultaneously that which society produces and that which produces society – we encounter here that circularity which characterizes the performative utterance. Modern power is immanent in the very relations that structure the social order. It is this aspect of modern power – its impersonal and omnipresent nature – which is most disturbing, since it threatens to enmesh the subject in a network of domination. Yet Foucault's theory seems to offer an escape from the totality of this domination by maintaining that the social field cannot be totalized, that it is crossed by an array of different and even competing discourses. In the ruptures sparked by this competition, in the interstices of their network, pockets of resistance form.

I don't think anyone has ever stopped to wonder if these contradictory discourses would, in fact, necessarily enable resistance; perhaps this is because Foucault banished all the psychoanalysts from his republic. For, while it seems logical to expect that the different subject positions one is summoned to occupy would come into conflict with each other, psychoanalysis has developed a logic that allows us to understand how one might simultaneously hold two contradictory positions; how one might hold to one term and repress its contrary; how a society could be founded on a nonrecognition of the contradictions it contains.

It is this last possibility which interests us at the moment and we turn to *Totem and Taboo* where the conditions of this possibility are elaborated by Freud in his description of the totemic form of society. How is this society formed? The primal father – the father who kept all the power and all the enjoyment to himself – is slain by the brothers.[11] In order to inscribe the parricide as a *fait accompli*, in order for the brothers to assure themselves that they will all be equal henceforth, that no one will take the place of the dead father, society is installed under the banner of the son who signifies the father's absence. Since the primal father is the principle of *jouissance*, of excess enjoyment, the signifier of his absence will be the son who promises to protect society from the trauma of *jouissance*'s return. The son stands for the evacuation, or drying up, of excess enjoyment and thus for the possibility of pleasure's even apportionment. In Lacanian terms, it is the object (a) which the son evicts, for if you recall, it is the object which is the excess in the subject, that causes the subject to be eccentric to, or other than, itself. This eviction of excess pleasure forms the son as an ideal father, 'mild and provident' in the words of de Tocqueville, 'kinder and gentler' in the words of George Bush's speech writer,

Peggy Noonan. He is the place to which all our questions are addressed, the place of knowledge; he is therefore often imagined under the traits of the educator (take for example Noonan's ideal: America's new 'educational President'). The ideal father installs a badly needed certainty in the place of the devastating uncertainty, the crisis of legitimation, that follows in the wake of the primal father's murder.

Now, it seems to me that Foucault's description of modern power resembles this description by Freud. *Discipline and Punish* begins with the spectacle *not* of monarchical power, as Foucault claims – he has isolated only a moment and not the structure of this earlier form of power – but with the spectacle of the obscene, traumatizing *jouissance* of the primal father constructed *retroactively* by the society of brothers. The body of Damiens is ripped apart, totally shattered in order to feed his enjoyment. His parricide is then marked in Foucault's text by a recitation of some of the rules 'for the House of young prisoners in Paris'. Reading these rules we can see that the law has now assumed a tutelary form: it instructs, it guards, it protects, and it guides the prisoner throughout his day. Not only that, it *constructs* the day and the prisoner along with it. The law comports the affirmative, positive force of the symbolic, it causes the world to come into being by naming it. Lacan called this form of the law the paternal metaphor, or the Name-of-the-Father. A symbolic coalescence of knowledge and power, it bathes the prisoner in the bright light of intelligibility. As we have said, it subjects the prisoner totally, since it is the cause of its existence as well as its visibility. And yet the hope of transgression is never distant from the disciplinary society Foucault analyses. The possibility of the overthrow of power haunts the structure like a phantom. Why is this?

Again, Foucault's point is that it is because there is a multiplicity of discourses that this promise is held out. But Freud's analysis of the totemic form of society of brothers, offers a different answer. The ideal father, the number one son in the society of brothers, only affirms, only becomes the principle of the regulation of alliances *by forbidding excess enjoyment*, only becomes the principle of knowledge and intelligibility by casting out the object (a) that marks the point at which the order of intelligibility collapses. Foucault wanted to found his analysis of disciplinary power on the expulsion of the notion of the repressive father. He thought he accomplished this by describing a mild and provident form of law, an ideal father, in psychoanalytic terms. The problem is that in expunging the primal father, the one who commands *jouissance*, and replacing him with the ideal father (the law of power/knowledge), Foucault installed the very principle he meant to eject: the principle of interdiction. For the ideal father *is* the father who interdicts – *jouissance*. He is only able to shelter and protect because he interdicts excess pleasure. According to Freud, it is his interdictions (therefore not the other contradictory discourses or subject positions), his *interdictions* which give the subject a whiff of hope; it is they which suggest the possibility of transgression. In forbidding excess enjoyment, they appear to be its only obstacle; the subject/prisoner is thus free to dream of their removal and of the bounty of pleasure which will some day be his.

But how can we be so sure that Foucault is incorrect, that it is not the potential collision of different discourses that provides the possibility of transgression? Because in a totemic society, a society ruled by a tutelary power, the contradictions among discourses are largely unacknowledged and conscientiously guarded against. The totemic is a pluralistic society. America is a good example. The scrupulous autonomy and independence of the brothers is assured in this fraternity. The field may be glutted with contradictions without disturbing the society in the least. This is not to say that the social order remains stable; we claimed earlier that it does not. As Freud makes clear in *Civilization and its Discontents*, the more one renounces enjoyment, the more one is obliged to renounce it. Every sacrifice of pleasure strengthens the demand for sacrifice. In a society ruled by a provident power, an ideal father, interdictions grow more and more numerous. Witness the fresh lot of interdictions that besiege us daily: barriers (from gates, to moats, to guard dogs) have begun to encircle our homes and to forbid entry to any strangers; injunctions are posted on everything from walls to milk cartons – don't smoke here, don't smoke there, don't eat this, don't eat that, and above all don't abuse your children. If you need any proof that a tutelary power is fundamentally the signifier of the death of the primal father (the one who enjoys), you will find none better than this current obsession with child abuse. The primal father is primarily the father who seduces the child – at least this is the guise under which he appears most often to psychoanalysis, in the complaints of the hysterics. More generally we could say that the campaign against the primal father is visible in the increasing abhorrence of the pleasure of others. In fact, the intolerable other *is* pleasure in today's society. What have increased as of late are

interdictions. These are the mechanisms that construct the phenomenon that Foucault calls surveillance.

BELONGING TO NO-ONE

You may have recognized here what we earlier called the
unvermögender Other; the ideal father is 'a man without means'. The
only way to be master of desire, which is what the ideal father is
supposed to be, is to be either impotent or dead. The fraternity this
father constructs is equally impotent, paralysed by the interdictions
which are required to stave off the conflict between the brothers. The
best literary illustration of this is James Joyce's *Dubliners*. Language,
country, religion. Three ideal fathers and a mass of interdictions. Such
a society cannot continue indefinitely. The law of the ideal father is
eventually repealed and the despotic primal father returns. A
totalitarian regime takes over.

It is essential to recognize that totalitarianism is not simply the
reinstatement of some earlier form of despotism, a reversion to an
especially brutal monarchical order, for example. If, as we stated at the
start, totalitarianism is a specifically *modern* form of power, this is
because it is dependent on the democratic revolution's privileging of
the individual, of the *people* rather than the king, or some other leader.
The totalitarian leader's power 'comes from below', as Foucault would
say, his is only the power that the people confer on him – by placing
him in the position of their ego ideal, as Freud says in *Group
Psychology and the Analysis of the Ego*. This is so clearly the case that
Gustav Le Bon does not bother to say very much at all about the leader
of the totalitarian group and, though Freud notes this as a criticism,
neither does he. Yet where Le Bon had focused on the relations among
the members of the group, Freud insisted that it was their common,
pre-existing relation to the leader that determined the totalitarian
formation of the group.

Psychoanalysis does not, however, as is sometimes proposed, argue
that all groups are basically totalitarian in nature. Instead it provides an
analysis which allows us to see how totalitarianism follows, though not
inevitably, from democracy. But under what conditions can
democracy be maintained and totalitarianism forestalled? Lefort's
formula is still the best: 'Power is and becomes democratic [only]
when it proves to belong to no one ... *when it proves to belong to no
one*'. The phrasing is exact, but in need of elaboration, for by itself it

admits of more than one interpretation. Have we not argued that a totemic society is founded on this very same principle, that of the *exclusion* of the primal father from the community of brothers? And hasn't Foucault made the same argument about the modern, disciplinary society: that no one need occupy the central tower in the panopticon, no one need possess power, for power to exert itself? And yet we have also argued that a totemic society initiates the *subversion* of democracy and have criticised Foucault for collapsing different forms of modern power, for failing to distinguish democracy from its subversion in totalitarianism. Isn't it precisely this notion of 'no one' which justifies the collapse? Justifies, no, but facilitates, certainly, by lending to Foucault's theory just that quiver of paradox that has so far proved seductive: at the very moment when power began to be wielded by no one, everyone became subjected to it. We may as well state at the outset that the 'no one' of Foucault's theory does not seem to be quite the same as the 'no one' of Lefort's.

What exactly does Foucault say about this 'no one' who occupies the place of power?

> [I]t does not matter who exercises power. Any individual, taken at random, can operate the machine ... Similarly, it does not matter what motivates him: the curiosity of the indiscreet, the malice of a child, the thirst for knowledge of a philosopher, or the perversity of those who take pleasure in spying or punishing.[12]

In other words, this no one is, more properly, *no one in particular*, anyone. It may seem unfair to put too much emphasis on a statement made with reference to Bentham's panopticon, since this architectural device may be insufficient to support the complex theory of Foucault. But the essential point remains that in his theory the notion that power 'belongs to no one' is attached, as here, to the observation that since the modern form of power, or law, has no external guarantees, it may be seen to guarantee itself. This means that the discourse of power or the statement of law does not derive its power from the person who speaks it; it is not by virtue of any quality, power, or interest of the enunciator that the discourse possesses its force. In fact, the discourse or statement annuls all qualities, powers, or interests of the enunciator, it effaces all contingent characteristics in order to fill this empty, anonymous space with its own tautological truth. The enunciator coincides with his function, that of enunciator; the bureaucracy

294

'automatizes and disindividualizes power', creating as its product the anonymous, impersonal bureaucrat.

From this angle the paradox of the modern form of power begins to look more familiar. Is this not the same paradox which is manifest in scientific statements, historical statements, maxims, that nineteenth-century class of statements whose badge of truth was their erasure of all the traces of their enunciation? If Foucault's work was so easily accepted as a theory of the nineteenth-century novel, this is because the realist novel had already been theorized in his terms. It had already been argued that the narrator was nobody in particular, nobody but a generalized consciousness. And if, despite all the well-meaning and careful attempts, by Foucault and others, to dispel the 'paranoid' interpretations of his theory, power, as he described it, still seems inescapable, then this is surely the result of the fact that by announcing themselves in such a neutral, general form (that is, as coming from nowhere), the discourses of power seem to embrace everyone in their address.

When Lefort says that power belongs to no one, he means something different from this. His 'no one' is attached not to the fact that the law guarantees itself, but to the fact that *there are no guarantees*. Democracy, Lefort argues, is 'the dissolution of the ultimate markers of certainty'. The discourse of power, the law, that gives birth to the modern subject can guarantee neither its own nor the subject's legitimacy. There where the subject looks for justification, for approval, it finds no one who can certify it. The modern subject encounters a certain blind spot in the Other, a certain lack of knowledge – an ignorance – in the powerful Other.

Historians are undoubtedly correct to point out that a great gathering of information was begun in the nineteenth century. The moment the individual subject became visible as a social value, it also became the object of an intense scrutiny. But it must also be remembered that this information proliferated as verificationism collapsed. Which resulted in what? A mass of information that could not be verified. It was the combination of these two conditions – and not simply the fact that the individual subject became the object of several new 'human sciences' – that produced the modern democratic subject. It is to the fact that power is *disjoined* from knowledge, that the force which produces the subject is blind, that the subject owes its precious singularity. For, if there is a *lack of knowledge* in the Other, then there is necessarily a *surplus of meaning* in the subject, an excess for which the Other cannot account, that is to say, there is something in the subject that escapes social recognition.

DOUBT

How to conclude? The space inhabited by indeterminate subjects will never be harmonious; a democracy is not a utopia. First of all, the attendant paradoxes that we referred to earlier through the example of universal suffrage contribute to a great deal of neurotic insatisfaction. It seems that the pre-eminent form of modern power is also the source of 'modern nervousness'. Additionally, since there where the 'markers of certainty' are erased, there enjoyment breaks out, democracy seems designed, if not to brew up more dissatisfaction, at least to acknowledge the impossibility of its alleviation. For as Freud says in *Totem and Taboo*, 'Sexual needs are not capable of uniting men,' they separate men.[13] In other words, once you admit enjoyment into the system, you have, unavoidably, a conflictual space, one that will not lie down flat, as on a grid. Yet it is just this conflict which preserves democracy. It is only this dissatisfaction and this struggle over the definition of the subject and of its relations to other subjects that prevents us from surrendering this power of definition to the Other. It is only because I doubt that I am therefore a democratic citizen.

NOTES

[1] Jacques Lacan, 'Seminar on "The Purloined Letter" ', trans. Jeffrey Mehlman, *Yale French Studies* 48 (1973), which is a partial translation of the essay published in *Écrits*; an earlier version of Lacan's argument appears in *The Seminar of Jacques Lacan II: The Ego in Freud's Theory and in the Technique of Psychoanalysis*, trans. Sylvana Tomaselli, New York, Norton, 1988.
[2] 'Intersubjective' is not to be taken here in the psychological sense; it does not refer to a relation between subjects who can identify with either the position or thinking of each other.
[3] Roland Barthes, 'The realistic effect', *Film Reader* 3 (1978), trans. Gerald Mead from 'L'effet de reel', *Communications* 11 (1968), pp84-9.
[4] See Ernest Mandel, *Delightful Murder: A Social History of the Crime Story*, London, Pluto Press, 1984.
[5] Richard Alewyn, 'The Origin of the Detective Novel', *The Poetics of Murder*, (eds) Moste and Stowe, New York, Harcourt, Brace, Janovich, 1983, p65. Whenever the link between detective fiction and democracy is made, it is usually attributed to the establishment of laws of evidence. See, e.g., Howard Haycraft, *Murder for Pleasure*, New York, Appleton-Century, 1942, pp312-18.

6 I here acknowledge my debt to the brilliant work of Claude Lefort who has theorized modern democracy not simply as a form of government, but more radically as a 'mutation of the symbolic order'. This paper is an introduction to a much longer study of the contributions of detective and Gothic fiction to this mutation.

7 Alexis de Tocqueville, *Democracy in America*, Pt II, New York, Knopf 1945, pp3-7. In his unpublished seminar on *'Extimité'* (1985-1986), Jacques-Alain Miller also stresses the relation between Cartesianism and democracy as he simultaneously develops the relation of these two terms to psychoanalysis. Miller's discussion of this point is much more extended and sophisticated than de Tocqueville's.

8 In describing her father Dora used the phrase *'ein vermögender Mann* [a man of means]', behind which Freud detected the phrase *'ein unvermögender Mann* [a man without means, unable, impotent]'. In proffering her description Dora was declaring her demand for a master, in reinterpreting her, Freud was indicating the sort of master the hysteric prefers.

9 Lefort uses this paradox to make a slightly different point, which is that universal suffrage prevents the notion of 'the people' from materializing, since numbers are inimicable to substance. They desubstantify the very image of 'the people'. Lefort, *Democracy and Political Theory*, Minneapolis, Minnesota Press, 1988, pp18-19.

10 De Tocqueville, p319.

11 The distinction between the primal and the ideal or Oedipal father on which this part of my discussion is based is drawn by Michel Silvestre in 'Le pere, sa fonction dans la psychanalyse', *Ornicar?*, no 34 (July-Sept. 1985), pp14-40.

12 Michel Foucault, *Discipline and Punish*, New York, Vintage, 1979, p202.

13 Sigmund Freud, *The Standard Edition of the Complete Psychological Works of Sigmund Freud*, trans. James Strachey, London, The Hogarth Press and the Institute of Psycho-Analysis, 1955, vol. XIII, p74.

A Symptomology of an Authoritarian Discourse

The Parliamentary Debates on the Prohibition of the Promotion of Homosexuality

Anna Marie Smith

Section 28 of the Local Government Act 1987-8
Prohibition on promoting homosexuality by teaching or publishing
material

28–(1) The following subsection shall be inserted after section 2 of the
Local Government Act 1986 (prohibition of political publicity) –

2A – (1) A local authority shall not –
(a) intentionally promote homosexuality or publish material with
the intention of promoting homosexuality;
(b) promote the teaching in any maintained school of the
acceptability of homosexuality as a pretended family relationship.

(2) Nothing in subsection (1) above shall be taken to prohibit the
doing of anything for the purpose of treating or preventing the
spread of disease.

(3) In any proceedings in connection with the application of this
section a court shall draw such inferences as to the intention of the
local authority as may reasonably be drawn from the evidence before
it.

(4) In subsection (1)(b) above 'maintained school' means –

(a) in England and Wales, a county school, voluntary school, nursery school or special school, within the meaning of the Education Act 1944; and

(b) in Scotland, a public school, nursery school or special school, within the meaning of the Education (Scotland) Act 1980.

(2) This section shall come into force at the end of the period of two months beginning with the day on which this Act is passed.

Section 28 of the Local Government Act 1987-8, which passed into British law on 9 March 1988, first appeared in the context of a private member's Bill introduced in the House of Lords by Lord Halsbury on 12 December 1986. According to the original wording of this first Bill, local authorities were to be prohibited from giving 'financial or other assistance to any person for the purpose of publishing or promoting homosexuality'. During its Third Reading in the House of Lords, the Bill was amended, such that the teaching of the acceptability of homosexuality as a 'pretended family relationship' would also be prohibited. In the Commons, it passed through Second Reading and received unanimous support at the Committee stage. Like most private members' Bills, however, this first Bill failed to progress beyond the Committee stage; its significance was more symbolic than juridical.

The Bill was none the less effective in preparing the way for the anti-gay elements in the subsequent 1987 Conservative Party election campaign. One official party poster featured four books with the titles *Young, Gay and Proud, Police Out of School, Black Lesbian in White America*, and *Playbook for Children About Sex*. The main text of the poster stated 'Labour's idea of a good education for your children'.[1] The play of racial and sexual images in this poster was by no means incidental; as Stuart Hall notes, the construction of the equivalence, Labour = 'excessive' local government = high rates = 'loony Left' = permissiveness = radical blackness, gayness, feminism = erosion of the entire social order, was central to the 1987 campaign.[2]

In the new session of the House, a local government Bill was introduced which aimed to force authorities to award works contracts only through competitive tendering and to dismantle all their contract compliance schemes relating to the employment of minorities. The 'free market' was to replace interventions by local bodies. As the forty-fourth piece of legislation on local government introduced since 1979, the Local Government Bill 1987-8 on one level simply constituted yet another attack on the autonomy of a local authorities, one more attempt to reduce them to de-politicized service delivery points. At the Committee stage, however, a version of Lord Halsbury's Bill to prohibit local authorities from promoting homosexuality was added as a new clause. The motion to make the clause stand as part of the Bill passed at that sitting without a vote, although the Opposition could have insisted on a division.

Clause 28 received disproportionate consideration throughout the subsequent debates in the House and the Lords. In the Lords, amendments to the Clause were passed, most notably the amendment which prohibited the 'intentional' promotion of homosexuality. These amendments were accepted by the House and the entire Bill received Royal Assent on 9 March 1988. Section 28 came into effect two months later. From its introduction to the final division, discussion of this particular clause accounted for approximately 26 per cent of the debates on the entire Bill.[3]

Clause 28 was therefore a late addition to an anti-local government, anti-union, anti-black, and anti-feminist Bill. The unique location of this legislation on homosexuality in a local government Act is not accidental. Local authorities had to a limited extent become a counterweight to central government in the late 1970s and early 1980s. In some cases, such as that of the Greater London Council (GLC), local governments became the sites of new leftist coalitions, in which the demands of feminists, black activists, and lesbians and gays were granted an unprecedented degree of legitimacy. However, instead of recognizing the democratic character of these modest advances in the representation of popular demands at the local level, the Thatcher government responded with the abolition of the GLC, the redefinition of progressive policy changes as the will of un-British pressure groups, and the demonization of elected local councillors as the tyrannical 'loony Left'.

The abolition of the GLC was fully in line with the centralist project of Thatcherite 'parliamentarism',[4] which aims to reduce the political terrain to two spheres, the enterprising individual and her family on the one hand, and central government on the other. No interruption in the simple relation between these two spheres is tolerated. What must be underlined, however, is that the organization of consent for centralization, through the equation of local government autonomy with the illegitimate subversion of the social order, was not a natural phenomenon. It was achieved through complex discursive initiatives, one of which was the strategic invention of a crisis around the

301

promotion of homosexuality. The Clause 28 discourse on homosexuality was not an irrational product of prejudice, that is to say, a 'homophobia', but was instead a coherent deployment of highly charged images, a strategic 'anti-gayness'.

THE EVIDENCE GAME

What were these discursive initiatives which created the appearance of a crisis around the promotion of homosexuality? In what follows, I shall examine the discourse of the supporters[5] of Clause 28, with specific emphasis on the parliamentary debates. I shall attempt to show that this discourse can be usefully considered as a complex ensemble of strategies. The most salient strategy in this discourse is organized around truth claims and the provision of 'evidence' to substantiate these claims. The supporters were able to set into motion a self-reinforcing circulation of their truth claims, such that each claim became situated in what could be called an 'evidence game'. The problem with this evidence game is that it is extremely seductive; when truth-claiming is located on a site in which uncertainties and anxieties have become concentrated, we can become seduced by the game's play of truths and counter-truths. Although we may think that we are resisting the original truth-claiming by providing counter-evidence, we may actually be reinforcing the game itself.

For example, the arguments of the supporters of the clause were based first and foremost on the proposition that a campaign to 'promote homosexuality' by local authorities *did exist* and that its subversive effects were devastating. Several speakers, such as Dame Jill Knight, specialized in the provision of 'evidence' in a complex circulation of mythical figures. A wide variety of texts was cited, ranging from GLC policy statements, to children's sex education materials produced wholly independently of local authorities, to a political manifesto written by a non-governmental gay and lesbian group. These disparate texts were listed as if they were equivalent, as if they were but the few of the many, and were invariably misattributed, misquoted, discussed out of context, and quoted selectively. At one point, Knight quotes a passage from a sex education text, which she incorrectly claims to have been 'promulgated by a local council'; she then directly proceeds to situate her 'evidence' by quoting passages from a radical critique of the family by the Gay Liberation Front written in 1971.[6] The argument is presented as if it were self-explanatory; any effort to place homosexuality on an equal plane with heterosexuality is seen to constitute a subversive 'promotion', because behind even the most apparently harmless tolerance of homosexuality lies a deep conspiracy to undermine the entire social order of the nation. 'Promotion' can be 'proven' in this context merely by referring to discourses in which homosexuality is included as a legitimate element; the citation of exact cases of the actual and explicit promotion of homosexual acts to minors is unnecessary.

Early speakers in the debates make several fallacious charges. It is claimed that lesbian and gay books were displayed in two Lambeth play centres, that the book *Young, Gay and Proud* was recommended for children by the Inner London Education Authority and stocked by a Haringey library, and that the text *Jenny Lives with Eric and Martin* was stocked at an ILEA teacher centre and its publisher grant-aided by the GLC. These fallacies then become self-perpetuating: later speakers cite the same 'evidence' as if its legitimacy and significance were already well known. In the final debates, simply citing the names of five local authorities, Camden, Haringey, Lambeth, Brent, and Ealing, is deemed sufficient to evoke the figure of the 'promoter' of homosexuality. Local councils' support for lesbian and gay youth groups and discos is presented as if the local councils invented these activities to brainwash teenagers, though of course they actually originated in the gay community, rather than in any local authority plot. Furthermore, although the speakers claim to be concerned with the welfare of children, they also cite publications and policies aimed at adults.

The most forceful truth-claiming in support of the clause is organized around interpretations of popular opinion. Opinion polls in which 83 per cent of the respondents stated that they 'do not approve of schools teaching that homosexuality is on par with heterosexuality', 43 per cent stated that they 'do not approve of homosexual relationships between consenting adults', and 85.9 per cent agreed that the promotion of homosexuality should be prohibited,[7] are offered as conclusive evidence of the necessity of the clause. The relatively few public protests in support of the clause are presented as the true expression of the opinions of the 'average ratepayer'. With these claims, the evidence game becomes even more complex. Supporters can agree that the 'promotion of homosexuality' is a mythical construction, but they can nevertheless argue that the signs of popular concern irrefutably indicate the necessity of prohibitive legislation.

Patrick says, for example,

> I accept that [the clause] is needed ... I know that parents often object to the fact that such teaching *appears* to be available in the schools. Whether it is in fact available is not the argument.[8]

The supporters never recognize, however, the context of these 'popular' concerns – the fact that widespread anxiety and misinformation about AIDS, and the supporters' own fallacious claims about local government activities, preceded these poll findings and protests. The supporters also do not admit that most of the leaders of such protests were not 'average ratepayers' but members of right-wing activist groups. Through the evidence game, a mythical narrative is constructed; first, there were the excesses of the 'promoter', then, the expressions of popular concern, and, last, the legitimate response of the supporters in the form of the clause. The truth-claiming conceals the extent to which the supporters' discourse is constitutive of that which appears to be its enemy, the 'promotion campaign', and of that which it appears to be representing, 'popular opinion'.

Furthermore, the truth-claiming of the supporters constitutes a framework which organizes both the supporters' discourse and, for the most part, the opposers' discourse. For example, when the clause is introduced in Committee, Cunningham, the Labour spokesman on local government affairs, emphasizes that it has never been the policy of the Labour Party to promote homosexuality. What Cunningham does not do is question the manner in which the supporters express their concerns about homosexuality, or defend the existing policies of Labour-led local governments; he attempts only to distance the Labour Party from the alleged phenomenon. In his intervention in the same Committee debate, Grant, a back-bench Labour MP, takes an entirely different approach. Instead of arguing about whether or not a campaign to promote homosexuality actually exists, he presents a detailed defence of Haringey's modest proposals for changes in school curricula. Reading from a council report, Grant states that the aim of responsible teaching is to ' "reflect the reality of actual experiences of children" ' and to give the children ' "the confidence to manage their relationships with integrity" ' and to encourage them to establish non-exploitative friendships and relationships based on ' "equality and respect" '.[9] From this and other similar contributions to the debates, it can be seen that, while it is true that a very small number of local authorities established lesbian and gay units, offered support to gay organizations, and explored the possibilities of promoting 'positive images' of lesbians and gays through their programmes, these initiatives were very few in number, were often merely proposed changes, and were shaped by measured, principled, and cautious thinking.

However, within the opposers' discourse, interventions such as Grant's were exceptional. The opposers generally pursued Cunningham's line of argument, in an attempt to show that a campaign to promote homosexuality simply did not exist. Whereas Grant directly confronts the 'loony Left' and 'promotion of homosexuality' figures deployed in the supporters' discourse, most of the opposers focus on demonstrating that the supporters' claims are untruthful.[10]

The problem with this counter-truth strategy is that the charges of the supporters, for all their fictitious character, were tremendously effective in popular terms; not only were they widely believed, but they moved many people to positive action; to repeat the charges to others, or to write to their MP. The signifying function of discourse on the promotion of homosexuality was to represent and to give permission to otherwise disorganized or unspoken anxieties; and that function could not be nullified through counter-truths. The senselessness of the supporters' charges did not in any way diminish the authority of their claims. Anyone who felt that the supporters' claims 'spoke' to her was perfectly capable of saying, 'Well, I know very well that some of these stories are untrue, but we still have to do something about this crisis.'[11] The 'promotion of homosexuality' in this context is not a hypothesis which can be rationally proven or disproven; it is a symptom of underlying ruptures in the social. Even if one symptom could be treated with the remedy of counter-truth, the ruptures it conceals will produce other symptoms, forming a chain of elements. The symptom-work, condensation and displacement, representation and iteration, can never been completed. The symptom is situated on the terrain of excess,[12] a permanent, futile, and yet highly productive struggle of representation. In this context, the counter-truth discourse, in so far as it also 'believes in' truth, can even escalate the symptom-evidence game by taking the truth claims seriously.

HOMOSEXUALITY AS RADICAL DIFFERENCE: INVADER, SEDUCER, PRETENDER

Instead of playing the evidence game by offering counter-truths, it is more important to analyse the conditions of effectiveness of truth claims. In the place of counter-truth-claiming, we should engage in 'symptomology', an investigation of the structure, and the strengths and weaknesses, of the supporters' truth-claiming discourse. Why was this expression of anxiety around homosexuality, in this particular form, so persuasive? Why did the conception of the erosion of the social order through the promotion of homosexuality seem to 'sum up' otherwise disparate concerns, concerns about disease, morality, children, and the family, and the relations between central government and local government? Why did the devotion of extensive official discourse to this conception of homosexuality, at this particular time, appear to be a legitimate exercise?

In the late 1980s, discourse on homosexuality is almost inevitably permeated by discourse on AIDS. In terms of the Clause 28 supporters' discourse, discourse on AIDS plays a key role in two different ways. First, the AIDS phenomenon is strategically interpreted such that homosexuality no longer appears to be one social element among many, but is represented as a threat to the very existence of other social elements. Knight, for example, mentions AIDS at several junctures and argues that Clause 28 is of the greatest importance in that 'AIDS starts with and comes mainly from homosexuals' and only 'spreads to others' later.[13] This interpretation of AIDS, such that 'homosexuality' appears to be equivalent to 'threat to others', is of course only one possible interpretation. The AIDS syndrome does not live in an empirical group of people; indeed, the groundless equation, gayness = AIDS, is an extremely dangerous strategy of denial by heterosexuals of their own risks and responsibilities.[14] The HIV virus associated with AIDS is transmitted by practices which cut across all social groupings, and an individual's imaginary location in a so-called 'low risk group' provides absolutely no prophylactic protection from the virus. Condoms, not fantasies about identities, stop the virus. The search for the origin of AIDS is in turn nothing more than an attempt to ground this denial of the risks to heterosexuals; claims about the origins of AIDS are shaped more by racist and anti-gay fantasies than by reputable medical research.

It is none the less important to analyse the statements about AIDS by the supporters of Clause 28. Through these statements, we can begin to understand the context of the Clause 28 discourse. The construction of the myth of the promotion of homosexuality is effective in part because it is preceded by the articulation, homosexuality = threat to all other elements in the social. Discourse on AIDS, both by officials like Knight and by the popular press, prepared the way for Clause 28. However, discourse on AIDS is also re-represented in the discourse on Clause 28. AIDS 'hysteria' has generated a great deal of hostility towards lesbians and gays, from everyday discrimination to 'queer-bashing'. Clause 28 gives this expression of hostility a legitimate and apparently disinterested form. Many individuals would not consider violent or hostile acts towards homosexuals as socially acceptable. By contrast, agreeing with an elected official that our children are being threatened by a campaign to promote homosexuality is more readily understood as a socially acceptable act.

The statements about AIDS by the Clause 28 supporters are also useful for symptomology in that they are organized according to a precise structure which is reproduced throughout their discourse. In her claim about AIDS, Knight appears to be expressing her fears about the threat of *illness*. It is, however, important to note that this expression takes a form which is central to the tradition of western philosophy, or, in Derridean terms, the 'metaphysics of presence'. In any text within this tradition, there is always some stated or implied recognition of radical difference,[15] but there are also attempts to use radical difference against itself, to conceal its primordiality through various strategies, one of which is the deployment of 'inside'/'outside' figures. In Knight's discourse on AIDS, there is a recognition both of radical difference, and of its threatening potential. There is 'homosexuality' as opposed to 'the norm', and homosexuality is equated with a disease which later spreads into not-otherness, the 'norm', which it contaminates. By representing radical difference as an 'invader' figure, however, the discourse of the supporters paradoxically creates a sense of a threatened space, the 'natural social order', the 'inside'. More than this, already in the very terms of the presentation of radical difference, there is no simple opposition, the norm versus homosexuality. There is instead a complex of spaces, and fundamental attributes are ascribed to each space as if they were inherent characteristics. The 'norm' appears to have been there first, as the natural space, and homosexuality appears to have come later, as that which essentially wants to contaminate the natural space from the outside. But it is of course only with the invader figure that the 'norm' takes on this appearance. The threat of radical difference is reworked to produce that which it could otherwise interrupt, the sense of the primacy, completedness, and closure of the 'norm' as the original space. Thus Knight's discourse only appears to be about nothing more than illness. The anxieties she voices are actually about the disruption of the social order in general. In other words, these are anxieties about radical difference. The hegemonic interpretation of the AIDS phenomenon is, for example, actually a representation of radical difference, situated within a long tradition of similar representations of 'other' social elements. This AIDS discourse is linked genealogically to popular anxieties about various diseases, communist infiltration, immigrant populations, crime 'waves', drug 'crazes', etc. Each of these is seen to invade the social order from the outside or to threaten it from within. Fundamental anxieties are organized around this interruption, and a simulated consensus is forged against the figure of the 'invader' or the 'enemy within'. We have a sense of a Thatcherite Britishness, for example, only by virtue of a series of staged confrontations: resistances to the belligerent Argentinian invader, the swamping by black immigrants, the revolutionary plot of the communist miners, etc. Knight's presupposed sexual norm appears as such only through its representation in opposition to diseased and uncontained homosexuality. The hegemonic discourse on AIDS is therefore an expression of anxieties about radical differences; it is a representation of the threat of radical difference in the figure of the diseased homosexual invader, and it offers compensation for anxieties about radical difference by creating a sense of consensus.

The supporters' discourse on Clause 28 is structured in part in a manner similar to the hegemonic AIDS discourse. It is taken for granted that a space of sexual normalcy exists as the primordial and natural space, and that, although that space is threatened by the homosexual invader, it remains for the time being uncontaminated. At the same time, however, the supporters' discourse is contradictory, for it contains a vision of the space of the sexual norm as already thoroughly contaminated by homosexual otherness. In this second representation of the threat of radical difference, homosexuality is not simply a threatening invader from the outside, but has taken on the properties of a seducer, a floating element whose corrosive effects are already experienced throughout the space of the norm.

This second representation becomes particularly striking in the context of the supporters' expressions of their views on the development of sexuality. The supporters unanimously agree that

A Symptomology of an Authoritarian Discourse

sexuality is not fixed biologically at birth and that virtually every child and teenager is vulnerable to sexual corruption through 'improper' teaching. Quoting from the Wolfenden Report, the Earl of Halsbury argues that because ' "people's sexual orientation [is] not fixed at any particular stage, but is stabilised around the middle twenties" ', school-leavers are still 'open to seduction', and must be protected until that age.[16] In contrast to Knight's taking-for-granted of the resilience of sexual normalcy as a primordial space, here there is no such certainty: anyone is open to seduction.

With the assumption of the universality of the possibility of corruption, an obsessive surveillance of the sexual space of young people follows. Homosexuality must be displaced from the childhood space in which 'true' sexuality is carefully nurtured; if homosexuality is to emerge, it must do so later. The paradoxes are of course obvious: homosexuality is represented as potentially present in the originary moment of childhood, and yet must be made to come later; heterosexuality, the 'natural' sexuality, does not 'naturally' develop but must be produced through intervention; if every 'normal' child can be seduced by the not-normal, then there is something in the essence of normalcy that turns the 'normal' against itself; the 'normal' would not be 'normal' without its relation to the not-normal; thus the very idea of normalcy depends on an ever-present threat from the not-normal; with the play of contamination and dependency between the two terms, the distinction between the 'normal' and not-normal ultimately fails, etc. This self-contradictory thinking does not collapse into incoherence, however, but fuels an obsessive concern for the production of normalcy in a world in which nothing can be taken for granted, especially the sexual development of the most apparently 'normal' child. 'Natural' sexual development, then, cannot be left to 'nature' but must be actively created through an intensely interventionist project of social transformation.

Having examined these discursive operations of the supporters' discourse, its representation of radical difference, we are now in a position to make intelligible the precise terms of the clause. The supporters say that they do not want to eliminate services for lesbians and gays, and that they do recognize the importance of discussing homosexuality in the classroom. Many emphasize that they are not against homosexuals *per se*. A Government spokesman defends the inclusion of the vague term homosexuality in the clause, instead of the more precise 'homosexual acts', because he is concerned that local authorities are attempting to 'sell' the 'whole gamut of homosexuality, homosexual acts, homosexual relationships, even the abstract concept'.[17] Homosexuality becomes a threat to the extent that it takes the form of radical difference, to the extent that it invades the space of the norm from the outside, or circulates throughout this space as a seductive floating element. Whereas the *homosexual* is defined as a someone who is inclined towards erotic acts with a member of her own sex, *homosexuality* is defined as the *manifestation* of sexual desire towards a member of one's own sex.[18] The crisis which the supporters' discourse aims to forestall relates to uncontained homosexuality, this showing of radical difference. The problem is not the existence of an invisible sexual minority, or the acts of consenting adults in private, it is the disruption of the social order by radical difference. The dangerous potential of this radical difference is realized in so far as its circulation is encouraged and made public, that is, in so far as it is 'promoted'. Consequently, the main section of Clause 28 does not refer to persons (homosexuals) or acts (sodomy), but prohibits the 'promotion' of 'homosexuality'.

An account of the second part of the clause, the prohibition of the 'teaching of the acceptability of homosexuality as a pretended family relationship', can also be given in terms of the representation of radical difference in the supporters' discourse. The supporters say that they want to make illegal any discourse organized by a local authority which 'portrays' homosexuality as 'the norm',[19] grants homosexuality a 'more favourable treatment, a more favourable status, or wider acceptance [than heterosexuality]',[20] or suggests that the '[homosexual] lifestyle is desirable over another'.[21] Homosexuality not only wants to invade the space of the norm from the outside, and to circulate seductively throughout the space of the norm, it also wants to take the place of the norm by presenting itself as the pseudo-norm. The crisis here is the possibility of deception: the possibility that homosexuality may be accepted as legitimate, as a norm. The supporters' discourse instead names homosexuality as a false norm, its family relations as simulacra, and attempts to make a distinction in law between the pretender and the real thing. Here again their discourse is grounded in paradox: they believe that the distinction between the pretender and the real thing is necessary, and that drawing this distinction is a task appropriate for official discourse; yet the very necessity of such a distinction is indicative of its impossibility. Necessary and yet impossible, but always productive; these are the hallmarks of the

310

supporters' discursive project.[22]

THE 'GOOD HOMOSEXUAL/BAD GAYNESS' DIVISION

The supporters' discourse is opposed to homosexuality in so far as it takes the form of radical difference, the invader, seducer, and pretender. There is a distinction, then, between homosexuality as a radical difference, which disrupts the social order, and homosexuality as a simple difference, which not only does not disrupt the social order, but must be included in the social order for strategic purposes. This distinction is made in explicit terms throughout the supporters' discourse. The law-abiding and not-diseased *subject* who keeps her expression of difference strictly behind closed doors in a monogamous relationship with another adult, the 'good homosexual', is distinguished from the publicly flaunting *element* which strives to reproduce itself by seducing the innocent young. This element is 'bad gayness'. Lord Halsbury, for example, argues that it is important to distinguish between 'responsible' homosexuals and their 'exhibition[ist]', 'promiscuous', and 'proselytizing' counterparts. He argues that lesbians belong to the former category because they are not 'wildly promiscuous' and do not 'molest little girls', 'indulge in disgusting and unnatural practices', or 'spread venereal disease'.[23] Lord Monson says that he recognizes the 'genuine' rights and freedoms of homosexuals, but emphasizes that these rights pertain only to the 'bedrooms of consenting adults' and not to 'propaga[tion]'.[24]

Other Clause 28 supporters recognize that the gay community is currently facing a violent backlash, but they attribute that backlash to the work of bad gayness, rather than to their own discourse. Conservative MP Wilshire says that it is the 'arrogan[ce], self-assertive[ness], aggressive boastfulness and self-glorification' of some homosexuals which has offended the 'majority of people'.[25] Dickens, another Tory MP, argues that lesbians and gays who want support against the 'queer-bashers' should accept the decriminalization of homosexuality 'gently and steadily and not expect too much'. He concludes:

> [homosexuals] are only likely to get that support [against violent attacks] if they stop continuing to flaunt their homosexuality and thrusting it down other people's throats.[26]

The distinction between the good homosexual and bad gayness is made on both qualitative and ontological grounds. The good subject is *closeted* in every sense of the term, hidden and contained within closed frontiers, while the bad element *comes out of the closet*, shows itself and refuses to be contained. The goodness of the homosexual consists precisely in her self-limiting, fixed subjecthood status, an otherness which knows her proper place. The badness of bad gayness lies in its unfixity and 'excessiveness', its insatiable drive towards expansion and self-reproduction, its contamination of the space of normalcy through its entry of the wrong orifices, and, above all, its pursuit of unlimited bodily pleasure.

ANTI-GAYNESS AND ANTI-BLACKNESS

Having demonstrated this distinction between homosexuality as radical difference and homosexuality as simple difference, the strategic necessity for the supporters of the clause simultaneously to include the latter and to exclude the former from their vision of the social order remains to be shown. First, however, it is important to note that the strategies of the supporters' discourse are not 'new', but have already been developed in discourses on other social elements. The manufacturing of a crisis in a mythical but effective evidence game; the use of otherness as a common enemy against which the concealment of social ruptures becomes possible; the representation of that otherness as an invader, a floating interruption, and a pretender; the division of otherness into legitimate and illegitimate camps; the pseudo-acceptance of the former as harmless difference and the exclusion of the latter as dangerous difference; all these strategies are also at work in the New Right discourse on race and nation. The 'panic' about the numbers of 'new Commonwealth' immigrants (the technical euphemism for blacks) in the later 1960s was the product of an evidence game organized by Powellite discourse. Through opposition to blackness, and, later, to a chain of equally subversive signifiers – the student movement, the peace movement, Irish nationalists, etc. – Powellism was able to create a new sense of nation.[27]

The Conservative Party campaign poster cited above makes sense only because it works within this tradition. The sense of invaderness is not fixed in terms of a single concrete enemy, but circulates to new figures. The reader of the poster is prompted to think: 'As we fought against the blacks to exclude them (through the immigration laws) and to regulate their dangerous difference (through new policing discourses), so too must we join togther to exclude and to regulate gayness.' The white line of the immigration queue and the thin blue line of inner city policing is reproduced in anti-gay discourse in the form of an obscure division between 'proper' and 'improper' teaching on homosexuality.

In New Right discourse, whiteness, Britishness, and heterosexuality are represented as if they ought to correspond to a given set of people; at the same time, radical difference is seen as potentially subversive of these essential attributes. The very whiteness-Britishness of school-children is held to be vulnerable to corruption by radical blackness, which is seen to take a particularly insidious form in 'multiculturalism' and putatively illegitimate versions of the history of the empire.[28] Regardless of actual skin pigmentation, parenting, and apparent 'normalcy', the white child is seen as someone who needs protection from these subversive elements; her true identity must be actively produced through proper teaching.

The current problematization of the space and frontiers of the classroom with regard to the otherness of blackness follows from the thinking of identities as always susceptible to illegitimate influences, and this is precisely the thinking that runs through the supporters' discourse on Clause 28. There are close correspondences between discourse on the 'promotion of homosexuality' and discourse on race. In the Clause 28 debate, Lord Halsbury says, for example:

> We have for several decades past been emancipating minorities who claimed that they were disadvantaged. Are they grateful? Not a bit. We emancipated races and got inverted racism. We emancipate homosexuals and they condemn heterosexism as chauvinist sexism, male oppression and so on. They will push us off the pavement if we give them a chance.[29]

Rights and freedoms are here defined as privileges bestowed by a generous and 'permissive' society.[30] Furthermore, the products of 'permissiveness' are represented as disruptive social movements, each of which follows the same pattern. It is interesting to note, for example, that the worst villains in the 'promotion of homosexuality' story – teachers, cultural workers, and intellectuals in general – are also the villains of Powellite and Thatcherite discourse on race. In Powell's speeches, for example, the most treasonous enemy is not blacks, but the apparently harmless intellectual, the journalists, lecturers, politicians and even church officials who spread the corrosive message of tolerance. The Powellite/Thatcherite argument – which is reproduced in the discourse of the supporters of Clause 28 – is that the most sinister advances of the 'left', including blackness, gayness, and socialism, have been made on the terrain of moral and intellectual reform, or 'social engineering'. From this perspective, the role of the intellectual is seen as critical in that it is through intellectual activity that the movement of difference is regulated; the crime of the 'permissive' intellectual is the weakening of the frontiers which would otherwise facilitate the exclusion and neutralization of radical difference. It is not accidental, then, that Section 28 prohibits the *intentional* promotion of homosexuality; what this encourages is an intellectual self-examination, a policing of one's own intentions.[31] Section 28 is therefore also located within a particularly effective tradition of anti-intellectualism – the tradition of insidious incitement to self-censorship.[32]

THE EXCLUSION AND INCLUSION OF DIFFERENCE

When the supporters of Clause 28 speak of a distinction between the good homosexual and bad gayness, then, they are not saying anything 'new', but are speaking within a tradition. In both anti-blackness and anti-gayness discouse, threatening difference is divided into radical difference and simple difference; anti-British blackness and flaunting gayness versus the entrepreneurial, assimilated black and the closeted homosexual. Why then is this distinction, and the combination of the exclusion of radical difference with the inclusion of simple difference, strategically necessary? First, this operation facilitates the concealment of the exclusionary dimension of the discourse; it makes it possible to argue coherently, and effectively, 'We are not really against blacks and gays, we include most of them and only exclude the few "bad apples",' etc. That which is included, however, is a neutralized, simple difference; the 'cost' of inclusion is never explicitly recognized. Second, this double manoeuvre opens up the tremendously productive possibility of self-division and self-surveillance *within* an element of otherness, practised at a local level, in local discourses. I shall return to this theme below. Third, it allows the space of Britishness and the norm to be represented as invulnerable; it permits the British to say, 'Look at how strong our nation is, we can actually live together with so many different peoples and still maintain our Britishness,' etc. We are doubly reassured here: we congratulate ourselves on our ability to tolerate, indeed to enjoy included difference; yet we enjoy it in a safe, neutralized space – a walk in a zoo rather than a walk on the wild side. Finally, the exclusion of radical difference produces consensus, a sense of common purpose. The exclusion of radical difference is necessary for the creation of a sense of unity (our nation, our shared norm), yet the inclusion of simple difference is a necessary support for that exclusion. The movement of difference is therefore taken up, rather than suppressed, through the exclusion/inclusion matrix, but, paradoxically, in the reworking of difference through this matrix, an appearance of consensus and closure is created and preserved.

It is of course true that some of the supporters of Clause 28 do not participate in these complex manoeuvres *vis-à-vis* radical difference. When Smith, a Labour MP, cites the escalation of physical attacks on lesbians and gays in general, and the arson attack on the offices of the community newspaper *Capital Gay* in particular, Kellett-Bowman, a Conservative MP, responds:

Quite right ... there ought to be intolerance for evil.[33]

Fairburn, a Conservative MP, claims incorrectly that homosexuality is classed as a 'psychopathological perversion' and lists unlimited aggression, sadism, masochism, and criminality as equivalents of homosexuality.[34] Others further equate homosexuality with the total destruction of the social order, the institution of the family, and even civilization itself.[35] The 'promotion of homosexuality' is represented as the 'thin edge of the wedge', or the first step on a slippery slope towards total anarchy. Lord Monson argues that lesbian and gay pride weeks cannot be publicly funded because there would then be no grounds to refuse support to 'bondage pride weeks'; in his view, 'the possible permutations are endless'.[36] Wilshire says that if the promotion of homosexuality were made legal simply because homosexual acts are now decriminalized, this would 'lead to an "everything goes" in this country'. In an almost impossible twist of logic, he concludes that if the promotion of homosexuality were allowed, then other promotions of illegitimate elements, such as the promotion of racial hatred, would also have to be permitted.[37]

This discourse of bigotry, though not typical of the supporters' discourse, is put to use within it. Contrasting themselves to the bigots

315

on the one side, and the 'loony Left' on the other, the supporters are able to locate themselves as the centrist representatives of the moderate majority,[38] in a situation where they would otherwise be recognized themselves as extremist reactionaries. They actually express concern regarding the current backlash against lesbians and gays, yet argue that the clause is the best remedy in that it will 'remove the source of the disquiet',[39] namely the 'unacceptable activities of a few extremist councils'.[40] The 'good homosexual' is therefore represented as the innocent victim of a backlash against homosexuals which ought properly to be directed against local authorities; indeed, it is implied that it is in the true interest of the lesbian and gay community itself to support the clause. The arguments of both the bigots and the opposers of Clause 28 are represented in this context as equivalents, as equally disruptive extremisms – and the supporters' response to the crisis is represented as the only possible strategy for the restoration of order.

THE LOGIC OF FANTASY AND THE SYMPTOM: THE FAMILY VERSUS GAYNESS

The supporters' discourse on Clause 28 takes place, as I have suggested above, within certain traditions; its strategies *vis-à-vis* radical difference were already prepared in similar discourses on AIDS and on race-nation identities. In addition to these elements, however, there is also an abundance of references to particular conceptions of the 'family', the 'parent', and the 'child'. These figures are often presented in New Right discourse in the context of the constant problematization of the space of the classroom. The classroom must perform an impossible task, that of completing the natural development of the child. The 'proper' space for the development of racial and sexual identities is, however, the space of the family. In the context of the Clause 28 debates, the supporters argue that teachers and other local government officials are 'strangers' from 'outside the home', and that the teaching of sexuality ought to 'start in the family unit'.[41] The teacher, then, should only complete the work of the parents and should not interfere (but is there not already something lacking in the parent-child relationship that a teacher should be necessary?). It is implied that it is only in the hyper-normal space of the family, a space of known blood relatives and organized hierarchical relations, that radical differences can be adequately resisted.

What must be underlined here is that these figures, the family, the parent, and the child, are *imaginary*. Though the New Right claims to be concerned about actual families, many of its policies, such as its housing legislation, the poll tax, and the freezing of child benefits, have contributed directly to family breakdown. The family is also represented in New Right discourse as a super-safe place; yet statistics on the sexual and physical abuse of married women and children in actual families fundamentally contradict that vision. In any event, if the Clause 28 message about the dangers to children posed by the promotion of homosexuality were received by actual parents alone, then it would work with only a small proportion of the population. The appeal of the arguments put forward by the supporters of the clause is not limited to a fixed audience precisely because of the metaphorical character of their references. Speaking about the innocent child who is 'at risk' from the promotion of homosexuality is effective because the image of the 'child within', or, in metaphysical terms, a pure 'inside', is universal. Speaking to the anxious parent is effective because the movement to protect the vulnerable space of the child is also universal. Discourses within the tradition of the 'metaphysics of presence' are always caught up in a necessary and yet impossible movement of 'parenting' the innocent 'child' or the pure 'inside', that is, the always unfinished mission to circumscribe perfectly that 'inside' space with a barrier which allows the entry of simple difference and simultaneously repels radical difference. Our experience of actual families may not correspond with these imaginary figures, but the references are none the less effective.

Like other strategies of the supporters' discourse, the deployment of these figures – the family, the parent, the child – becomes intelligible when understood in terms of the management of the threat of radical difference. Attempts to exclude and neutralize radical difference are never fully successful; but there must always be some promise of the possibility of a final solution. A scenario in which radical difference is completely neutralized must be offered to allow the forgetting of the impossibility of this final operation. This scenario, or fantasy,[42] is a simulacrum which offers compensation for the irresolvability of radical difference. The figures of the idealized family, and the eternal English nation, play this key function in New Right discourse. They are imaginary fantasy spaces utterly purified of radical difference. Furthermore, these particular fantasies are not innocent day-dreams. References to fantasy figures like the idealized family or the eternal nation make possible an otherwise impossible authoritarian strategy, that of speaking and acting as if the social were/ought to be a closed space, when it is everywhere apparent that this is simply not the case. The authoritarianism of Thatcherism and of New Right discourse therefore owes everything to these fantasies of the idealized family and the eternal nation as exemplary spaces of closure.

What must be emphasized is that there is no fully constituted desire which precedes the fantasy. It is not as if there is first an entity, such as the British people, which naturally dreams of an authoritarian society, and that, second, the New Right merely offers to that entity appropriate fantasy figures for the fulfilment of its desire. The construction of fantasy figures is a fundamentally constitutive operation. We learn 'how to desire' through fantasy; that is, through fantasy figures, the exemplars of closure, we learn to pursue the impossible, the defence of closure against radical difference.

These fantasies, however, cannot play their compensatory role unless some explanation is given for the gap between the actual impossibility of fully neutralizing radical difference and the perfection of the imaginary fantasy. Blame for any failure to complete the neutralization of radical difference must be displaced on to some other element – the symptom. The symptom can be represented as wholly external to the fantasy space, as an external 'cause' for the failure to neutralize completely radical difference. The symptom is therefore the necessary support for the fantasy, in that it facilitates the concealment of the impossibility of pure spaces. Only with the symptom figure can the impossible be promised; we will have unity, purity, and a return to our true essence, but only after we have dealt with this symptom, and that symptom, and now this other symptom, etc. We *will* be as one as a people, our English identity *will* be fully restored, the primacy and perfection of the family *will* be realized, our society *will not* be marked by crime, disease, and moral decay, etc., but only after we have finally solved the problems about these blacks and gays (or, elsewhere, 'acid house' parties, pornography, prostitution, terrorists, drug dealers, communists, foreigners, Jews, etc.).

It makes sense, then, that the New Right is obsessed with blackness and gayness, and the family and the nation. The fantasies which support its authoritarian symbolic structure each have their corresponding object of fascination: the ideal family has flaunting gayness and the ideal nation has radical blackness. Every new invocation of the ideal family and the ideal nation is twinned with yet another demon figure of gayness and blackness. The very structure of this discourse ensures the endless production of a chain of symptom-figures. Because it is engaged in a simultaneous expansion of social ruptures, or radical difference, on the one hand, and the generation of compensatory ideal fantasies which support authoritarian thinking on the other, New Right discourse endlessly produces and reproduces symptom-figures which underpin its contradictory strategies of rupture and compensation.

THE 'PRETEND CONSENSUS' OF THE NEW RIGHT

What is the product of these attempts to manage the threat of radical difference? It has been argued above that these strategies create a sense of unity where there might otherwise be dispersion – but what is the status of this unity?

In popular mobilization against the promotion of homosexuality, New Right intellectuals championed the anti-gayness and religious fundamentalism of the black and Jewish communities as exemplary figures of true British morality.[43] The anti-black and anti-Semitic traditions of the New Right were temporarily suppressed to allow for mobilization around a single common opposition to the particular symptom-figure of the day, which was flaunting gayness. What was at stake here was not the formation of a fixed and identifiable 'bloc' united by shared support for actual policies and beliefs. Such a bloc is by definition an impossibility; there can only ever be the construction of a 'pretend consensus', organized around a complex and contradictory anti-will (anti-radical blackness, anti-flaunting gayness, anti-revolutionary worker, etc.).[44] It is only with reference to these symptom-figures that there can be any collective sense of 'consensus', and the simulated bloc of the 'pretend consensus' is then re-represented as if it were a positive body organized around a positive system of beliefs. In this manner, the appearance is created of a unified 'us' opposed to a unified 'them' – a mythical 'us' which is also seen to have issued a positive mandate to 'our' representatives. Positive mandates in the political sphere are therefore actually created retrospectively through the re-representation of an anti-will; a will to contain the threat of radical difference.

RADICAL DIFFERENCE AND THE IDENTITIES OF LESBIANS AND GAYS

In the above discussion of the combination of the exclusion of radical difference with the inclusion of simple difference, reference was made to the incitement of self-division and self-surveillance within the element of otherness. This theme will now be taken up in relation to my remarks on the construction of consensus. In the parliamentary debates on Clause 28, the Earl of Halsbury reads a letter which he says is from a 'male homosexual'.

> I want to say how fed up I am with my fellow homosexuals. They have brought it upon themselves, their unpopularity. They are too promiscuous, too aggressive and exhibitionist. I cannot stand the sight of them. I wish they would keep themselves to themselves.[45]

The distinction in the letter between the good homosexual and bad gayness is repeated in many other texts which are written by lesbians and gays ourselves. The New Right discourse speaks persuasively to the element within lesbians and gays which 'wants to be good'; it seems to offer to the good homosexual full inclusion in the pretend consensus.

The New Right does not say 'no' to all homosexuality, but actually encourages the development of a self-limiting homosexual subject. This subject is imbued with the sense of a moral imperative; a sense, for example, that we (lesbians and gays) ought to conduct ourselves as 'good citizens', to control our excessive members or to expel them, to welcome heterosexuals to all our events, etc. We are encouraged not to suppress our difference, but to assert a difference of a neutralized type. What could have been an expression of radical difference, a challenge to the entire order of social relations around gender and sexuality, is encouraged to become an expression of simple difference, the demands of a fixed interest group seeking legitimacy.

The ideal of goodness, and full inclusion in that space of normalcy, is of course impossible. Virtually no element is offered this complete inclusion; even the Lords and royalty have had their legitimacy questioned in New Right discourse. However, some inclusion of simple difference must take place; the mere exclusion of radical difference is ineffective. The survival of the body of the norm depends upon taking within the body the very element which threatens its life, but in a particular form, like a vaccine against a disease. Authoritarian discourse dreams of closure, and its simulation of closure is produced by the assimilation and neutralization of difference. Neutralizations of radical difference, however, are never successful if they remain 'top down' exercises of domination. Radical difference must be regulated at local sites, from multiple centres, and that regulation must be expressed in local discourses, such that it appears to be achieved by lesbians, gays, blacks, workers, etc., ourselves. The organization of consent among lesbians and gays, and the pseudo-inclusion of the good homosexual in the pretend consensus, is therefore necessary rather than accidental to New Right discourse.

The perfectly good homosexual always remains, however, a contradiction in terms: no one can ever be perfectly closeted. What the discourse of Clause 28 produces – in tandem with other discourses – in lesbian and gay discourse is an escalation of the tendencies within ourselves and our communities to demonize our own 'bad' or subversive elements. To our credit, there has been a great deal of solidarity across otherwise separate camps, between men and women, for example. But, although we have engaged in many resistances in the context of the AIDS phenomenon and Section 28, we should also take responsibility for the tradition of ongoing demonizations within our community. Expressions of hostility towards political 'trouble-makers' or excessive drag queens, expressions of blame and guilt around the circulation and contraction of the HIV virus, and expressions of the necessity of 'legitimate' interest group strategies, are common in the letters pages of our community publications. Besides this 'conservative' tendency, there is also a 'radical activist' tendency which is likewise structured around a sense of moral imperative and self-perfection. We may find ourselves, in the face of tremendous pressures, trying to become 'super' lesbians and 'super' gay men, to formulate perfect identities which, however, never quite fit us. Here the problem is not so much one of retreat to conservatism, but one of rigidification of the meaning we ascribe to lesbian-ness and gay-ness. A rigid conception of lesbian-ness, for example, is used in criticisms by 'radical' lesbians of the sexual practices of other lesbians, and of the production by other lesbians of erotic images. In these demonizations, any deviation from the lesbian norm is identified as a dangerous enemy within, an anti-lesbian-ness.

It should be emphasized that the New Right promotion of self-division and self-surveillance is an operation which could potentially work with any social identity. Any pursuit of the ideal of goodness, whether it occurs in 'their' terms and 'their' space, or in 'our' terms and 'our' space, perpetuates the illusion that our identities, which, by definition, are always imperfect, can be perfected. In this sense, it is simply one more variant of the universal attempt to achieve a total neutralization of radical difference. Radical difference disrupts every social identity; yet we come to experience that disruption as something for which we are guilty, as something caused by the badness within.

Blaming an enemy figure, an enemy 'outside' or badness within, is not, however, inevitable. Instead of becoming caught up in this seductive, futile, and dangerously rigidifying game, we could begin with the rcognition that our identities, in this case, as lesbians and gays, are never singular, but always plural. There is a plurality of lesbian-nesses which share only a resemblance, and no lesbian-ness is the correct one. Identities are always shifting and refracting; they make sense only in limited and temporary contexts. At their best moment, they make possible resistances. We can use identities productively in our resistances, and, at the same time, recognize that even if all our anti-gay enemies disappeared, there would be no revelation of a true lesbian-ness or gay-ness. Paradoxically, we can, and we must, engage in a contradictory movement, deploy our identities in ways that are limited and strategic, and, at the same time, create the space for their weakening and eventual dissolution. It is precisely in a moment of 'crisis' such as the AIDS phenomenon and Clause 28 that identities should be simultaneously deployed and questioned. We cannot choose to stand outside the movement of difference, even by virtue of our oppressed status. Whether or not we do recognize the impossibility of our identities, a true lesbian-ness and gay-ness will remain for ever beyond our grasp. If we continue to pursue these impossible goals, it is inevitable that the extremely damaging blaming games will continue, the blaming of 'badness' in our own community and within ourselves.

In other words, what is needed is a rethinking of the standard responses to radical difference. The strategies which have been outlined above – the representations of the threat of radical difference as the invader, seducer, pretender, the division of radical difference, the exclusion of radical difference and the inclusion of simple difference, and the offering of a fantasy space purified of radical difference and supported by the symptom – all pertain to an authoritarian type of discourse, a discourse which has everything staked on the simulation of closure, a completed consensus. Lesbian and gay discourses are as subject as any others to these authoritarian initiatives and are deeply affected by them. The risk is that we may find ourselves responding with our own version of closure, a construction of rigid models of legitimate or 'super' lesbian-ness and gay-ness. This incitement to closure must somehow be refused, and the difficult task of rethinking an approach to radical difference must somehow be explored.[46]

THE LIMITATIONS OF THE OPPOSERS' DISCOURSE

It is precisely on this 'ground' – the 'ground' of a potential radical difference – that the discourse of the opposers of Clause 28 becomes ineffective. The opposers' discourse fails in three ways. First, as noted above, it fails to confront directly the 'loony Left' charge, and tends to conceal its own pro-gay elements, especially those within the Labour Party. Second, its position on the clause itself is often equivocal. Several prominent speakers, including Cunningham, the Labour spokesman on local government affairs, speak in favour of the clause in the first instance and only reverse their position after much lobbying from the grassroots of the party.[47]

Most important, however, is the failure of the opposers to recognize the impossibility of identities. Their discourse is largely structured around the proposition that the clause is nonsensical because everyone's sexuality is fixed at birth, such that no promotion of any sexuality is possible.[48] Well-intentioned as they may be, the opposers, in arguing that homosexuality simply 'is', undermine the importance of the construction of alternative sexual identities and communities. If heterosexuality and homosexuality are marked at birth as clear affiliations to separate groups, and if sexual categories are inevitably fixed, then sexuality ceases to be a terrain of struggle. From this perspective, it would appear that homosexuals ought to organize merely to guide each individual to their 'true calling', and to constitute themselves as simply one more bloc in a pluralist society. That the actual lesbian and gay movements are engaged in so much more than this – interrupting *everyone's* experience of sexuality and gender, and even questioning the structure of sexual categorization itself – appears nonsensical and even illegitimate from this perspective. Yet the thinking of homosexuality as a naturally fixed bloc in a system of separate and competing blocs was common in many discourses of opposition against the clause.[49] The popularity of this approach

323

indicates the extremely underdeveloped status of the thinking about identities in general, and sexuality and gender in particular, in many 'leftist' discourses in Britain.

What the left often fails to recognize is that homosexual, gay, and lesbian identities cannot be taken for granted, for, as historical constructs, they developed only in certain contexts, and will disappear in other contexts. Indeed, the very conception that democratic principles such as genuine choice and self-determination have a legitimate place in the sphere of sexuality is a relatively recent and fragile development. The slogan 'The personal is political' has had a very short career indeed. It is only by not taking the emergence of these principles for granted, by emphasizing their historical character, that we can become more conscious of the dangers which threaten them, and equip ourselves to engage in their defence.[50]

THE CENTRALITY OF THE PROMOTION OF HOMO-SEXUALITY FOR RADICAL DEMOCRACY

The opposers' discourse is excellent on one particular point, namely its insistence on the fact that the prohibition of the promotion of homosexuality is a thoroughly anti-lesbian and anti-gay measure. The opposers were able to demonstrate that opposition to bad gayness is essentially opposition to all gayness, since, as we have shown, the 'good homosexual' is an impossibility. Clause 28 thus gives symbolic licence to anti-lesbian and anti-gay bigotry.

Yet there remains a tremendous absence in the discourse of the opposers: the argument that homosexuality *can* and *ought to be* promoted. We can partially account for this absence in terms of short-term strategies; clearly, it would have been a counter-productive argument in some contexts during the Clause 28 debate. It is important, however, to recognize the limitations in suppressing this argument, and the importance of taking up this proposition wherever possible. It is a myth that homosexuals constitute, and will always constitute, 10 per cent of the population, and that homosexuality pertains only to this fixed group. The promotion of homosexuality involves the circulation of one amongst many possible representations of radical difference, the promotion of the interruption of spaces which cannot tolerate radical difference. Were this radical difference to be thus 'promoted', both heterosexuals *and* homosexuals would increasingly question the fixity and necessity of their sexuality. The promotion of homosexuality would of course by no means render non-homosexuality impossible. Radical gayness is not necessarily contradictory to all conceptions of the family and heterosexuality, just as radical blackness is not necessarily contradictory to all whitenesses and Britishnesses. Radical gayness is contradictory only to an exclusionary and authoritarian conception of the family which falsely presents itself as the only moral possibility for collective living. It is contradictory only to a 'compulsory heterosexuality' which claims to be the only legitimate form of sexual expression. It is contradictory only to the discourses which stake everything on the blocking of the circulation of a non-neutralized difference. For precisely these reasons, the promotion of homosexuality is central to the radical democratic project because of the work that it does, its interruption effects, its challenge to the necessity of some of the most authoritarian spaces and logics in modern society: to patriarchal power relations, the moral policing of the 'public'/'private' spheres, and the idealization of the family.

The centrality of the promotion of radical difference for the radical democratic project is not limited to sexuality. Sexual identities are not 'more' chosen, and are not more subject to the movement of difference, than other identities, such as race. No identity is fixed in biological matter; all identities are socially constructed on a discursive terrain. That terrain is never a configuration of our choosing, and we always experience it as a field into which we have been 'thrown', but these discourses are, necessarily, always caught up in the movement of difference. There is always the possibility of interruption and subversion. The effects of the radical black movements in Britain since the 1960s can be compared with the effects of the lesbian and gay movements, in terms of their interruption of categories which present themselves as 'natural'. Through this interruption, not only has the identity 'black' become thinkable, but the unity and necessity of whiteness and Britishness have been called into question. Radical gayness and radical blackness are central to a radical democratic resistance; their interruption effects make visible the circulation of non-neutralized difference where there is supposed to be only simple difference. The fundamental fear expressed in the authoritarian response to gayness and blackness is not simply a fear of AIDS or a blackened Britain, but is, first and foremost, the fear of radical difference.

325

'THATCHERISM' AS A FLOATING SIGNIFIER

As a postscript, the terms I have used to designate contemporary British authoritarianism should be clarified. Although the names 'New Right' and 'Thatcherism' have been used in this discussion, it would be misleading to suggest that these discourses can be easily located. There is no relation of absolute proximity between the signifier and the signified here. Using terms such as 'New Right' is immediately problematic, since it perpetuates the vision of two partisan elements, the Conservatives and Labour, whose so-called 'natural' constituencies are the middle class, industrial and finance capital, etc., versus the workers, blacks, women, gays, etc. We have named the opposing sides in the Clause 28 debate as the 'supporters' and the 'opposers' precisely because anti-gayness, and attempts to neutralize the threat of radical difference in general, have no natural socio-political home; they can be found on the right and on the left, in any class fraction, and even among lesbians and gays ourselves. This lack of a natural home is not limited to anti-gay initiatives alone, but characterizes virtually all the strategies commonly identified as 'Thatcherite'; thus we cannot rule out the possibility of the strategies of Thatcherite discourse being reproduced by a Labour-led bloc in the future. Thatcherism, one variant of authoritarian discourse, must be understood as a floating signifier, and not as a project which naturally belongs to a fixed constituency and which is naturally opposed by another fixed constituency. We are witnessing today the first visible signs of fundamental weaknesses in the Thatcherite project; in that context, an examination of the non-partisan character of Thatcherism is especially important.

Such an examination will call attention to fundamental anxieties about the threat of radical difference – anxieties (partially) resolved within authoritarian discourse through strategies for the neutralization of this threat and constitutive fantasies of a final solution. Even in our resistances to this authoritarianism, we may find ourselves re-creating its images of closure, through truth-games, self-division, self-surveillance, and 'our own' fantasies of complete identities.

NOTES

I would like to thank Tessa Boffin, Erica Carter, and Parveen Adams for their helpful comments.

1 *Out on Tuesday*, Abseil Productions, Channel Four television series, 14 February 1989.

2 S. Hall, 'Blue election, election blues', *Marxism Today* (July 1987), 32-3.

3 These estimates are based on an approximate count of Hansard columns devoted to various topics in the debates. The debates were not limited by governmental 'guillotine'.

4 Raymond Williams, quoted in S. Watney, 'Taking liberties', in S. Watney and E. Carter (eds), *Taking Liberties: Aids and Cultural Politics* (London: Serpent's Tail, 1989), 25-6.

5 I am using the terms 'supporters' and 'opposers' to the clause to indicate the non-partisan nature of these discourses.

6 *Official Report*, House of Commons, 8/5/87, cols 997-8.

7 The first two statistics are from a Harris poll cited by Lord Manson, while the third statistic is from a MORI poll cited by Lord Campbell and Lady Saltoun. *Official Report*, House of Lords, 2/2/88, col. 999; 1/2/88, col. 874; and 2/2/88, col. 1007.

8 Emphasis added; *Official Report*, Standing Committee 'A', 8/12/87, col. 1220.

9 *Official Report*, Standing Committee 'A', 8/12/87, Cunningham, cols 1211-14 and Grant, cols 1223-4.

10 Hall argues that the 'traditionalist' left, which has become hegemonic in the Labour Party, not only refuses to engage with the 'loony Left' image but actually colludes with it, by returning to a 'respectable, moderate, trade unionist, male-dominated working-class' image in which the traces of the feminist, black, and gay struggles are suppressed; *op.cit.*, 34.

11 This denial is none the less coherent and resembles the logic of the fetishist, cf. S. Žižek, *The Sublime Object of Ideology* (London: Verso, 1989), 30-3.

12 The Lacanian conception of the symptom is drawn from Žižek, ibid., 9-83, while the conception of representation is located on the terrain of excess is taken from S. Watney, *Policing Desire: pornography, AIDS and the media* (London: Methuen, 1987).

13 *Official Report*, House of Commons, 8/5/87, col. 999. For a critique of the common myth that AIDS has an African origin, see Cindy Patton's essay in *New Formations* Spring 1990.

14 S. Watney, 'Psychoanalysis, sexuality and AIDS', in S. Shepherd and M. Wallis (eds), *Coming On Strong* (London: Unwin Hyman, 1989), 33-7.

15 For the purposes of discussion, the term 'difference' will be used in three ways. First, reference will be made to *radical difference*, an irresolvable, non-neutralizable difference which is prior to all coherence and regularity. It functions as the condition of possibility for any appearance of closure, but is simultaneously the condition of impossibility of closure, permanently subverting and postponing the completion of that which it makes possible. Second, the term *movement of difference* will be used to emphasize that every discourse is caught up in the 'play of differences'; there is never a 'choice' concerning whether or not strategies will be deployed to rework the threat of radical difference. Possibilities for this reworking include the strategies of representing radical difference as an invader, a seducer, and a pretender. Another possible manoeuvre is the attempt to divide radical difference and to

transform some of this difference into *simple difference*. It will be argued that although some form of difference must always be 'included' in every discourse, the potential subversiveness of difference can be muted to the extent that it is made to take the form of simple difference. While the attempt to neutralize totally radical difference always fails, it is none the less productive. A purely simple difference, like the category of the accidental, does not 'interrupt' spaces and orders, but is compatible with closure. In a discourse which is staked on the creation of the semblance of closure (although the attainment of full closure is ruled out from the beginning), radical difference is never only 'excluded', but is also always partially transformed and 'included' as a form of simple difference. These distinctions, and the application of these terms, are derived from a reading of Derrida's conception of *différance*, particularly as it is employed in *Of Grammatology* (London: Johns Hopkins University Press, 1976).

[16] *Official Report*, House of Lords, 16/2/88, cols 593-4.

[17] Earl of Caithness, *Official Report*, House of Lords, 16/2/88, cols 611-12.

[18] Paraphrase of entries in Webster's Dictionary (Springfield: G. & C. Merriam, 1977).

[19] Howard, *Official Report*, House of Commons, 15/12/87, col. 1019.

[20] Earl of Caithness, *Official Report*, House of Lords, 1/2/88, col. 889.

[21] Baroness Blatch, *Official Report*, House of Lords, 16/2/55, cols. 599-600.

[22] Conservative MPs continue to lobby against lesbian and gay parenting. In a recent development, MP Ann Winterton tabled an Early Day Motion on 26 October 1989, which expressed 'profound concern' that lesbians had received artificial insemination by donors at a London pregnancy advisory service clinic. Winterton intends to lobby for the introduction of an amendment to prohibit the provision of this service to unmarried women, and to order the compulsory registration of all sperm donoors, in forthcoming legislation on embryo research.

[23] *Official Report*, House of Lords, 18/12/86, col. 310.

[24] *Official Report*, House of Lord, 16/2/88, col. 594.

[25] *Official Report*, House of Commons, 9/3/88, cols 406-7.

[26] *Official Report*, House of Commons, 9/3/88, cols 406, 417.

[27] A. Smith, 'An analysis of the speeches of Powell: a contribution to the genealogy of Thatcherism', *Department of Government Working Papers*, University of Essex, 1989.

[28] There have been extensive debates in the 1980s in Britain about the teaching of 'multiculturalism' and 'anti-racism', the content and form of the British history curriculum, and the appropriate quantitative mix of children from different ethnic backgrounds in places such as Dewsbury. Many of these debates originate in the New Right journal, the *Salisbury Review*. Cf. G. Seidel, 'The white discursive order', in I. Zavala *et al.* (eds), *Approaches to Discourse, Poetics and Psychiatry* (Amsterdam: Benjamins, 1987), 39-66.

[29] *Official Report*, House of Lords, 18/12/86, col. 310.

[30] For a critique of the myth of the 'permissive' moment, see J. Weeks, *Sex, Politics and Society* (London: Longman, 1981), 249-72.

[31] The Earl of Caithness says that the clause is intended to make any local authority involved in an initiative concerning homosexuality 'ask itself' about

its legal position, and 'decide what its purpose is' in that activity. *Official Report*, House of Lords, 1/2/88, col. 951.

[32] Wilshire, who introduced the clause, says it stands as a 'warning to the liberal and the trendy that you can go too far for society to tolerate'. A spokesperson for the National Council of Civil Liberties further comments, 'It's the self-censorship, the decisions taken by councils behind closed doors that make Section 28 so dangerous.' *Guardian* (11 October 1989), 27.

[33] *Official Report*, House of Commons, 15/12/87, col. 1009.

[34] *Official Report*, House of Commons, 9/3/88, cols 372, 382.

[35] *Official Report*, House of Lords, 16/2/88, Baroness Strange, col. 611; Baroness Blatch, col. 610; Viscount Buckmaster, col. 607.

[36] *Official Report*, House of Lords, 16/2/88, col. 594.

[37] *Official Report*, House of Commons, 15/12/87, col. 1006.

[38] *Official Report*, Wilshire, House of Commons, 9/3/88, col. 404; Lord Ritchie, House of Lords, 16/2/88, col. 604.

[39] *Official Report*, Howard, House of Commons, 9/3/88, col. 421.

[40] *Official Report*, Earl of Caithness, House of Lords, 16/2/88, col. 643.

[41] *Official Report*, Patrick, Standing Committee 'A', 8/12/87, cols 1219-20.

[42] This interpretation of the Lacanian conception of fantasy, and the symptom's role in terms of fantasy, is drawn from Žižek, *op.cit.*, especially 47-9, 72-5, 118, and 124-8.

[43] Conservative MP Greenway says that he organized a 'conference on the family' in response to Ealing's policies on homosexuality, and he emphasizes that representatives of the Anglican, Catholic, Sikh, Muslim, and Hindu communities attended. He also insists that it is taught in all these communities, and in the Jewish community, that homosexuality is 'wrong'. *Official Report*, House of Commons, 15/12/87, col. 1000.

Mercer notes that groups of black parents were involved in the protests against the proposed 'positive images' campaign in Haringey, and that anti-gayness in the black community has become particularly evident with the AIDS phenomenon. K. Mercer, 'Aids, racism, and homophobia', in R. Chapman and J. Rutherford (eds), *Male Order: Unwrapping masculinity* (London: Lawrence & Wishart, 1988), 153-61.

[44] Analysts who argue that Thatcherism is a rather weak political phenomenon, because there is no majority bloc of positive support for specific policies, are therefore asking the wrong questions.

[45] *Official Report*, House of Lords, 1/2/88, cols 874-5.

[46] One possibility for this rethinking is the conception of 'negotiation' developed by Homi Bhabha in 'The commitment to theory', *New Formations*, Summer 1988, 5-23 reprinted in this book.

[47] See, for example, Cunningham's speeches, in which he first says that he is opposed to the promotion of homosexuality, urges all committee members to vote for its inclusion in the Bill, and forgoes any amendment of, or division about, the clause (*Official Report*, Standing Committee 'A', 8/12/87, cols 1211-14); then, in the Third Reading, he says that the clause must be amended to preserve the rights of lesbians and gays to 'equal treatment' but that he still supports it in principle (House of Commons, 15/12/87, cols 996-7); and then, in the final debates, he says that he has always been 'fundamentally opposed to

the Clause' (House of Commons, 9/3/88, col. 373).
[48] *Official Report*, Roberts, Standing Committee 'A', 8/12/87, col. 1215; and, in the House of Commons, Pike, 15/12/87, col. 1014; Hughes, 9/3/88, cols 340, 390; Livingstone, 9/3/88, col. 417; Fisher, 9/3/88, col. 394.
[49] J. Marshall, 'Flaunting it: the challenge of the 1990s', *Gay Times* (January 1989), 12-13.
[50] E. Laclau, 'Community and its paradoxes: Richard Rorty's "liberal Utopia" ', unpublished paper.

Notes on Contributors

Ien Ang is senior lecturer in the School of Humanities and Director of the Centre for Research in Culture and Communication at Murdoch University, Australia. She is author of *Watching Dallas* (1985), *Desperately Seeking the Audience* (1991) and *Living Room Wars* (in press).

Homi Bhabha is a professor of English at the University of Chicago and visiting professor at the School of Oriental and African Studies and University College, London.

Charlotte Brunsdon teaches Film Studies at Warwick University. She is editor of *Films for Women* (1986) and a regular contributor to *Screen*.

Joan Copjec teaches in the English and Comparative Literature Departments at the University at Buffalo where she is also Director of the Centre for the Study of Psychoanalysis and Culture. Formerly Senior Editor of *October*, she is editor of *Shades of Noir: A Reader* and *Supposing the Subject* (1994). She is also author of *Read My Desire: Lacan Against the Historicists* (1994).

Mladen Dolar teaches philosophy at the University of Ljubljana.

Stuart Hall is Professor of Sociology at the Open University. He has written widely on politics, culture and race and is co-editor of *New Times* (1989) and editor of *Formations of Modernity* (1992).

Dick Hebdige is Dean of Critical Studies at the Centre for the Study of Cultural Diversity, California Institute of the Arts. He is author of *Subculture: The Meaning of Style* (1979) *Cut'n'Mix* (1987) and *Hiding in the Light* (1988).

Kobena Mercer has worked at the BFI, London and currently teaches at the Centre for the Study of Cultural Diversity, California Institute of the Arts.

331

Satya P. Mohanty teaches English at Cornell University.

Chantal Mouffe is Programme Director at College International de Philosophie, Paris. She is co-author (with Ernesto Laclau) of *Hegemony and Socialist Strategy* (1985), editor of *Radical Democracy* (1992) and author of *The Return of the Political* (1993).

Jacqueline Rose has a chair in English at Queen Mary and Westfield College, University of London. Her most recent publications are *The Haunting of Sylvia Plath* (1991) and *Why War? Psychoanalysis, Politics and the Return to Melanie Klein* (1994).

Susan Willis teaches English at Duke University. She is author of *Specifying: Black Women Writing The American Experience* (1987), *A Primer for Daily Life* (1991), and co-author of *Inside the Mouse: Work and Play at Disney World* (1995).

Anna Marie Smith is Assistant Professor of Political Theory in the Department of Government, Cornell University. Her publications include *New Right Discourse On Sexuality, Britain 1968-1990* (1994).